# FOLIAGE

ASTONISHING COLOR AND TEXTURE BEYOND FLOWERS

# FOLIAGE

NANCY J. ONDRA

PHOTOGRAPHY BY ROB CARDILLO

 Storey Publishing

*The mission of Storey Publishing is to serve our customers by publishing practical information that encourages personal independence in harmony with the environment.*

Edited by Gwen Steege and Carleen Madigan Perkins

Art direction and cover design by Cynthia McFarland

Text design by Cynthia McFarland and Blue Design

Text production by Erin Dawson

Indexed by Susan Olason, Indexes & Knowledge Maps

**front cover:** *Ipomoea batatas* 'Blackie' (Chanticleer, PA)

**front flap:** *Euphorbia myrsinites*

**back cover:** *Colocasia esculenta* var. *antiquorum* 'Illustris' (The Gardens at Ball, IL)

**back flap:** *Capsicum* 'Black Pearl' with celosia

**page 2–3:** *Agave scabra*

**page 4 (left to right):** *Sambucus racemosa* 'Sutherland Gold' with *Artemisia* 'Powis Castle', *Cercis canadensis* 'Forest Pansy', *Plectranthus* 'Silver Shield', *Euphorbia marginata*

Text © 2007 by Nancy J. Ondra
Cover and interior photography © Rob Cardillo, except for the following:
© cfgphoto.com, 123 bottom; © Saxon Holt, 50 left, 167 left, 178 right, 216 left, 274 right; © Nancy Ondra, 235 bottom

The information in this book is true and complete to the best of our knowledge. All recommendations are made without guarantee on the part of the author or Storey Publishing. The author and publisher disclaim any liability in connection with the use of this information. For additional information please contact Storey Publishing, 210 MASS MoCA Way, North Adams, MA 01247.

Storey books are available for special premium and promotional uses and for customized editions. For further information, please call 1-800-793-9396.

Printed in China by R.R. Donnelley
10 9 8 7 6 5 4 3 2 1

**Library of Congress Cataloging-in-Publication Data**

Ondra, Nancy J.
    Foliage / Nancy J. Ondra.
        p. cm.
    Includes index.
    ISBN-13: 978-1-58017-648-4; ISBN 10: 1-58017-648-8 (pbk. : alk. paper) –
    ISBN-13: 978-1-58017-654-5; ISBN-10: 1-58017-654-2 (hardcover-jacketed : alk. paper) 1. Foliage plants.
    2. Leaves. 3. Gardening. I. Title.

SB431.O53 2007
635.97'5—dc22
                                                                            2006038133

# ACKNOWLEDGMENTS

*Once again, I owe boundless thanks to everyone at Storey for their encouragement, patience, and vision throughout the entire process of turning this relatively simple concept into a beautiful reality. Special thanks, too, to Sandy White of Floral & Hardy in Skippack, Pennsylvania, for sharing some exceptional variegated plants for research and photography.*

—NANCY ONDRA

*My warmest thanks to the author and my friend, Nancy Ondra for committing herself to this book. Nan's dedication to her craft and encyclopedic knowledge of the world of plants are only matched by her skills as a gardener. Her horticulturally rich and exquisitely well-designed yard was the setting for many of the dynamic combinations and plant portraits seen throughout this book. And her mother bakes some of the finest cookies I've ever tasted.*

*I also applaud the thoughtful and creative publishing team at Storey Publishing: Gwen Steege carefully nurtured this book in the beginning, Carleen Perkins became a responsive and insightful editorial midwife, and Cindy McFarland and Erin Dawson wove a beautiful design out of words and pixels. Thanks also to Kevin Metcalfe for cheery technical support and to Laurie Figary for keeping on top of the image flow.*

*Additionally, the individuals, nurseries, and gardens whose names appear on page 281 provided access for photography or assisted me in some significant way in completing this book. My deepest gratitude to all of you!*

—ROB CARDILLO

# CONTENTS

# 1 | EXPLORING YOUR OPTIONS

ABOVE: **Earning their keep.** Many perennials formerly known for their flowers now contribute color all season long, thanks to selections with showy foliage (such as × *Heucherella* 'Stoplight').

OPPOSITE: **Who needs flowers?** Borders based on foliage colors, textures, and forms make blooms practically incidental. (Hobbs garden, Vancouver, BC)

For most of us, it's the beauty of flowers that lured us into gardening in the first place. Velvety red roses, sunny-eyed daisies, icy blue irises, and countless other combinations of flower forms and colors catch our eye and our heart, inspiring us to devote hours and years to planting and nurturing them. Somewhere along the way, though, the allure of these floral glories gets tempered with a dose of reality. Weather that's too dry, too wet, too hot, or too cold can blemish perfect petals or fade flowers quickly, disappointing our hopes for a bounty of blooms. Fickle weather also interferes with our attempts at creating (or re-creating) spectacular floral combinations. If just one plant blooms a few days late or early, the effect we've waited all year to enjoy can be ruined for the entire growing season.

Eventually, even the most ardent flower lover realizes that a garden based only on blooms leaves something to be desired — something that's sure to add visual interest no matter what the season, no matter what the weather. Catalogs and garden shops are filled with all kinds of ornaments and statuary that can serve this purpose, but too many of these accents can bring on a whole other kind of visual disaster. So, what's a gardener to do?

Why, look to the leaves, of course!

# FANTASTIC LEAF FORMS

*HOSTA 'ZEBRA STRIPES'*

*ECHEVERIA METALLICA*

*DICENTRA 'KING OF HEARTS'*

*EUPHORBIA CHARACIAS*

*PSEUDOPANAX FEROX*

*JUNIPERUS HORIZONTALIS 'LIME GLOW'*

*SALIX BABYLONICA 'CRISPA'*

*DRYOPTERIS ERYTHROSORA*

*CAREX BUCHANANII*

# THE FOLIAGE FACTOR

Flowers may come and go, but as long as a plant is actively growing (and sometimes even when it's not), the foliage has an undeniable presence in our gardens. But instead of serving merely as a space filler before and after blooming, foliage that is attractive in its own right greatly extends the seasonal interest of individual plants, and of the garden as a whole. The qualities that make foliage attractive are essentially the same that apply to flowers: shape, size, texture, and color.

## Striking Outlines

Ask a non-gardener to draw a leaf, and chances are she'll draw a straight line enclosed by two arcing lines, with an extra bit of straight line at one end: the classic outline of a simple leaf. Ask a botanist to do the same thing, and she'll want a lot of specifics first: a simple or a compound leaf? What overall shape? What kind of margins? What kind of base, and what kind of tip? When you study the outlines of leaves, you'll see that there is a dizzying array of ways they can be shaped. Many common garden plants, however, have rather "ordinary" foliage; the leaves may be a little rounder or skinnier than usual, but they're not all that distinctive. What catches our eye are the extremes: those that are very narrow, or perfectly circular, or obviously arrow-shaped, for instance.

There are fancy terms for all the various leaf shapes, and we gardeners use some of them, but mostly we use less precise but more easily envisioned descriptions. To start with, there are *simple* and *compound* leaves. A simple leaf is just that: one single leafstalk surrounded by leafy tissue. Compound leaves, on the other hand, are made up of several to many smaller leaves, called leaflets. Those leaflets may all radiate from one point (an arrangement commonly called *palmately compound*) or be attached at different points along a central stalk; botanists refer to this as *pinnately compound*, but gardeners often describe it as featherlike or, if there are many small leaflets, as ferny or fernlike. (When discussing true ferns, by the way, the entire leaf is referred to as a frond.)

The edges of leaves can also add visual interest. Foliage with smooth, shallow-toothed, or lightly scalloped margins is fairly ordinary-looking, but leaves with distinctly jagged or deeply lobed edges have an interesting, lacy look that's often very appealing. When the lobes point toward the central leaf vein, the leaf is said to be *pinnately lobed*; when they all appear to point to one spot at the base, the leaf is *palmately lobed*.

RIGHT: **Absolutely elegant.** The palmately lobed leaves of this Japanese maple (*Acer palmatum* 'Shaina') create a delightfully delicate appearance.

From a practical standpoint, knowing the proper terms for the different types and shapes of leaves isn't nearly as important as developing an appreciation of the various forms that foliage can take. Then, when you're trying to choose the perfect partner for a particular plant, or if you're searching for something to add excitement to a bland bed or border, you'll remember that contrasting leaf shapes can be very pleasing and perhaps use that to guide your choice of companion. Remember, too, that unusually shaped leaves work best when used in moderation. A border made up of all lacy leaves or all ferny foliage generally isn't any more interesting than one composed of more-mundane leaf shapes.

LEFT: **Definitely different.** These oreganos (*Origanum*) all have fairly similar leaf shapes, but their varying sizes, textures, and colors give each one a distinctive appearance in the garden.

## Sizing Them Up

Combining plants with different leaf sizes is another designer trick for creating interesting beds and borders. An additional consideration is whether you'll keep the overall size range of the foliage in scale with the site. Tiny-leaved plants have minimal appeal in gardens viewed from a distance but can be fascinating when admired close up in a small space, next to a bench, or along a path. Large-leaved plants are more flexible from a design standpoint, adding drama to a small space while easily holding their own from some distance away.

It's easy to overdo small leaves but challenging to have too many big leaves, unless you're using mostly tropical plants, which create a deliberately lush look with a charm all its own. Among hardy garden plants for temperate climates, freakishly large leaves — such as those of giant gunnera (*Gunnera manicata*) — simply aren't that common, and even smaller-scale-but-still-big leaves often prefer much more moisture than is found in most beds and borders. Little wonder, then, that many plantings suffer from a surfeit of medium-sized to small leaves — and that often, the addition of just one or two clumps of big, bold foliage makes all the difference.

## LOOKS AREN'T EVERYTHING

Shape, size, and color are the most obvious qualities that leaves contribute to our gardens, but foliage doesn't just please the eye; it can delight our other senses as well.

**The right touch.** Velvety or fuzzy leaves, such as those of lamb's ear (*Stachys byzantina*, pictured), practically beg to be stroked, and very fine-textured grasses, such as feather grass (*Nassella tenuissima*), are fun to run your fingers through. Even spiny-looking leaves can be tempting to touch; you know they're probably going to be sharp, but you still can't resist the urge to put your fingers on them!

*Stachys byzantina*

**Good scents.** Fragrant foliage is common among plants typically classified as herbs (such as 'Purple Ruffles' basil, pictured), and many of these work just as well in ornamental plantings as they do in kitchen and herb gardens. Some primarily decorative plants, such as southernwood (*Artemisia abrotanum*) and bigroot geranium (*Geranium macrorrhizum*), also have interesting foliage aromas. Most leaves don't release their scent unless you brush, rub, or crush them; one exception is eglantine rose (*Rosa eglanteria*), which has a distinctive fruity scent when it gets wet.

*Ocimum basilicum*
**'Purple Ruffles'**

**Savor the flavor.** Besides great fragrance, many herbs — including 'All Gold' lemon balm (*Melissa officinalis*) — offer great-tasting foliage, either for cooking or for nibbling right in the garden. A number of vegetables, including kales, lettuces, and chards, also earn a place in ornamental plantings for their outstanding leaf colors and textures. Even some fruits fall into the fabulous-foliage category, such as golden-leaved alpine strawberry (*Fragaria vesca* 'Golden Alexandria') and purple-leaved grape (*Vitis vinifera* 'Purpurea'), to name just two.

*Melissa officinalis* **'All Gold'**

### On the Surface

The term *texture* is used a couple of ways in relation to leaves. First, it applies to the look of the leaf's surface — whether it's glossy or matte (dull); rough or smooth; flat, rumpled, or pleated; plain, powdery, or fuzzy. The ways these various features can combine with size, shape, and color add an exciting dimension to leaf interest, and to the overall value of foliage in creating beautiful gardens. Glossy leaves, for example, reflect light, so they are terrific for brightening up shady spots; fuzzy foliage, on the other hand, makes a great contrast to satiny smooth flower petals in bright sites. Pleats, velvety coverings, and other unusual textures also make some leaves irresistibly touchable,

providing an extra element of pleasure to your plantings.

The term *texture* also refers to a combination of leaf shape and size, and how those factors interact to produce a plant's overall visual effect. Grassy, strappy, and swordlike leaves produce a spiky effect, while deeply lobed to finely dissected leaves have a lacy look. Plants with small or short and narrow to needlelike leaves are usually described as fine-textured; those with big, broad leaves are said to be bold or coarse. "Medium-textured" is a catchall category for most of those that don't fall neatly into one group or another.

TOP: **Changeable characters.** While grasses generally have a spiky texture in leaf, some — such as tufted hair grass (*Deschampsia cespitosa*) — develop a much softer appearance when their flowers form. (Tuscan Farm Gardens, Langley, BC)

BOTTOM: **A study in contrasts.** Soft and subtle by itself, the fuzzy gray foliage of *Tradescantia sillamontana* becomes bold and dramatic when set against the much smaller and smoother leaves of golden creeping Jenny (*Lysimachia nummularia* 'Aurea').

# TEXTURAL TOUCHES

AEONIUM 'ZWARTKOP'

'NERO DI TOSCANA' KALE

AGAVE PARRYI

MAMMILLARIA

PLECTRANTHUS 'SILVER SHIELD'

ALBIZIA 'SUMMER CHOCOLATE'

ABIES ALBA 'SILVER CLOUD'

GERANIUM 'CHERYL'S SHADOW'

ALTERNANTHERA FICOIDEA
'RED THREADS'

### Chase the Rainbow

Plant nerds wax poetic about contrasting leaf shapes and textures, but for many people, a garden that's not filled with color — and specifically, colors other than green — isn't much of a garden at all.

In a room, a car, or a piece of clothing, green is easily recognized as a color, but where plants are concerned, we *expect* them to be green; maybe that's why it's so easy to overlook the amazing range of greens there are in the plant world. Developing an appreciation of them is definitely worthwhile, and creating an interesting garden based entirely on varying shades of green foliage can be a challenging and rewarding design exercise. But why limit yourself to greens when there are so many other colors that leaves come in? Red, orange, yellow, green, powder blue, and purple, and even pink, brown, black, and silver: you name the hue (except true blue, it seems), and some plant somewhere probably has leaves of that color. And we're not just talking about solid colors; there may be two, three, or even more colors in each leaf, in all matter of spots, splashes, stripes, and speckles.

So what makes one leaf green and another anything but? Chlorophylls are the pigments we perceive as green, but they're not the only ones present in leaves; there are also xanthophylls (yellow), carotenes (red, orange, or yellow), and anthocyanins (red, blue, and purple), among others. These non-green pigments, in various combinations, tend to be most visible when chlorophyll isn't as abundant. Often, this is when the foliage is emerging in spring or getting ready to drop in autumn, but they can be prominent during the growing season, too, depending on light levels, sap pH, temperature, and other factors. Leaf parts that lack pigment appear white; air spaces just beneath the leaf surface produce a silvery effect. Waxy and hairy leaf coverings also influence the leaf color.

LEFT: **Elegant echoes.** Non-green foliage is invaluable for echoing flower colors, or even for replacing flowers altogether, supplying a dependable show throughout the growing season.

OPPOSITE: **A tapestry of color.** For most of us, knowing *why* leaves appear different colors isn't as important as the possibilities they present for creating eye-catching combinations. (Ondra garden, PA)

# COLORFUL CHARACTERS

*CAPSICUM* 'BLACK PEARL'   × *HEUCHERELLA* 'STOPLIGHT'   *COTINUS COGGYGRIA*   *HOSTA SIEBOLDIANA* 'ELEGANS'   *ATHYRIUM NIPONICUM VAR. PICTUM*   *DAPHNE* 'BRIGGS MOONLIGHT'

## FINDING EXCEPTIONAL FOLIAGE PLANTS

If you always do your plant shopping locally, you can just look at the leaves and know whether you think they're interesting, or if they'll contrast nicely with the plants you intend to combine them with. When you're reading mail-order catalogs, however, things are a lot less clear. Pictures usually focus on the flowers, even if the leaves are attractive, too, so you can't depend on them to tell the whole story. Catalog descriptions also leave much to be desired when it comes to foliage, giving it a passing mention if any at all.

### The Name Game

Sometimes, all you have to go on is the plant's name. You may find clues to foliage features in the "specific epithet" (the second word in the scientific name). If you know that *argentea* refers to a silvery appearance, for example, then you might presume that a plant with a name like *Salvia argentea* will have silvery foliage. Cultivar names — the word or words enclosed in single quotes at the very end of a botanical name — may also highlight foliage features; it's easy to guess what a hosta named 'Blue Mouse Ears' might look like. This approach isn't foolproof, though, because the botanical and/or cultivar names may relate to the flowers

LEFT: **Cool companions.** The names *Plecostachys serpyllifolia* (with silver foliage) and *Scaevola aemula* (with purple-blue flowers) may not roll trippingly off the tongue, but fortunately, you don't have to pronounce them to know that the plants look great together.

instead of the leaves. For instance, in the Japanese kerria (*Kerria japonica*) cultivar name 'Golden Guinea', "Golden" refers to the blooms, but in the cultivar name 'Chiba Gold', "Gold" alludes to the bright yellow foliage. Still, it's worthwhile to be aware of these clues, so check out the other What's in a Name? boxes in chapters 2 through 5 for words to watch for when you're poring over plant catalogs.

## Adventures in Cyberspace

Luckily for us foliage fanatics, the electronic age gives us another option: Internet searches. If you want to learn more about the leaves of a particular plant, simply type its name and the word *foliage* into a search engine, and you'll probably find out way more than you ever wanted to know. Don't forget about image searches too. Often, photos posted by home gardeners focus on plant features ignored by glossy catalog pictures.

---

## WHAT'S IN A NAME?

To those in the know, botanical names tell a lot about a plant's leaves. Here are some common shape terms you'll run across and what they mean.

### Referring to Shapes

*acutifolia, -um, -us* (pointed-leaved)

*cordifolia, -um, -us* (heart shaped)

*diversifolia, -um, -us* (with many shapes)

*ensifolia, -um, -us* (sword shaped)

*filicifolia, -um, -us* (fernlike)

*filifolia, -um, -us* (threadlike)

*flabellifolia, -um, -us* (fan shaped)

*integrifolia, -um, -us* (with entire or uncut leaves)

*longifolia, -um, -us* (long-leaved)

*oblongifolia, -um, -us* (oblong-leaved)

*obtusifolia, -um, -us* (blunt-leaved)

*ovalifolia, -um, -us* (oval-leaved)

*renifolia, -um, -us* (kidney shaped)

*rhombifolia, -um, -us* (diamond shaped)

*rotundifolia, -um, -us* (rounded)

*sagittifolia, -um, -us* (arrow shaped)

*spathifolia, -um, -us* (spatula shaped)

### Referring to Width

*angustifolia, -um, -us* (narrow-leaved)

*latifolia, -um, -us* (broad-leaved)

*tenuifolia, -um, -us* (slender-leaved)

### Referring to Size

*grandifolia, -um, -us* (large-leaved)

*minutifolia, -um, -us* (tiny-leaved)

*parvifolia, -um, -us* (small-leaved)

### Referring to Number of Leaflets

*simplicifolia, -um, -us* (simple-leaved, no leaflets)

*unifolia, -um, -us* (one-leaved)

*unifoliata, -um, -us* (with one leaf)

*bifolia, -um, -us* (two-leaved)

*bifoliatus, -um, -us* (with two leaves)

*ternifolia, -um, -us* (leaves in groups of three)

*trifolia, -um, -us* (three-leaved)

*trifoliata, -um, -us* (with three leaves)

*quadrifolia, -um, -us* (four-leaved)

*quinquefolia, -um, -us* (five-leaved)

*centifolia, -um, -us* (hundred-leaved)

*millefolia, -um, -us* (thousand-leaved)

### Miscellaneous Leaf Terms

*cerefolia, -um, -us* (waxy-leaved)

*crassifolia, -um, -us* (thick-leaved)

*densifolia, -um, -us* (with dense leaves)

*paucifolia, -um, -us* (with few leaves)

*perfoliata, -um, -us* (with the leaves joined around the stem)

*pinguifolia, -um, -us* (plump-leaved)

*planifolia, -um, -us* (flat-leaved)

*sessilifolia, -um, -us* (lacking a leafstalk)

*tortifolia, -um, -us* (twisted-leaved)

## CREATING EXCITING COMBINATIONS

The same principles that make for great flower-based pairings work just as well when you're working with foliage. First, of course, all of the plants should have compatible growth needs. Silver-leaved lavender with a silver-spotted pulmonaria, for example, could be an attractive combination, but it probably won't work well in the garden because one needs sun and good drainage while the other prefers shade and evenly moist soil. Partners that share soil and light needs thrive with the same basic care, so your gardens will look beautiful and stay healthy with minimal primping and pampering.

### Unity and Diversity

From an aesthetic standpoint, the most pleasing combinations usually have a balance of harmony and contrast. If the partners are too similar, they'll blend right into each other; if they have nothing in common, the effect can be either remarkably dramatic or unbearably chaotic. So if you're trying to build a combination around a particular plant's foliage, consider the four basics — shape, size, texture, and color — then look for partners that are similar in one or more of these categories and different in others. Starting with a large, heart-shaped, smooth green leaf? A similarly green partner with small or medium-sized, lacy, ferny, grassy, or needlelike foliage could provide just enough visual contrast to prevent boredom.

Color difference tends to be the most obvious characteristic in foliage combinations, so if you're working with dissimilar colors, it's usually best to keep other contrasts to a minimum, unless you're really looking for shock value. The more limited your color palette, the more imperative it is to bring in interest from varying sizes, shapes, and textures.

Besides looking at individual leaves, it's important to consider the overall *form* of the plants you're considering as companions. Ground-hugging mats, creeping carpeters, rounded mounds, airy "clouds," and spiky clumpers are just some of the distinct growth habits that add drama or harmony to a combination. As with color, form makes a strong visual statement, so a little contrast goes a long way in most foliage combinations!

RIGHT: **Cool hues.** The lacy blue foliage of dill stands out against the striking, bold purple-leaved perilla.

OPPOSITE: **High contrast.** Pairing the spiky, bright red foliage of Japanese blood grass (*Imperata cylindrica* var. *koenigii* 'Rubra') with the lacy, silver foliage of 'Powis Castle' artemisia creates a strong statement for a sunny site. (Ondra garden, PA)

## Other Considerations

Location can also influence your choice of partners for particular foliage combinations. If you're planting a site that's seen at close range, such as near a doorway, next to a patio, or in a container, it's a perfect opportunity to play with contrasting shapes and textures while keeping the color range fairly limited (all green, for instance, or just greens and blues). In gardens seen from a distance, these subtle details will hardly be visible, so contrasting colors and forms are more useful for providing visual impact.

Small spaces and containers, by the way, are also very useful as testing grounds for new combinations. Besides letting you see

**LEFT: Red light, green light.** This simple but dramatic pairing of 'Immortality' iris foliage with 'Crimson Pygmy' barberry (*Berberis thunbergii*) becomes absolutely magical when backlit by the setting sun.

**OPPOSITE: Raising the stakes.** Want to experiment with different lighting effects on your foliage plants? Growing them in containers lets you move them around to find just the right site, and their raised position makes it easier for slanting rays of sunlight to shine through them. (Beds and Borders, NY)

how the plants themselves will perform in your growing conditions, they also give you a chance to live with the pairings for a while. If the plants grow well and you like the effect, great; if not, it's a simple matter to add or remove partners, or to take them all out and start over. Far better to see how that pink-and-black combo you've envisioned really looks in person before you create an entire border around it!

Looking at the ways light interacts with foliage is a rather esoteric consideration when it comes to planning combinations, but it may provide exciting insights into ways you can create breathtaking garden pictures. Backlighting (where the sun is behind the leaves) is especially effective. It can silhouette striking shapes or shine right through the foliage, dramatically changing its color. Red, purple, and green leaves, in particular, glow like stained glass, creating eye-catching results. To take advantage of backlighting, situate foliage plants where the rising or setting sun will shine through them; the taller the plants you're working with, the easier this is. (Containers can be very helpful here, because they raise the leaves and increase the chance of interesting backlighting.)

# GROWING GREAT-LOOKING FOLIAGE

There are no big secrets to getting the very best out of your foliage plants: basic garden care and a willingness to experiment are all you really need! A good trowel and spade help, too, because you'll probably be moving your plants around now and then to find the perfect spot for them.

## Getting the Site Right

Giving all of your plants the growing conditions they prefer keeps them healthy and vigorous, which is just as important for good foliage as it is for flowers. Still, it's possible to tweak matters in favor of the foliage. Being a little more generous than usual with fertilizers (especially those rich in nitrogen) and organic soil amendments (such as aged manures) usually encourages foliage production, which helps you get the best from large-leaved plants in particular. It's also useful for promoting overall vigor in plants that appreciate ample fertility, which translates into more leaves and thus to even more foliage interest. Being free-handed with fertilizer doesn't benefit all foliage plants, however. Those that are accustomed to leaner soil (some plants with silvery leaves, for example) may also grow more lushly where nutrients are abundant, but they may not be as intensely colored; plus, they may be more prone to leaf-disfiguring diseases, and that defeats the whole purpose! Soft, lush growth can also be particularly enticing to insects and animal pests.

Soil moisture has an effect similar to that of soil fertility where foliage is concerned. Plants typically need lots of moisture to support leafy growth, but those that have adapted to do without will suffer if they get too much. Here again, the key is to find out what each plant prefers and then do your best to provide the ideal conditions. Hostas, for example, thrive with ample fertility and moisture; if they don't get both, their leaves will be smaller than usual and may become brown and crispy. To keep them happy, work lots of organic matter into the soil to help it retain moisture and boost fertility; use an organic mulch to reduce water loss from evaporation; and water during dry spells. With a silvery-leaved sage (*Salvia*), though, all this pampering would probably produce weak growth and lead to the overall decline of the plant; it can also contribute to winter losses in areas where you'd normally expect a particular plant to be cold-hardy. For plants such as these, holding off on soil improvement, fertilizing, and watering is much more likely to produce the best foliage effect.

ABOVE: **A bright idea.** The reddish markings of 'Vancouver Centennial' geranium (*Pelargonium*) are most distinct in full sun.

OPPOSITE: **Lush and lovely.** Moist, fertile soil supports an abundance of bold foliage. (Plant Delights, NC)

Light levels seem to be the most flexible of plant needs when it comes to promoting top-quality foliage. It takes a great deal of energy to produce flowers and seeds, and because plants need light to fuel that process, it's hardly surprising that ample sunlight is a must for gardeners in search of the biggest and brightest blooms. When you're focusing on foliage, though, you'll find that many typical sun-lovers will produce loads of luxuriant leaves in shadier sites; they'll simply flower less abundantly in exchange. Those of you who live where summers are hot may find that plants commonly touted as needing full sun actually perform much better with light, all-day shade or with morning sun and afternoon shade. Of course, not all light-loving plants are able to adapt to less than full sun — especially those with silvery, hairy leaves — but enough of them can to make it worthwhile experimenting. If they don't thrive, simply move them back to a brighter spot and try something else.

Getting handy with a trowel or spade is also useful for fine-tuning the appearance of colored foliage in your lighting conditions. Too much shade can cause yellow-leaved and variegated plants to turn greenish; too much sun will burn very pale leaves. Between those two extremes, though, is plenty of opportunity for softening or intensifying foliage colors without harming a plant. Just don't get too carried away with moving your plants around; it's usually

BELOW: **Making a point.** Gray-blue *Agave scabra* is a striking accent for sunbaked sites.

best to give them at least a month or two (ideally, a year or two) in their new home, so you can see how they adapt.

Also, keep in mind that although a plant can easily adjust to a shadier site without immediate harm, moving any leafed-out plant from shade to full sun is likely to give it a bad case of sunburn, in the form of tan patches, browned edges, or an overall scorched appearance. Providing some afternoon shade during the first few days (cover it with a bushel basket or a piece of screening, for example) will go a long way to helping a plant get accustomed to its brighter site. If a plant that's been in place for a week or two still scorches, give it some extra water and mulch it well. Often, having ample moisture will enable a plant to tolerate more sun than it usually would.

### Other Care Considerations

Foliage typically takes a lot less fussing to look good than flowers need, but a bit of grooming now and then can really make it look top-notch. Just as you deadhead flowering plants (in other words, pinch or cut off their faded blooms), you'll want to occasionally "deadleaf" foliage that is discolored, distorted, damaged, or overcrowded. When many of the leaves are imperfect, or if they have faded from their bright spring coloration, you could nip back all of the stem tips, or even cut off all of the foliage at ground level, to promote fresh new growth. This trick works with many perennials and a few shrubs, but not all, so it's best to do some research on your particular plants before you do anything drastic in the pruning department.

Although most foliage plants also produce flowers, these blooms take away energy from the leaves, so you may decide to remove them. Of course, if the blooms are attractive, it makes more sense to take them into consideration when you plan combinations, so you can get the most possible enjoyment out of an entire plant. But when the blossoms aren't particularly interesting — as on coleus and many hostas, for example — cutting or pinching them off will help the foliage stay in top form.

RIGHT: **A pinch in time.** Regularly removing the flower buds on coleus (such as the *Solenostemon scutellarioides* 'Picture Perfect Rose' shown here) keep your attention right where it should be: on the fabulous foliage!

It's fun to grow plants with oddly spotted, streaked, or jagged-edged leaves, but it's a pleasure only if the foliage is *supposed* to look like that. If those silvery spots are actually caused by a fungal disease, or those notched edges are due to weevils, for example, you'll have to decide if you're going to take action, and how. Here are a few common foliage problems and tips on how to handle them.

**Fungal diseases.** White or gray spots or patches are a common symptom of powdery mildew; orange-brown spots and streaks are the calling cards of rust. Other fungal diseases cause yellow, brown, or black spots of various sizes (pictured, top). Pinching off and destroying affected plant parts as soon as you notice these symptoms may be enough to stop the spread of the disease; sulfur-based sprays or dusts applied every 10 to 14 days may also help to prevent further infection. If fungal diseases are a problem on the same plants each year, move them to a site with better air circulation, replace them with disease-resistant cultivars (if available), or try completely different plants in their place.

**Viruses.** Leaves that are mottled with white, yellow, or light and dark green patches may be infected by a virus or they may simply be variegated — or they may be both!

Some plants prized for their showy foliage, such as the yellow-specked 'Thompsonii' flowering maple (*Abutilon × pictum*), get their variegation from a virus; in this example, the virus doesn't really harm the plant. In other cases, though, viruses can gradually weaken the growth and stunt a plant. Viruses are spread mostly by insects as they feed, so it's tough to prevent them, and once plants are affected, the only "cure" is to remove and destroy them.

**Slugs and snails.** These slimy pests are notorious foes of foliage because they chew large, ragged holes, sometimes leaving behind nothing but the tough leaf veins. Slugs and snails thrive in moist, cool conditions, so if they are a problem in your garden, consider holding off on spring mulching until early summer, when the soil surface has dried out a bit. Handpicking them off your plants at night, or trapping them under boards, cabbage leaves, or grapefruit rinds and then scraping the collected pests into a bucket of soapy water every afternoon, will eventually reduce slug and snail populations, but you need to do it daily for several weeks, at least. Where these pests are a serious problem, you may have to rely on local advice on which plants to avoid and which plants don't seem to be bothered by them.

**Black spot**

**Beetle damage**

**Caterpillars.** The larvae of moths and butterflies, these wormlike creatures can cause damage similar to that of slugs and snails; caterpillars, however, are usually visible during the day. You may have to look closely, though, because many of them blend in remarkably well with the foliage they're feeding on. Handpick them, or spray with *Bacillus thuringiensis* var. *kurstaki* (Btk) as a natural control. If you spot large, plump green caterpillars with black and yellow banding, move these to dill or parsley plants growing in a less visible area. Known as parsleyworms while in this larval form, they'll mature into beautiful black swallowtail butterflies.

**Beetles.** Damage from beetles ranges from notched edges or tiny holes in the leaves to completely skeletonized plants, with nothing left but the leafstalks and veins (pictured, bottom). These pests may be barely visible or up to an inch long (some are even bigger). Most are active during the day, but a few — like weevils — feed only at night. If you spot them, picking them off and dropping them in a can of soapy water immediately stops the damage. (*Caution:* It's smart to wear gloves, as some beetles can irritate your skin.) Applying parasitic nematodes to your soil can help control beetle larvae (grubs); rotenone and/or pyrethrin sprays may help control adult beetles.

**Spider mites and thrips.** Barely visible to the unaided eye, these tiny pests suck plant sap from leaves. The feeding of spider mites usually produces yellow to tan stippling, while damage from thrips is typically more like silvery streaks or speckling. Insecticidal soap sprays can help control both pests.

**Aphids.** These tiny insects cluster underneath leaves and along shoot tips, sucking out the plant sap and causing discolored growth; heavy infestations seriously weaken plants and cause leaves to fall. Besides spreading diseases as they feed, aphids release a sticky substance that falls on lower leaves and supports the growth of a black coating called sooty mold. Rubbing off these pests with your fingers is one control approach; another is to spray with insecticidal soap. Once you control the aphids, rain will usually wash away the sooty mold.

**True bugs.** Plant bugs, lace bugs, and other true bugs produce damage similar to that caused by aphids — including discolored, deformed leaves — as well as sunken brown spots on the foliage. Handpick pests and drop them into soapy water, try insecticidal soap every three to five days for two weeks, or use rotenone as a last resort.

**Leaf miners.** Pale, winding tunnels or blotches that appear under the leaf surface are a sign of these tiny pests. Picking off and destroying affected leaves is the most direct and dependable control option, although you could try weekly insecticidal soap sprays as soon as you notice the first symptoms to try to prevent further damage.

**Nutrient or pH imbalance.** Sometimes leaf damage is due to a lack or an excess of nutrients rather than to a pest or pathogen. The pH (acidity or alkalinity) of the soil has a definite effect on the amounts and types of nutrients that are available to plants. For instance, leaves that are chlorotic (yellow with green veins) are a common symptom on azaleas, rhododendrons, hollies (*Ilex*), and other acid-loving plants growing in soil that isn't acidic enough (in other words, the pH is too high). Sometimes the pH is fine but the nutrients simply aren't present in the soil in the right amounts. Symptoms of possible nutrient imbalances include yellowed new or old leaves, browned leaf tips, and an overall purplish cast to the foliage (especially in cool weather). If you suspect a nutrient imbalance, take a soil test to check the pH and nutrient levels, and add fertilizer to supply missing nutrients, lime to raise the pH, or sulfur to lower the pH, if needed.

# 2 GO FOR THE GOLD

When it comes to adding long-lasting beauty to beds and borders, colorful leaves simply can't be beat. And of all the various foliage colors, yellows and golds are the most likely to create a dramatic response from the people who view them in your garden. The exact nature of that response depends on personal tastes, of course: some love the way golden foliage combines with other colors to create vivid contrasts, while others think it just looks sickly. The latter group does have a point — yellowing foliage *can* be a sign of nutrient deficiencies — but it's certainly possible to use yellow-leaved plants in a way that makes them look deliberate and cared for, and not simply like testaments to poor fertilizing practices. This is a great excuse for using *lots* of gold foliage (and other colors, too) throughout your gardens: a single clump of yellow leaves might appear to be unhealthy, but an abundance of different yellow-leaved plants couldn't be interpreted as anything but intentional, especially when it's paired with other non-green foliage.

ABOVE: **Let there be light.** Clearly yellow in full sun, the fine-textured foliage of 'Angelina' sedum takes on much more of a greenish yellow cast in some shade.

OPPOSITE: **High impact, low maintenance.** Dotted into a carpet of creeping ajuga (*Ajuga reptans*), color-rich clumps of Bowles' golden sedge (*Carex elata* 'Aurea') create a striking color contrast throughout the growing season. (Chanticleer, PA)

## GETTING STARTED WITH GOLD

Leaves that are naturally yellow owe their coloration primarily to pigments called *carotenoids,* such as red lycopene, orange-yellow carotene, and yellow xanthophyll. Usually, carotenoids are covered up by the green chlorophyll and red-purple anthocyanin pigments, but when these other pigments are reduced or absent, the foliage may appear yellow-green, clear yellow, or orange-yellow. Carotenoids are always present in leaves and last much longer than chlorophyll; that's why some leaves turn yellow only when chlorophyll production declines in fall (and when weather conditions don't favor the formation of reddish pigments).

If a plant that's green starts turning yellow during the growing season, it's possible that it's producing new shoots that will stay all-yellow. (This phenomenon is called *lutescence.*) It's far more likely, though, that there's some nutrient imbalance in the soil; usually, more than one plant will show symptoms. This *chlorosis* is often due to a lack of nitrogen, magnesium, or iron. When nitrogen is deficient, the leaves tend to turn pale green and then yellow, usually starting at the tips and then working toward the main stem; the oldest (bottom) leaves are affected first. Magnesium deficiency also tends to show in the oldest leaves first, but it mostly discolors the tissue between the leaf veins; the veins stay green. Iron-deficiency symptoms resemble those of magnesium (yellow leaves with green veins), but in this case, the new leaves show symptoms first.

Phosphorus, calcium, sulfur, manganese, and copper imbalances can also cause various patterns of leaf yellowing. Little wonder, then, that many people think yellow foliage simply isn't healthy. Sometimes these problems correct themselves: if the weather gets warmer, for example, or if watering or rainfall increases soil moisture, making it easier for roots to take up the needed nutrients. In other cases, you may need to add fertilizer (as a short-term solution) and/or build up soil fertility with ample amounts of organic matter (for long-term health) so plants that are supposed to be green *stay* green. (Don't worry about healthy, fertile soil turning your naturally golden-leaved plants green; it will just make them grow better and help them produce more of that sunny yellow foliage.)

LEFT: **The early show.** The bright yellow spring foliage of some plants, including 'Goldheart' bleeding heart (*Dicentra spectabilis*), loses its rich color as temperatures rise.

OPPOSITE: **Changing with the times.** Cool temperatures tend to favor purple and red pigments, so don't be surprised to see orange or bronze tints on the new foliage of yellow-leaved plants, such as this golden catalpa (*Catalpa bignonioides* 'Aurea').

### Getting the Site Right

When you're considering yellow or golden foliage for your garden, keep in mind that the wide range of tints and shades has a big influence on how it will grow and how it will look with other plants. The exact kind of yellow you're dealing with depends on the plant itself, as well as on the season and the growing conditions.

The secret to getting the best from any kind of golden foliage is choosing cultivars that will thrive in the growing conditions you have available (or, of course, seeking out the right site in your yard for the plant that you've already purchased). Three major factors influence the golden effect.

**The amount of sunlight.** Some yellow-leaved plants, such as 'Gold Leaf' forsythia, need at least a partial day of shade; otherwise, they may bleach out to a pale yellow-green, develop an overall tan cast, or turn crispy brown on the leaf edges. Other yellow-leaved selections demand full sun, fading to a boring yellowish green or even plain green if they get too much shade.

**The intensity of sunlight.** Climate, too, often plays a role in determining ideal planting sites for yellow foliage. A certain plant may thrive in full sun in cooler climates but suffer in the strong sunlight of a southern summer. Golden hops (*Humulus lupulus* 'Aureus'), for example, typically thrives in all-day sun in mid Zone 6 and north; farther south, it tends to "scorch" (turn brown) unless it gets a bit of afternoon shade.

**Soil moisture levels.** Soil moisture affects how yellow-leaved plants perform in a particular area. They may look lush and lovely in full sun if the soil is evenly moist, but turn limp or crispy in the same amount of sunlight if the soil dries out during the growing season. Golden meadowsweet (*Filipendula ulmaria* 'Aurea'), 'All Gold' lemon balm (*Melissa officinalis*), and yellow-leaved toad lilies (*Tricyrtis*) and dead nettles (*Lamium maculatum*) are a few golden-foliage plants that are particularly prone to leaf scorch if they get lots of light but not enough water.

RIGHT: **Wow power.** Beautiful in its own right, golden foliage also provides exciting opportunities for creating traffic-stopping combinations, such as this pairing of 'Golden Jubilee' anise hyssop (*Agastache foeniculum*) and Johnny-jump-ups (*Viola tricolor*). (Morris Arboretum, PA)

## GOLDEN PLANTS THAT BASK IN FULL SUN

*Agastache foeniculum* 'Golden Jubilee'

*Alopecurus pratensis* 'Aureovariegatus'

*Carex elata* 'Aurea'

*Caryopteris* Sunshine Blue ('Jason'), 'Worcester Blue'

*Catalpa bignonioides* 'Aurea'

*Chamaecyparis obtusa* 'Fernspray Gold', 'Lynn's Golden', others

*Choisya ternata* Sundance ('Lich')

*Cornus mas* 'Aurea'

*Cotinus coggygria* Golden Spirit ('Ancot')

*Deutzia gracilis* Chardonnay Pearls ('Duncan')

*Erica carnea* 'Ann Sparkes', 'Golden Starlet', others

*Filipendula ulmaria* 'Aurea'

*Humulus lupulus* 'Aureus'

*Ipomoea batatas* 'Margarita', 'Sweet Caroline Light Green', others

*Jasminum officinale* Fiona Sunrise ('Frojas')

*Juniperus horizontalis* 'Lime Glow', 'Mother Lode', others

*Leycesteria formosa* Golden Lanterns ('Notbruce')

*Liriope muscari* 'Pee Dee Gold Ingot'

*Mirabilis jalapa* 'Limelight'

*Origanum vulgare* 'Aureum', 'Aureum Crispum', others

*Phaseolus coccineus* 'Sun Bright'

*Physocarpus opulifolius* 'Dart's Gold', 'Nugget', others

*Picea abies* 'Aurea', 'Gold Drift', others

*Rhus typhina* Tiger Eyes ('Bailtiger')

*Sedum rupestre* 'Angelina'

*Spiraea* 'Gold Mound', 'Golden Elf', others

*Taxus baccata* 'Aurea', 'Summergold', others

*Thuja occidentalis* 'Europe Gold', 'Rheingold', others

*Tradescantia Andersoniana* Group 'Chedglow', 'Sweet Kate'

*Veronica prostrata* 'Aztec Gold'

*Weigela* Briant Rubidor, 'Looymansii Aurea'

So how do you know what kind of conditions a given golden plant will prefer? Checking the information on the plant label or catalog description is a good starting point, but what if that's not available? Seeing how the plant in question performs in other gardens in your area—by going on garden tours, visiting botanical gardens and arboreta, observing nursery display beds, and checking out friends' gardens — is a good idea. If that's not an option, keep the plant in a pot for the first summer and set it where you think it will look good. If you see signs of scorching during the first few weeks (if the leaves bleach out to a pale yellow-green, develop an overall tan cast, or turn crispy brown), move the pot to a slightly shadier spot.

OPPOSITE: **Practical partnerships.** In sites where the soil doesn't stay dependably moist, taller companions may cast just enough shade to keep Bowles' golden sedge (*Carex elata* 'Aurea') and other yellow-leaved beauties looking good well into the summer. (Chanticleer, PA)

If the leaves turn green, gradually move it to a sunnier site. Some yellow-leaved plants, such as golden wood millet (*Milium effusum* 'Aureum'), will turn greenish in summer regardless of light levels. Thus, if changing the light level doesn't enhance the color, situate the plant wherever its green-leaved counterparts normally thrive and it should perform well there too; then, keep its seasonal color change in mind when planning combinations. (In some cases, cutting back the plant by a half to two-thirds will encourage a flush of more-colorful new growth; it's worth a try, at least on your perennials.)

Another approach to testing golden foliage is to plant it right in your garden, in growing conditions that are similar to what the all-green version likes. Getting a little too much or too little sun isn't likely to kill a plant, and it may settle in and adapt to the site after a few weeks. If it's still showing

LEFT: **Seasonal surprises.** The orange tones of 'Brigadoon' hypericum (*H. calycinum*) are most intense in the spring and fall, often disappearing completely during the summer months.

signs of scorching, providing a taller companion on the south side may supply just enough shade during the hottest part of the day to prevent further damage; conversely, removing an overshadowing companion will provide more light. If all else fails, dig up the golden plant and move it!

One other consideration when it comes to light: strong sun will really change the look of some golden leaves. A plant that bears clear yellow foliage in partial shade, for example, may take on brassy yellow or even distinctly orange tones when grown in full sun. (*Weigela* Briant Rubidor is one that comes to mind.) This isn't necessarily a bad thing — it doesn't seem to have a major influence on the health or vigor of the plant — but it's something you need to keep in mind when you're deciding where to site a new yellow-leaved acquisition, as well as when you're choosing companions for it.

## WHAT'S IN A NAME?

When you're seeking a new yellow-leaved plant to try, it will be easy to spot when you're shopping at a garden center. Just be sure to double-check the tag or label to make sure that the plant is **supposed** to be that color; sometimes weather conditions or a lack of fertilizer will cause normally green potted plants to turn yellowish. Buying by mail–order, especially from a catalog without pictures, makes the search a little trickier, but you can get a clue to the foliage color if you spot any of these terms in a plant's name.

This isn't foolproof, of course, because these terms can just as easily refer to the flowers as to the leaves. But when you're hunting for gold foliage, they're enough of a clue to make further research worthwhile.

| | | |
|---|---|---|
| amber | dawn | moon, moonbeam, moonlight |
| *aurata, -um, -us* (marked with gold) | daybreak | nugget |
| *aurea, -um, -us* (gold) | *flava, -um, -us* (bright yellow) | *ochracea, -um, -us* (pale yellow, cream) |
| *aureata, -um, -us* (with gold) | *flavescens* (yellowish) | *ochroleuca, -um, -us* (pale yellow white) |
| *aureola, -um, -us* (golden) | *flavida, -um, -us* (yellowish) | *ogon* (gold bullion, usually translated simply as gold) |
| *aurescens* (turning yellow) | gilt | ore |
| banana | glow | pineapple |
| blond | gold, golden | primrose |
| bullion | *icterina, -um, -us* (jaundice-yellow) | sulfur, sulphur |
| butter, buttercup | ingot | sun, sunburst, sunlight, sunny, sunrise, sunset, sunshine |
| canary | Klondike | *xanthina, -um, -us* (yellow) |
| chiffon | lemon | yellow |
| *chrysophylla, -um, -us* (with golden leaves) | lime | |
| citron, citrus | *lutea, -um, -us* (yellow) | |
| cream | *lutescens* (yellowish) | |
| | Midas | |

# HUES OF GARDEN GOLDS

**ERICA DARLEYENSIS 'MARY HELEN'**

**CHOISYA TERNATA SUNDANCE**

**HYPERICUM CALYCINUM 'BRIGADOON'**

**TANACETUM PARTHENIUM 'AUREUM'**

**IPOMOEA BATATAS 'SWEET CAROLINE BRONZE'**

**PICEA ORIENTALIS 'SKYLANDS'**

# GOLD IN THE GARDEN

Once you develop an appreciation of yellow-leaved plants, you'll find ample opportunities for using them in your garden. In sunny spots, they are invaluable for adding flowerlike color, even when blooms themselves are scarce. And in shady sites, a scattering of yellow foliage mimics the effect of dappled sunlight, adding welcome touches of brightness amid darker greens and blues.

A single clump of yellow foliage makes an eye-catching accent; a block of three or more plants makes a dramatic color statement. Where space is limited, it's fine to tuck single clumps of different golden plants throughout a bed or border. The repeated color helps to unify the design, while the diverse habits and leaf shapes keep things from getting monotonous.

When planning combinations with golden foliage, keep in mind that the leaf color can vary widely through the growing season. Some selections, such as 'Belsay Gold' comfrey (*Symphytum*), are bright yellow in spring, then turn green as the seasons progress. Sometimes cutting them back to the ground will encourage a flush of colorful new growth, but this trick doesn't always work. These changeable cultivars work best for an amazing early display; you'll need to use other plants for later color. Or base your combinations on yellow-leaved plants that hold their color well all through the growing season, such as Sunshine Blue caryopteris (*Caryopteris incana* 'Jason'). These dependable selections are the cornerstone of combinations that will look good throughout the growing season.

## Yellow Bedfellows

Planning pleasing combinations with yellow flowers and foliage is definitely a gardening challenge. Generally, the more similar the yellows, the more attractive the pairing; brassy orange-yellows against greenish yellows usually don't have enough of either contrast or harmony to really "work" together.

LEFT: **Brighten the mood.** Masses of willowy Mellow Yellow spirea (*Spiraea thunbergii* 'Ogon') make a cheerful complement to more-subdued hues of purple and green. (Chanticleer, PA)

RIGHT TOP: **Plan ahead.** Yellow-leaved plants that also have bright flowers, such as Briant Rubidor weigela, can be a little overwhelming in full bloom, so think carefully before planting large groupings of them. Often, a single clump is all you need!

RIGHT BOTTOM: **Don't lose the blues.** Purple and blue flowers tend to disappear into a background of green foliage, so why not try them against a backdrop of bright yellow instead? 'Sweet Kate' spiderwort (*Tradescantia* Andersoniana Group) combines both colors in a single plant.

When you combine similar shades of yellow, however, you need to include a good dash of at least one other color to prevent them from blending into each other. For example, a simple grouping of southern bush honeysuckle (*Diervilla sessilifolia*) in front of Tiger Eyes sumac (*Rhus typhina* 'Bailtiger') supplies a cheerful display of yellow all summer without being an indiscriminate mass of one color, because the bush honeysuckle's bright lemon blooms are scattered over its abundant, bright green foliage, providing just enough yellow to echo the sumac's bright chartreuse leaves. If you're looking for a more dramatic effect, try golden foliage with yellow-flowered plants that have purple, black, or pink leaves. 'Albury Purple' hypericum (*Hypericum androsaemum*), for example, has bright yellow blooms atop dusky purple foliage, which makes a vivid contrast to an underplanting of sunny yellow 'Sweet Caroline Light Green' sweet potato vine (*Ipomoea batatas*).

LEFT: **Bold and beautiful.** Yellow foliage can be so visually intense that pale-colored companions simply fade into the background. That's certainly not a problem with this pairing of 'Cherry Profusion' zinnia and 'Margarita' sweet potato vine (*Ipomoea batatas*), however!

If you want to extend a yellow theme throughout a planting, yellow-variegated leaves make a great "bridge" between like-colored flowers and golden foliage. The narrow, yellow-banded leaves of 'Gold Bar' miscanthus, for instance, provide a perfect visual link between the chartreuse mounds of Chardonnay Pearls deutzia (*Deutzia gracilis* 'Duncan') and the tall, greenish yellow blossoms of giant scabious (*Cephalaria gigantea*). Looking to leaves alone for color? Try yellow-variegated foliage to separate masses of different yellow-leaved plants, such as blue-and-gold 'Tokudama Flavocircinalis' hosta between golden elderberry (*Sambucus nigra* 'Aurea') and golden creeping Jenny (*Lysimachia nummularia* 'Aurea'). Solid-yellow foliage partners are also valuable for drawing attention to variegated companions with somewhat subtle yellow markings, such as 'Innocence' mock orange (*Philadelphus*) and 'Oehme' palm sedge (*Carex muskingumensis*)

*Carex buchananii*

## A STUDY IN BROWN

Of all the foliage colors to choose from, selecting plants with brown foliage takes the most horticultural chutzpah. Planning combinations around a plant that already looks dead definitely requires an adventurous design sense — or at least a good sense of humor! These oddities are tailor-made as accents, because for better or worse, they never fail to attract attention.

Brown leaves often have pink or orange tones in them, so you may be able to choose harmonious companions with flowers in those colors; yellow flowers and foliage are pleasing partners as well. Browns paired with silvers and blues are kind of dicey, but if you're going to give brown foliage a try, why not go all the way and do something really wild? You can always change it next year!

When you're shopping in a nursery or garden center, brown-leaved plants typically stand out easily from their more traditional counterparts. Most retail outlets don't carry many of these oddballs, though, because they're not strong sellers. When you're ready to expand your color horizons, start scouring mail-order catalogs and Web sites for these bizarre beauties. Color pictures are your best resource, but the names of the plants can often help clue you in to rust- or coffee-colored candidates.

In the plant-by-plant guide in this chapter, you'll find entries for some of the lightest brown leaves; darker browns are discussed in the Rousing Red to Basic Black chapter, starting on page 88.

| | | |
|---|---|---|
| amber | coffee | peach, peachy |
| auburn | copper | *rubiginosa, -um, -us* (rusty) |
| autumn | *cuprea, -um, -us* (coppery) | russet, rust, rusty |
| bronze | *cuprescens* (copper-colored) | *squalida, -um, -us* (dirty) |
| brown | *ferruginea, -um, -us* (rust-colored) | sunrise, sunset |
| cappuccino | | tawny |
| caramel | khaki | *testacea, -um, -us* (brick-colored) |
| *carnea, -um, -us* (flesh-colored) | marmalade | toffee |
| | ocher | |

## Yellow with Blue and Purple

Yellow-leaved plants make perfect partners for blue and purple flowers. In fact, you can often find this exact combination in a single plant: 'Gold Bullion' mountain bluet (*Centaurea montana*) and 'Aztec Gold' speedwell (*Veronica prostrata*) are just two examples. The more intense the color of the bloom, the more dramatic the combination will be. Pale blue and lavender hues often fade into the background against light green leaves, but they really benefit from the bright cheer of yellow foliage. Chartreuse and blue leaves (such as those of many hostas) look cool and stylish together, and deep purple leaves make a vibrant contrast to any kind of golden foliage.

LEFT: **Stunning simplicity.** Rising up through the lacy leaves of 'Goldenvale' white-stemmed bramble (*Rubus cockburnianus*), the green shoot tips of 'Black Pearl' pepper (*Capsicum annuum*) quickly turn deep purple, creating a dramatic color contrast.

RIGHT: **Perfect partners.** This container combination of Fiona Sunrise common jasmine (*Jasminum officinale* 'Frojas'), 'Sweet Caroline Purple' sweet potato vine (*Ipomoea batatas*), and heliotrope (*Heliotropium arborescens*) has it all: rich color, textural interest, and great fragrance, too!

ABOVE: **A vivid image.** Shocking pink flowers against chartreuse foliage make 'Limelight' four-o'clock (*Mirabilis jalapa*) an unforgettable garden annual.

OPPOSITE: **Out of the ordinary.** For a somewhat softer effect, pair the pink flowers of kangaroo paws (*Anigozanthos*) with Fiona Sunrise common jasmine (*Jasminum officinale* 'Frojas') and a purple-leaved sweet potato vine (*Ipomoea batatas*).

### Yellow with Pink and Red

Yellow foliage paired with pink flowers is not a combination everyone enjoys, but apparently it appeals to Mother Nature, because she's provided us with that very combination in many spirea selections, as well as in 'Goldheart' bleeding heart (*Dicentra spectabilis*) and 'Limelight' four-o'clock (*Mirabilis jalapa*). For an even richer contrast, try yellow-leaved plants that have red flowers, such as golden hardy fuchsia (*Fuchsia magellanica* 'Aurea'), 'Tip Top Mahogany' nasturtium (*Tropaeolum majus*), and 'Sun Bright' runner bean (*Phaseolus coccineus*). Or choose green-leaved companions with rich red, pink, and maroon blooms, such as wine-red knautia (*Knautia macedonica*), cardinal red 'Jacob Cline' bee balm (*Monarda*), or bright pink 'Versailles Tetra' cosmos (*Cosmos bipinnatus*). Rich purplish pinks — like the blooms of 'Plum Crazy' hibiscus — also look great with yellow leaves. Unlike light blues and purples, pale shades of pink generally don't show off to advantage against golden foliage.

Think you'd like to pair yellow and pink foliage? As with flowers, deeper shades of pink tend to give the most satisfying contrast. For a really dramatic combination, consider the effect of golden foliage with red leaves, such as those of Japanese blood grass (*Imperata cylindrica* var. *koenigii* 'Rubra').

For a really knock-your-socks-off combo, it's tough to beat golden foliage paired with magenta flowers. Let the vining stems and bright blooms of *Petunia integrifolia* wind their way up through a mass of 'Giant Exhibition Limelight' coleus, for instance, or use the golden-leaved, magenta-flowered 'Anne Thomson' geranium as an underplanting for the purple-pink 'Moje Hammarberg' rose (*Rosa rugosa*).

### Yellow with White

Crisp white blooms are elegant against golden foliage. Single selections with that very combination include golden mock orange (*Philadelphus coronarius* 'Aureus') and 'Goldenvale' white-stemmed bramble (*Rubus cockburnianus*). Separate white-flowered plants work well too, particularly when the white blossoms have distinct yellow anthers or markings that echo the color of their golden-leaved partners. White-variegated plants, on the other hand, typically don't make pleasing partners for yellow foliage, perhaps because they are both so eye-catching and fight each other for attention.

## Yellow with Other Colors

Without a doubt, yellow leaves make excellent bedmates for burgundy, black, and dark green foliage. You might, for example, pair the grassy, golden foliage of 'Pee Dee Gold Ingot' lilyturf (*Liriope muscari*) with the broad, chocolate brown leaves of 'Burnished Bronze' foamy bells (× *Heucherella*). Or try the "ever-yellow" tufts of golden greater woodrush (*Luzula sylvatica* 'Aurea') as an underplanting for evergreen stinking hellebore (*Helleborus foetidus*) to create a splendid winter combination. These simple but stunning partnerships are easy to create and seldom fail to please. Admittedly, there are a few gardeners who scorn yellow-and-burgundy pairings as being unsophisticated *because* they're so easy to make. But if you're gardening for beauty and love those colors together, don't be deterred from using them.

LEFT: **Guaranteed to please.** Set against a dark background — in the form of foliage, hardscaping, or garden ornaments — the glowing leaves of 'Key Lime Pie' heuchera are sure to attract attention.

OPPOSITE: **A bright idea.** The new foliage of 'Limelight' licorice plant (*Helichrysum petiolare*) is vibrant enough to hold its own against any silver-leaved companion.

Pairing yellow foliage with silver and gray leaves takes a more adventurous spirit. Generally, the results are most satisfying when the partners have some strongly contrasting feature (form or texture): fuzzy lamb's ears (*Stachys byzantina*) against the small, smooth leaves of golden oregano (*Origanum vulgare* 'Aureum'), for example. If the foliage you're working with is bright silver and rich yellow — as with 'Powis Castle' artemisia and 'Lemon Princess' spirea (*Spiraea japonica*) — then the color contrast may be enough to carry off the pairing effectively.

The combination of brown and yellow foliage is a matter of taste. The contrast is undeniably eye-catching, but whether it's pleasing depends on how you feel about brown foliage to begin with. Think you want to try? Consider bronzy *Carex comans* surrounded by a pool of yellow 'Angelina' sedum (*Sedum rupestre*), or 'Sweet Caroline Bronze' sweet potato vine (*Ipomoea batatas*) as a ground cover around Golden Lanterns Himalayan honeysuckle (*Leycesteria formosa* 'Notbruce').

Two other flower colors to consider for yellow-leaved partners are orange and green. Matching the intensity of the orange and yellow usually gives the most attractive results. Bright orange cannas look smashing

in front of golden yellow 'Sutherland Gold' elderberry (*Sambucus racemosa*), for instance; peachy Orange Meadowbrite coneflower (*Echinacea* 'Art's Pride') looks lovely with greenish yellow 'All Gold' lemon balm (*Melissa officinalis*). To complement green flowers (which are typically on the yellow-green side), choose foliage partners in the same color range. Two of my favorite pairings in this range are *Nicotiana langsdorffii* with yellow-leaved hostas and 'Envy' zinnia with golden catalpa (*Catalpa bignonioides* 'Aurea').

## EXPANDING YOUR PLANT PALETTE

To help you find the perfect foliage option for any combination, the plant-by-plant entries in each chapter are organized by overall texture, indicated by the icons below.

SPIKY     BOLD     MEDIUM     FINE     LACY

Throughout this book, you'll notice that many plant names are enclosed in single quotes (for example, 'Frosty Fire' dianthus); these are cultivar names. When particular plants also have trademarked names, these appear without single quotes (as in Tiger Eyes sumac).

## ALOPECURUS
*Foxtail grass*

**Height: 1 foot**
**Leaf size: 6–10 inches long;**
**⅛–¼ inch wide**
**Full sun to partial shade**
**Zones 4–8**

Golden meadow foxtail (*Alopecurus pratensis* 'Aureovariegatus'; also known as 'Aureus' or 'Variegatus') is an out-of-the-ordinary option for adding spiky, sun-bright foliage to your spring and fall garden. This perennial grass grows in loose tufts of narrow, upright foliage that's semievergreen in mild climates, spreading slowly by rhizomes to form handsome, easy-to-control patches. It also qualifies as a variegated plant because some of its blades are striped with bright green, but other leaves are solid yellow and the whole plant looks yellow from a distance. Slender, spike-like flower clusters bloom atop slender stems usually 2 to 3 feet tall; they don't add anything to the show, though. A single plant or a small grouping makes a good accent in a border; a larger mass makes an interesting cool-season ground cover. It's particularly stunning interplanted with bright blue Siberian squill (*Scilla siberica*) or blue forget-me-nots (*Myosotis*).

**GROWING TIPS:** Golden meadow foxtail keeps its brightest yellow in full sun; in partial shade, it ages to a softer greenish yellow. Evenly moist but well-drained soil is ideal, although it will adapt to average border conditions. Shear off the flower spikes to keep the plants looking tidy; if needed, trim the plants to the ground in mid- to late summer to make way for fresh fall growth.

**ALTERNATIVES:** Golden grassy-leaved sweet flag (*Acorus gramineus* 'Ogon' or 'Wogon') has fine green striping on glossy yellow leaves to 1 foot tall. 'Minimus Aureus' is bright yellow in spring, aging to greenish yellow; 3 inches tall. Both grow in moist soil or even standing water with full sun to partial shade. Zones 6 to 10.

*Alopecurus pratensis* 'Variegatus'

*Carex elata* 'Aurea'

## CAREX
*Sedge*

**Height: Varies**
**Leaf size: Varies**
**Full sun to partial shade**
**Zones vary**

For shade or sun, average soil to standing water, sedges (*Carex*) can fit into just about any part of your garden. Besides ranging in height and habit (from distinctly upright to elegantly arching), they also come in a range of colors, including the bright yellow to bronzy brown selections discussed here. Enjoy them at the front of a mixed border or foundation planting, as accents in water gardens or container plantings, or in masses as grasslike ground covers. Sedges do flower, but the greenish to brown inflorescences aren't especially interesting.

*With yellow foliage.* For pure color power, it's tough to beat Bowles' golden sedge (*C. elata* 'Aurea'; also sold as 'Bowles Golden'). Its deciduous, upright clumps grow 18 to 30 inches tall, with 18- to 24-inch-long, ¼-inch-wide blades that are bright yellow with barely visible green stripes. 'Knightshayes' is similar but has no green at all. Both of these thrive in full sun with constantly wet soil to several inches of standing water; they will take slightly drier conditions with some shade. Zones 5 to 8. *C. siderosticha* 'Lemon Zest' is also deciduous but has much broader leaf blades — about 1 inch wide and 6 to 10 inches long. They are bright yellow from spring into summer, aging to greenish yellow (especially in shade), and grow in slowly expanding clumps 10 inches tall and about as wide. Partial to full shade with evenly moist to wet soil. Zones 5 or 6 to 9.

*With brown foliage.* Commonly called New Zealand or hair sedges, these curiously colored "ever-brown" perennials create distinctively different accent plants. True, the brown doesn't appeal to everyone, but many adventurous gardeners enjoy the challenge of finding the perfect sites and partners to show off these elegant oddities. (Use them to echo the color of browning seedheads on other perennials and shrubs, so you'll have an excuse not to bother with deadheading!) New Zealand sedges grow in full sun to partial shade. Evenly moist soil is especially important in sunny sites. Plants in partial shade will tolerate slightly drier conditions, although their colors may not be as rich. Good drainage, especially in winter, is important in any site. Most of these are rated as winter-hardy only in Zones 6 or 7 to 10, but gardeners in cooler climates (even as far north as Zone 4) are reporting success with some of them. If you live where these sedges are questionably hardy and don't want to risk losing them, consider bringing them indoors for the winter.

There are many brown-leaved sedges to choose from and new ones are available every year. Whether mounding or upright, the glossy foliage is typically 18 to 30 inches long and about ⅛ inch wide. The leaf colors range from tan to pinkish (coppery) brown to orange-brown to greenish brown, so you're best off selecting species and cultivars in person if you want a specific color for a combination.

Mounding New Zealand sedges have long, slender, arching leaves that look lovely cascading out of a container, over a wall, or on a slope. Options in this group are 1-foot-tall *C. comans* 'Bronze' ('Bronze Form') and 2-foot tall *C. comans* 'Milk Chocolate'. Plants sold under the names *C. tenuiculmis*, *C. secta* var. *tenuiculmis*, 'Bronzina', and 'Cappuccino' are in the 1- to 2-foot-tall range; so are *C. flagellifera* and *C. flagellifera* 'Toffee Twist'.

Other New Zealand sedges tend to stay in more upright, V-shaped clumps, although they, too, may appear mounding as their older leaves start to arch outward. They also develop curly leaf tips. Options in this group are leatherleaf sedge (*C. buchananii*) and the aptly named *C.* 'Bad Hair Day'. Both grow about 2 feet tall; *C. petriei* is about 1 foot tall.

**GROWING TIPS:** Although sedges are rather adaptable, you'll get the best results with the least amount of work if you select those that are best suited to the normal growing conditions your garden has to offer. Cut off the dead growth of deciduous sedges before new growth starts in spring. On the "ever-browns," use a rake or your fingers to pull out the dead leaves; you may also want to trim off the flowers to prevent the plants from self-sowing.

**ALTERNATIVES:** *Libertia peregrinans* bears upright, olive to golden green leaves shaded with orange, especially in cool weather; about

2 feet tall. Full sun to partial shade; average, well-drained soil. Zones 8 to 11. New Zealand wind grass (*Anemanthele lessoniana* or *Stipa arundinacea*) has arching, orange-tinged green leaves that turn solid orange-brown in winter; 2 to 4 feet tall. Full sun average to dry, well-drained soil; Zones 7 or 8 to 10.

## HAKONECHLOA
*Hakone grass*

**Height: 12–18 inches tall**
**Leaf size: 8–12 inches long;**
**about ½ inch wide**
**Partial to full shade**
**Zones 5–8**

Finding ornamental grasses for shade — and especially *golden* grasses — can be a real design challenge. Thanks to 'All Gold' Hakone grass (*Hakonechloa macra*), we now have an elegant option to fill that distinctive texture and color niche. Held on thin, upright-then-arching stems, its long, narrow leaves are bright golden yellow where light is ample and greenish yellow in deep shade, with orange to reddish shading in fall. Airy clusters of yellow-tan flowers and seedheads appear in late summer. Let 'All Gold' arch over the edge of a planter or hanging basket, or use it to create pools of sun-bright color in a woodland garden. It makes a superb textural contrast to bold-leaved partners and a striking color contrast to dark green, purple, and black foliage.

**GROWING TIPS:** All-day shade is ideal in hot-summer areas;

*Hakonechloa macra 'All Gold'*

morning sun with afternoon shade brings out the best color in cooler climates. Fertile, evenly moist but well-drained soil is ideal, although the plants will withstand average garden conditions. Hakone grass tends to be slow-growing, but planting in compost-enriched soil, keeping the soil evenly moist, and mulching well with compost will encourage faster growth.

**ALTERNATIVE:** *Pleioblastus auricomus* 'Chrysophyllus' (also listed under *P. viridistriatus*) is a bamboo with light yellow to greenish yellow foliage; about 3 feet tall in fast-spreading clumps. Keep in a container, or mow a wide strip around it regularly to contain it. Best in morning sun and afternoon shade or light all-day shade; average, well-drained soil. Usually rated for Zones 7 to 11, but may survive into Zone 4.

*Liriope muscari* 'Pee Dee Gold Ingot'

## LIRIOPE
*Lilyturf, liriope*

**Height: 10–12 inches**
**Leaf size: About 1 foot long;**
   **⅓ inch wide**
**Full sun to full shade**
**Zones 5 or 6–10**

Sunny yellow foliage is a great color accent during the growing season, but it's even more welcome in the winter landscape. Like other lilyturfs, *Liriope muscari* 'Pee Dee Gold Ingot' (also listed as 'Peedee Ingot') is a sturdy, adaptable choice that makes a fantastic border accent as well as a gorgeous ground cover for just about any garden site. It grows in spreading mounds of arching, narrow leaves that are bright green-tinged yellow when new, aging to lighter yellow later in the season. Spike-like clusters of small, purple-blue blossoms in mid- to late summer make an eye-catching complement to the foliage.

**GROWING TIPS:** 'Pee Dee Gold Ingot' tends to hold its brightest color in full sun with evenly moist but well-drained soil. In average garden soil, a site with morning sun and afternoon shade or light all-day shade is usually ideal. The foliage normally holds up well through the winter, but if it becomes tattered-looking, mow or trim off the top growth in late winter to early spring to make room for the new leaves.

**ALTERNATIVE:** The narrow, glossy leaves of golden greater woodrush (*Luzula sylvatica* 'Aurea') are greenish yellow when new and bright yellow when older (especially in sun). Great as an "ever-yellow" ground cover, border accent, or container plant. Morning sun and afternoon shade or light all-day shade; average, well-drained soil. Zones 6 to 9.

## TRADESCANTIA
*Spiderwort*

**Height: 1–2 feet**
**Leaf size: 8–12 inches long;**
   **½–1 inch wide**
**Full sun to partial shade**
**Zones 3–9**

Spiderworts (*Tradescantia* Andersoniana Group) may have their place — they flower for a good part of the growing season, after all — but their rather floppy nature, scattered blooms, and overall lack of "wow" power keeps them off most gardeners' top-ten lists. With the addition of bright yellow foliage, however, a lot can be forgiven, particularly when it's paired with rich purple-blue blooms from early summer into fall. Looking much like a compact, golden-leaved ornamental grass, the spreading clumps of 'Sweet Kate' (also sold as 'Blue and Gold') offer both color and texture to beds and borders from spring to frost. 'Chedglow' is similar, but its flowers are more pinkish purple. These moisture-loving perennials also make a striking addition to pond- or streamside plantings.

**GROWING TIPS:** Yellow-leaved spiderworts keep their brightest color in full sun, but evenly moist to wet soil is a must to keep the leaves from browning there. With morning sun and afternoon shade or light all-day shade, they will grow quite happily in average, well-drained soil. Clip off the faded flowers to prevent self-sowing and encourage rebloom. If the plants start to sprawl, turn greenish yellow, or simply look scruffy by midsummer, cut all of the stems to the ground and water well. Fresh growth will quickly appear and stay great-looking through the fall; plants will probably flower again as well.

**ALTERNATIVE:** Golden wood millet (*Milium effusum* 'Aureum'), also known as Bowles' golden grass, grows in loose, 1-foot-tall clumps of long, arching, bright yellow leaves that fade to greenish yellow by midsummer. A perfect partner for spring bulbs and early-flowering perennials in mixed borders or spring-sunny woodland gardens; in summer, it prefers light shade (especially if the soil doesn't stay dependably moist). Zones 5 to 9.

*Tradescantia* 'Sweet Kate'

## CATALPA
*Catalpa, Indian bean tree*

**Height: 30–40 feet (tree form)**
**Leaf size: 6–10 inches long and**
**wide**
**Full sun**
**Zones 5–9**

If you're looking for bold yellow foliage on a grand scale, golden catalpa (*Catalpa bignonioides* 'Aurea') could be just the ticket. Let it grow into its natural tree form, and its broad, rounded crown will light up the landscape from the time it leafs out in spring until midsummer, when the leaves turn greenish. Or treat it as a cut-back shrub (pruned to a 1- to 2-foot-tall framework every year in early spring) to get larger, brighter leaves on 6- to 10-foot-tall stems; this way, you can enjoy it as a big border shrub. The new growth of this deciduous tree is often tinged with purple or bronze, turning bright yellow and then aging to greenish yellow or light green. Tree-form plants produce clusters of white flowers in late spring to early summer, followed by long, narrow seedpods. *Note:* The species is considered invasive in some areas.

**GROWING TIPS:** Golden catalpa needs full sun but is more flexible about its soil conditions, adapting to just about any well-drained site. This vigorous, fast-growing plant is sensitive to late frosts when young, so plan on supplying some frost protection for the first few years. Catalpas are susceptible to a number of pests and diseases, but they usually recover on their own by producing a new set of leaves and/or sending up new shoots.

**ALTERNATIVES:** 'Golden Shadow' paper mulberry (*Broussonetia papyrifera*) has lobed to heart-shaped leaves that are bright yellow through most — if not all — of the growing season. Unpruned, it's a large tree to 30 feet tall or more; pruned back to 1 to 2 feet, it stays 6 to 10 feet tall. Zones 6 to 9. *Note:* The species is considered invasive in some areas. 'Golden Glory' Harlequin glorybower (*Clerodendrum trichotomum*) has heart-shaped, bright yellow new leaves, aging to yellowish green. Normally a large shrub or small tree, it often dies back to the ground in the coldest parts of its range. Zones 6 or 7 to 9. Full sun to partial shade; average, well-drained soil.

*Catalpa bignonioides* 'Aurea'

## HOSTA
*Hosta*

**Height: Varies**
**Leaf size: Varies**
**Full sun to partial shade**
**Zones 3–8**

Ask a gardener to name some classic shade perennials, and chances are that hostas (*Hosta*) will be at the top of the list. But shade isn't the only place these versatile plants can grow; in fact, yellow-leaved hostas typically produce their best colors in full sun. As one of the few options that combine bold texture and golden foliage on a compact, hardy perennial, gold-leaved hostas are invaluable for a dramatic splash of color and structure to mixed borders.

When choosing yellow-leaved hostas, it pays to do your homework before you buy. Don't rely on a book or catalog picture, or the color of a cute little container-grown plant in a spring garden center display, because that shows just one moment in time. You see, some hostas emerge in spring the most glorious yellow you can imagine, then turn yellowish green by midsummer; others come up greenish and take a while to develop their full yellow effect; then there are those that offer fairly consistent coloring throughout the growing season. If it's important to you to have a certain color intensity in a certain season, visit local display gardens at that time of year to see the plants for yourself.

There are many dozens of gold-leaved hostas to choose from in a wide range of leaf shapes, leaf sizes, and plant sizes, and new ones appear every year, so it's not possible to give more than a brief sampling of them here. Among the smallest selections (up to about 1 foot tall and 2 feet wide in leaf) are 'Chartreuse Wiggles', with very narrow, wavy-edged

*Hosta* 'Piedmont Gold'

*Xanthosoma* 'Lime Zinger'

leaves that emerge greenish yellow and age to greenish; 'Cheatin Heart', with bright yellow, heart-shaped leaves; and 'Little Black Scape', with lance-shaped leaves that are greenish at first and bright yellowish green by summer, with contrasting deep purple flower stems.

In the 1- to 2-foot-tall, 2- to 3-foot-wide range, check out 'Dawn's Early Light', with broad, bright yellow leaves that age to light yellow or greenish yellow; 'Gold Regal', with bright yellow to yellowish green, heart-shaped leaves on vase-shaped plants; 'Richland Gold', with narrower, heart-shaped leaves that emerge greenish yellow and age to pale or rich yellow; and 'Piedmont Gold', with broad, yellowish green leaves that turn bright yellow for summer.

Have a really big space to fill? Consider some of the super-sized, broad-leaved selections, which grow 20 to 30 inches tall and eventually spread to 3 to 4 feet wide — or even wider! 'Squash Casserole' emerges green and turns bright greenish yellow; 'Zounds' has even larger, puckered and cupped leaves that start out light green and age to bright yellow. 'Sun Power' has a more upright habit, emerging yellowish green and aging to light or bright yellow. The biggest of the bunch is 'Sum and Substance', which forms massive clumps of broad, glossy, yellow-green to light yellow foliage.

**GROWING TIPS:** Yellow-leaved hostas thrive in full sun if the soil is evenly moist; in average, well-drained soil, try them with morning sun and afternoon shade. It's not unusual to see some leaf browning on yellow hostas during their first growing season. If the problem continues, though, water them regularly or move them to a slightly shadier site. Clip off the flower stems after the blooms fade to tidy the clumps.

**ALTERNATIVE:** Fast-growing 'Belsay Gold' comfrey (*Symphytum*) produces sizable mounds (2 to 3 feet tall and wide) of large, fuzzy leaves that emerge bright yellow in spring. The foliage turns greenish by midsummer, but if you cut back the whole plant to the ground, new yellowish-green growth will appear. Full sun to partial shade; average to moist, well-drained soil. Zones 5 to 8.

## XANTHOSOMA
*Xanthosoma,* elephant's ears

**Height: 10–12 feet (where fully hardy)**
**Leaf size: 1–2 feet long; 8–12 inches wide**
**Partial to full shade**
**Zones 8–11**

*Subtle* is definitely not a word that comes to mind where 'Lime Zinger' xanthosoma (*Xanthosoma mafaffa* or *X. aurea*) appears in a combination. Also known as 'Chartreuse Giant', 'Golden Delicious', and 'Lime Green', this heat-loving, tender perennial bears bright yellow leaves where light is abundant and yellow-green to light green foliage in more shade. Grow it in the ground or enjoy it in a large-scale container (it usually stays 3 to 4 feet tall and wide in a pot); either way, the big bold leaves will add a touch of the tropics to any planting. 'Lime Zinger' looks absolutely amazing paired with dark foliage, such as purple-leaved coleus or the equally large 'Black Magic' colocasia (*Colocasia esculenta* 'Black Magic').

**GROWING TIPS:** Light all-day shade or morning sun with afternoon shade is ideal; the leaves may bleach out in too much sun. Fertile, evenly moist soil is best. Ample warmth, moisture, and fertilizer produce the biggest leaves and most vigorous growth. Where 'Lime Zinger' isn't hardy, bring it indoors in fall before temperatures drop much below 60°F (15°C) and grow it as a houseplant if you have the space. Otherwise, allow it to go dormant and store it in a cool, dry place.

**ALTERNATIVE:** For a bold effect from a hardier perennial, consider 'Hollard's Gold' bear's breeches (*Acanthus mollis;* also known as 'New Zealand Gold' and 'Fielding Gold'). Its dense, 3- to 4-foot-tall and -wide clumps of broad, lobed, glossy leaves emerge bright yellow, usually softening to greenish yellow or mostly green in summer. Full sun to light shade; humus-rich, average to evenly moist but well-drained soil. Zones 5 or 6 to 9.

## AGASTACHE
*Anise hyssop*

**Height: 2–3 feet**
**Leaf size: 2–3 inches long;**
**        2 inches wide**
**Full sun to partial shade**
**Zones 5 or 6–9**

Fragrant foliage, beautiful blooms, *and* golden foliage on an easy-to-grow perennial — what more could you ask for? 'Golden Jubilee' anise hyssop (*Agastache foeniculum*) has it all, making it an outstanding multi-season addition to a border, foundation planting, or container. It's absolutely glorious in spring, with bright yellow shoots that may be bronze-tinged at the tips; by midsummer, the older leaves turn greenish yellow. Spikes of small, light purple-blue flowers appear in late spring to early summer and continue all the way into fall. If you let the spikes dry on the plant and don't cut them down, you can enjoy their form well into winter. The entire plant has a licorice-mint or root beer scent when you rub it, so it's tempting to place it near a path or bench; be aware, though, that bees really love the blooms.

**GROWING TIPS:** 'Golden Jubilee' will adapt to a wide range of growing conditions, but it's at its best in full sun with evenly moist but well-drained soil. Even if it's not hardy in your area, you can enjoy it as an annual because it blooms the first year from seed.

The plants often self-sow freely, so once you've grown them through a full season, you'll probably always have "volunteers" coming up each year. If the foliage gets dull-looking during the summer, shearing back the plants by about a third will encourage a flush of brighter new shoots.

**ALTERNATIVE:** If you're more interested in foliage than flowers, golden orach (*Atriplex hortensis* 'Golden') makes a lovely color accent from early spring to late summer. This easy annual grows 3 to 6 feet tall, with upright stems bearing lance-shaped to triangular, smooth, light yellow leaves. Full sun; average to evenly moist but well-drained soil. *Note:* The species is considered invasive in some areas.

*Agastache foeniculum* 'Golden Jubilee'

*Aquilegia vulgaris* 'Woodside Gold'

## AQUILEGIA
*Columbine*

**Height: 2–3 feet**
**Leaf size: About 1 inch long; ½–**
**        1 inch wide (individual leaflet)**
**Full sun to partial shade**
**Zones 3 or 4–8**

Columbines (*Aquilegia*) have long been treasured for their nodding, spurred, late-spring to early-summer blooms, but they normally don't have much to offer for the rest of the year. Those with golden foliage, though, extend their season of interest from early spring well into summer, so they make a more significant contribution to beds, borders, and woodland gardens. Columbines grow in rosettes of compound leaves made up of small, lobed leaflets, with separate, upright flowering stems. *A. vulgaris* 'Mellow Yellow' has clear yellow new leaves softening to light yellow, with white to pale blue flowers. *A.* 'Roman Bronze' has bright yellow new leaves that develop a light orange shading, with deep purple flowers. *A.* 'Sunburst Ruby' has bright yellow foliage with deep pinkish red blooms. *A. vulgaris* 'Woodside Gold' ('Woodside Golden') foliage emerges bright yellow and ages to light yellow or greenish yellow, with pink, blue, or white flowers.

**GROWING TIPS:** Columbines will adapt to a range of growing conditions, but they thrive in morning sun and afternoon shade or light all-day shade with humus-rich, evenly moist but well-drained soil. Cut off most of the flowering stems once the blossoms fade. Columbine plants tend to die out after a few years, so let a few blossoms set seed; that way, you'll always have young plants coming along. They likely won't have the same flower colors as the parent plants, but they'll probably have yellow foliage. (Pull out any all-green seedlings.) Cut the whole plant to the ground in midsummer, and it will produce a flush of bright new foliage for the rest of the season.

**ALTERNATIVE:** 'Sunningdale Gold' masterwort (*Astrantia major*) is another beauty for the spring garden. This 12- to 18-inch-tall, clump-forming perennial emerges in spring with eye-catching, medium to light yellow, deeply lobed leaves that gradually age to greenish yellow and then solid green in summer (cut to the ground for bright new growth). Full sun (in cool climates) to partial shade; average to moist but well-drained soil. Zones 4 to 7.

## CHOISYA
*Mexican orange blossom*

**Height: 5–7 feet**
**Leaf size: 2–3 inches long; about**
**    1 inch wide (individual leaflet)**
**Full sun to partial shade**
**Zones 7 or 8–10**

Sundance Mexican orange blossom (*Choisya ternata* 'Lich'): to see it is to want it! At its best, this bushy shrub is a stunning sight, with three-part leaves that are bright to medium yellow when new, eventually aging to light yellow or chartreuse and staying attractive all year long. Sometimes, though, it can be challenging to get — or keep — the richly colored new growth. In too much sun, it may scorch (turn brown); in too much heat (especially with warm nights), it can be a not-as-appealing greenish yellow; and in too much shade, it may be mostly or entirely green. Still, it's worth

*Choisya ternata* Sundance

trying to find the perfect spot so you can enjoy the handsome foliage, as well as the fragrant white flowers that may appear in spring and possibly again in fall. Where it's hardy, Sundance is lovely in a mixed border or foundation planting; elsewhere, enjoy it in a container for the summer and bring it into a protected place for the winter. Goldfingers ('Limo') is a newer selection with longer, narrower leaflets that create a more fine-textured effect.

**GROWING TIPS:** In cooler areas, golden Mexican orange blossom grows well in full sun; in warmer climates, morning sun and afternoon shade will reduce the chance of scorching but still encourage a good yellow color. Average to moist but well-drained, acidic soil is ideal. If there are some winter-damaged leaves, clipping about 6 inches from the shoot tips in late spring is a good way to remove them and encourage a flush of colorful new growth as well.

**ALTERNATIVE:** Left unpruned, deciduous golden privet (*Ligustrum* 'Vicaryi') forms a rounded shrub 8 to 12 feet tall and wide, with bright yellow leaves through the growing season if in full sun; in shadier sites, they turn yellowish green or all green. Average, well-drained soil. Zones 5 to 8. *Note:* Several species of privet are considered invasive in many areas; this one, however, currently doesn't appear to be a problem.

## CORNUS
*Dogwood*

**Height: Varies**
**Leaf size: Varies**
**Full sun to partial shade**
**Zones vary**

Dogwoods (*Cornus*) are a terrific choice for multi-season interest: not just golden foliage, but also showy flowers, bright berries, and/or colorful winter stems. They also tend to be a lot hardier than are many yellow-leaved woody plants, so they're especially useful for cooler climates.

Golden Cornelian cherry (*C. mas* 'Aureus') is an unusual deciduous shrub or small tree that grows 10 to 15 feet tall over time, with light yellow new leaves usually aging to green-tinged yellow or yellowish green for summer, then turning purplish in fall. The mature leaves are 3 to 4 inches long and 1 to 2 inches wide. Small but abundant yellow flowers bloom in late winter to early spring, ripening into bright red berries by midsummer. Older trees develop attractively peeling bark that extends the show into winter. Zones 4 to 8.

Among the shrubby dogwoods are golden red-twig dogwood (*C. alba* 'Aurea'), which grows about 6 feet tall and wide, and larger 'Sunshine' western red osier dogwood (*C. sericea* var. *occidentalis* or *C. stolonifera*), which can reach 10 feet tall and wide. Both have bright yellow new growth and tend to hold their color well

*Cornus sericea* 'Sunshine'

through the season if they get plenty of light. Their mature leaves are typically 4 to 5 inches long and about 3 inches wide. They also produce clusters of white flowers followed by white berries, but these features aren't especially noticeable. Be aware that plants sold as 'Sunshine' sometimes have variegated leaves instead of solid-gold foliage, so it's best to buy in person or confirm the leaf color before buying by mail order. Zones 2 to 8.

**GROWING TIPS:** Golden Cornelian cherry can be a little tricky to situate just right — in too much sun, the leaves will bleach out or scorch; in too much shade, they will be mostly green. A site with morning sun and light afternoon shade and average, well-drained soil is usually ideal. The shrubby dogwoods are at their best in full sun and moist soil, although they will adapt to partial shade with average, well-drained soil. Pruning these types heavily in late winter controls their size and encourages the production of more-colorful young stems; either remove up to a third of the oldest stems at the base of the plant each year or cut all of the stems to 6 to 12 inches above the ground every other year.

**ALTERNATIVES:** The leaves of golden forsythias (*Forsythia*) are so bright, the plants look like they're blooming all through the growing season. Two of the most commonly available choices are *F. × intermedia* 'Gold Leaf' ('Goldleaf'), which grows 5 to 7 feet tall and wide, and *F. koreana* 'Suwan Gold', usually 3 to 4 feet tall and wide. Best in partial shade with average, well-drained soil. Zones 5 to 9.

## COTINUS
*Smoke tree*

**Height: Varies**
**Leaf size: 3 inches long;**
   **2–3 inches wide**
**Full sun to partial shade**
**Zones 4–8**

Train it as a small tree or keep it as a bushy shrub: either way, Golden Spirit smoke tree (*Cotinus coggygria* 'Ancot') is an out-of-the-ordinary addition to a mixed border, shrub border, or foundation planting. Other smoke tree selections are prized for their airy flower clusters and/or deep purple foliage, but this one stands out for its glowing bright to light yellow, deciduous leaves, which may also be tinged with orange to red when new. It can also produce the usual pinkish, smokelike plumes in summer, by the way, and its fall color is excellent, too (usually a mix of yellow, red, and orange), so it has a lot to offer. Left unpruned, it can reach 10 feet tall or more. If you cut it back to a 1- to 3-foot framework each year in early spring, the stems may still reach 6 to 8 feet tall; they usually won't flower, but they'll have somewhat larger-than-usual leaves.

**GROWING TIPS:** Full sun brings out the richest yellow coloring in the leaves, although they may also be prone to scorching unless the soil is evenly moist. In average, well-drained soil with morning sun and afternoon shade, or light all-day shade, the color is still an attractive green-tinged yellow.

**ALTERNATIVE:** 'Hearts of Gold' redbud (*Cercis canadensis*) is another small, deciduous tree (about 15 feet tall), with heart-shaped, red-blushed yellow spring leaves and brilliant yellow fall foliage. In cool climates, where it can take full sun, the yellow leaf color may hold through most of the summer; elsewhere, it prefers some summer shade and usually turns yellow-green or all green until fall. Average, well-drained soil. Zones 4 to 9.

*Cotinus coggygria* Golden Spirit

*Deutzia gracilis* Chardonnay Pearls

## DEUTZIA
*Deutzia*

**Height: 3–4 feet**
**Leaf size: 2–3 inches long;**
**    1 inch wide**
**Full sun to partial shade**
**Zones 4 or 5–8**

Deutzias (*Deutzia*) don't often get much attention for their foliage; usually, it's their abundance of white or pink flowers that earns them a place in the garden. Chardonnay Pearls slender deutzia (*D. gracilis* 'Duncan'), however, is a star on both counts. Its narrow,

deciduous leaves emerge bright yellow and (if the plants get plenty of light) typically hold their color well through the growing season; in some shade, they'll be a cool greenish yellow by summer. From mid-spring to early or midsummer, clusters of rounded flower buds open into starry, pure white, lightly fragrant blossoms that add an extra touch to this terrific, trouble-free shrub. Its compact size and long season of interest make it a great choice for borders and foundation plantings.

**GROWING TIPS:** Chardonnay Pearls will usually adapt to either full sun or partial shade with average to moist but well-drained soil. (In hot-summer areas, a site with morning sun and afternoon shade, or light all-day shade, may reduce the chance of leaf scorch during dry periods.) If you want to shape the plant or control its size, cut out a few of the oldest stems immediately after flowering. You can remove dead stems at any time.

**ALTERNATIVES:** Deciduous golden alpine currant (*Ribes alpinum* 'Aureum') grows 2 to 3 feet tall, with lobed, bright yellow new leaves aging to light yellow or yellow-green. Zones 2 to 6. Golden flowering currant (*R. sanguineum* 'Brocklebankii') grows about 4 feet tall, with small, lobed leaves that are a bright yellow when new, usually softening to yellowish green. Zones 5 or 6 to 8. Morning sun and afternoon shade; average, well-drained soil.

## DICENTRA
*Bleeding heart*

**Height: 2–3 feet**
**Leaf size: 2–3 inches long and wide**
**    (individual leaflet)**
**Partial shade**
**Zones 3–8**

Gardens are filled with a veritable rainbow of magnificent colors in spring, but 'Goldheart' bleeding heart (*Dicentra spectabilis;* also commonly listed as 'Gold Heart') is a guaranteed star among stars. Granted, it's a poor choice for those of you who can't stand pink and yellow together.

But for the rest of us, this stunning perennial is a treasure from the time its ferny, bright yellow foliage emerges in spring (often with an orangey tinge on the newest leaves) through its display of dangling pink hearts on arching stems lasting into early summer. In moist soil (especially in cooler areas), the foliage may continue to look good through the rest of the growing season. Elsewhere, don't worry if the clumps die back to the ground in summer; they'll return next spring for another fabulous display.

*Dicentra spectabilis* 'Goldheart'

**GROWING TIPS:** Although 'Gold-heart' glows in spring sun and continues to hold its color with plenty of light, the leaves may scorch unless the soil stays evenly moist but not soggy. A site with afternoon shade (or all-day shade in hot climates) and average, well-drained soil is usually a good compromise. If the foliage starts to look scruffy by midsummer, cut back the whole plant to the ground and tuck some coleus or other annuals into the empty space to fill the gap, being careful not to damage the bleeding heart's thick but brittle roots.

**ALTERNATIVES:** 'Golden Panda' corydalis (*Corydalis flexuosa*) is also at its best in spring, with 10- to 12-inch-tall mounds of lacy, greenish yellow to yellowish green leaves. It definitely prefers cool climates and can be a little temperamental in warm-summer areas. Partial shade; humus-rich and moist but well-drained soil. Golden mukdenia (*Mukdenia rossii* 'Ogon'; also listed under *Aceriphyllum rossii*) is another treasure for shady sites, with bronzy yellow new growth; deeply lobed, yellow summer foliage; and often attractive fall colors as well. Established clumps spread slowly by thick rhizomes to form handsome patches. Golden mukdenia takes some searching to track down, but it's worth the effort! Partial shade; average to moist but well-drained soil. Zones 4 to 8 for both plants.

# DURANTA
*Pigeonberry*

**Height: 3–5 feet (in most areas)**
**Leaf size: 2–3 inches long;**
**    about 1 inch wide**
**Full sun to partial shade**
**Zones 8–11**

Seldom seen just a few years ago, selections of pigeonberry (*Duranta erecta;* also sold as *D. repens*) have quickly become favorites with gardeners always on the hunt for colorful and easy-to-grow additions to borders and container plantings. In its native tropics, pigeonberry is an evergreen shrub or tree; elsewhere, it stays much smaller — typically 3 to 5 feet tall and wide — and you can keep it even shorter with a bit of trimming. It's also known as sky flower and golden dewdrop because of its pendent, spike-like clusters of fragrant, light blue flowers, which appear throughout the growing season, and its rounded, yellow to orange-yellow fruits. The leaves are usually a rich green, but there are a number of cultivars with bright yellow foliage: names to look for are 'Aurea', 'Cuban Gold', 'Gold', 'Gold Mound', and 'Sunstruck'. These selections often don't flower abundantly, particularly in cool climates, but the leaves are really the main feature. Unlike many other yellow-leaved plants, golden pigeonberries thrive in heat and humidity, holding on to their rich color even through the dog days of summer — a fact

*Duranta erecta* 'Gold Mound'

that endears them to southern gardeners in particular. *Caution:* All parts of these plants are poisonous if ingested, so keep them away from kids and pets.

**GROWING TIPS:** Golden pigeonberries will grow in just about any light conditions, but they're most likely to bloom in full sun or with morning sun and afternoon shade. Average, well-drained soil is fine. In Zone 8, the top growth is usually winter-killed, but the plants can resprout from the roots. Even if the stems aren't damaged, cutting them back to the ground in spring is a good way to encourage lower, bushier growth.

**ALTERNATIVE:** Golden bay (*Laurus nobilis* 'Aurea') is another handsome "ever-yellow" shrub or tree for mild climates; elsewhere, it's a gorgeous container plant. Its aromatic leaves emerge bright yellow, then may develop some greenish tinges, especially if they get some shade. The plants can eventually reach to 40 feet, but they're slow-growing, and you can keep them more compact with regular pruning. Some shelter from winter winds is a plus. Like regular bay or bay laurel, golden bay leaves can be used in cooking. *Caution:* Handling the leaves may irritate sensitive skin. Full sun to light shade; average to moist but well-drained soil. Zones 8 to 11.

## FILIPENDULA
*Meadowsweet*

**Height: About 1 foot in leaf**
**Leaf size: 8–12 inches long;**
  **3–4 inches wide**
**Sun to partial shade**
**Zones 3–8**

Meadowsweet (*Filipendula*) isn't among the trendiest of perennials, so it doesn't get much attention in gardening magazines and mail-order catalogs. Maybe that's why golden meadowsweet (*F. ulmaria* 'Aurea') is one of the best-kept secrets when it comes to fantastic foliage. It grows in dense clumps of pinnately compound leaves with toothed and deeply lobed tip leaflets and much smaller side leaflets, all of which emerge bright yellow and stay that way if they get plenty of sun; in some shade, they age to a still pleasant greenish yellow. Plumelike clusters of tiny, creamcolored flowers bloom atop 2- to 3-foot-tall stems in summer; they're nice, but you may decide to cut them off so they don't draw attention from the foliage.

**GROWING TIPS:** Golden meadowsweet will grow in full sun or partial shade, but the more sun you give it, the more important it is for the soil to stay evenly moist. Remove the faded flowers to tidy the plants and prevent self-sowing. If the foliage looks tattered or turns brown, cut the entire plant to the ground and water thoroughly to encourage a flush of bright new growth for fall.

**ALTERNATIVE:** For a similar effect — at least in spring — from an even more uncommon perennial, consider golden valerian (*Valeriana phu* 'Aurea'). It grows in dense, 8- to 12-inch-tall, moderately spreading clumps that are bright yellow in spring, aging to medium green by early to midsummer. Full sun with evenly moist soil; otherwise, morning sun and afternoon shade or light all-day shade with average, well-drained soil. Zones 4 to 8.

*Filipendula ulmaria* 'Aurea'

## HEUCHERA
*Heuchera*

**Height: 8–12 inches**
**Leaf size: 4–5 inches long and wide**
**Full sun to partial shade**
**Zones 3 or 4–8**

Purple-leaved heucheras (*Heuchera*) are practically a must-have for foliage-appreciating perennial gardeners, and now they come in a whole new color range. From clear yellow through coppery orange, selections are appearing every year to provide exciting opportunities for creative color combinations.

Among the distinctly yellow varieties are the similar 'Key Lime Pie' ('Dolce Key Lime Pie') and 'Lime Rickey', both with bright yellow new growth that ages to green-tinged yellow, and sporting airy clusters of tiny white flowers to about 18 inches tall.

Quite a number of cultivars offer yellow, pink, and orange shades in their foliage, including 'Amber Waves', 'Crème Brûlé' ('Crème Brulee' or 'Dolce Crème Brûlé'), 'Marmalade', 'Peach Flambé', 'Peach Melba' ('Dolce Peach Melba'), and *H. villosa* 'Caramel'. If you're a fanatic for exact color matching, don't make the mistake of planning combinations with these simply from a photograph, because the look of their leaves varies greatly depending on the time of year and the amount of light they receive. Some people find the orangey browns unappealing, but for adventurous gardeners who want to expand their color horizons, these unusual hues make great companions for a wide array of foliage and flowering partners — particularly those

*Heuchera* 'Key Lime Pie'

in shades of yellow, pink, purple, and blue.

**GROWING TIPS:** Golden heucheras typically perform best with morning sun and afternoon shade or light all-day shade. Those with more orange in the foliage usually tolerate more sun but will also do well in partial shade, although they're often more greenish there. Good drainage is a must in any site because heucheras hate soggy soil, but those in full sun do appreciate occasional watering; otherwise, the foliage may turn brown on the edges. Removing the flowers after they fade makes the plants look better and helps promote rebloom. Clip off any damaged leaves as needed.

**ALTERNATIVES:** Yellow-leaved foamy bells (× *Heucherella*) aren't as tough as heucheras, but in cool-summer areas, they're outstanding for spring color impact. 'Sunspot' has bright yellow leaves with a small red center splash; 'Stoplight' has a larger red patch. 'Gold' ('Strike It Rich Gold') leaves are deeply lobed with red center veining. All are about 6 inches in leaf. Partial shade; average to moist but well-drained soil. Zones 4 to 8. 'Cool Gold' piggyback plant (*Tolmiea menziesii*) offers fascinating form as well as extra color impact, especially in spring. Starting out medium to light yellow and aging to greenish yellow, the plant also has the curious habit of producing new plantlets directly from its existing leaves. The leafy clumps are about 8 inches tall. Partial shade; average, well-drained soil. Zones 6 to 8.

# HUMULUS
*Hops*

**Height: 15–20 feet**
**Leaf size: 4–6 inches long and wide**
**Full sun to partial shade**
**Zones 4–8**

This is no delicate climber for a cute little trellis: golden hops (*Humulus lupulus* 'Aureus') gets big and it grows *fast!* This deciduous twining vine can easily reach 6 to 8 feet tall the first year you plant it, and after another year or two, it can shoot up from ground level to 15 feet or more by midsummer. The broad, lobed leaves are bright yellow in spring. While the older leaves age to greenish yellow or light green (especially in shade), the newest leaves are usually still yellow, creating an interesting two-tone effect through the rest of the growing season. The foliage is the main reason to grow this vine; however, it also produces greenish summer flowers that mature to interesting conelike fruits in autumn. Plants sold as 'Bianca' and 'Gold Nugget' are similar, if not identical, to 'Aureus'.

When you're choosing a site for golden hops, think big: train it over a fence or sturdy arbor; let it scramble up into a tree; or give it wires, twine, or trellis panels to twine around. It makes a fantastic summer and fall privacy screen around a pool or patio, and it's terrific for covering a large tree stump, a chain-link fence, or an ugly shed. Keep in mind that golden hops grows outward as well as upward, with thick but

*Humulus lupulus* 'Aureus'

shallow creeping rhizomes. It's not difficult to pull up the ones you don't want while the shoots are just emerging in spring, as long as you don't have other, more delicate plants growing close by. You can create amazing combinations by letting clematis or other vigorous vines mingle with golden hops, but keep them several feet apart so the hops vine doesn't smother its companion. Another option is to sow an annual vine in front in late spring to early summer, so the annual can clamber up through the already-tall hops. Morning glories (*Ipomoea*) and hyacinth bean (*Lablab purpureus*) are two good candidates.

**GROWING TIPS:** Golden hops are usually at their best in full sun with evenly moist soil, but in hot climates, even ample moisture may not be enough to prevent some leaf bleaching or scorching. A site with morning sun and afternoon shade — or even light all-day shade with average, well-drained soil — is a good compromise. The vines die back to the ground, so feel free to clear away most or all of the top growth any time from late fall to early spring. *Caution:* It's smart to wear gloves and long sleeves when working around hops vines, because the rough leaves and stems can easily irritate your skin.

**ALTERNATIVE:** 'Fenway Park' Boston ivy (*Parthenocissus tricuspidata*) creates a similar effect, and it thrives in the same growing conditions, but it clings to vertical surfaces with adhesive tendrils instead of by twining stems. It can eventually climb to 60 feet. The rich yellow to yellow-green foliage turns orange to red in fall. *Note:* The species is considered invasive in some areas. Zones 4 to 8.

# HYDRANGEA
*Hydrangea*

**Height: 3–6 feet**
**Leaf size: 6–8 inches long;**
   **4–6 inches wide**
**Full sun to partial shade**
**Zones 5 or 6–9**

You know how some golden-leaved plants are absolutely glorious and some frankly look a little sickly? For some reason, many gardeners seem to put golden-leaved hydrangeas (*Hydrangea*) in the latter group, even though the foliage colors of these deciduous shrubs are no different from those of many popular plants

*Hydrangea quercifolia* 'Little Honey'

in this category. Perhaps it's the pinkish tinge that hydrangeas tend to have in their flowers (some people don't like pink and yellow together, after all), or maybe it's the brassy tints the leaves take on when they get too much sun. If you're already hesitant about using golden foliage in your garden, you're probably best off starting with another option (such as weigela), or at least taking a good look at the plants in person before you buy. For the rest of you, don't hesitate to track down these beauties; you won't be disappointed! They look absolutely amazing with a wide range of harmonious or contrasting companions, from powder blue hostas and deep green ferns to rich purple heucheras and black snakeroots (*Cimicifuga*).

Among the classic bigleaf hydrangeas (*H. macrophylla*) are several selections with bright yellow to greenish yellow leaves, such as 'Lemon Daddy', 'Lemon Zest', and Sun Goddess ('Yellowleaf'). These have the usual broad leaves on 4- to 6-foot-tall stems, with clusters of summer flowers that are pinkish in neutral to alkaline soil and bluish in acidic soil. 'Golden Sunlight' (*H. serrata;* also listed as *H. macrophylla* var. *serrata*) is similar but more compact (usually 3 to 4 feet tall), with light green summer color. 'Little Honey' oakleaf hydrangea (*H. quercifolia*) has white summer

flowers and deeply lobed lemon yellow leaves that turn red in fall.

**GROWING TIPS:** Golden-leaved hydrangeas will grow in full sun or partial shade and prefer moist but well-drained soil. In hot-summer areas especially, a site with morning sun and afternoon shade or light all-day shade usually brings out the best leaf color. On bigleaf hydrangeas, the flower buds are often winter-killed in the northern parts of their hardiness range, but the blooms are basically secondary to the showy foliage anyway; prune any damaged or dead shoots back to the emerging growth in spring.

**ALTERNATIVES:** Viburnums (*Viburnum*) enjoy similar growing conditions. The lobed leaves of 8- to 12-foot-tall golden European cranberry-bush (*V. opulus* 'Aureum') are bright yellow (and often red-tinged) in spring; they may bleach out or turn greenish later. Zones 3 to 8. Golden wayfaring tree (*V. lantana* 'Aureum' or 'Aurea') has broadly oval, yellow leaves; 10 to 15 feet tall. Zones 4 to 8. *Note:* Both species are considered invasive in some areas.

# HYPERICUM
*Hypericum, St.-John's-wort*

**Height: Varies**
**Leaf size: 3–4 inches long;**
   **1–2 inches wide**
**Full sun to full shade**
**Zones vary**

Hypericums (*Hypericum*) often earn a place in the garden for

their sunny yellow summer blooms, reddish fall fruits, and neat mounded form. Now there's another reason to consider them for your garden: golden foliage. Deciduous *H. androsaemum* 'Golden Tutsan' grows 2 to 3 feet tall and 3 to 4 feet wide, with brilliant yellow foliage, summer-long flowers, and deep red fall berries that ripen to black. Zones 6 to 9. *H. × inodorum* 'Summergold' ('Summer Gold') is also deciduous but slightly taller — in the range of 3 to 5 feet — with bright yellow to greenish yellow spring foliage that turns yellowish green to medium green. Like 'Golden Tutsan', it blooms all summer and has red berries that change to black in fall. Zones 6 or 7 to 9. "Ever-yellow" to "semi-ever-yellow" 'Brigadoon' hypericum (*H. calycinum*) has more of a carpet form, typically growing about 1 foot tall but spreading widely by stolons. Its arching to trailing stems bear lemon yellow to greenish yellow foliage that's often tinged heavily with peach to orange in cool weather. It flowers in late spring to early summer. Zones 5 or 6 to 8. A sheltered site will help prevent damage from drying winter wind.

**GROWING TIPS:** Yellow-leaved hypericums will grow in full sun (with plenty of moisture) to full shade (even dry shade), although morning sun and afternoon shade with average, well-drained soil is usually ideal. A yearly trim

*Hypericum calycinum* 'Brigadoon'

before growth begins encourages the production of vigorous, richly colored new shoots. In some climates (particularly the Pacific Northwest), hypericums are prone to fungal rusts, which disfigure the foliage; in these areas, consider other options for golden foliage.

**ALTERNATIVES:** 'Canyon Creek' abelia (*Abelia*) has orange-tinged, light yellow spring leaves that turn green in summer, then bronzy red in fall; 4 to 6 feet tall. Selections of glossy abelia (*A. × grandiflora*) that have similar color changes are sold under various names, including 'Aurea', 'Gold Sport', 'Gold Spot', and 'Gold Strike'; they are usually 3 to 6 feet tall. Full sun or partial shade; average, well-drained soil. Zones 5 or 6 to 9.

## IPOMOEA
*Sweet potato vine*

**Height: About 6 inches**
**Leaf size: 6–8 inches long;**
  **5–6 inches wide**
**Full sun to partial shade**
**Zones 9 or 10–11**

Creeping along the ground or cascading out of containers, sweet potato vines (*Ipomoea batatas*) are top-notch choices for easy-care summer and fall color. Their long stems can creep or trail 10 feet or more, and they take root where the stems touch the soil, so they will cover quite a large area by the end of the growing season. That makes them an excellent choice for a temporary ground cover or for filling the "empty" areas among properly spaced perennials or shrubs in a newly planted border.

'Margarita' (which is also sold under a variety of other spellings, including 'Margarite', 'Marguerita', and 'Marguerite') is an extra-vigorous spreader with heart-shaped, medium yellow to greenish yellow leaves. 'Terrace Lime' has similar foliage but is more compact. 'Sweet Caroline Light Green' is also bright yellow to greenish yellow, but with deeply lobed leaves and a much bushier habit (and sometimes with a narrow red leaf rim). Its more restrained growth rate makes it a far better choice for most containers than the enthusiastic 'Margarita'.

'Sweet Caroline Bronze' shares the habit and leaf shape of 'Sweet Caroline Light Green', but its color is in a class by itself. Depending on the amount of light it gets, as well as the weather, the foliage will be anything from a rich hot-chocolate color to pinkish brown to pale caramel-yellow; multiple shades of these colors often appear on the same plant at the same time. With its changeable nature, 'Sweet Caroline Bronze' offers exciting opportunities for unusual color combinations.

**GROWING TIPS:** Sweet potato vines thrive in full sun, but they will tolerate partial shade too. Average to moist, well-drained soil is fine. You can overwinter sweet potato vines by taking cuttings in fall and growing them as houseplants in a warm, bright spot, or by digging up the large tuberous roots and storing them in a cool, dry place.

**ALTERNATIVE:** For a trailing container plant just a few inches tall, you might consider 'Buttercup' English ivy (*Hedera helix*). Its lobed leaves are bright to pale yellow in bright sites and greenish yellow in too much shade. A site with morning sun and afternoon shade is usually ideal; average to moist but well-drained soil. Zones 5 to 9. *Note:* The species *H. helix* is considered invasive in some areas.

*Ipomoea batatas* 'Margarita'

## LEYCESTERIA
*Himalayan honeysuckle, pheasantberry*

**Height: 4–8 feet**
**Leaf size: 4–6 inches long;**
**3–4 inches wide**
**Full sun to partial shade**
**Zones 6–9**

Sure, golden foliage is great, but when you find a plant that offers showy flowers and fascinating fruits as well, you've really got something! Golden Lanterns Himalayan honeysuckle (*Leycesteria formosa* 'Notbruce') never fails to please from the time its red-tinged yellow foliage emerges in spring. By early summer, the foliage is clear yellow to greenish yellow. Throughout the summer, clusters of small white flowers with purplish red bracts dangle from the stems; in fall, they turn into red berries that ripen to deep purple. In most areas, after the leaves drop in fall, the greenish stems add winter interest. In Zone 6 (and even some parts of Zone 5), the plants usually die back to the ground in winter.

**GROWING TIPS:** Golden Lanterns is at its best in full sun, but it will perform well in partial shade, too. Average to moist but well-drained soil is fine. Even where the stems survive the winter, cutting them down in early spring is a good way to keep the clumps tidy. Although the berries are gorgeous, be aware that the plants will self-sow abundantly in some conditions. *Note:* The species wasn't officially considered invasive in this country at the time this was written, but it has become a problem elsewhere, so check its status in your area before you plant.

**ALTERNATIVE:** 'Golden Arrow' persicaria (*Persicaria amplexicaule* or *P. amplexicaulus*) offers lance-shaped leaves that are bright yellow in spring, turning greenish yellow during the summer. This clump-former is 2 to 3 feet tall and about as wide. Full sun (in cooler areas) to partial shade; average to moist but well-drained soil. (The more sun the plants get, the more moisture they need.) Zones 5 to 8.

*Leycesteria formosa* Golden Lanterns

*Lysimachia congestiflora* 'Golden Harvest'

## LYSIMACHIA
*Loosestrife, lysimachia*

**Height: Varies**
**Leaf size: Varies**
**Full sun to full shade**
**Zones vary**

Loosestrifes (*Lysimachia*) are a good choice for low-growing golden foliage — *if* you use them wisely! They all have a tendency to spread, which is a plus if you need something to trail out of a planter, window box, or hanging basket or to serve as a ground cover. Some loosestrifes, however, are a little *too* good at making themselves at home, and their overenthusiastic nature can turn them from a pleasure into a problem.

*Lysimachia congestiflora* 'Golden Harvest' is a beauty for containers and as a garden annual for Zones 6 and north, and is usually not a thug even where it's hardy (Zones 7 or 8 to 10). It creates a 4- to 8-inch-tall carpet of roughly oval leaves that are about 2 inches long and 1 inch wide and range in color from bright yellow to a pale greenish yellow, depending on the amount of light the plant gets. Clusters of golden yellow flowers bloom at the shoot tips in spring and summer.

Golden creeping Jenny (*L. nummularia* 'Aurea') is alluring in photographs, and it looks so demure and dainty in small pots that many an unwary gardener has been swayed by its undeniable charm. The rounded to oval leaves are only ½ to ¾ inch long and wide, and with enough light they'll stay brilliant yellow throughout the growing season. (Even in deep shade, the color is still an attractive greenish yellow.) The plants also produce cupped, bright yellow blooms through the summer, but you'll hardly notice them against the similarly colored foliage.

Golden creeping Jenny is fine for containers; letting it loose in the garden, however, is a rather tricky proposition. In sites where it's not happy, it may die a slow, lingering death or just suddenly disappear, while in the moist to wet soils it loves, you may end up with an area of nothing *but* golden creeping Jenny before you know it. The ground-hugging stems readily take root wherever they touch the soil, stopping only when they reach very dry conditions or expanses of paving. Along the edge of a pond or water garden, the stems can even reach right into the water; planted near the front of a bed or border, they'll readily creep over any edging strip and root into adjacent lawn areas. It's not difficult to pull out rooted stems, and regular trimming will prevent them from creeping out of bounds, so if you're willing to keep after them, their 1-inch-tall, "golden carpet" effect can be worth the extra effort. Zones 3 to 8. *Note:* The species *L. nummularia* is considered invasive in many areas.

**GROWING TIPS:** Both of these yellow-leaved loosestrifes can grow anywhere from full sun to full shade, although they prefer a bit of shade in the afternoon — especially if the soil isn't dependably moist. *L. congestiflora* 'Golden Harvest' usually does best with soil that's fairly well drained, though, and golden creeping Jenny will grow in even soggy soil. Snip off any all-green shoots that appear.

**ALTERNATIVE: Desert Skies Chinese plumbago (*Ceratostigma willmottianum* 'Palmgold') is a small, spreading, deciduous shrub with upright, 2- to 3-foot-tall stems clad in bright yellow leaves, which may turn reddish in autumn. Cut back by one-half to two-thirds in early spring to promote bushy growth. Full sun to light shade; average, well-drained soil. Zones 7 or 8 to 10.**

*Melissa officinalis* 'All Gold'

## MELISSA
*Lemon balm*

**Height: 1–2 feet**
**Leaf size: 2–3 inches long;**
**about 2 inches wide**
**Full sun to partial shade**
**Zones 4–8**

If you enjoy foliage that's fragrant as well as colorful, golden lemon balm (*Melissa officinalis* 'All Gold'; also sold as 'Gold Leaf') may be a perfect choice for your garden. Its upright stems form dense, slow-spreading mounds of toothed leaves that are bright yellow through spring. With ample light, they turn light to pale yellow by summer; in shade, they age to greenish yellow. Tiny white to pinkish flowers appear in summer, but they aren't showy. The leaves release an intense lemon fragrance when you rub them, so try to site them next to a path or near a bench, so you can easily reach them. Keep in mind that some nurseries sell this golden-leaved herb as 'Aurea'; others use 'Aurea' to describe a selection with yellow-and-green leaves. *Note:* The species is considered invasive in some areas.

**GROWING TIPS:** Golden lemon balm keeps its most intense foliage color in a bright site, but if it gets too much sun, the leaves may bleach out or turn crispy brown. Where the soil is dependably moist, it may be fine in full sun (especially in the North); otherwise, a site with morning sun and afternoon shade and average to moist but well-drained soil is a good compromise. Cutting down the plants to the ground in early to midsummer prevents self-sowing and encourages a flush of bright new foliage for fall. If you allow the plants to go to seed, the seedlings usually have yellow leaves too.

**ALTERNATIVE: Another addition to the elegant-edible category is golden alpine strawberry (*Fragaria vesca* 'Golden Alexandria'). Its 4- to 8-inch-tall, perennial clumps of toothed, three-part leaves emerge bright yellow and stay that way in full sun as long as the soil is evenly moist; in partial shade with average, well-drained soil, they'll still be an attractive greenish yellow. The plants don't produce runners, so they're great for beds and pots. Comes true from seed. Zones 5 to 9.**

*Mirabilis jalapa* 'Limelight'

## MIRABILIS
*Four-o'clocks, marvel-of-Peru*

**Height: 2–4 feet**
**Leaf size: 2–4 inches long;**
 **1–3 inches wide**
**Full sun to partial shade**
**Zones 8–11**

Four-o'clocks (*Mirabilis jalapa*) have long been favorites for the flower garden due to their abundant, colorful blooms that tend to open in late afternoon and close sometime the next morning. (The cooler or cloudier it is, the longer they stay open). The flowers first appear on the upright, bushy plants in early to midsummer and continue into fall. While the species normally has solid green leaves to complement its bright blooms, the selection known as 'Limelight' (also sold as 'Limelight Rose') goes one better, with lemon yellow to greenish yellow leaves that make an amazing backdrop for its shocking pink flowers. (Some of the leaves may also have some green sections in them.) It's not a flower-and-foliage combination that most color-shy gardeners are comfortable with, but if you like to walk on the wild side, 'Limelight' is guaranteed to please. *Note:* The species is considered invasive in a few areas of the country.

**GROWING TIPS:** Full sun generally brings out the best foliage color, but then it's important that the soil stays moist if you want vigorous growth. In hot climates, or in a site with average, well-drained soil, morning sun and afternoon shade or light all-day shade should provide good results. Four-o'clocks are perennial in mild areas, but it's easy to grow them as annuals anywhere; simply sow the seeds directly in the garden in late spring. The plants will then self-sow, so you'll likely have plenty of volunteer seedlings each year after that without starting them again yourself. You can also dig up the large, elongated tubers and overwinter them indoors in a cool, dry place.

**ALTERNATIVE:** 'Sunshine' cape fuchsia (*Phygelius* × *rectus*) grows 3 to 4 feet tall in spreading clumps, with bright yellow to greenish yellow leaves. It laughs at heat and humidity, so it's terrific for southern gardens. Cut back by about half in summer if plants start to sprawl. Full sun to partial shade; average to moist but well-drained soil. Zones 7 to 10; may be hardier with good drainage and snow cover.

## PELARGONIUM
*Geranium, pelargonium*

**Height: Usually 1–3 feet**
**Leaf size: 2–4 inches long and wide**
**Full sun to partial shade**
**Zones 8 or 9–11**

Some experienced gardeners dismiss zonal geraniums (*Pelargonium* × *hortorum*) as being "too common," but there's nothing common about the selections with golden foliage! Although there are several dozen named cultivars in this color range, you'd be lucky to find more than one or two at your local garden center. For a much wider selection, check out mail-order nurseries that specialize in these gems. Here's a sampling of just a few golden-leaved geraniums; they produce the usual upright, bushy plants, differing mainly in leaf shapes and flower colors. To a greater or lesser extent, their foliage also shows the dark ring or "zone" that gives the zonal geraniums their name.

*With rounded leaves.* Geranium aficionados use the term *fancy-leaved* to refer to cultivars grown mainly for their colorful, shallowly lobed foliage. 'Mrs. Quilter' has bright to light yellow leaves with a large red to brownish zone and single light pink to salmon pink flowers. 'Occold Shield' has a big maroon-brown zone that usually covers most or all of the leaf center, with a light yellow to greenish yellow border and scarlet flowers. The foliage of 'Persian Queen' is basically green-tinged yellow with very little visible zoning; blooms are neon pink.

*With pointy leaves.* "Stellar" geraniums have fan-shaped foliage with distinctly pointed lobes, as well as "starry" flowers. The

*Pelargonium* 'Lotusland'

leaves of 'Golden Staph' are light yellow to greenish yellow with a faint reddish zone; its flowers are orange-red. 'Ken's Gold' is also light yellow to greenish yellow, with a more noticeable reddish zone and double, bright pink flowers. 'Vancouver Centennial' leaves have a deep reddish brown center and a bright to light yellow edge; its single flowers are orange-red. 'Lotusland' looks almost identical but has pink flowers.

**GROWING TIPS:** Golden-leaved geraniums produce their brightest leaf colors with lots of light, although too-intense sun may bleach them out. Morning sun with light afternoon shade is usually ideal. Average, well-drained soil is fine. Remove the faded flowers regularly. Before frost, bring your favorite plants indoors and enjoy them as houseplants for the winter. Wait until after the last frost date in spring to set them out again.

**ALTERNATIVE:** Another favorite with beginning gardeners for their easy-care nature and abundant blooms, annual nasturtiums (*Tropaeolum majus*) are also popular with foliage fanatics for their distinctive circular leaves. Seed strains with green or variegated leaves are easy to find, but 'Tip Top Mahogany' is unique, with greenish yellow foliage in 6- to 12-inch-tall mounds. Full sun; fertile, evenly moist but well-drained soil. Sow indoors in early spring or outdoors in mid-spring.

## PHASEOLUS
*Runner bean*

**Height: 6–8 feet**
**Leaf size: 3–5 inches long and wide**
**Full sun to partial shade**
**Zones 10 and 11**

Want to deck your walls with golden foliage? 'Sun Bright' runner bean (*Phaseolus coccineus*) offers not only bright yellow to yellow-green, three-part leaves, but also showy scarlet flowers that are a magnet for hummingbirds. As a bonus, you can eat the green pods, the seeds, *and* the blossoms! That makes this vibrant vine a great choice for the vegetable garden as well as for ornamental plantings. Try pairing it with hyacinth bean (*Lablab purpureus*), which has purplish foliage and magenta pods that contrast nicely with the runner bean's bright leaves and flowers. Runner bean is actually a perennial in very warm climates, but most gardeners enjoy it as an annual because it begins blooming within a month or two after planting and continues until frost.

**GROWING TIPS:** Full sun produces the brightest foliage color; plants in partial shade tend to be greenish. Fertile, average to evenly moist but well-drained soil is ideal. Put in place some kind of support — strings, netting, or bamboo poles are ideal — *before* sowing seed after all danger of frost has passed (when the soil is 50°F/10°C). Keep the twining vines well mulched, and water during dry spells to encourage vigorous growth. Save the seeds to plant next spring, or dig up the tuberous roots and overwinter them indoors as you would dahlias.

**ALTERNATIVE:** 'Lemon Lace' silver fleece vine (*Fallopia baldschuanica* 'Lemon Lace'; also listed under *F. aubertii* and *Polygonum aubertii*) is a fast-growing deciduous climber that can reach 15 to 25 feet tall. Its slender, twining, red-tinged stems are clad in bright lemon yellow leaves throughout the growing season. Besides growing *up*, the plants also spread *out* by creeping rhizomes. Full sun; partial shade with average, well-drained soil. Zones 5 to 9. *Note:* This species is considered invasive in some areas.

*Phaseolus coccineus* 'Sun Bright'

## PHYSOCARPUS
*Ninebark*

**Height:** Varies
**Leaf size:** 3–4 inches long;
   2–3 inches wide
**Full sun to partial shade**
**Zones 2–7 or 8**

Ninebarks (*Physocarpus opulifolius*) have been around for ages, but it's only recently that these deciduous shrubs have gotten some well-deserved attention for their easy-care nature and multi-season features. In late spring to early summer, domed clusters of white to pinkish flowers bloom along the arching stems, ripening into reddish seed capsules later in the summer. The fall color is

*Physocarpus opulifolius* 'Dart's Gold'

usually yellow to orange; it's not one of the most dramatic color changers, but it's still attractive. Then in winter, you can enjoy the attractive peeling bark on the mature stems.

Selections with golden foliage complete the cycle of year-round interest with bright yellow young leaves that make the plants look like full-bloom forsythias. The colorful effect lasts to midsummer, when the leaves typically turn yellowish green to light green. Golden ninebarks are handsome enough to serve as specimen shrubs, but they also look great in mixed or shrub borders and as informal hedges. 'Luteus', the original yellow-leaved cultivar, grows 8 to 10 feet tall. 'Dart's Gold' (also sold as 'Dart's Golden') is somewhat shorter — usually 5 to 7 feet tall — and tends to hold its yellow color longer into the summer. 'Nugget' is often billed as being more compact than 'Dart's Gold', but it's typically 6 to 8 feet tall, with slightly smaller leaves that give it a finer texture.

**GROWING TIPS:** Ninebarks produce the brightest foliage and hold their yellow color longest in full sun, but they will grow well in partial shade too. They'll adapt to just about any well-drained soil conditions, but they're most vigorous in evenly moist, acidic soil. Pruning away a few of the oldest stems at their base each spring helps to keep the plants vigorous and control their size. Or if the plants are overgrown, cut down

all of the stems to about 6 inches to get lots of good-looking new shoots.

**ALTERNATIVES:** Golden spike winter hazel (*Corylopsis spicata* 'Aurea') is a wide-spreading, deciduous shrub with bright yellow new leaves aging to green by summer; 6 to 8 feet tall. Full sun to partial shade; acidic, average to moist but well-drained soil. Zones 5 to 8. Golden hazel (*Corylus avellana* 'Aurea') produces a similar effect on larger plants (usually 10 to 12 feet tall). Full sun to partial shade; average, well-drained soil. Zones 3 to 8.

## SOLENOSTEMON
*Coleus*

**Height:** 1–3 feet
**Leaf size:** Usually 3–5 inches long;
   2–4 inches wide
**Full sun to partial shade**
**Zones 10 and 11**

When you're looking for a dependable dash of summer and fall foliage interest for beds, borders, and containers, coleus (*Solenostemon scutellarioides*, formerly *Coleus blumei*) can be an excellent choice. The upright, bushy plants grow quickly, and their colorful foliage comes in pure hues, magical multicolors, and even out-of-the-ordinary shades to provide unlimited opportunities for classic or offbeat color combinations. There are dozens of selections in the yellow-to-orange range, so here are just a few highlights. Check out the selection at your local garden center to find the exact

colors and sizes you need, or explore the far more diverse offerings of mail-order nurseries that specialize in coleus.

*Solid yellow.* 'Giant Exhibition Limelight' (also sold as 'Giant Exhibition Lime') and 'Golda' have broad leaves that are bright yellow in sun and greenish yellow in some shade. 'Butter Kutter' ('Butter Cutter') has the same colors but looks decidedly different because of its very narrow, jagged-edged leaves.

*Yellow with red to purple markings.* 'Pineapple Queen' is a classic with bright to brassy yellow leaves with deep red stems and leaf bases. The foliage of 'Pineapplette' is lemon yellow to greenish yellow flecked with red, on reddish stems. 'The Line' has clear yellow to yellow-green leaves with a deep red midrib; 'Gay's Delight' has much heavier deep purple leaf veining. Seed-grown 'Wizard Pineapple' is bright yellow tinged or mottled with green and occasionally splashed with red.

*Orange-yellow to tan.* If your color tastes run to the unusual, consider 'Penney' (also sold as 'Penny'). In shade its leaves are pale yellowish green backed with greenish pink, and in sun they appear tan backed with purplish pink. 'Pineapple Prince' and 'Orange King' are usually in the medium yellow to yellowish tan range, with pink-blushed leaf bases, edges, and undersides. All of these combinations may have a coppery orange appearance when the sun shines through them.

*Solenostemon 'Pineapple Queen'*

**Rusty orange.** For a distinctly orange effect, look for 'Copper Glow', 'Klondike', or 'Rustic Orange', with pinkish orange to reddish orange foliage narrowly rimmed with yellow-green. 'Sedona' ranges from an excellent clear orange or pink-mottled orange through brick red and even pale peach, depending on the growing conditions. It's a beauty for combinations based on sunset shades.

**GROWING TIPS:** Light levels and temperatures make a big difference in the colors on yellow- to orange-leaved coleus. Full sun generally produces the most intense colors, but in very strong sun, the foliage of some of the older cultivars (such as 'Pineapple Queen' and 'The Line') may bleach out. A site with morning sun and afternoon shade (especially in southern gardens) is usually a good compromise. The more light the plants get, the more important it is that their soil is evenly moist (but not soggy). Pinching off the shoot tips every few weeks encourages bushy growth and discourages flowering. To preserve your favorite plants from year to year, take cuttings in late summer or fall (they're easy to root), then keep them in a sunny spot indoors or under plant lights through the winter. Wait until after the last frost date to set them back outside.

**ALTERNATIVES:** Golden parrot leaf (*Alternanthera ficoidea* 'Chartreuse' or 'Chartreuse Form') bears narrow, bright yellow to greenish yellow leaves in dense clumps; 4 to 8 inches tall. Full sun; average to moist but well-drained soil. Zones 9 to 11. 'Golden Delicious' pineapple sage (*Salvia elegans*) has fragrant, greenish yellow to bright yellow foliage in bushy, 3-foot-tall clumps. Full sun to light shade (especially in hot-summer areas); average, well-drained soil. Zones 8 to 11.

## TALINUM
*Jewels-of-Opar, fameflower*

**Height: 12–18 inches**
**Leaf size: 3–4 inches long;**
    **1–2 inches wide**
**Full sun to partial shade**
**Zones 9–11**

Not all gold-leaved plants produce gold-leaved seedlings, but those that do, such as golden jewels-of-Opar (*Talinum paniculatum* 'Kingwood Gold'; also sold as 'Aureum'), are a real boon for gardeners who want lots of bright color without spending a bundle. It's perennial in only the warmest zones, but it's easy to grow as an annual elsewhere, producing bushy clumps of fleshy leaves that are bright greenish yellow in sun and yellow-green to pale green in some shade. From midsummer to frost, the plants are topped with 18- to 24-inch-tall, airy clusters of small reddish pink flowers that ripen into coppery red seedpods. A single plant is great for adding a splash of color as well as intriguing texture to a mixed container. In the garden, enjoy a group of golden jewels-of-Opar at the front of a border, or tuck them into gaps left when early-flowering bulbs and perennials go dormant in early to mid-summer. When you're searching for this plant, you'll more often find it under the misspelled name 'Kingswood Gold'.

**GROWING TIPS:** Full sun is best, but the plants will tolerate partial shade too. Average, well-drained soil is fine. Bring a few plants indoors as winter houseplants, if you like, but it's just as easy to gather the dried seedpods in fall and start new transplants by sowing the seed indoors in early to mid-spring or else directly in the garden in late spring. Where they're happy, the plants are apt to self-sow abundantly, so you may not even need to sow more seeds; simply pull out or transplant the volunteers that aren't where you want them. If you find they self-sow too prolifically in your conditions, you may want to keep the flower stems clipped off.

**ALTERNATIVE:** Another sow-and-grow annual that makes a great cool-season filler is 'Australian Yellow' lettuce (*Lactuca sativa*). It's the same kind of looseleaf lettuce you grow in the vegetable garden, but its dense, 8-inch-tall clumps of crinkled, greenish yellow leaves earn it a place in ornamental borders too. Start indoors in cell packs or sow directly in the garden. Full sun to partial shade; average to moist but well-drained soil.

*Talinum paniculatum* 'Kingwood Gold'

## TRICYRTIS
*Toad lily*

**Height: 1–3 feet**
**Leaf size: 3–5 inches long;**
**    1–2 inches wide**
**Partial to full shade**
**Zones 4–9**

One look at the exquisite, orchid-like blooms of toad lilies (*Tricyrtis*), and it's often love at first sight for perennial gardeners on the hunt for lovely late summer and fall flowers. Now there are selections with glorious golden foliage as well, so the plants earn their keep from the time they emerge in spring until Jack Frost makes a return appearance in autumn. There are quite

a few named toad lily cultivars with bright yellow new leaves that typically age to a softer yellowish green during the summer, plus white flowers that are lightly to heavily spotted with purple from late summer into fall. Most of them grow about 2 feet tall, although they will be shorter or taller depending on the growing conditions. Names to look for are *T. hirta* 'Gold Leaf', 'Golden Gleam', and 'Lime Mound'; *T. formosana* 'Gates of Heaven' and 'Gilty Pleasure'; and hybrids 'Lemon Lime' and 'Moonlight'.

**GROWING TIPS:** Toad lilies typically prefer partial shade with humus-rich, evenly moist but well-drained soil. In cool climates, they will tolerate full sun with lots of moisture, and the ample light tends to bring out the most intense leaf color; in hot climates, they may perform better in full shade but quickly turn greenish there. A site with morning sun and afternoon shade is a good compromise in any area. Although toad lilies don't like constantly soggy soil, ample moisture encourages tall stems; the same selections growing with less moisture are usually much shorter. Too-dry soil causes the leaves to turn brown. Toad lilies spread to varying degrees by rhizomes but rarely enough to be considered aggressive; if needed, divide the plants in early spring to control their size. The new shoots are prone to frost damage, so be prepared to protect them from late-spring frosts.

*Tricyrtis hirta* 'Golden Gleam'

*Weigela* Briant Rubidor

**ALTERNATIVES:** For multi-season interest in a brighter spot, consider 1- to 2-foot-tall golden red raspberry (*Rubus idaeus* 'Aureus'), for Zones 4 or 5 to 7, or 3-foot-tall golden salmonberry (*Rubus spectabilis* 'Golden Ruby'), for Zones 5 to 9. Both spread by suckers to form broad patches of prickly stems clad in deciduous, bright lemon yellow to greenish yellow (and sometimes red-tinged) foliage. Full sun to partial shade; average to moist but well-drained soil.

## WEIGELA
*Weigela*

**Height: Varies**
**Leaf size: 3–4 inches long;**
**    1–2 inches wide**
**Full sun to partial shade**
**Zones 4 or 5–8**

Long gone are the days when weigelas (*Weigela*) could be dismissed as single-season shrubs. They still produce the same large, funnel-shaped blooms in late spring to early summer, but now they come

in a wide range of leaf colors too. Admittedly, the gold-leaved selections aren't to everyone's taste, but if you like your borders on the bright side, these easy-care shrubs will create quite a splash both in and out of bloom. Established plants have arching branches and an overall mounded form, which is particularly noticeable when they're in full spring bloom. It's not unusual for scattered blossoms to appear later in the season as well. You may notice a reddish blush on the new leaves, especially in cool weather.

The best known of the bunch is Briant Rubidor (also sold as 'Rubidor', 'Rubigold', and 'Olympiade'), with brilliant yellow new foliage that holds its color through most of the growing season in bright light, turning greenish yellow in more shade. Some leaves may also have solid-green markings. The flowers are deep red to rich rosy pink, creating a nice contrast with the foliage. Briant Rubidor typically grows 5 to 8 feet tall. 'Jean's Gold' is similar but slightly taller (to about 10 feet). If your nerves can't stand that much color contrast, consider 'Looymansii Aurea', with softer greenish yellow foliage and rosy pink to pale pink flowers on plants about 6 feet tall. Weather conditions during bloom time can influence the colors of the flowers on any of these weigelas, so don't be surprised if their effect varies from year to year.

**GROWING TIPS:** It may be tricky to find just the right site for golden-leaved weigelas. In cooler areas, they can usually take full sun; elsewhere, too much sun may cause the foliage to bleach out. Conversely, too much shade tends to turn the leaves either yellowish green or light green. A site with morning sun and afternoon shade is a good compromise. Average, well-drained soil is fine. Trim lightly after the flowers fade to maintain a neat, mounded shape. On established plants, removing a few of the oldest stems at their base before new growth starts each spring will help keep the shrubs vigorous.

**ALTERNATIVE:** Another wonderful flowering shrub for foundation plantings and mixed borders is golden mock orange (*Philadelphus coronarius* 'Aureus'), with bright yellow spring foliage that ages to yellowish green; 6 to 10 feet tall. It generally grows best in morning sun and afternoon shade or else light all-day shade; strong sun causes the leaves to bleach or scorch. Moist but well-drained, humus-rich soil is ideal. Zones 4 or 5 to 8.

# CAMPANULA
*Bellflower*

**Height: Varies**
**Leaf size: Varies**
**Full sun to partial shade**
**Zones vary**

Bellflowers (*Campanula*) are classic border favorites for their beautiful blue blossoms, and now they come dressed up with golden foliage. You have your choice between an upright grower and two carpeting creepers, all with bright yellow spring foliage that typically softens to greenish yellow by midsummer. 'Kelly's Gold' peachleaf bellflower (*C. persicifolia*) grows in tidy, spreading rosettes of narrow leaves (usually 4 to 8 inches long and about ½ inch wide) that may be "ever-yellow" in mild areas. The rosettes elongate into 18- to 24-inch-tall stems bearing cupped, white to palest blue flowers from early to midsummer. 'Dickson's Gold' Adriatic or Gargano bellflower (*C. garganica;* also sold as 'Aurea') grows outward instead of upward, forming a dense, 3- to 6-inch-tall carpet of toothed, heart-shaped leaves that are 1 to 1½ inches long and wide, accented with starry, light purple-blue blooms in early to midsummer. Zones 4 or 5 to 8. Golden Dalmatian bellflower (*C. portenschlagiana* 'Aurea') looks similar, but its darker purple-blue flowers also have wider petals. Zones 4 to 8. These low growers are ideal for edging borders and for planting atop low walls and among rocks.

**GROWING TIPS:** Bellflowers generally perform best with full sun in cool climates; in warm-summer areas, a site with morning sun and afternoon shade or light all-day shade usually provides better results. Average to moist but well-drained soil is ideal. Cutting off the upright stems of peachleaf bellflower or shearing the low-growers to the foliage as soon as the flowers fade may encourage another flush of blossoms later in the growing season. The creepers spread quickly where their growing conditions are ideal; divide them in spring or fall to control their growth.

**ALTERNATIVES:** 'Illuminator' yellow meadow rue (*Thalictrum flavum*) emerges with ferny, light yellow to peachy yellow leaves that turn light green; 3 to 5 feet tall. 'Amy Jan' columbine meadow rue (*T. aquilegifolium*) has equally delicate-looking, light yellow spring leaves that age to yellow-green; 18 to 24 inches tall. Full sun and moist but well-drained soil in cool climates; partial shade with average soil in warmer areas. Zones 4 to 8.

*Campanula garganica* 'Dickson's Gold'

*Chamaecyparis obtusa*
'Fernspray Gold'

## CARYOPTERIS
*Caryopteris, bluebeard, blue mist shrub*

**Height: 2–4 feet**
**Leaf size: 2–3 inches long;**
**½–1 inch wide**
**Full sun to partial shade**
**Zones 5–9**

Blue flowers are a treat any time of year, but they're especially welcome in late summer and fall, when shades of yellow, orange, and red are most abundant. But their flower color isn't the only thing that makes caryopteris (*Caryopteris*) a splendid choice for sunny beds, borders, and foundation plantings: the dense, bushy plants look good during the rest of the growing season, too, and they don't demand any

special care in return. And now, if their usual grayish green leaves don't quite fill your craving for color, you can choose cultivars with eye-catching yellow leaves instead.

The foliage of *C.* × *clandonensis* 'Worcester Gold' is usually at its best from early spring until mid- to late summer, with narrow, bright lemon yellow leaves that are about 2 inches long and ½ inch wide. By the time the clustered, purplish blue blooms appear in late summer, the foliage is usually light yellow to yellowish green.

*C. incana* Sunshine Blue ('Jason') is a newer selection that's showing signs of eclipsing 'Worcester Gold', due to its more intense, long-lasting foliage color and even later bloom time. It too has a shrubby form, with sharply toothed leaves that are 2 to 3 inches long and about 1 inch wide. The foliage emerges brilliant yellow in spring and stays distinctly yellow through its early- to mid-fall flowering period, even in light shade, and the flowers are a more intense blue.
**GROWING TIPS:** Full sun is ideal, but the plants will still perform well with either morning or afternoon sun; the foliage just won't stay colorful as long. Average, well-drained soil is fine. In the cooler parts of their hardiness range, golden caryopteris may die back partly or completely to the ground in winter, but they normally sprout up again from the base, so you can cut the plants

*Caryopteris incana* Sunshine Blue

back hard in spring. (Wait until you see new growth appearing, even if that isn't until mid- or late spring.) Where they don't experience winter damage, it's still a good idea to cut them back by at least half — even all the way to their base — to encourage lots of vigorous new growth and control their size. Unpruned plants will be closer to 3 or 4 feet in height and spread instead of 1 to 2 feet.
**ALTERNATIVES:** Yellow-leaved cultivars of Japanese barberry (*Berberis thunbergii*), such as 4- to 6-foot-tall 'Aurea' and 2-foot Bonanza Gold ('Bogozam'), offer some of the best golden foliage you can find, and they grow practically anywhere. Be aware, though, that this species is considered seriously invasive in some regions. Even if Japanese barberries are still sold where you live, please check the status of the species in your area *before* you buy them.

## CHAMAECYPARIS
*False cypress*

**Height: Varies**
**Leaf size: ¼ inch or less (individual needlelike or scalelike leaves)**
**Full sun**
**Zones vary**

For their sheer variety of heights, shapes, and colors, false cypresses (*Chamaecyparis*) are tough to beat. Selections with golden foliage are especially abundant, providing lots of exciting opportunities for adding "ever-yellow" color and fine-textured foliage to borders, foundation plantings, and even

containers. Here's an overview of some of the more compact golden cultivars currently available; for many other options, check out the selection at your local nursery, or seek out specialty conifer nurseries. The sizes below are approximate, reflecting the heights that the plants can reach after about 10 years. These selections of Hinoki false cypress (*C. obtusa*) and Sawara or Japanese false cypress (*C. pisifera*) are typically rated for Zones 4 or 5 to 8.

For feathery, medium to light yellow foliage in a tight spot, choose slow-growing cultivars such as mounded-to-pyramidal *C. obtusa* 'Nana Lutea' and globe-shaped *C. pisifera* 'Vintage Gold', both of which typically reach just 2 to 3 feet tall in 10 years. Slightly taller options — in the range of 3 to 5 feet — are *C. obtusa* 'Lynn's Golden' (also known as 'Lynn's Golden Ceramic' or 'Golden

Christmas'), with a conical to pyramidal habit; 'Meroke', with a narrowly upright cone shape; and 'Verdon' ('Verdoni'), which forms a broad, somewhat irregular pyramid. 'Fernspray Gold' reaches about 6 feet in 10 years but eventually gets much taller, with twisted, fernlike foliage and a broadly upright habit. 'Golden Fern' looks similar but is more compact.

The false cypresses with feathery or ferny foliage are lovely, but selections of *C. pisifera* that are described as "thread-leaved" are especially elegant. As you can guess from the name, their foliage is held in slender, stringlike branchlets that weep at the tips, providing a distinctive textural effect that few other plants can match. Broadly conical 'Filifera Aurea' (commonly called gold thread cypress or gold thread-leaf false cypress) is a classic choice; it grows slowly but will eventually reach 15 feet or more in height. 'Golden Mops' (which is also known under a variety of similar names, including 'Filifera Golden Mops', 'Gold Mops', and just plain 'Mops') has a much lower, mounded form in the range of 3 to 5 feet. 'Sungold' falls in between with 4- to 8-foot-tall, flat-topped mounds; unlike the other two, which have deep to medium yellow foliage all year long, this one is medium to light yellow in spring and more of a yellowish green the rest of the year.

**GROWING TIPS:** False cypresses thrive in humus-rich, evenly moist but well-drained soil. The yellow-leaved selections are brightest in sun, but too much strong sun will cause browning, so try a site with some afternoon shade. Protection from strong wind is beneficial too. Water during dry spells for the first few years to help young plants get established.

**ALTERNATIVES:** For a vertical accent or hedge, try a golden Leyland cypress (× *Cupressocyparis leylandii*), such as 'Castlewellan' ('Castlewellan Gold') or 'Gold Rider'. Zones 6 to 9. Monterey cypress (*Cupressus macrocarpa*) also has several yellow to yellow-green cultivars, including broadly pyramidal 'Gold Crest' ('Goldcrest') and columnar 'Golden Pillar'. Zones 7 to 10. All of these can reach 10 to 20 feet tall in 10 years but stay smaller with pruning. Full sun; average, well-drained soil.

## ERICA
*Heath, heather*

**Height: 6–12 inches**
**Leaf size: ⅛–¼ inch long;**
**⅛ inch wide**
**Full sun**
**Zones vary**

Heaths (*Erica*) aren't suited to every garden, but where they're happy, they're tough to beat for flowers, foliage, and overall year-round beauty. There are hundreds of species and selections, varying widely in height, hardiness, and foliage and flower color; in general, though, they all share short, needlelike leaves and tiny, bell-shaped to globe-shaped flowers in white or shades of purple

*Erica carnea* 'Golden Starlet'

to pink, usually from winter to early spring. Many of them have different foliage colors in winter and summer, so even though the leaves are present all year long, you can create eye-catching combinations that change through the seasons. Try *that* with a typical evergreen shrub! Heaths look particularly good planted in groups as ground covers, on slopes, in containers, or among other acid-loving shrubs and dwarf conifers.

Spring heath (*E. carnea*) is one of the hardiest and most adaptable species, so it's a great one to start with if you're new to growing these plants. You probably won't find more than a few selections at your local garden center, so you'll need to track down a mail-order source to explore the large number of cultivars available — including those with golden to orange foliage. (These nurseries can also be very helpful in recommending selections that are well suited to your particular climate and conditions.) Among the many available cultivars are 'Ann Sparkes', with deep yellow foliage tipped with red in winter, along with rosy pink to purple flowers; 'Foxhollow', with medium yellow to yellow-green foliage tipped with orange in winter, sporting pink flowers; and 'Golden Starlet', with bright to light yellow leaves that turn yellow-green in cooler weather, and clad in white flowers. Zones 3 or 4 to 7.

Bell heath or bell heather (*E. cinerea*) is slightly less hardy (usually Zones 4 or 5 to 8) and blooms from midsummer to early fall. It, too, offers several selections with golden foliage. 'Celebration' is deep yellow in summer and yellow-green in winter, with white flowers. 'Fiddler's Gold' has bright yellow summer foliage tinged red in winter, with pinkish purple blooms. 'Golden Sport' is yellow to yellow-green shaded with pinkish red in winter, and has pinkish purple flowers. 'Windlebrook' has deep yellow foliage that turns orange-red in winter, and boasts purplish pink flowers. *Note: E. cinerea* is considered invasive in some areas.

**GROWING TIPS:** Heaths grow best in full sun with acidic soil, but they will tolerate light shade. Good drainage is a must (heaths hate soggy soil), but they also appreciate some moisture, especially when they're young. Water regularly for the first year or two; after that, established heaths are fairly drought-tolerant. Trim lightly in early to mid-spring to shape the plants and keep them dense and bushy. Mulching with pine needles and/or pine boughs will help prevent winter damage. If heavy snows flatten or break the stems, or if drying winds or fluctuating temperatures kill some or all of the top growth, cut back to the live growth or to the base if necessary, and hope that they'll resprout.

**ALTERNATIVES:** Heather (*Calluna vulgaris*) looks like heath and enjoys the same conditions. 'Beoley Gold' and 'Gold Haze' are light yellow; deep yellow 'Boskoop' turns reddish orange in winter; 8 to 12 inches tall. Zones 4 to 7. 'Sunset Gold' breath-of-heaven (*Coleonema pulchrum* or *C. pulchellum*; also sold as 'Golden Sunset' or under *Diosma ericoides*) offers a similar look for Zones 8 to 11; 2 to 3 feet tall. Full sun to light shade; average, well-drained soil.

## FUCHSIA
*Fuchsia*

**Height:** Varies
**Leaf size:** 1–2 inches long;
    ½–1 inch wide
**Full sun to partial shade**
**Zones vary**

Fuchsias (*Fuchsia*) aren't the most handsome plants as far as their overall form is concerned, but their showy flowers make them a pleasing addition to containers and borders. Add in colorful foliage, and you have the makings for some intriguing combinations.

The best known of the yellow-leaved cultivars is commonly sold as either *F.* 'Genii' or *F. magellanica* 'Aurea'. With a mixture of arching and upright red stems, it creates a loose, 2- to 3-foot-tall clump with small leaves that are deep to medium yellow in full sun and greenish yellow in partial shade. In fall, the foliage often develops reddish veins, and it

*Fuchsia magellanica* 'Aurea'

usually lasts through the winter. Small red-and-purple flowers dangle from the stems from late spring until heavy frost, providing an extra dash of color. Zones 7 to 9 or 10.

'Autumnale' could just as easily fit in the following chapter (Rousing Red to Basic Black), but I've included it here because it usually starts off in spring with yellow to yellow-green foliage. As the growing season progresses, it develops orange to red shading that gradually expands to cover most or all of the leaves by fall, creating an amazing spectacle. 'Autumnale' has the same reddish stems as 'Genii' and very similar flowers, but its leaves are typically somewhat wider and its branching habit is even more distinctly horizontal, so it usually isn't much more than 1 foot tall. It shows off splendidly in a container or basket or atop a low wall, where its stems can arch gracefully.

Reports of its hardiness vary; most likely Zones 8 or 9 to 11.

**GROWING TIPS:** Golden fuchsias produce their most-intense leaf colors with ample light. In cool-summer areas, they're best in full sun; elsewhere, try morning sun and afternoon shade or light all-day shade. Fertile, moist but well-drained soil is ideal. In spring, cut out any dead or winter-damaged stems and trim as needed to shape the plants.

**ALTERNATIVE:** Golden Mexican heather or elfin herb (*Cuphea hyssopifolia* 'Aurea'; also sold as 'Golden', 'Golden Foliage', and 'Gold Leaf Form') grows in dense, 1- to 2-foot-tall mounds of small, bright yellow leaves that usually soften to yellowish green in summer. Full sun to partial shade; average, well-drained soil. Cut back by half or more in spring to promote bushy new growth. Zones 7 or 8 to 11.

## HELICHRYSUM
*Licorice plant*

**Height:** 1–2 feet
**Leaf size:** 1–1½ inches long
    and wide
**Full sun to partial shade**
**Zones 9 or 10–11**

For many gardeners, container plantings simply aren't complete without licorice plant (*Helichrysum petiolare*; also sold as *H. petiolatum*). Its velvety leaves create an interesting textural contrast to the smooth surfaces of most foliage, and its trailing stems show off beautifully when allowed to cascade out of a planter or hanging basket. Licorice plants look quite handsome as garden plants, too, forming low mounds or carpets that spread several feet across. (The stems may also take root where they touch the soil, extending their coverage even farther.) In a border, the stems will weave their way through other low growers and even clamber up through taller companions.

The usual silvery gray species form is lovely in its own right, but the selection known as 'Limelight' is even more eye-catching, with its combination of woolly leaves and yellowish shading. Its exact color varies depending on the season and the light conditions, from medium to pale yellow in brightly lit spots in spring to a light yellowish green to pale green later in the year or in sites with less sun. Small clusters of tiny cream-colored flowers may appear in midsummer. Licorice plants tend to put on their best growth before that time, especially in areas with hot, humid summers, where the foliage may be prone to leaf rot. The leaves are also a favorite food of some butterfly larvae, which can defoliate an entire plant. Still, 'Limelight' is so beautiful that it's worth growing if only for its spring to midsummer color. *Note:* The species appears to be invasive in some areas (mostly in very mild coastal regions).
**GROWING TIPS:** Bright light brings out the most-intense leaf color on 'Limelight', but too much sun can bleach out the leaves,

so a site with morning sun and afternoon shade or light all-day shade is usually best. Neutral to alkaline, well-drained soil is ideal. Although licorice plants are commonly touted as being drought-tolerant, they are usually much happier with regular watering. If the plants spread too vigorously, trim them back as needed. Clip off any flowers that appear.
**ALTERNATIVE:** For even daintier foliage better suited to small-scale containers or basket plantings, consider 'Gold 'n' Pearls' bacopa. You may see it sold under *Sutera* or *Bacopa* or as 'Olympic Gold', and under any of these names it is just as apt to have solid-yellow leaves as green-splashed yellow ones (and sometimes solid-green ones too). To 4 inches tall. Partial to full shade; average to moist soil. Zones 9 to 11.

## JUNIPERUS
*Juniper*

> **Height:** Varies
> **Leaf size:** ¼–½ inch long; about ⅛ inch wide
> **Full sun**
> **Zones vary**

Whether you need a low-growing ground cover, a space-filling mound-former, or an eye-catching vertical accent, "ever-gold" junipers (*Juniperus*) make marvelous additions to sun-drenched borders and foundation plantings. When you're selecting golden junipers, keep in mind that the intensity and persistence of their yellow color varies depending on climate as well as the site and the

season. Like other golden conifers, junipers may also take on darker tints in winter; some describe them as "bronzed" while others dismiss them as "browned." Before you commit to a mass planting or spend a bundle on a single specimen, it's smart to visit local arboreta or display gardens in winter or to talk to growers in your area to find out how particular cultivars perform in your region. Here's an overview of just a few popular selections in a variety of habits. Common juniper (*J. communis*) is typically hardy in Zones 2 to 6 or 7; creeping juniper (*J. horizontalis*) is normally hardy in Zones 4 to 9; and plants sold under *J. × pfitzeriana, J. chinensis,* and *J. × media* are usually rated for Zones 3 to 9.

*Spreading junipers.* For a ground-hugging golden juniper barely 6 inches tall but spreading to 6 feet wide or more, look for *J. horizontalis* 'Mother Lode' (also sold as 'Motherlode' and 'Golden Wiltonii'). Its distinctly horizontal shoots are bright yellow in spring, creamy yellow in summer, and orange-tinged in winter. Quite a few other cultivars have a broadly vase-shaped habit. *J. horizontalis* 'Lime Glow' ('Limeglow') reaches just 18 to 24 inches tall but spreads to 3 feet wide, with bright greenish yellow growth fading to yellowish green, shaded with orange to purple in winter. *J. × pfitzeriana* (or *J. chinensis* or *J. × media*) 'Gold Sovereign' is about the same size, but holds its bright to light yellow color

*Helichrysum petiolare* 'Limelight'

*Juniperus horizontalis* 'Lime Glow'

all through the year. Among the slightly taller selections (2 to 3 feet tall and roughly 3 to 5 feet wide) are *J. chinensis* 'Golden Glow' and *J. × pfitzeriana* (or *J. chinensis* or *J. × media*) 'Saybrook Gold'; they, too, usually stay medium to deep yellow all year long. *J. × pfitzeriana* (or *J. chinensis*) 'Old Gold' is similar but may be tinged with orangey brown in summer. Slightly taller selections (3 to 4 feet tall and 4 to 6 feet wide) are medium to deep yellow *J. × pfitzeriana* (or *J. chinensis* or *J. × media*) 'Gold Coast', deep yellow Gold Coast Improved ('Monsan'), and bright yellow-tipped Gold Star ('Bakaurea'). All three stay well colored in winter, too. *J. × pfitzeriana* (or *J. chinensis* or *J. × media*) 'Pfitzeriana Aurea' is the tallest in this group, reaching 6 to 10 feet and 15 to 20 feet across. It's at its best in spring and summer, with light yellow to greenish yellow tips, gradually aging to yellowish green or light green later in the year.

*Upright junipers.* One golden juniper with a distinctly upright habit is *J. chinensis* 'Mac's Golden', with an overall greenish yellow appearance (4 to 6 feet tall). *J. communis* 'Gold Cone' forms a narrow, 6- to 8-foot-tall column of golden yellow to light yellow foliage that's usually brightest in spring to early summer. It tends to turn yellow-green or even mostly green during the summer in hot climates, and may show some bronzing in winter.

**GROWING TIPS:** Golden junipers typically keep their brightest color in full sun, although some benefit from light midafternoon shade to prevent sun scorch. Average to dry, well-drained soil is fine. The plants seldom need any special care; just trim any wayward shoots if you want to.

**ALTERNATIVES:** For a site with morning sun and afternoon shade, or light all-day shade, try a golden-leaved Canada hemlock (*Tsuga canadensis*). 'Everitt Gold' (also sold as 'Everitt Golden', 'Everitt's Golden', and 'Aurea Compacta') forms dense, light yellow to yellowish green pyramids eventually 3 to 5 feet tall. Faster-growing, pyramidal 'Golden Splendor' can reach 15 feet tall, with medium to creamy yellow foliage. Moist but well-drained soil. Zones 3 or 4 to 7.

## LAMIUM
*Dead nettle*

**Height: 6–8 inches**
**Leaf size: 1–2 inches long;**
    **about 1 inch wide**
**Partial to full shade**
**Zones 3 or 4–9**

Spotted dead nettles (*Lamium maculatum*) are a popular choice for shady gardens, mainly because their silver-splashed selections supply a color not often seen in shade-loving perennials. But silvery foliage isn't their only claim to fame: they also come in yellow-leaved cultivars that produce attractive, carpet-forming growth and clustered flowers in late spring to early summer.

*Lamium maculatum* 'Aureum'

*L. maculatum* 'Aureum' has bright yellow to greenish yellow foliage with a silvery white center stripe, plus purplish pink flowers. 'Cannon's Gold' is similar but usually lacks the white stripe, as does 'Beedham's White'; the latter also has white flowers instead of purplish pink ones. Yellow-leaved dead nettles are sometimes a little touchier about their growing conditions than their silver-leaved relatives are, but where they're happy, they bring lovely sunny color to beds, borders, planters, window boxes, and even hanging baskets. *Note: L. maculatum* is considered invasive in some areas of the country.

**GROWING TIPS:** Bright light usually brings out the best foliage color, but too much sun can scorch the leaves, especially if the soil isn't dependably moist. A site that gets morning sun and afternoon shade or light all-day shade with evenly moist but well-drained, humus-rich soil is ideal. If the foliage starts to turn greenish, shear the plants to an inch or two above the ground in midsummer to encourage a flush of bright new shoots that'll look good well into winter. If you choose not to trim them in midsummer, then do it in early spring before new growth begins.

**ALTERNATIVES:** Common or lesser periwinkle (*Vinca minor*) is another classic ground cover. 'Aurea' has clear yellow leaves; 6 to 8 inches tall. Light shade; evenly moist but well-drained soil. Zones 4 to 9. *Note:* The species is considered invasive in some areas. Ground-hugging Scotch moss or golden pearlwort (*Sagina subulata* 'Aurea') has needlelike, bright greenish yellow leaves. Full sun to partial shade; evenly moist but well-drained soil. Zones 4 or 5 to 9.

## LONICERA
*Honeysuckle*

**Height: Usually 3–5 feet**
**Leaf size: ½ inch long; ¼ inch wide**
**Full sun to partial shade**
**Zones 6 or 7–9**

This is not your usual honeysuckle! 'Baggesen's Gold' boxleaf honeysuckle (*Lonicera nitida*) isn't a twining vine with large, colorful flowers; instead, it's a low-growing shrub with narrow, glossy, "ever-yellow" to partially deciduous foliage and tiny, yellowish white spring blossoms that are barely noticeable. Its small leaves are typically deep to medium yellow in spring and summer, aging to yellow-green by fall and often taking on pinkish to purplish tinges for winter. Left unpruned, the plants tend to have a loose form with arching, feathery-looking shoots; they also respond well to pruning, so you can easily keep them bushier or even shear them into low, formal hedges or topiary shapes. 'Baggesen's Gold' blends prettily into mixed borders and shows off beautifully in planters too.

**GROWING TIPS:** A site with full sun and average to moist, well-drained soil is usually ideal. Afternoon shade may be better in hot climates to prevent leaf bleaching or scorching; with too much shade, however, the leaf color will be more in the light yellow to light green range. Shelter from drying winter winds helps to keep the foliage looking good through the colder months. Trim as needed to remove wayward shoots and keep the plants nicely shaped. If they get too leggy, trim them almost to the ground in spring to encourage dense new growth.

**ALTERNATIVES:** Japanese holly (*Ilex crenata*) looks somewhat similar but is slightly hardier (Zones 5 or 6 to 9). 'Golden Dwarf Helleri' (also sold as 'Golden Heller' and 'Golden Helleri') and 'Golden Gem' are medium to light yellow; 2 to 3 feet tall. 'Lemon Gem' is greenish yellow; 12 to 18 inches tall. Full sun to afternoon shade; acidic, average to moist but well-drained soil. *Note: I. crenata* is considered invasive in some areas.

*Lonicera nitida* 'Baggesen's Gold'

## ORIGANUM
*Oregano, marjoram*

**Height: Varies**
**Leaf size: ½–1½ inches long;**
**½–1 inch wide**
**Full sun to partial shade**
**Zones 5–9**

Ornamental oreganos (*Origanum*) lack the rich flavor of their culinary cousins, but they share the aromatic foliage, summer flowers, and handsome mounding habit that make for great garden plants. Golden-leaved selections also offer rich leaf colors that complement both bright and pastel flowering and foliage partners in beds, borders, foundation plantings, and containers. Planted in groups, golden oreganos make eye-catching ground covers.

There are several selections to choose from, and they all grow in spreading clumps that are bright yellow in spring and green-tinged yellow by summer. The plants are 6 to 10 inches tall in leaf and 12 to 15 inches tall in bloom, with pale pink to white flowers. The most widely available option in this group is commonly called golden oregano (*O. vulgare* 'Aureum'); plants with similar traits are sold under the names *O.* 'Norton Gold' ('Norton's Gold'), *O. onites* 'Aureum', 'Thumbles' ('Thumbles'

*Origanum vulgare* 'Aureum'

Variety'), and 'Thea's Gold'. *O. vulgare* 'Aureum Crispum' ('Curly Gold') has rounded, crinkled leaves instead of the usual smooth, oval-shaped foliage.

**GROWING TIPS:** Full sun helps to keep the leaf colors bright, but it can also scorch the foliage if the soil gets too dry. Morning sun and afternoon shade with average, well-drained soil is a good compromise. Shearing the plants by half just before flowering encourages dense, bushy growth. The clumps develop woody bases that benefit from being divided every two to four years in spring.

**ALTERNATIVE:** In partial to full shade, try 'Harvest Moon' strawberry begonia (*Saxifraga stolonifera*; also listed as *S. sarmentosa*). It grows in "ever-gold" clumps of rounded, light yellow to yellowish green leaves that are maroon underneath. The foliage may also be blushed with red in cool weather. The plants spread by slender stolons to form dense carpets to about 6 inches tall. Humus-rich, evenly moist but well-drained soil. Zones 7 to 10.

## PICEA
*Spruce*

**Height: Varies**
**Leaf size: ½–1 inch long;**
    **less than ⅛ inch wide**
**Full sun to partial shade**
**Zones vary**

Cool-climate gardeners may envy those who can grow a wide range of colored foliage year-round, but northern gardens have the advantage when it comes to many conifers, including most spruces (*Picea*). These handsome evergreens form dense, conical to pyramidal trees that seldom need pruning, and their needle-like leaves come in an array of green, blue, and yellow shades. Although spruces are typically quite tall, there are a number of selections in every color group

*Picea orientalis* 'Skylands'

that are short or slow-growing enough to stay in scale with the average home landscape. Here's a sampling of just a few "ever-yellow" spruces that usually take 10 years or more to reach 10 feet tall. Nurseries that specialize in conifers offer many more and can suggest those likely to perform best in your particular climate. Keep in mind that although some people adore the appearance of golden spruces, others find them rather sickly looking, so you might want to think twice about putting them in a high-visibility setting, such as a front yard.

Among the compact, golden selections of Norway spruce (*P. abies*) are bright yellow to yellow-green 'Aurea' and the even more intense 'Jacobsen' (also sold as 'Aurea Jacobsen'); both have a pyramidal form that can reach 5 to 10 feet tall in 10 years. Gorgeous 'Gold Drift' is bright yellow in spring and still a pleasing greenish yellow in winter; let it trail on a slope or over a wall, or stake it to create an upright plant with weeping branches. 'Vermont Gold' ('Repens Gold') forms brilliant yellow, spreading mounds about 1 foot tall but several feet across. Zones 3 to 7 or 8.

'Aureospicata' Oriental spruce (*P. orientalis*) and the slightly earlier-to-grow 'Early Gold' both have bright yellow spring shoots that turn deep green by late summer, on pyramidal plants about 6 to 8 feet tall. Narrowly pyramidal 'Skylands' is also bright yellow in spring, turning light yellow-green

in summer and holding that color well into winter. It's usually 5 to 8 feet tall in 10 years but may grow faster once it's established. (This one seems particularly prone to scorching, so afternoon shade is a must for it in many areas.) Zones 4 to 7 or 8.

Conical Colorado spruce (*P. pungens*) is best known for its silvery blue selections, so its golden cultivars are definitely something different; they too, though, typically have blue-green older needles. 'Aurea' and 'Sunshine' have bright yellow new growth and hold some yellow through most of the year; they're usually 4 to 6 feet tall. 'Walnut Glen' has light yellow to cream new growth, appearing cream-frosted blue by winter (5 to 6 feet tall). Zones 3 to 7 or 8.

**GROWING TIPS:** Spruces normally prefer full sun, but the golden forms often benefit from afternoon shade, especially when young. They appreciate acidic, evenly moist but well-drained soil. Careful attention to watering during the first few years helps get young spruces off to a good start.

**ALTERNATIVE:** True cedars (*Cedrus*) are an elegant "ever-gold" option for warmer climates (Zones 6 to 10). Most get quite tall, but 'Golden Horizon' Himalayan cedar (*C. deodara*) is just 3 to 5 feet. It has an overall spreading habit, with horizontal to arching branches clad in fine, medium greenish yellow to light yellow needles. Clip upright shoots to preserve the mounded form. Full sun; average, well-drained soil.

## SEDUM
*Sedum, stonecrop*

**Height: 2–6 inches**
**Leaf size: Varies**
**Full sun to partial shade**
**Zones vary**

Tough and trouble-free, golden sedums (*Sedum*) are a real treat for busy gardeners who want lots of color without a lot of fussing. These easy "ever-yellow" perennials will adapt to a wide range of growing conditions, so they make compatible companions for many different plants, and they show off superbly in a variety of settings, from edging beds, borders, and paths to covering slopes; cascading out of baskets, window boxes, and planters; and trailing over low walls. Their starry, yellow, late-spring to early-summer flowers are pretty, but you'll hardly notice them against the bright foliage.

Of the two best selections for golden foliage, *S. makinoi* 'Ogon' (sometimes sold as 'Limelight') is more delicate-looking. Held on pinkish stems, its tiny, light yellow to greenish yellow leaves are barely ⅓ inch long and wide. They may also be blushed with pink or peach tones in cool weather. 'Ogon' grows in dense, spreading mats that are just 2 to 3 inches tall and 1 foot or more across. Zones 6 or 7 to 10.

*S. rupestre* 'Angelina' (also listed under *S. reflexum*) is anything but subtle. Its 6-inch-tall stems are densely clad in short, needlelike leaves that start out rich, deep yellow often tinged with orange at the tips, then turn bright

*Sedum makinoi* 'Ogon'

greenish yellow for the summer. When cool weather returns, the upper sides of sun-exposed leaves take on a deep orange shade that makes an amazing accent in the winter garden. 'Angelina' forms a dense, spreading carpet that holds its leaves throughout the winter in most areas; you can shear plants in spring to remove any discolored shoots, or just let the vigorous new growth cover them. You may also choose to shear off the yellow flowers, as they don't add much extra interest and may produce self-sown seedlings. Zones 3 to 9.

*S. acre* 'Aureum' is yet another sedum you may find for sale. It's tipped with yellow only in spring, though, turning light green for the rest of the year. It will grow just about anywhere in Zones 3 to 8 and spreads far and wide in no time at all, so it qualifies as aggressive in the garden and can be invasive in natural areas as well. 'Ogon' and 'Angelina' are much better choices for adding golden foliage to beds, borders, and containers.

**GROWING TIPS:** 'Angelina' is at its best and brightest in full sun, but it can still be a respectable yellow-green in partial shade. 'Ogon', on the other hand, actually looks better with afternoon shade or light all-day shade; strong sun may bleach the leaves to very pale yellow or nearly white. Clipping off the faded flowers isn't absolutely necessary, but it helps to keep the plants tidy and prevents self-sowing. Sedums are incredibly easy to divide any time during the growing season if you want to control their spread or expand your plantings.

**ALTERNATIVE:** Golden false clover is sold under a variety of names, including *Oxalis spiralis* 'Aurea', *O. spiralis* subsp. *vulcanicola* 'Copper Glow', and *O. vulcanicola* 'Copper Glow'. Looking like a cross between a clover and a sedum, it has succulent red stems clad in small leaves that are usually light yellow to pinkish or peachy yellow; 6 to 9 inches tall. Let the plants trail out of a basket or pot, or use them in masses as a ground cover. Full sun to light shade; average, well-drained soil. Zones 9 to 11.

## SPIRAEA
*Spirea*

**Height:** Varies
**Leaf size:** 1–3 inches long; ½–1 inch wide
**Full sun to partial shade**
**Zones 4 or 5–9**

For their foliage alone, golden spireas (mostly selections of *Spiraea* × *bumalda*; also listed as *S. japonica* and *S. thunbergii*) are amazing color accents for mixed borders, foundation plantings, and even containers. They come in a range of heights but tend to form bushy mounds that are in perfect scale with both perennials and other small shrubs. Many also undergo striking color changes from spring to summer (from orange-red to yellow) as well as from summer to fall (usually turning back to orange and/or red). Spireas don't demand any special care, and they adapt readily to all sorts of growing conditions.

So why don't we see golden spireas in everyone's garden? Probably because of the late-spring to early-summer flowers, which are almost always some shade of pink. It's one thing when they bloom against clear yellow foliage (even that combination is unappealing to some), but when the clustered pink flowers blossom among the orange-red new shoots that many golden spireas retain until bloom time, the effect can be rather shocking (as well as difficult to plan combinations around). If you're crazy about color no matter where it comes from, golden spireas are a great choice for you; otherwise, consider shearing off the flowers before they open, choosing one of the few options with white blooms, or selecting another shrub altogether. *Note:* Both *S. japonica* and *S. thunbergii* are considered invasive in some areas of the country.

Options are plentiful among the pink-flowered golden spireas. Two- to 3-foot-tall 'Goldflame' is one of the best known, but it's not the best; it tends to turn mostly green in summer, it may revert to solid-green shoots, and it's prone to powdery mildew. Two- to 3-foot-tall Limemound ('Monhub') and 3- to 4-foot-tall 'Gold Mound'

*Spiraea thunbergii* Mellow Yellow

('Goldmound') hold their yellow a few weeks longer, but they still turn greenish in summer. Some selections with medium to light yellow foliage that holds its color well through summer are 'Candlelight' ('Candle Light'), 'Firelight' ('Fire Light'), Magic Carpet ('Walbuma'), and Golden Princess ('Lisp'), all of which are in the 2- to 3-foot-tall range. More-compact cultivars are the 1- to 2-foot-tall 'Flaming Mound' (with particularly bright red new growth) and the 12- to 15-inch-tall Dakota Goldcharm ('Mertyann') and 'Lemondrop'. The smallest selection to date is 'Golden Elf'; it grows just 6 to 12 inches tall and has the added feature of flowering only sparsely, if at all.

If white flowers are more to your liking, look for the wonderful 3-foot-tall selection called 'White Gold', with bright yellow new growth that usually softens to light yellow or yellow-green by the time the white flowers appear. Or check out the distinctly different *S. thunbergii* Mellow Yellow ('Ogon'), which produces fragrant white flowers along its arching branches in late winter to early spring, just before the very narrow, bright yellow leaves appear. The foliage tends to turn yellowish green in the heat of summer, then changes to shades of pink, orange, and/or red for fall. It's typically 3 to 5 feet tall.

**GROWING TIPS:** Golden spireas stay brightest in full sun, although they will look acceptable with just morning sun and afternoon shade (in fact, they may prefer that in hot-summer areas, or anywhere the soil tends to be dry). Average, well-drained soil is fine. If your plants are getting a little taller than you'd like, shear them back by about a third in early spring. You'll probably also want to shear off the brownish spent flower clusters to improve the appearance of the plant for summer (this may promote rebloom as well).

**ALTERNATIVE:** For similarly fine foliage on an "ever-gold" shrub, consider golden false holly (*Osmanthus heterophyllus* 'Ogon'). The spiky-looking leaves are bright yellow to orange-yellow when new, softening to light yellow in summer and turning green when fresh shoots appear the following spring. Eventually about 6 feet tall. Shelter from winter wind. Partial shade is usually best, with average to moist but well-drained, acidic soil. Zones 6 or 7 to 10.

## TAXUS
*Yew*

**Height: Varies**
**Leaf size: ½–1 inch long;**
**⅛–¼ inch wide**
**Full sun to partial shade**
**Zones vary**

Good-looking and easy to grow, yews (*Taxus*) have long been a popular choice for foundation and landscape plantings in many parts of the country. As with many other widely grown conifers, they've produced quite a few variants over the years, with different heights, habits, and needle colors. Yews that are described as golden are actually more correctly variegated, because they typically keep a thin strip of green along the center of each glossy needle. But since the needles are so fine and so abundant, those with yellowish markings produce plants that have an overall golden appearance for at least part of the year. Below is an overview of just a few of the available yews in this color group. Selections of English yew (*T. baccata*) are usually best suited to Zones 5 to 7 or 8, while those of Japanese yew (*T. cuspidata*) are typically rated for Zones 4 or 5 to 8.

*Options abound* if you'd like a golden yew with a low, spreading form. *T. baccata* 'Repandens Aurea' (also sold as 'Repens Aurea') grows only 2 to 3 feet tall but can spread to 10 feet wide or more, with yellow- to cream-edged needles that hold their color through the winter. 'Summergold' tends to be slightly shorter (in the range of 1 to 2 feet), while 'Watnong Gold' is closer to 3 to 5 feet tall; both have a somewhat brighter effect than does 'Repandens Aurea', especially in summer. *T. cuspidata* 'Aurescens' (also sold as 'Nana Aurescens') eventually reaches 3 to 5 feet tall and 6 feet wide or more, with bright greenish yellow new growth that softens to light yellow or yellow-green and usually stays that way into winter. It grows anywhere from 1 to 3 feet tall and 3 to 6 feet across. 'Dwarf Bright Gold' is similar but slightly larger (2 to 4 feet tall and 4 to 6 feet wide).

If you're looking for a vertical accent instead of a spreader, check out plants sold as *T. baccata* 'Aurea', which commonly

*Taxus cuspidata* 'Aurescens'

have a rounded to broadly conical form, and 'Standishii' or 'Stricta Aurea', which form a narrower column. They all have light yellow needles and reach 6 to 8 feet tall in 10 years, eventually maturing closer to 15 or 20 feet if left unpruned.

*Caution:* Yew is quite toxic if ingested; it's not something kids would normally eat, but be sure to keep the clippings away from pets and livestock. Also be aware that the species *T. cuspidata* is considered invasive in some areas of the country.

**GROWING TIPS:** Golden yews tend to burn in strong sun, but too much shade will turn them greenish; a site with morning sun and afternoon shade should be ideal. Average to moist but well-drained soil is fine. Shelter from winter wind is a plus. Yews are quite attractive when allowed to develop their natural bushy or upright forms, but they also tolerate regular pruning well if you want to control their size or their shape.

**ALTERNATIVES:** Golden Japanese black pine (*Pinus thunbergii* 'Ogon'), for Zones 5 to 8, and 'Louie' Eastern white pine (*P. strobus*), for Zones 3 to 7, have an upright form and usually grow 10 to 15 feet tall in 10 years. 'Gold Coin' Scotch pine (*P. sylvestris*) typically matures at 6 to 8 feet; Zones 2 to 7. Full sun to afternoon shade; average, well-drained soil. *Note: P. thunbergii* is considered invasive in some areas.

# THUJA
*Arborvitae*

**Height: Varies**
**Leaf size:** ¼–½ inch long;
   to ¼ inch wide (individual
   scalelike leaves)
**Full sun to partial shade**
**Zones vary**

When the topic of new and exciting plants comes up, arborvitaes (*Thuja*) rarely get a mention; after all, they're one of the most widely chosen evergreens for landscapes and foundation plantings in many parts of the country. But don't overlook them just because they're common: they'll tolerate a wide range of growing conditions, and they don't demand a lot of maintenance to look respectable all year long. To take advantage of their good points and indulge your craving for colorful foliage at the same time, consider adding one or more of the many "ever-gold" arborvitaes to your mixed borders or year-round container plantings.

Below is a brief overview of golden selections from American arborvitae or eastern white cedar (*T. occidentalis*), which is usually recommended for Zones 2 or 3 to 7, and western red cedar or giant arborvitae (*T. plicata*), typically suggested for Zones 5 or 6 to 8. Nurseries that specialize in conifers offer many others as well. Unless indicated otherwise, the heights given below refer to the approximate size the plants will reach in 10 years.

Need an arborvitae that's on the smaller side? *T. plicata* 'Rogersii' is one of the smallest (to about 2 feet), with bright yellow foliage that's tinged with orange to bronze in winter on a broadly pyramidal plant. Bright to light yellow *T. occidentalis* 'Golden Globe' has a distinctly rounded form typically 2 to 4 feet tall. And then there's the readily available, broadly conical 'Rheingold', with deep yellow to orange-tinged yellow foliage that turns bronzy yellow in winter; it's 3 to 4 feet tall.

Taller options abound among the golden arborvitaes, with either broad or narrowly upright forms. Two broadly pyramidal selections of *T. occidentalis* are the 4- to 8-foot-tall 'Sunkist' and the 10- to 15-foot-tall Techny Gold ('Walter Brown'); the 4- to 6-foot-tall 'Collyer's Gold' and the 10-foot 'Sunshine' are cultivars of *T. plicata*. All of these have medium to light yellow foliage that holds its color well throughout winter. If you'd prefer a more narrowly upright form, check out 5- to 8-foot-tall *T. occidentalis* 'Europe Gold' ('Europa Gold'), with bright to deep yellow foliage that's tinged with orange in winter, or 8- to 10-foot-tall 'Yellow Ribbon', with medium to light yellow foliage all year.

**GROWING TIPS:** Golden arborvitaes grow in full sun to partial shade (morning sun and afternoon shade is usually ideal, especially in the warmer parts of

*Thuja plicata* 'Sunshine'

their hardiness range). They prefer evenly moist but well-drained soil, although they will adjust to drier conditions once they've been in the ground for a few years. Arborvitaes usually stay dense and bushy without pruning; they don't mind being trimmed regularly, however, if you want to control their size.

**ALTERNATIVE:** Golden false arborvitae (*Thujopsis dolabrata* [*T. dolobrata*] 'Aurea') looks similar to true arborvitaes, with glossy, medium to light yellow foliage that may be tinged with orange in winter. The broadly pyramidal to conical plants grow to about 5 feet tall in 10 years (eventually to about 20 feet). Full sun to partial shade; acidic, evenly moist but well-drained soil. Zones 5 to 8.

## VERONICA
*Speedwell, veronica*

**Height:** Varies
**Leaf size:** Varies
**Full sun to partial shade**
**Zones vary**

Speedwells (*Veronica*) are best known for their beautiful blue flowers, but that's not the only reason to make a place for them; there are some exquisite gold-leaved cultivars.

*V. prostrata* 'Trehane' is the old standard in this group, forming low, spreading, 6- to 8-inch-tall mounds of bright yellow spring leaves that are about 1½ inches long and ½ inch wide. By the time the spikelike clusters of tiny blue flowers appear in early summer, the leaves are usually a softer yellow to yellowish green. It's usually recommended for Zones 4 to 8. The stunning

*V. prostrata* 'Aztec Gold' is a newer selection with a similar growth habit and bloom display, but its leaves are brilliant yellow, and they hold their rich color through the growing season if they get plenty of light. It's rated for Zones 4 to 8.

"Ever-yellow" *V. repens* 'Sunshine' is the lowest growing of the gold veronicas, forming a dense, spreading mat of oval, ½-inch-long and -wide leaves that reach barely 1 inch tall. The foliage is lemon yellow in sun to yellow-green in some shade. Palest blue to white flowers may appear in spring, but don't depend on them for much of an impact.

**GROWING TIPS:** Full sun brings out the brightest yellow leaf color on 'Aztec Gold' and 'Sunshine'; morning sun and afternoon shade or light all-day shade is usually better for 'Trehane', which can otherwise be prone to leaf scorch. All three prefer soil that stays evenly moist, but good drainage is a must, too — especially in winter. If 'Aztec Gold' or 'Trehane' clumps lose their dense, bushy habit after flowering, shear the plants by half to two-thirds.

**ALTERNATIVES:** For drier sites, consider thymes (*Thymus*) with tiny, aromatic, bright yellow to yellow-green leaves. They're usually attributed to *T. × citriodorus* but may also be listed under *T. pulegioides* or *T. vulgaris*. Names to look for include 'Archer's Gold', 'Bertram Anderson', and 'Clear Gold'. Full sun; average to dry, well-drained soil. Zones 4 to 9.

*Veronica prostrata* 'Trehane'

## ACER
*Maple*

**Height:** Varies
**Leaf size:** 2–4 inches long and wide
**Full sun to partial shade**
**Zones vary**

Maples (*Acer*) are a mainstay of home landscapes in many parts of the country, and with good reason: they're beautiful, adaptable, and virtually trouble-free. These deciduous trees are well known for their fantastic fall colors, but many of them undergo striking color changes earlier in the season as well. Below is a sampling of some marvelous maples that have golden foliage in spring

and/or summer. Some are small enough to do well in a container, at least for a few years; others are better suited for large mixed borders or as single specimens.

Many selections of the popular Japanese maple (*A. palmatum*) have deeply lobed, yellowish spring foliage that is tinged and/or edged with red to orange in spring, turning green in summer. 'Kashima' is very dwarf (just 3 to 5 feet tall) with yellow fall color. Slightly larger cultivars (6 to 8 feet tall) are 'Tsuma-gaki', with red-edged yellow leaves in autumn, and 'Wou-nishiki', with bright red fall color. In the range

*Acer shirasawanum* 'Aureum'

of 12 to 18 feet tall with orange-and-yellow fall color are 'Katsura', 'Ueno-homare', and 'Ueno-yama'. Zones 5 or 6 to 8. *Note:* This species is considered invasive in some areas; Japanese maples can self-sow into woodlands and other natural areas.

Golden fullmoon maple (*A. shirasawanum* 'Aureum') is a great choice if you're looking for foliage that stays yellow through most of the growing season. This slow-growing small tree will eventually reach 15 to 20 feet tall, with lobed leaves that are greenish yellow in spring, light yellow through the summer, and a mix of yellow, orange, and red in fall. It also has showy reddish flowers, seeds, and leaf stems. 'Autumn Moon' has pink- to orange-tinged new growth that gradually ages to light yellow, turning orange to reddish again in fall. Zones 5 to 7 or 8.

'Auratum' and 'Kelly's Gold' box elders (*A. negundo*) aren't as elegant as fullmoon maples, but they, too, hold their light yellow to greenish yellow color throughout the season, and they grow much more quickly. They can reach 25 to 30 feet tall, but if you cut out some of the oldest stems each year, you'll keep them smaller. Zones 3 or 4 to 8. *Note:* This species is considered invasive in some areas.

**GROWING TIPS:** Golden maples vary in their sun tolerance. They need enough light to keep their brightest leaf colors but not so much that they bleach or scorch. A site with morning sun and afternoon shade is ideal for most; box elders will usually take more sun. Evenly moist but well-drained soil is ideal for all of these maples.

**ALTERNATIVES:** Golden locust (*Robinia pseudoacacia* 'Frisia') is a much taller golden tree (to about 30 feet), with bright yellow leaflets that turn yellow-green for the summer and then back to yellow or yellow-orange before dropping in fall. Zones 4 to 9. 'Sunburst' honey locust (*Gleditsia triacanthos* var. *inermis*) has even smaller, lemon yellow leaflets that age to green by summer; to 40 feet. Zones 3 to 9. Full sun; average, well-drained soil.

## DRYOPTERIS
*Male fern*

**Height: 18–30 inches**
**Leaf size: 18–30 inches long;**
    **4–6 inches wide (whole frond)**
**Partial to full shade**
**Zones 5 or 6–9**

Ferns get plenty of attention from texture-attuned gardeners, but they don't often come to mind as dramatic color accents. Although it's not unusual for the newly emerging fronds of some ferns to have a purplish tint, most quickly turn green and stay that way for the rest of the growing season. Not so with autumn fern (*Dryopteris erythrosora*). Also known as Japanese shield fern, this easy, adaptable perennial brings many of the colors of fall to the spring garden, with slow-spreading clumps of deep purple new fronds that turn various shades of orange, copper, or old-gold before aging to medium to deep, glossy green for summer. Fronds keep emerging through most of the growing season, so there's usually a range of colors on each plant into autumn, when all of the fronds turn orange-bronze again. (The backs of the arching fronds are also dotted with attractive red spore cases at this time.) Autumn fern may hold its foliage all winter in mild areas but it's usually deciduous. 'Brilliance' is noted for its particularly bright coppery fronds.

**GROWING TIPS:** Autumn fern grows in partial to full shade and prefers acidic, compost-enriched, well-drained soil. It can tolerate quite a bit of drought once it's been growing in the same spot for a few years; it prefers evenly moist (but not soggy) soil, however, and will grow most vigorously there. Cut off the old fronds at the base in late winter or early spring to clear the way for the stunning spring display.

**ALTERNATIVE:** For something really different, check out golden Boston fern (*Nephrolepis exaltata* 'Aurea'; also sold as 'Golden Boston', 'Bostoniensis Aurea', and 'Rita's Gold'). It forms the same dense clumps of arching fronds as does the usual Boston fern, but in this case, they're a rich creamy yellow to yellowish green. Light all-day shade; evenly moist but well-drained soil is ideal. Zones 9 to 11; a gorgeous winter houseplant in cooler climates.

*Dryopteris erythrosora*

# GERANIUM
*Geranium*

**Height: Varies**
**Leaf size: 3–5 inches long and wide**
**Full sun to full shade**
**Zones vary**

Hardy geraniums (*Geranium*) get lots of attention for their flowers, but their handsome foliage also makes a significant contribution to beds and borders. Those that have deeply lobed leaves are quite attractive for their lacy texture, and some have showy fall foliage color too, but it's the selections with golden foliage that really add an unexpected color splash. They're typically at their best in spring (it's not unusual for them to show pinkish or reddish tinges over the bright yellow base color), but in the right site, some of them stay yellow well into summer. Plus, they have the usual colorful blossoms.

While none of the golden geraniums is exactly common, the hybrid 'Ann Folkard' is the most readily available of the bunch. It's a big one, growing anywhere from 2 to 4 feet tall with a possible spread of 3 to 6 feet. It starts out as a central mound, then sends out long, trailing stems that like to weave among or climb up through its companions. The lacy, bright yellow to light green leaves look great anywhere they pop up, but the saucer-shaped, black-centered, magenta-pink flowers have the potential for creating spectacular color clashes; they appear in varying abundance from late spring or early summer well into fall. It's usually rated for Zones 5 or 6 to 9. 'Anne Thompson' (also sold as 'Ann Thompson' and 'Ann Thomson') is essentially a more compact version, reaching about 1 foot tall and spreading 3 to 4 feet. Zones 4 to 9.

If those two don't satisfy your cravings for golden geraniums, specialty nurseries offer several other selections worth notice, such as sun-loving, 1-foot-tall hybrids 'Diva', with purplish pink flowers, and 'Blue Sunrise', with medium blue to purplish blue blooms. Shade-lovers include 1-foot-tall, pink-flowered 'Heronswood Gold' wild geranium (*G. maculatum*) and 12- to 18-inch-tall, purple-flowered 'Golden Spring' and 'Mrs. Withey Price' mourning widow (*G. phaeum*). These are usually hardy in Zones 4 or 5 to 9.

**GROWING TIPS:** Sun brings out the brightest yellow color, but too much will scorch or bleach out the leaves; in deep shade, on the other hand, the leaves quickly turn green. A site with average to moist but well-drained soil that gets morning sun and afternoon shade is usually ideal for sun and shade lovers alike.

**ALTERNATIVES:** For geranium-like foliage on a grand scale, consider 'Golden Palms' coltsfoot (*Petasites frigidus* var. *palmatus*). The deeply lobed, bright yellow to greenish yellow leaves can easily reach 1 foot across, in partly shaded, moist- or wet-soil sites. It's typically about 2 feet tall, with creeping rhizomes that spread many feet in all directions. For a more restrained option, seek out 'Chedglow' stinking hellebore (*Helleborus foetidus*; also sold as 'Gold Bullion'), with deeply lobed, "ever-yellow" foliage on upright stems; 18 to 24 inches tall. Partial shade; average, well-drained soil. Zones 5 to 9 for both.

*Geranium* 'Blue Sunrise'

# JASMINUM
*Jasmine*

**Height: 10–20 feet**
**Leaf size: 2–3 inches long;**
**1½ inches wide**
**Full sun to partial shade**
**Zones 7–9**

Fiona Sunrise common or poet's jasmine (*Jasminum officinale* 'Frojas') is an elegant option for fine foliage on a sturdy but controllable climber. Its twining stems bear compound leaves with narrow leaflets that are brilliant yellow (sometimes tinged with orange) in spring, turning light yellow for summer and aging to medium or deep yellow for fall.

*Jasminum officinale* Fiona Sunrise

The leaves are eventually deciduous, but they often hang on into late fall or early winter. The easy-care nature and glorious foliage of Fiona Sunrise are more than enough to earn it a place of honor in gardens or containers, but there's an added benefit: small but fabulously fragrant white flowers that appear throughout the summer. Let the vines sprawl or weave among other companions, or support them with a trellis. For extra color, combine Fiona Sunrise with another small-scale climber, such as a hybrid clematis.

**GROWING TIPS:** This adaptable jasmine bears its richest yellow color in full sun but is still a bright greenish yellow in partial shade. Average to moist, well-drained soil is fine. Fiona Sunrise seldom needs any special attention; simply prune it as needed if you want to keep it shorter. Where it's not hardy, bring it indoors in fall and enjoy it as a houseplant for the winter.

**ALTERNATIVE:** Love that lacy foliage but need a shrub instead of a vine? Look for 'Goldenvale' white-stemmed bramble (*Rubus cockburnianus*; also sold as 'Golden Vale' and 'Aureus'). It forms dense thickets of arching, prickly, white-frosted purple stems for winter, with vivid yellow to greenish yellow foliage through the growing season; 5 to 7 feet tall. Full sun to partial shade; average to moist but well-drained soil. Zones 5 to 9.

*Rhus typhina* Tiger Eyes

# RHUS
*Sumac*

**Height: 6–12 feet**
**Leaf size: 3–4 inches long; about**
**    2 inches wide (individual leaflet)**
**Full sun to partial shade**
**Zones 4–8**

Staghorn sumac (*Rhus typhina*) rarely earns a place on most gardeners' wish lists, due in large part to the notorious skin-irritating properties of its "most unwanted" relative, poison sumac (*Toxicodendron vernix,* formerly *R. vernix*). Luckily for texture-loving gardeners, this lacy-leaved shrub doesn't cause the same problems — and better yet, it now comes in a gorgeous golden-foliage form too. A sport of cutleaf sumac (*R. typhina* 'Laciniata'), Tiger Eyes ('Bailtiger') shares its parent's 1- to 2-foot-long leaves

with deeply cut leaflets and stout, upright stems that are covered with a velvety fuzz when young. What makes Tiger Eyes a real standout, though, is its stunning clear yellow to green-tinged yellow foliage, which lights up the landscape from spring to late summer and then — in some conditions at least — takes on glowing shades of red and orange for the fall season.

Like the regular staghorn sumac, Tiger Eyes can send up suckers several feet away from the main plant, although it doesn't appear to spread quite as vigorously. If you're concerned about the suckers, reduce the possibility of them appearing by siting the plant where you're not likely to dig into the roots (such as in a lawn area instead of a

border). Tiger Eyes also looks fantastic growing in a large container, perhaps a wooden half-barrel; enjoy it alone as a graceful patio accent or underplant it with sun-loving coleus, salvias, or verbenas for an intense summer and fall display. In the garden, pair Tiger Eyes with rosy pinks to echo the pinkish color of its leaf stems; liven it up with bright orange, red, and purple companions; or contrast its lacy leaves with bold foliage, such as dark-leaved 'Australia' canna.

**GROWING TIPS:** Tiger Eyes is brightest in full sun but will grow in partial shade too. Average, well-drained soil is fine; it will even take a hot, dry site. If you want to keep the plants compact, cut out one or two of the tallest stems at ground level each spring. Another recommendation: choose its planting site carefully, then leave it there. If you dig it up to move it, the roots left behind will send up lots of new shoots.

**ALTERNATIVES:** Golden elderberries (*Sambucus nigra* 'Aurea' and *S. nigra* var. *canadensis* 'Aurea') are spreading shrubs with bright yellow, compound leaves aging to greenish yellow. 'Plumosa Aurea' European red elder (*S. racemosa*) is similar in color but has a lacier texture; also-lacy 'Sutherland Gold' is more sun-tolerant. To 15 feet or more; stays 6 to 8 feet if cut back hard in spring. Morning sun and afternoon shade, or light all-day shade; average to moist soil. Zones 3 to 9.

## TANACETUM
*Feverfew, tansy*

**Height: Varies**
**Leaf size: Varies**
**Full sun to partial shade**
**Zones 4–8 or –9**

Feverfew (*Tanacetum parthenium*; also listed under *Chrysanthemum parthenium* and *Matricaria parthenium*) and tansy (*T. vulgare*) have long had a place in herb gardens, but you don't often see either species in ornamental plantings, probably because of their propensity to spread freely. But the golden-leaved forms are so beautiful that it's worth putting in a little extra effort to control them. The deeply lobed, brilliant yellow, aromatic leaves emerge very early in spring, so they make colorful companions for bulbs, pansies (*Viola × wittrockiana*), and early-flowering perennials. Later, the feverfew and tansy foliage expands to fill the gaps as their partners go dormant in summer.

Golden feverfew (*T. parthenium* 'Aureum') has 2- to 3-inch-long, 1½-inch-wide leaves that usually turn yellowish green by midsummer. It reaches 12 to 18 inches tall in bloom, with many small, yellow-centered, white-petaled daisies from early to late summer. Golden feverfew is often a short-lived perennial, but you can also grow it as an annual (sow indoors in early spring) for flowers in late summer and fall. The plants also self-sow prolifically, so you may want to clip off most of the spent blooms. Just leave one or two to drop seed and create replacement plants. Occasionally, you'll see yellow-leaved plants sold under the names 'Golden Feather' and 'Golden Moss'. Some sources claim that 'Golden Feather' has more deeply cut leaves and that 'Golden Moss' is more compact, but others use golden feather and golden moss as alternate common names for the regular golden feverfew.

Golden tansy (*T. vulgare* 'Isla Gold') is more dependably perennial, spreading by rhizomes to form broad patches of very lacy leaves (3 to 5 inches long and about 2 inches wide) that tend to hold their color through the summer. The 2- to 4-foot-tall flowering stems are topped with clusters of deep yellow, buttonlike blooms in mid- to late summer. They're not very showy and don't complement the lighter yellow foliage, so some gardeners cut them off before they open.

**GROWING TIPS:** Golden feverfew and golden tansy are brightest in full sun, but too much strong sunlight may bleach or scorch the leaves if the soil is at all dry, so afternoon shade is a benefit in hot-summer climates. Average, well-drained soil is fine; the plants appreciate evenly moist soil, but that can cause tansy to spread even faster. Deadheading is a must to avoid overenthusiastic self-sowing; dividing golden tansy every two or three years will help control its spread. *Caution:* Handling the foliage of these plants may irritate sensitive skin, so it's wise to wear gloves while working around them.

**ALTERNATIVE:** For another ferny-foliaged golden herb, check out 'Golden Phoenix' wormwood (*Artemisia vulgaris*). Its lacy, bright yellow leaves make a terrific addition to container plantings for both texture and color. In a pot, it stays 1 to 2 feet tall. In the ground, it can reach 3 to 6 feet tall and is a rampant spreader. Full sun; average to dry, well-drained soil is best. Zones 4 to 8.

AT RIGHT: **A fall surprise.** For most of the growing season, Arkansas bluestar (*Amsonia hubrichtii*) is a rather undistinguished green, but its distinctive autumn foliage makes it a handsome color and textural accent in late-season beds and borders. (The Landscape Arboretum at Temple University Ambler, PA)

*Tanacetum parthenium* 'Aureum'

# 3 ROUSING RED TO BASIC BLACK

ABOVE: **Getting an edge.** A bright green rim gives the moody purple foliage of 'Flame Leaf' euphorbia a neat, crisp appearance.

OPPOSITE: **Something special.** In a border based on rich reds and purples, green becomes an exciting accent instead of a boring background color. (Atlock Flower Farm, NJ)

Welcome to the dark side! Whether you're a confirmed fan of "purple" foliage or considering it for the first time, you'll never get tired of using these shady characters in beds, borders, and container combinations. Looking for maximum color impact? Pair dark leaves with bright silver, white, orange, or yellow for dramatic contrast. Prefer understated elegance? Combine dark foliage with grays, blues, and greens in a variety of textures for an effect of subtle sophistication, or indulge in the sultry richness of velvety purple paired with deep crimson. Really want to live on the edge? Experiment with off-beat pairings, such as near-black leaves with magenta to pink flowers and foliage, or deep burgundy set against coppery browns in foliage or hardscaping. Long limited to just a few old standbys, gardeners today simply can't get enough of these dusky-leaved beauties, especially the many exciting introductions that are coming on the market every year. Annuals, perennials, shrubs, trees, vines, and even edibles, suited for sun or shade, moist or dry soil: dark foliage in all its forms deserves a place in gardens everywhere.

## GETTING STARTED WITH DARK FOLIAGE

Although most dark leaves are commonly referred to as purple foliage, they actually vary widely in color, from near-black to brownish green and from rich burgundy to true red. These colors are most often the result of compounds within the leaves called *anthocyanins*. These water-soluble, red, blue, and purple pigments form in the cell sap. They're not always present, and when they are, their abundance depends on many factors. Sunlight encourages the production of anthocyanins; so do cool temperatures and dry conditions. Nutrient levels can also influence their appearance. Low nitrogen, for instance, enhances reddish or purplish colors; abundant nitrogen may cause leaves to appear more on the green side. Phosphorus deficiency can also cause foliage to develop a purplish cast.

When anthocyanins are present, the colors they produce depend a good deal on the pH of the sap. Acidic conditions promote reds, while a more neutral pH promotes purples. (Keep in mind that the pH of the leaf sap is not always the same as the pH of the soil the plant is growing in. Adding lime to raise the pH or sulfur to lower it won't necessarily affect the intensity of the red or purple of the foliage.)

LEFT: **Light it up.** Dark foliage, such as the leaves of 'Forest Pansy' redbud (*Cercis canadensis*), often takes on a very different appearance when the sun shines through it.

RIGHT: **Know what to expect.** Black mondo grass (*Ophiopogon planiscapus* 'Nigrescens') holds its dark color throughout the year, while Japanese blood grass (*Imperata cylindrica* var. *koenigii* 'Rubra') turns from mostly green in summer to totally red by fall. (Scott Arboretum, PA)

So why do plants bother to produce reddish pigments? In some cases, these compounds appear to help protect cells from damage due to ultraviolet radiation, but in other situations, their purpose isn't clear. Of course, to us gardeners, the *why* doesn't matter nearly as much as the *when*. Quite a few plants — 'Gerald Darby' iris and many astilbes, epimediums, and peonies, for example — have reddish or purplish new growth in spring, then become all green in summer. On other plants, the actively growing shoot tips may stay reddish while the older leaves turn green (as in cleyeras, photinias, and some hybrid roses). Some "evergreens" are actually green only in summer and fall, developing purplish colors that hold through the winter into spring; examples here are many abelias, bergenias, and leucothoes, as well as several conifers. Then, of course, there are plants that are dependably purple from the time they emerge until the end of

the growing season. Among these are heucheras, dark-leaved selections of ninebark (*Physocarpus opulifolius*), and weigelas.

## Making the Most of Dark Foliage

In general, purple-leaved forms of sun-loving plants also prefer sun. Dark-leaved selections of shade plants usually also thrive in shade, although they may develop deeper colors if you give them more light. Unlike the many variegated and yellow-leaved plants that produce their best colors in spring, most plants that are purple or reddish in spring and green in summer don't respond well to being cut back hard, so just enjoy their early colors and plan on them being green for the rest of the season. On those that produce reddish or purplish new growth all summer, pruning lightly every few weeks through midsummer encourages the plants to produce more shoot tips and thus more color. Plants that develop dark foliage only in winter tend to be most purplish in sun, so make sure they get plenty of light if you want to encourage that; those in a sheltered

RIGHT: **Light and dark.** Pairing dark foliage with brighter greens and golds is a great way to keep it from looking too gloomy. (Hortulus Farm Gardens, PA)

## DARK FOLIAGE FOR FULL SUN

*Acalypha wilkesiana* 'Curly Q', 'Raggedy Ann', others

*Alternanthera dentata* 'Rubiginosa', others

*Atriplex hortensis* var. *rubra*

*Beta vulgaris* 'Bull's Blood', 'MacGregor's Favorite'

*Canna* 'Australia', 'Intrigue', others

*Capsicum annuum* 'Black Pearl', 'Explosive Embers', others

*Cercis canadensis* 'Forest Pansy'

*Cordyline fruticosa* 'Button Black', 'Maroon Magic', others

*Cotinus coggygria* 'Royal Purple', 'Velvet Cloak', others

*Dahlia* 'Bishop of Llandaff', 'Fascination', others

*Eucomis comosa* 'Oakhurst', 'Sparkling Burgundy'

*Euphorbia cotinifolia*

*Geranium pratense* 'Black Beauty', 'Purple Haze', others

*Heuchera* 'Bressingham Bronze', 'Purple Petticoats', others

*Hibiscus acetosella* 'Jungle Red', 'Red Shield'

*Ipomoea batatas* 'Blackie', 'Sweet Caroline Purple', others

*Iresine herbstii* 'Brilliantissima', 'Purple Lady'

*Loropetalum chinense* var. *rubrum* 'Burgundy', others

*Ocimum basilicum* 'Osmin', 'Red Rubin', others

*Pennisetum setaceum* 'Eaton Canyon', 'Rubrum'

*Phormium* 'Merlot', 'Platt's Black', others

*Physocarpus opulifolius* Diabolo ('Monlo'), others

*Ricinus communis* 'Carmencita', 'Sanguineus', others

*Sambucus nigra* 'Guincho Purple', 'Thundercloud', others

*Sedum* 'Black Jack', 'Purple Emperor', others

*Tradescantia pallida* 'Purpurea'

*Weigela* 'Dark Horse', 'Ruby Queen', others

## DARK FOLIAGE FOR SHADY SITES

*Alocasia reginula* 'Black Velvet'

*Begonia* 'Raspberry Crush', 'Venetian Red', others

*Caladium bicolor* 'Florida Cardinal', 'Thai Beauty', others

*Cimicifuga simplex* 'Black Negligee', 'Brunette', others

*Cryptotaenia japonica* f. *atropurpurea*

*Geranium maculatum* 'Elizabeth Ann', 'Espresso'

× *Heucherella* 'Burnished Bronze', 'Chocolate Lace'

*Kaempferia* 'Alva', others

*Ligularia dentata* 'Britt-Marie Crawford', others

*Ophiopogon planiscapus* 'Black Knight', 'Nigrescens'

*Oxalis triangularis* 'Atropurpurea', 'Charmed Wine', others

*Rodgersia podophylla* 'Braunlaub', 'Rotlaub'

*Viola riviniana* Purpurea Group

ACALYPHA
WILKESIANA

COTINUS
'ROYAL PURPLE'

PHYSOCARPUS
OPULIFOLIUS
DIABOLO

STROBILANTHES
DYERIANUS

SEDUM SPURIUM
'RED CARPET'

OPHIOPOGON
PLANISCAPUS
EBONY KNIGHT

spot (as on the north side of a building) tend to stay greenish year-round.

## Do Your Homework

To be fair, I should warn you that some of the most beautiful dark-leaved plants are also troublesome thugs—not just in your garden, but in natural areas as well. On the home-garden level, some examples of problem purples are purple fringed loosestrife (*Lysimachia ciliata* 'Purpurea'), which spreads rapidly by creeping roots, and purple perilla (*Perilla frutescens* var. *purpurascens*), 'Chocolate' white snakeroot (*Eupatorium rugosum*), and 'Chameleon' euphorbia (*Euphorbia dulcis*), all of which can produce many unwanted seedlings. You may also decide to avoid Japanese barberry (*Berberis thunbergii*). It has many stunning purple-foliaged cultivars, but it's also a serious invasive threat in several parts of the country, because its seedlings can quickly crowd out native woodland vegetation. Fortunately, there are still plenty of other dark beauties that are safe to enjoy, so go ahead and give them a try — just do some research *before* you plant.

LEFT: **In black and white.** Diabolo ninebark (*Physocarpus opulifolius* 'Monlo') offers high contrast during its early summer bloom period; later in the summer, its red seed capsules create an entirely different effect against the dark foliage.

## WHAT'S IN A NAME?

When you're ready to shop for dark foliage, local nurseries are the best place to start. There, you can easily see the exact shade of red or purple you're dealing with, and you'll get an idea of whether the color might change in different seasons. Once you've exhausted local options, it's time to resort to mail-order catalogs. To help you key into offerings that boast dark foliage, here are some clues to look for in the name.

amethyst
*atropunicea, -um, -us* (dark reddish purple)
*atropurpurea, -um, -us* (dark purple)
*atrorubens* (dark red)
*atrosanguinea, -um, -us* (deep red)
black
blackbird
blood, bloody
brass, brazen
bronze
brunette
burgundy
cardinal
*cardinalis* (red)
charcoal
cherry
chocolate
cinnamon
claret
copper
cranberry
crimson
*cruenta, -um, -us* (blood red)
dark
demon
dusk, dusky
ebony
ember
*erubescens* (reddening)

*erythrophylla, -um, -us* (red-leaved)
espresso
fire
*fusca, -um, -us* (dark)
garnet
grape
grenadine
ink
intrigue
jungle
lava
licorice
magenta
mahogany
maroon
merlot
midnight
moody
mystery
night
*nigra, -um, niger* (black)
*nigrescens* (blackish)
obsidian
Othello
oxblood
pink
plum
*punicea, -um, -us* (reddish purple)
purple
*purpurascens* (purplish)

*purpurata, -um, -us* (purple)
*purpurea, -um, -us* (purple)
raspberry
raven
red
rose, rosy
*rosea, -um, -us* (rose-colored)
rouge
*rubella, -um, -us* (reddish)
*rubens* (red)
*rubescens* (reddish)
*rubra, -um, ruber* (red)
*rubrifolia, -um, -us* (red-leaved)
ruby
*sanguinea, -um, -us* (blood red)
*sanguinolenta, -um, -us* (blood red)
scarlet
shadow
sooty
storm, stormy
strawberry
thunder
velvet
Vesuvius
*violacea, -um, -us* (violet)
violet
voodoo
wine

## DARK FOLIAGE IN THE GARDEN

No matter what colors you enjoy in your garden, pairing them with some dark foliage is the perfect recipe for turning so-so pairings into exciting and memorable combinations. Are your pastel plantings just a little too sweet for words? Spotting in a few plants with dusky foliage can be just what's needed to set off those soft colors. Could your bright borders use a touch of darkness to balance the richly hued blooms? Purple-leaved plants can add that invaluable bit of moodiness that makes other colors all the more intense.

**LEFT: Simple, yet satisfying.** For many foliage fanatics, the combination of purple and gold foliage never fails to please. Planted beneath or as a background, dark foliage makes bright companions "pop"; when it's in the foreground — as with this 'Blackie' sweet potato vine (*Ipomoea batatas*) — the dark foliage looks stunning against the golden backdrop.

**RIGHT: A dark secret.** When the new foliage of 'Oakhurst' pineapple lily (*Eucomis*) emerges in spring, it's a deep reddish purple; during the summer, the purple appearance is much less obvious. Keeping color changes like this in mind is a key part of creating combinations for different seasons. (Beds and Borders, NY)

As with all foliage colors, it's possible to have too much of a good thing here, so don't get too carried away with adding maroon- and purple-leaved plants to your garden and landscape. If you overdo the dark foliage, you run the risk of creating a black-hole effect; masses of dark leaves will blend in with the mulch and leave the impression of large gaps between clumps of other colors, especially in shady sites. But when you scatter it judiciously through beds and borders, dark foliage provides exciting opportunities for both dramatic and subtle combinations.

All "purples" aren't created equal, so whenever possible, it's best to have the plants in front of you when choosing companions. Pictures in books and catalogs don't always do justice to the true leaf color, because appearances vary widely depending on lighting conditions as well as the age of the leaf and the time of year. A photograph is just one moment in time, after all, but you'll be looking at the plants you choose all through the growing season, and at various times during the day. A single "purple" leaf may look near-black in direct mid-day sun, take on a bluish cast with side lighting, and appear blood red with backlighting. Plus, different people use color terms differently: one might describe a particular leaf as purple while another says it's burgundy and another calls it plum. If you're using the dark foliage just for contrast or as a background for blooms, the exact shade doesn't matter quite so much. But when you're trying to echo specific flower colors or markings, finding the perfect color match can make all the difference.

## Dark Foliage with Purple and Blue

If you grow lots of blue and purple flowers, you already know they look cool mixed with green foliage and cheerful when contrasted with yellow foliage. But did you know that you can create a completely different mood by pairing them with dark-leaved companions? In sunny sites, combining light blue or lavender flowers and powder blue foliage with somber, deep purple leaves creates an edgy effect: not quite as striking as a black-and-white contrast, but close. In shade, the result is more soothing, with the dark foliage helping the paler partners to stand out, though still retaining a sense of color harmony. Of course, purple foliage is also tailor-made for partnering with plum-colored blooms, such as *Allium atropurpureum*, 'Basye's Purple' rose, 'Black Ball' cornflower (*Centaurea cyanus*), 'Black Barlow' columbine (*Aquilegia × hybrida*), 'Jungle Beauty' daylily (*Hemerocallis*), and 'Queen of Night' tulip.

LEFT: **Pale in comparison.** In borders based primarily on pastel colors, dark-leaved plants — such as 'Purple Majesty' millet (*Pennisetum glaucum*) — can add a touch of intensity.

RIGHT: **Pretty in purple.** 'Purple Knight' alternanthera creates a pleasing harmony with 'Victoria' mealy-cup sage (*Salvia farinacea*).

## Dark Foliage with Greens

If sophistication is the effect you're after, you simply can't go wrong by combining foliage of different textures in shades of green and purple. The dark foliage acts almost like a shadow among the lighter-colored greens, making it easy to admire the amazing array of leaf shapes and structures — particularly deeply lobed or cut leaves, such as those of *Syneilesis aconitifolia* and many ferns. For extra visual interest, create a bridge between the greens and solid-colored darks by using plants with green leaves that are spotted, striped, edged, or centered with purple. Green flowers, too, make great partners for purple foliage; they'll be much more visible against the dark background than against lighter green leaves.

LEFT: **Compare and contrast.** Deep purple partners are ideal for highlighting pale green leaves, which might otherwise get lost against other greens. (VanDusen Botanical Garden, Vancouver, BC)

BELOW: **Autumn abundance.** Moody maroon foliage is perfectly at home amid the rich colors of the fall garden. (Ondra garden, PA)

LEFT: **Naturally beautiful.** With pink and purple in every leaf, 'Tricolor' beech (*Fagus sylvatica*) doesn't need to bear showy blooms — its foliage alone offers more interest than many flowers do!

BELOW: **Shocking pink.** Bright pink flowers add pizzazz no matter where they appear, but when they're paired with near-black foliage, the effect is practically electric.

## Dark Foliage with Pink Partners

There are many moods of pink in flowers, and they all look exquisite paired with purple foliage. Pale pinks stand out nicely against the dark background, as do delicate peachy and salmon pinks. When the pinks intensify, so do the effects they create with dark partners. For eye-catching summer impact, consider hot pink Knock Out rose interplanted with deep red 'Hopi Red Dye' amaranth for sun, for example, or perhaps the feathery, clear pink blooms of 'Rheinland' ('Rhineland') astilbe against the bold, deep purple leaves of 'Britt-Marie Crawford' ligularia (*Ligularia dentata*) in a shadier spot. Dark foliage is also excellent in a pink-themed bed or border as a link between bluish to purplish pinks and peachy to coral-pink blooms, as well as between soft cotton-candy pinks and glowing magenta hues. As a bonus, many purple-leaved plants — including 'Forest Pansy' redbud (*Cercis canadensis*), 'Royal Purple' and 'Velvet Cloak' smoke trees (*Cotinus coggygria*), and a number of dahlias, heucheras, and sedums — also sport pink or pink-tinged flowers, so they do double duty in a pink-theme garden.

Tradescantia 'Blushing Bride'

### IN THE PINK

If dark red or purple foliage is a little too gloomy for your taste, how about something a little lighter — like pink? Pink leaves owe their color to the same pigments that cause purple foliage, but in this case, there's little or no chlorophyll in the pink parts. This lack of chlorophyll produces the pastel color instead of a deeper shade.

Not too many plants have distinctly pink foliage, but some come pretty close, including a number of phormium, rex begonia, and coleus cultivars. There are, however, quite a few green-and-white-variegated plants that include some pink in their leaves, among them 'Burgundy Glow' ajuga, 'First Blush' euphorbia, 'Pink Frost' sweet potato vine (*Ipomoea batatas*), 'Blushing Bride' tradescantia, and 'Tricolor' two-row sedum (*Sedum spurium*). The pink appearance is typically most prominent in cool weather, all but disappearing during the summer. Pink polka-dot plant (*Hypoestes phyllostachya* 'Pink Splash') keeps its colorful spots throughout the growing season, making it a great container companion for pink-flowered summer bloomers.

Pink-marked foliage is a perfect complement to pink flowers, and it looks terrific with purple leaves too. It shows off best where you can enjoy the delicate coloring up close — in a container, for example, or in a bed or border close to a walkway; from a distance, most pink foliage isn't all that striking.

## Dark Foliage with Red and Orange

Purple, maroon, and red leaves all look fantastic partnered with "hot"-colored flowers, such as cardinal red 'Jacob Cline' bee balm (*Monarda*) against the dark purple leaves of 'Black Lace' elderberry (*Sambucus nigra*), and glowing orange cosmos (*Cosmos sulphureus*) underplanted with maroon 'Merlot' lettuce. Sometimes you can even find the whole package in one plant, as with the lacy-leaved, orange-flowered 'Ellen Huston' ('Ellen Houston') dahlia or the broad-leaved, red-flowered 'Black Knight' canna. When you place scarlet or orange flowers directly in front of dark foliage, the bright blooms really sizzle; when you use masses of dark leaves next to or underneath red or orange, the foliage provides a place for your eye to rest before moving on to view the next grouping of colorful flowers.

While mixing bright blooms with dark foliage produces a festive, summery feeling, combining rich crimson and plum-purple flowers and berries with red and purple leaves creates a completely different look — one of velvety, sensual elegance. In a large area, the effect may be a little overwhelming, but in an intimate space, you can appreciate the beauty of individual blossoms, berries, seeds, and leaves.

## Dark Foliage with Yellows

Creating combinations based on dramatic color differences is often an easy way to ensure success, so pairing yellow flowers and/or foliage with dark leaves is a perfect starting point for a new planting. As with pastel pinks and blues, pale yellow blooms definitely show to advantage against dusky foliage, instead of getting lost against an equally light background. Clear yellow flowers produce a striking contrast against deep purple leaves, and sunny orange-yellow blooms are a perfect match for equally intense darkness. In foliage-based combinations, moody maroon and purple leaves are a perfect complement to chartreuse partners.

TOP: **Vividly vertical.** Spiky purple crinum (*Crinum procerum* var. *splendens*) makes an eye-catching complement to pink and red partners in borders and container plantings.

BOTTOM: **Get a little closer.** From a distance, the foliage of purple shamrock (*Oxalis triangularis* 'Atropurpurea') appears evenly dark. Up close, though, the intricate shading becomes apparent, especially when set against a brighter-leaved companion.

LEFT: **Feel the heat.** Dark-leaved dahlias can supply some spectacular foliage-and-flower pairings for summer and fall. (Chanticleer, PA)

*Phytolacca americana 'Silberstein'*

*Belamcanda chinensis*

## MORE PLANNING POINTERS

To add an extra touch of sophistication to your combinations, remember to look beyond the basic colors of flowers and foliage. Berries, seeds, and stems all come in a range of colors, and you can make the most of them by echoing their hues with bolder leaves and blooms in the same range. This trick is especially useful with purples and deep reds, which may fade into the background unless you emphasize them. Plus, there are so many possibilities that it's a shame not to take advantage of them! Many annuals and perennials, for instance, have purple stems, so plant them with similarly dark-leaved companions to draw attention to them. Try 'Silberstein' pokeweed (*Phytolacca americana*) underplanted with 'Blazin' Rose' beefsteak plant (*Iresine herbstii*), or 'Carin' Joe Pye weed (*Eupatorium maculatum*) next to Wine and Roses weigela (*Weigela florida* 'Alexandra'). The same concept works to bring out the best in black- or red-fruited

plants. Japanese blood grass (*Imperata cylindrica* var. *koenigii* 'Rubra'), for example, does a wonderful job echoing the reddish summer seed capsules of Diabolo ninebark (*Physocarpus opulifolius* 'Monlo'); the lacy, near-black leaves of many dahlias highlight perfectly both the bold green leaves and the black seeds of blackberry lily (*Belamcanda chinensis*).

Purple foliage is also fantastic for repeating the dark streaks, rings, or spots that appear inside or on the backs of many blooms. Think of the dark blush on the outside of some lilies, for instance, or the black blotches inside many Oriental poppies (*Papaver orientale*), or the dark streaks or "eyes" in the blooms of many dianthus, daylilies (*Hemerocallis*), and pansies. Daisy-type flowers with dark centers, such as black-eyed Susans and Gloriosa daisies (*Rudbeckia*), also make perfect partners for dark foliage: the leaves make the bright petals "pop" as they echo the black center buttons.

### Dark Foliage with White, Silver, and Gray

If high impact is what you're after, consider pairing dark leaves with silvers, whites, and grays in a "black and white" bed or border. Solid purples serve the obvious role of a shadowy backdrop for the light-colored partners, while purples that have a gray or silvery cast — such as 'Black Jack' and 'Purple Emperor' sedums, some cannas, and many heucheras — make a perfect bridge between darks and lights. All kinds of dark foliage can look particularly striking against light-colored hardscaping, such as pale gray pavers or silvery weathered-wood fencing. Galvanized metal containers also make a great backdrop for burgundy, maroon, and black leaves.

RIGHT: **Bold and brilliant.** This inspired pairing of metallic purple Persian shield (*Strobilanthes dyerianus*) and lacy silver *Senecio viravira* is the stuff great garden memories are made of. (Chanticleer, PA)

*Eucomis comosa* 'Oakhurst'

## EUCOMIS
*Pineapple lily*

**Height: 2 feet**
**Leaf size: 18–24 inches long;**
  **2–3 inches wide**
**Full sun to partial shade**
**Zones 6 or 7–9**

Purple pineapple lilies (*Eucomis comosa* 'Sparkling Burgundy' and 'Oakhurst') are guaranteed attention grabbers in any garden. They look exotic but are surprisingly hardy; even where they won't survive the winter outdoors, it's easy to overwinter them indoors

and then enjoy them in borders or containers for summer and fall. They're often rather slow to sprout in spring, but once you see the strappy, deep reddish purple leaves emerge, you'll know they were worth waiting for.

The leaves are distinctly upright at first, then gradually arch outward, and they turn more of a reddish green to light brown or olive green during hot weather. In mid- or late summer to early fall, thick, deep purple flower stalks appear, each with a dense, spikelike cluster of starry, creamy white to purplish pink blooms topped with a tuft of leaflike purple bracts to complete the "pineapple" effect. The flowers gradually develop into interesting seed capsules, so they remain attractive for well over two months. When cool weather returns, the new leaves are again deep purple, adding even more interest to the autumn appearance. Keep in mind that the leaves of pineapple lilies will cover quite a bit of ground when they start to spread (filling a space 2 to 3 feet across), so don't plant permanent companions too close to them. Instead, pair them with spring bulbs, early perennials, or cool-season annuals (such as pansies) that will go dormant by early to midsummer.

**GROWING TIPS:** Full sun generally encourages the best purple during cool weather, but the leaves typically turn greenish during the summer whether they're in full sun or partial shade. Evenly moist

but well-drained soil is ideal while the plants are actively growing, although they will tolerate dry conditions too. Where the bulbs aren't hardy, dig them up in fall, cut off any remaining top growth, and store them in a cool, dry place for the winter.

**ALTERNATIVES:** Purple-leaved crinum lilies (*Crinum*) look similar in leaf but tend to stay much more upright; usually 4 to 5 feet tall. They're sold under a variety of names, including *C. procerum* var. *splendens* and *C. asiaticum* var. *procerum* f. *splendens*; *C. augustum, C. amabile* 'Queen Emma', and 'Queen Emma's Purple'; and *C.* 'Sangria' (about 2 feet tall). Full sun to partial shade; evenly moist soil. Zones 9 to 11 for most.

## IMPERATA
*Japanese blood grass*

**Height: 12–18 inches**
**Leaf size: 12–18 inches long;**
  **¼–½ inch wide**
**Full sun to partial shade**
**Zones 5 or 6–9**

For really-and-truly red spiky foliage, Japanese blood grass (*Imperata cylindrica* var. *koenigii* 'Rubra'; also sold as *I. cylindrica* var. *rubra* or 'Red Baron') is one of the hardiest perennials you can find. Growing from creeping rhizomes, it produces slowly but steadily expanding patches of upright leaves that emerge bright green with clear red to purplish red tips. Over the summer, they gradually develop more coloring, becoming completely cranberry

*Imperata cylindrica* var. *koenigii* 'Rubra'

red in autumn and then turning coppery tan in winter. Japanese blood grass seldom blooms in most climates, but who needs flowers with foliage like this? It looks terrific at or near the front of a border, in a container, or in a mass planting as a unique ground cover. If possible, site it where you can see the rising or setting sun shining through the red blades — the effect is amazing! *Note:* The straight species (*I. cylindrica*), commonly known as cogon grass, is considered seriously invasive in many areas. So far, Japanese blood grass appears to be safe to grow, but if any all-green shoots appear, remove and destroy them immediately.

**GROWING TIPS:** Full sun brings out the richest red, but the plants perform well in partial shade too. Average, well-drained soil is fine. Japanese blood grass tends to look rather tattered by midwinter; cut it down any time before new growth starts to appear in spring.

**ALTERNATIVES:** Switchgrass (*Panicum virgatum*) offers several selections with reddish leaf tips on plants 3 to 4 feet tall in leaf. 'Shenandoah' colors up in early to midsummer and turns deep purple-red overall in autumn. 'Rotstrahlbusch' and 'Hänse Herms' ('Haense Herms') develop their red tips a few weeks later and tend to be more reddish in fall. Full sun to light shade; dry to wet soil. Zones 3 or 4 to 9.

## OPHIOPOGON
*Mondo grass*

**Height:** 6–8 inches
**Leaf size:** 8–12 inches long; ¼ inch wide
**Full sun to partial shade**
**Zones 5 or 6–10**

Lots of plants have dark foliage, but black mondo grass (*Ophiopogon planiscapus* 'Nigrescens'; also sold as 'Arabicus') is truly in a class by itself. This slow-spreading perennial isn't a true grass, but it grows in grasslike tufts of slender, arching, leathery leaves. Its foliage is such a deep purple that it really does appear to be true black, and it usually looks that way year-round. (Sometimes the new growth is greenish purple, but it quickly darkens.) Clusters of small, pale pink to white flowers appear in summer, followed by rounded, glossy black fruits, but they're nestled among the leaves and not especially showy. Very similar, if not identical, plants are available under the names 'Black Knight', 'Black Night', and Ebony Knight ('Ebknizam').

Black mondo grass looks fantastic in a mixed planter or in a pot of its own. Growing it in a raised container or window box, or siting it next to a pathway or bench, is a good way to make sure it gets noticed; from a distance, it may blend in with dark soil or mulch. To help it show up, try it with companions that have bright yellow, silvery blue, or variegated foliage for a dramatic contrast, or pair it with

partners that have green leaves but black stems, flowers, or fruits for an elegant echo. Black mondo grass is often billed as a ground cover, but that's usually practical only for very small areas, because it's very slow to fill in and rather expensive to buy in large quantities.

**GROWING TIPS:** Black mondo grass grows well in either full sun or partial shade with average to moist but well-drained soil. Water it regularly the first year or two during dry spells to help it get established. If the leaves become tattered in winter, trim them off before the new growth appears in spring.

**ALTERNATIVES:** Dark-leaved sweet Williams (*Dianthus barbatus*) are hardly a substitute for black mondo grass, but they're beautiful in their own right. The 6-inch-tall, biennial or short-lived perennial clumps are usually green their first year, blushing dark red in fall; the following spring's growth is deep maroon. Names to look for include 'Darkest of All', 'Nigrescens', Nigrescens Group, 'Nigricans', and 'Sooty'. Full sun; average, well-drained soil. Zones 4 to 9.

## PENNISETUM
*Fountain grass, millet*

**Height:** Varies
**Leaf size:** Varies
**Full sun**
**Zones 9 or 10–11**

Red-leaved fountain grasses (*Pennisetum*) produce such an abundance of dark, spiky

*Ophiopogon planiscapus* Ebony Knight

foliage, it's difficult to remember that they last only one growing season in most parts of the country. Plants sold as *P. setaceum* 'Rubrum', 'Purpureum', and 'Cupreum' (which are apparently properly attributed to *P. advena*) have long been the standard for their narrow, glossy, purplish red leaves (12 to 18 inches long and about ⅓ inch wide), as well as for their long, arching, fuzzy flower heads that are light tan heavily blushed with pink to burgundy. They grow in distinct clumps with a very upright habit that's usually 4 to 5 feet tall in full flower (from mid- or late summer to frost). 'Eaton Canyon' (also sold as 'Dwarf Rubrum', 'Rubrum Dwarf', and 'Red Riding Hood') is similar but typically reaches only 2 to 3 feet tall. Zones 9 to 11.

*P. macrostachyum* 'Burgundy Giant' is much bolder, growing up to 6 feet tall with broader leaves (to 1½ inches across). Zones 9 or 10 to 11. *Note:* The true *P. setaceum* is considered invasive in some areas, but these dark-leaved types seldom set viable seed.

Purple-leaved strains of pearl millet (*P. glaucum*) are much more recent introductions, but these grasses have quickly gained popularity for their speedy growth (from seed to several feet tall in a single growing season) and their exceptionally dark purplish

*Pennisetum glaucum* 'Purple Majesty'

brown, glossy foliage. Individual leaves are usually 2 to 3 feet long and 1 to 2 inches wide. Selections currently on the market include 'Purple Majesty', 4 to 5 feet tall; 'Jester', which is usually closer to 3 feet but may be taller; and 'Purple Baron', which tends to be in between at about 4 feet tall. Purple millets look much like 'Burgundy Giant' plants in leaf, but you'll see the difference when the plants are topped not with soft, arching flower heads, but instead with dense, upright, spikelike clusters that appear cream-colored in bloom, maturing into long-lasting, deep purple seedheads. Purple millets are commonly grown as annuals but are hardy in Zones 9 to 11. *Note:* The species is considered invasive in a few areas.

**GROWING TIPS:** Fountain grasses perform best in full sun and average, well-drained soil. They will tolerate dry conditions but grow more vigorously if the soil is moist. They thrive in heat, and tend to be scrawny and greenish where summers are cool and cloudy.

Plants sold as selections of *P. setaceum* don't grow from seed and are often difficult to winter indoors, so plan on buying new plants each spring. If you grow the plants where they're hardy, cut them to the ground in late winter to make room for the new foliage.

The trick to success with purple-leaved millets is to keep them growing steadily from the seedling stage. They don't like having their roots cramped, so if you

buy transplants that have been in their pots too long, they'll likely be stunted for the rest of the season. Fortunately, it's easy to start these annual grasses from seed: wait until late spring to sow indoors, then transplant the seedlings outdoors in small clumps in early summer, when they're just 2 to 3 inches tall. The foliage is light green to yellow-green (especially with 'Jester') for the first few weeks, but it usually darkens quickly once the weather heats up. A site that's sheltered from strong wind is ideal; otherwise, the taller plants are prone to falling over if they're not staked.

**ALTERNATIVE:** For spiky dark foliage on a grand scale, check out purple sugarcane (*Saccharum officinarum* var. *violacea;* also sold as 'Pele's Smoke'). It will grow anywhere from 6 to 15 feet or more in one growing season (the warmer the climate, the taller it usually gets). The long, straplike, upright-to-arching leaves are deep purple when new, aging to a purplish brown. Full sun; average to moist, well-drained soil. Zones 8 to 11.

## PHORMIUM
*Phormium, New Zealand flax*

**Height: 3–5 feet**
**Leaf size: 3–5 feet long;**
    **1½–3 inches wide**
**Full sun to partial shade**
**Zones 8 or 9–11**

Dependable and durable phormiums (*Phormium*) are a great choice for grassy to swordlike foliage, particularly in container plantings. There are quite a few

dark-leaved selections to choose from, and they hold their rich shades all through the growing season (even year-round in mild climates), so they're a terrific source of both color and texture. In mild climates, phormiums often flower in late spring to early summer, with small, tubular, usually orange-red flowers on tall, leafless stalks, but it's their leaves that garner most of the attention. Below is a sampling of some phormiums with foliage in the reddish range. Mild-climate gardeners have access to many more; cooler-climate gardeners will be lucky to find even a few. The sizes given here are the approximate height they can eventually reach in containers; in the ground, some may grow several feet taller.

For the very darkest of the dark-leaved phormiums, look for compact 'Platt's Black', with arching, deep purple to near-black leaves (2 to 3 feet tall); giant 'Merlot' (to 6 feet tall), with upright, deep reddish purple leaves that are silvery gray underneath; or the medium-sized 'Dark Delight', with slightly arching, dark reddish brown foliage (3 to 4 feet tall). A number of other selections also fall in the maroon-leaved category, from the grasslike 'Jack Spratt' (just 18 inches tall) and the slightly larger 'Tom Thumb' (2 to 3 feet) through 3- to 4-foot-tall 'Dusky Chief' and 'Monrovia Red' (*P. tenax* 'Atropurpureum Compacta'). Some larger options are 4- to 6-foot-tall

*Phormium tenax* 'Maori Queen'

'Bronze Baby' ('Redi Babe') and 6- to 8-foot-tall *P. tenax* 'Atropurpureum' (also sold as 'Purpureum' and 'Rubrum').

Looking for a slightly brighter effect? 'Dazzler' is deep red but has lighter red stripes; it grows 3 to 4 feet tall. A number of other phormiums offer leaves with distinct pink markings, a color that's easy to get in flowers but difficult to find in foliage. Cultivars with broad brownish green centers and pink edges include the 4- to 5-foot-tall 'Maori Chief' ('Rainbow Chief'), 'Maori Queen' ('Rainbow Queen'), and 'Pink Stripe'; the 6- to 7-foot-tall 'Guardsman'; and the even larger 'Sundowner' (to 8 feet or more). All of these tend to have an overall reddish appearance. For a stronger pink effect, look for selections with wide, peachy to reddish pink centers and narrow, brownish green

edges, such as 'Jester', 'Maori Maiden' ('Rainbow Maiden'), and 'Rainbow Warrior' — all usually 18 to 24 inches tall — and 'Flamingo' and 'Maori Sunrise' ('Rainbow Sunrise') — to about 3 feet tall.

**GROWING TIPS:** Dark-leaved phormiums develop their richest colors in full sun but will grow well in partial shade, too (particularly in hot climates). If possible, site them where the rising or setting sun shines through their leaves; the color effects are stunning. Established plants are somewhat drought-tolerant, but usually perform best with evenly moist but well-drained soil. Shelter from strong wind is ideal, especially in winter. Remove any off-color shoots as soon as you see them. Also, regularly cut off the older, faded leaves to keep the plants looking their best. Though some phormiums are hardy in the ground in Zone 8 and even parts of Zone 7, it's safest to bring them indoors in most areas north of Zone 9; give them a cool, bright spot and keep their soil on the dry side.

**ALTERNATIVES:** The long, narrow leaves of cordylines (*Cordyline*) grow from upright stems reaching to 30 feet tall outdoors (Zones 8 or 9 to 11); in pots, they're usually 2 to 4 feet tall. Several cultivars of *C. australis* have dark foliage, including reddish purple 'Red Sensation' and deep red to reddish brown 'Red Star' (*C. baueri* looks similar). There are many others. Full sun to light shade; average, well-drained soil.

## CALADIUM
*Caladium, angel wings, elephant's ears*

**Height: 1–3 feet**
**Leaf size: 6–12 inches long;**
   **6–8 inches wide**
**Full sun to full shade**
**Zones 9–11**

Colorful caladiums (*Caladium bicolor;* also known as *C.* × *hortulanum*) offer some of the truest reds and pinks you'll find in foliage. They also come in a variety of leaf shapes and patterns, providing endless possibilities for exciting combinations in beds, borders, and containers. Two of the most distinctly different caladiums in this color class are 'Thai Beauty' (with elongated, heart-shaped leaves that are light to rosy pink with a network of deep green veins often outlined in bright white) and *C. bicolor* var. *rubicundum* (with irregular pink spots on deep purple-black leaves that age to deep bronzy green); both are usually about 18 inches tall. Mail-order caladium specialists offer many more selections. Below is a sampling of just a few in each color category, typically in the 12- to 18-inch-tall range. Keep in mind that the exact color effect can vary widely, depending on the age of the leaf and the growing conditions.

*Red with green.* For heart-shaped leaves with red centers and green edges, consider 'Brandywine', 'Florida Cardinal', 'Florida Red Ruffles', and 'Frieda Hemple'. 'Festiva' is a medium to deep red overall with deep green veining.

*Pink with green.* For a bold splash of rich reddish pink, check out 'Fannie Munson', with just a touch of deep green veining. 'Kathleen' has solid medium pink centers shading to bright green along the leaf margins. 'Pink Beauty' also has large, light to medium pink centers, but with distinct deep green spotting mostly around the edges; 'Florida Elise' is similar but more heavily marbled with deep green. 'Rosebud' displays a bright pink center starburst shading out to white and then bright to deep green. 'Pink Symphony' has narrower, light to reddish pink leaves veined with white, sometimes with a bit of green shading around the edges.

*Caladium bicolor* 'Florida Cardinal'

**GROWING TIPS:** Compost-enriched soil that's evenly moist but not soggy is ideal. Although caladiums are traditionally considered shade plants, some cultivars will tolerate quite a bit of sun. Regular fertilizing encourages lush growth, but it can also bring out more green in the leaves (so will heavy shade). Where they're not hardy, lift the tubers in fall and store them indoors for the winter, or buy new tubers or started plants each spring.

**ALTERNATIVES:** Hybrid 'Alva' peacock ginger (*Kaempferia*) has oblong, 8- to 10-inch-long leaves

that tend to lay almost flat; they're deep chocolate brown marked with jagged silver bands. *K. rotunda* 'Raven' is much more upright and spiky-looking, with lance-shaped, purple-brown leaves that have a broad, irregular silvery edge and deep maroon backs; 18 to 24 inches tall. Partial to full shade; average, well-drained soil. Zones 8 or 9 to 11.

## CANNA
*Canna*

**Height: 4–7 feet**
**Leaf size: 18–30 inches long;**
    **8–12 inches wide**
**Full sun**
**Zones 7 or 8–10**

Cannas (*Canna*) are invaluable where you need height, rich color, and bold foliage on a fast-growing, easy-care perennial. Their thick, upright stems are clad in broad, paddle-shaped leaves and topped with showy flowers from midsummer into fall. There are many excellent dark-leaved cultivars to choose from, differing in their heights as well as their exact foliage and flower colors. For the most intensely dark leaves, 'Australia' (also known as 'Feuerzauber') is generally considered the winner, with glossy, nonfading, deep red to near-black foliage along with bright red flowers; it grows 4 to 5 feet tall. 'Red King Humbert' has a bit more green in its leaves but is still very dark, with scarlet flowers on 6- to 8-foot-tall stems. ('Roi Humbert' is very similar, if not identical.) 'Red Futurity' also has deep maroon

*Canna 'Australia'*

leaves but it grows just 2 to 3 feet tall, with red flowers.

Some cannas have a powdery white farina that gives their buds, stems, and leaves a somewhat grayish appearance. On selections that have purplish to maroon foliage, this smoky cast softens the intense color a bit, so they blend beautifully with pastels as well as bright companions, depending on their flower colors. 'America' (3 to 5 feet tall) and 'Black Knight' and 'Black Velvet' (5 to 6 feet tall) have bright red blooms, while 'Intrigue' (6 to 9 feet), 'Pacific Beauty' or 'Semaphore' (6 to 7 feet), and 'Wyoming' (3 to 5 feet) have orange flowers. For pretty pink blooms over dusty purple foliage, look to 'Constitution' (light pink), 'Madame Angele Martin' (peachy pink), or 'Madame Paul Caseneuve' (peachy pink to light pink); these are all usually in the range of 3 to 5 feet tall.

**GROWING TIPS:** Full sun encourages the richest leaf colors and most vigorous growth. Dark-leaved cannas tolerate partial shade but tend to be greenish there. The plants thrive in rich, fertile soil that's dependably moist; in fact, many will grow even in standing water. Fertilize often for lush growth. Remove individual damaged leaves as needed, or cut whole stems to the ground if their leaves look dull to promote new growth. Where they aren't hardy, dig them up in fall and store indoors for the winter, or buy new rhizomes each spring.

**ALTERNATIVE:** Red-leaved or red Abyssinian banana (*Ensete ventricosum* 'Maurelii'; also sold as 'Atropurpureum', 'Rubrum', and *Ensete maurelii*) has deep green, red-blushed leaves that can reach several feet long. In hot climates, the reddish color may hardly be visible; it's much more intense and long-lasting in cooler areas. About 20 feet tall where hardy; 6 to 10 feet tall elsewhere. Full sun; average, well-drained soil. Zones 8 or 9 to 11.

## COLOCASIA
*Colocasia*, elephant's ears, taro, coco yam, dasheen

**Height: 3–6 feet**
**Leaf size: 1–3 feet long;**
    **1–2 feet wide**
**Sun to partial shade**
**Zones 7 or 8–10**

Big and bold colocasias (*Colocasia*) offer some of the very darkest foliage you'll find. Their huge, heart- to shield-shaped leaves grow in shrub-sized masses that bring instant impact to moist-soil borders, pond-side plantings, and large containers. Several selections have solid purple-black foliage, often with a bit of a grayish cast on the newer leaves, on 5- to 6-foot-tall plants. Unfortunately, these cultivars tend to be somewhat muddled in the trade. Plants sold as *C. esculenta* 'Black Magic' and 'Jet Black Wonder' should have smooth-edged leaves and be mostly clump-forming; those sold as 'Black Runner' and 'Black Ruffles' typically have wavy-edged leaves and spread by runners to

*Colocasia esculenta* var. *antiquorum* 'Illustris'

form wide patches. *C. esculenta* var. *antiquorum* 'Illustris' (*C. antiquorum* 'Illustris') also spreads but is about half of the height, with leaves that are usually so heavily shaded with velvety black that only the bright green midrib and main veins are visible. *C. affinis* var. *jenningsii* (*C. affinis* 'Jenningsii') plants are even shorter — to about 18 inches tall — with roughly oblong leaves that are variably shaded with black between the main veins, sometimes with a grayish green center as well; it, too, can spread quickly. *Note:* *C. esculenta* is considered invasive in some areas.

**GROWING TIPS:** Colocasias generally thrive in full sun with evenly moist to wet soil (or even standing water); a little afternoon shade is beneficial in hot climates. Rich soil and regular fertilizing encourages fast growth and the largest leaves. Where the plants are not hardy, dig up the corms or bring potted plants indoors for the winter. Where they can stay outdoors all year, don't worry if they're slow to sprout; they may not come up until late spring or even early summer, but once hot weather arrives, they'll fill out quickly.

**ALTERNATIVES:** *Alocasia reginula* 'Black Velvet' grows in spreading clumps to about 18 inches tall, with broad, oblong, near-black leaves that are veined and rimmed with white. *A. × amazonica* 'Purpley' is taller (2 to 4 feet), with shield-shaped, practically black leaves that have prominently rippled edges; the midrib, main veins, and leaf edges are all outlined with white. Partial shade; evenly moist but not soggy soil. Zones 9 to 11.

## LIGULARIA
*Ligularia*

**Height: 2–3 feet**
**Leaf size: 8–12 inches long**
**and wide**
**Partial to full shade**
**Zones 3–8**

Large leaves have a lot of surface area to lose water from, so it's not surprising that most bold-foliage plants need a steady supply of soil moisture. Bigleaf ligularia (*Ligularia dentata*) definitely falls into that category, happily forming luxuriant mounds of rounded to kidney-shaped, toothed leaves in moist-soil borders, streamside plantings, and other damp areas. Ligularias are fantastic foliage perennials, but they do bloom as well, with clusters of yellow-orange, daisy-like flowers atop 3- to 4-foot-tall stems from midsummer to fall. The very similar 'Desdemona' and 'Othello' have long been the standard selections for dark purple-brown leaves, at least early in the season; by midsummer, their leaf surfaces are usually deep green, although the undersides stay a rich reddish purple, as do the leaf stems and flower stalks. Newer 'Britt-Marie Crawford' is quickly gaining popularity for its tendency to keep its glossy, dark chocolate-brown foliage color through most, if not all, of the growing season.

**GROWING TIPS:** Even where they have plenty of water, ligularias often droop dramatically in strong sunlight, but they also need plenty of light to produce their darkest leaf colors. A site with morning sun and some afternoon shade is a good compromise. Rich, reliably moist soil and shelter from strong wind encourage vigorous growth and lush leaves. Seed from dark-leaved ligularias often produces dark-leaved seedlings, but the exact leaf colors will vary.

**ALTERNATIVES:** Many rodgersias (*Rodgersia*) have somewhat bronzy or reddish foliage when they emerge in spring, and often again in fall. A few that hold their rich spring shading longer include 'Braunlaub' and 'Rotlaub' bronzeleaf rodgersia (*R. podophylla*) and 'Chocolate Wings' featherleaf rodgersia (*R. pinnata*); about 2 feet tall in leaf. Morning sun and afternoon shade or light all-day shade; evenly moist but well-drained soil. Zones 4 to 7 or 8.

*Ligularia* 'Britt-Marie Crawford'

## RICINUS
*Castor bean*

**Height: 6–15 feet or more**
**Leaf size: 12–18 inches long**
 **and wide**
**Full sun**
**Zones 9–11**

With fast-growing castor beans (*Ricinus communis*) on hand, even cool-climate gardeners can enjoy a touch of the tropics in their borders. These plants grow into gigantic shrubs in tropical areas, but most of us treat them as annuals, enjoying them as eye-catching accents in sun-drenched borders or in masses as a summer-and-fall screen planting around a pool, deck, or patio. Castor beans have thick, upright, branching stems (more like trunks, actually), with broad, lobed leaves that tend to be quite glossy when new. From midsummer into fall, they also produce spikes of pinkish female flowers above cream-colored male flowers; the females then mature into rounded, spiny seed capsules. A number of seed strains have deep red to brownish red leaves, differing mainly in the height they reach, although that also depends on their growing conditions. Seeds labeled 'Sanguineus' tend to produce the tallest plants (in the range of 8 to 12 feet in one season), while 'Carmencita' (also sold as 'Carmencita Red' and 'Carmencita Bright Red') is 6 to 8 feet tall. 'Carmencita Pink' is about the same size, but its seed capsules are distinctly pink instead of the usual bright red. Among the lower-growing strains (in the 4- to 6-foot-tall range) are 'Dwarf Red Spire', 'New Zealand Purple', and *R. communis* var. *gibsonii* ('Gibsonii'). 'Impala' tends to be especially dark red overall, on 4- to 5-foot-tall plants. *Note:* Castor beans are considered to be invasive in some areas; cutting off the flower spikes will prevent seed production.

**GROWING TIPS:** Castor beans thrive in full sun but will tolerate light shade. Average, well-drained soil is fine. The richer the soil and the more moisture they get, the taller they will be. A site that's somewhat sheltered from wind will help prevent damage to the leaves and minimize the chance of the plants getting knocked over. Castor beans are easy to grow from seed. Soak the seeds in water overnight, then sow indoors six to eight weeks before your last frost date or directly outdoors in late spring. The plants often self-sow if you don't deadhead them. *Caution:* All parts of castor bean plants (and especially the seeds) are toxic if ingested, and handling the plants or seeds may irritate sensitive skin. Wear gloves when handling them, and keep them away from kids and pets.

**ALTERNATIVE:** The broad foliage of purple-leaved catalpa (*Catalpa × erubescens* 'Purpurea') is so deep purple that it's nearly black in spring, eventually turning dark green in summer. It can grow into a deciduous tree to 50 feet tall, but if cut back to 1 to 2 feet tall in early spring, it stays in the 6- to 10-foot-tall range. Full sun; average, well-drained soil. Zones 5 to 9.

*Ricinus communis* 'Impala'

## ACALYPHA
### Copperleaf

**Height:** 2–4 feet (10–15 feet where hardy)
**Leaf size:** 4–8 inches long and wide
**Full sun**
**Zones 10–11**

With a name like copperleaf, it's not difficult to guess what color the kidney-shaped to roughly oval foliage of *Acalypha wilkesiana* tends to be. These bushy, "ever-brown" shrubs have glossy, toothed leaves that are commonly reddish brown, but it's not unusual for them to be edged, speckled, blotched, or otherwise marked with one or more other colors. These multicolors offer particularly exciting opportunities for creating fantastic combinations with a variety of flowering and foliage partners in beds and containers. Copperleafs bloom, too — with narrow, reddish to pinkish, fuzzy-looking, trailing clusters — but their flowers are

nowhere near as fabulous as the foliage.

There are lots of spectacular copperleafs to choose from, so it's not possible to give more than a sampling of them here. Among those with solid brownish to reddish purple leaves are 'Curly Q', with broad, curled leaves that have distinctly toothed edges; and 'Raggedy Ann' (also known as 'Razzle Dazzle'), with narrower, jagged-edged leaves. For a jazzier effect, consider a cultivar that sports a bright pink edge, such as 'Obovata', with large, curved leaves; 'Marginata', with large, flat leaves; 'Marginata Bronze', with much wider pink margins on flat leaves; or 'Cypress Elf' (also known as 'Mardi Gras'), with very narrow, drooping leaves on compact, lacy-looking plants. Broad, flat-foliaged 'Louisiana Red' and 'Macrophylla' have random red to pink markings over the whole leaf surface. For an even wilder

mix of colors, check out 'Jungle Dragon' (also known as 'Tequila Sunrise') and 'Macafeeana', both with broad leaves that may boast a variety of red, pink, orange, and tan to brownish markings.

**GROWING TIPS:** Full sun usually brings out the richest leaf colors, but the plants will perform well in partial shade too. Average to moist but well-drained soil is fine. Pinching or clipping off the shoot tips promotes bushier growth. To keep the plants from year to year, bring them indoors in early to mid-fall and keep them in a warm, bright, humid spot for the winter.

**ALTERNATIVE:** 'Amigo Mahogany Red' celosia (*Celosia argentea* Cristata Group) has deep reddish purple foliage; 6 to 12 inches tall. 'New Look Red' (Plumosa Group) has deep red leaves (12 to 18 inches); 'Forest Fire' and 'Wine Sparkler' are 2 to 3 feet tall. Purple-leaved cotton (*Gossypium herbaceum* 'Nigra') has broad, lobed, near-black foliage on bushy, upright plants; 2 to 3 feet tall. Full sun; average, well-drained soil. Grow both as annuals.

*Ajuga reptans* 'Mahogany'

*Acalypha wilkesiana*

## AJUGA
### Ajuga, bugleweed

**Height:** Varies
**Leaf size:** 3–4 inches long; about 1 inch wide
**Full sun to full shade**
**Zones 3 or 4–8**

Ajugas (*Ajuga reptans*) are invaluable for adding dark foliage right at ground level. Their rosettes of glossy, often ever-present leaves

send out runners that take root and produce new plants, quickly forming a weed-suppressing ground cover. Short spikes of small blue or purple-blue blooms appear from early or mid-spring to late spring or early summer. Dark-leaved ajugas can be a little gloomy-looking in shady spots, so pair them with bright greens, yellows, or silvers to provide some contrast. In brighter sites and container plantings, they add just the right touch of moodiness to set off more-vibrant companions. Just be careful about letting ajugas loose in your beds and borders, because they spread quickly and are likely to creep into nearby lawn areas as well. *Note:* The species is considered invasive in some areas.

Most common ajugas have leaves that are 3 to 4 inches long and about 1 inch wide, with

flowering stems to about 6 inches tall. 'Atropurpurea', 'Bronze', and 'Purpurea' are rather general names used for purplish to brownish ajugas; the plants themselves can be quite variable. For dependably dark foliage, look for reddish brown 'Braunherz', purplish brown 'Bronze Beauty', deep purple 'Purple Brocade', and purple-black 'Mahogany'. For a bit more textural interest, check out deep purple-black 'Black Scallop', with scalloped leaf edges, and reddish purple 'Ruffled Lace', with wavy edges.

For a somewhat bolder effect, there are a few selections that are about twice the usual size in both leaf and flower: 'Catlin's Giant' (also sold as 'Caitlin's Giant'), with brownish green leaves in bright sites, and 'Jungle Beauty' (also sold as 'Jungle Beauty Improved'), with deep purple to purple-green foliage. On the other end of the size spectrum is Chocolate Chip ('Valfredda'; also listed under A. × tenorii). It's just 3 to 4 inches tall in flower, and its narrow, dark brown leaves are even tinier: 1½ inches long and ½ inch wide. A. pyramidalis 'Metallica Crispa Purpurea' (also sold as 'Mini Crisp Red' and 'Mini Crispa Red') is another distinctly different selection, with heavily crinkled, 4-inch-long, deep purple leaves on slow-spreading plants.

**GROWING TIPS:** Purple-leaved ajugas will grow anywhere from full sun (in cooler climates) to full shade, but they tend to have

the darkest foliage and flower most abundantly when they get plenty of light. Those growing in deep shade may appear nearly all green. Fertile, evenly moist but well-drained soil keeps the plants looking their best. After the flowers have faded, use shears or a string trimmer to remove the bloom stalks and improve the foliage effect.

**ALTERNATIVE:** If enthusiastic spreaders don't alarm you, consider purple-leaved or Labrador violet. It's sold under several names, including *Viola riviniana* Purpurea Group and *V. labradorica* var. *purpurea*. The small, heart-shaped leaves are deep purple during the cooler months, usually turning mostly green with a purplish blush in summer; 2 to 3 inches tall. Morning sun and afternoon shade or light all-day shade; moist but well-drained soil. Zones 3 to 8.

## ATRIPLEX
*Orach, mountain spinach*

**Height: 3–6 feet**
**Leaf size: 3–5 inches long;**
   **2–3 inches wide**
**Full sun to partial shade**
**Annual**

You're more likely to find orach (*Atriplex hortensis*) listed in seed catalogs with edibles rather than with ornamentals, because this fast-growing annual is sometimes used as a summer substitute for spinach, either raw or cooked. But the red-leaved selections are so beautiful that they also make out-

standing color accents for beds and borders from early spring to late summer. The decidedly upright plants branch out near their base if they have the space; in more crowded conditions, they tend to stay quite narrow and spiky-looking. In midsummer, the stems are topped with small, nondescript flowers that mature into nodding clusters of small, flattened seedpods. Seeds labeled *A. hortensis* var. *rubra* and *A. hortensis* 'Rubra', 'Purpurea', 'Atrosanguinea', or similar names typically have pinkish purple shoot tips and smooth, deep reddish purple older leaves. 'Triple Purple' is deep purple with crinkled leaves. And then there's 'Magenta Magic', with a distinctly different but difficult-to-describe color: more of a coppery red than deep purple. The vertical habit of all of these looks great coming up through lower airy or mound-forming companions. Try to keep them in small patches, though, so their partners can fill in when the orach dies back in late summer to early fall. *Note:* The species is considered invasive in some areas of the country.

**GROWING TIPS:** Full sun to partial shade with average to evenly moist but well-drained soil is ideal. Some sources recommend waiting to sow until the soil is warm, but this cool-season annual usually germinates much better when you sow anytime between fall and late winter, thus exposing the seeds to

chilly temperatures. Pull out any greenish seedlings. Pinching off the shoot tips of young plants encourages lower, bushier growth. Cut off most of the seedheads, but allow some to mature so you can get self-sown seedlings.

**ALTERNATIVES:** Many stunning selections of amaranth (*Amaranthus*) offer deep red to purplish red foliage on upright stems. Strains such as 'Black Leaved', 'Hopi Red Dye', 'Intense Purple', and 'Red Cathedral' are 4 to 6 feet tall; 'Oeschberg' is usually more compact (3 to 5 feet tall) *A. lividus* subsp. *lividus* is 2 to 3 feet tall. Sow in the garden after the last frost date. Full sun; average, well-drained soil.

*Atriplex hortensis* var. *rubra*

## BEGONIA
### *Begonia*

**Height: Varies**
**Leaf size: Varies**
**Full sun to partial shade**
**Zones 9–11**

Begonias (*Begonia*) offer such an abundance of fantastic foliage, in such an array of sizes, shapes, and colors, that it's a challenge to know where to begin with them. Many of the major groups within the genus — canelike; rhizomatous and rex; semperflorens; and tuberous types, for example — include cultivars with red, purple, brownish, or pinkish leaves, all of which can be amazing additions to beds, borders, and container combinations during frost-free weather. The clustered flowers are a bonus. Here's just a sampling of the available selections.

*Canelike begonias.* Sometimes also called cane or angel-wing begonias, these have thick, sturdy stems that can eventually grow 8 feet tall or more, although regular pruning keeps them much smaller. The leaves grow to 1 foot long or more and about 6 inches wide; many of them are spotted or blotched with silver. 'Cracklin' Rosie' is a classic with reddish new leaves, aging to brownish green or very deep green with pink spots on top. 'Jeanne Jones' has jagged-edged, near-black leaves with silver spots on top. And then there's compact 'Little Miss Mummey', with glossy brownish black foliage that's dotted with silvery white. The leaves of all three, as well as those of

deep purple 'Linda Dawn', also have deep red undersides, adding even more color to the mix.

*Rhizomatous begonias.* These, as you might guess, grow from creeping rhizomes, with leaves that can be anywhere from a few inches to more than a foot long. 'Cleopatra' has jagged green foliage that's moderately to heavily shaded with brown to deep purple. The spiral-centered leaves of 'Midnight Twist' are a satiny near-black with deep red undersides. 'Plum Gorgeous' is reddish purple on top and reddish underneath, while 'Red Doll' has small reddish to reddish brown leaves marked with a small, pale green star, sometimes with some muted yellow-green mottling.

*Rex begonias.* Rex or Rex Cultorum begonias are a particular type of rhizomatous begonia with colorful leaves that are often fantastically shaded or patterned with silver. They may be low-growing or upright and branching, but they're commonly 8 to 18 inches tall. 'Boston Cherries and Chocolate' has small, deep purple to brown foliage with silvery pink to reddish pink markings. Jagged-edged 'Raspberry Crush' also has a spiral center with black veins and margins; the base color is deep red on younger leaves and pink to silvery on older foliage. 'Venetian Red' has small, red to reddish pink leaves with near-black shading along the main veins and edge.

*Semperflorens begonias.* Also known as wax begonias and

fibrous-rooted begonias, these bushy, 8- to 24-inch-tall plants are commonly grown as annuals, but they're perennial in frost-free areas. They're prized for their typically glossy, rounded leaves as much as for their red, pink, or white flowers, which appear throughout the growing season. Some seed strains include a mix of green- and bronze-leaved types; other strains include all bronze-leaved plants that differ only in their flower color. One of the best known is the bronze-leaved, single-flowered Cocktail Series, to which white 'Whiskey', pink-and-white 'Rum', pale pink 'Brandy', medium pink 'Gin', and scarlet 'Vodka' belong. Double-flowered bronze begonias are propagated by cuttings: 'Lady Carol' is red and 'Lady Francis' is pink.

*Tuberous begonias.* These upright or trailing plants are best known for their large, colorful summer flowers, but some of them have lovely leaves as well. 'Switzerland' is stunning, with near-black leaves and large, double, bright red blooms on plants that are 8 to 12 inches tall.

**GROWING TIPS:** Begonias generally thrive in morning sun and afternoon shade or light all-day shade with average to moist but well-drained soil. Semperflorens begonias normally grow well in full sun too. Many rex begonias detest direct sun; light all-day shade is usually best for them. The more shade your begonias get, the less red or purple and the more green they will be. You

can bring any begonias indoors if you want to hold them over from year to year in frost-prone areas. The tuberous types go dormant in fall, and the rex types sometimes do, too, but the others usually keep growing if you set them in a bright spot or under plant lights.

**ALTERNATIVES:** Zonal geraniums (*Pelargonium × hortorum*) get their name from the dark purplish to brownish band on their green, yellow, or multicolored leaves. 'Distinction' is just one green-leaved selection with a particularly prominent dark zone. 'Bird Dancer' and the Black Velvet Series have deep purple leaf centers and bright green edges; the scented geranium 'Chocolate Mint' has a purplish brown leaf center. Full sun; average, well-drained soil. Zones 8 or 9 to 11.

*Begonia* 'Linda Dawn'

*Cercis canadensis* 'Forest Pansy'

*Cotinus coggygria* 'Royal Purple'

## CERCIS
*Redbud*

**Height: 12–25 feet**
**Leaf size: 3–4 inches long and wide**
**Full sun to partial shade**
**Zones 5 or 6–9**

Redbuds (*Cercis canadensis*) have a lot in their favor, including bright purplish pink, early-spring flowers; attractive, heart-shaped summer foliage; and sometimes showy fall color too. But it's the addition of a rich purple to the foliage that took redbuds from relative obscurity to the top of many gardeners' must-have lists. The flowers of 'Forest Pansy' tend to be darker and come out a bit later than usual, so they're still around when the glossy, rich reddish purple leaves emerge. The fully expanded foliage darkens to a matte deep purple, then gradually turns purple-tinged green to dark green during the summer. In autumn, they often take on shades of orange to rusty red or reddish purple. 'Forest Pansy' makes a wonderful multi-season specimen tree for the home landscape. If you think the dark foliage is a bit too somber, lighten the mood with an underplanting of silver-spotted dead nettle (*Lamium maculatum*) or Japanese painted fern (*Athyrium niponicum* var. *pictum*).

**GROWING TIPS:** The leaves stay purple longest in full-sun sites, but the plants also perform well with full spring sun and partial summer shade (especially in warmer areas). Average to moist soil is fine. Be aware that gardeners in some areas have trouble with established trees dying suddenly. At this time, the cause is unknown, but some suspect it's due to overly wet soil; make sure the planting site is well drained.

**ALTERNATIVES:** Warm-climate gardeners have another terrific shrub or small tree to consider: loropetalum (*Loropetalum chinense* var. *rubrum*). 'Burgundy' reaches about 15 feet tall; 'Zhuzhou Fuchsia' is about 10 feet and somewhat hardier. Plants sold as 'Plum Delight', 'Pizzazz', 'Hines Burgundy', and 'Hines Purpleleaf' tend to be 6 to 8 feet tall. Full sun for best leaf color; acidic, moist but well-drained soil. Zones 7 or 8 to 9.

## COTINUS
*Smoke tree, smoke bush*

**Height: Varies**
**Leaf size: 3–4 inches long;**
    **2–3 inches wide**
**Full sun to partial shade**
**Zones 4–8**

It's a tree! It's a bush! It's smoke tree — or smoke bush. Known botanically as *Cotinus coggygria*, this deciduous species will reach 15 feet tall if you let it develop its natural, open-crowned, treelike form, with airy, pink-tinged, summer flower clusters that create the "smoke" effect they get their name from. Need a smaller-scale shrub? Cut back smoke trees to a 1- to 3-foot framework each year in early spring. The new stems reach a more compact 6 to 8 feet tall, making them a good back-of-the-border accent in mixed plantings. They usually won't flower, but they'll have somewhat larger-than-usual leaves, and that means even greater foliage interest in summer and fall. With purple-leaved selections, of course, foliage interest is the main attraction anyway. Two of the best for reddish purple to deep purple leaves through the summer (and shades of orange and red in fall) are 'Royal Purple' and 'Velvet Cloak'. Plants sold as *C. coggygria* f. *purpureus*, 'Purpureus', and 'Foliis Purpureus' typically have variable amounts of purple in their foliage. Hybrid 'Grace' has grayish pink new foliage; pinkish green older leaves; and an excellent mix of purple, orange, and red shades in fall.

**GROWING TIPS:** Smoke trees have the darkest leaves in full sun, but they will grow in partial shade as well. They look particularly good where you can see the rising or setting sun shining through the foliage. Average, well-drained soil is fine.

**ALTERNATIVES:** Japanese barberries (*Berberis thunbergii*) are among the most widely planted purple-leaved shrubs, ranging in size from rounded 'Concorde' (18 inches tall) to narrowly upright 'Helmond's Pillar' and spreading 'Royal Cloak' (both about 5 feet tall). Full sun to full shade; average soil. Zones 4 to 8. *Note:* Despite being readily available, barberries are a poor choice in areas where they're considered seriously invasive (particularly in the northeastern United States, but elsewhere too).

# EUPATORIUM
*White snakeroot*

**Height: 3–5 feet**
**Leaf size: 4–6 inches long;**
 **2–4 inches wide**
**Full sun to partial shade**
**Zones 4–9**

'Chocolate' white snakeroot (*Eupatorium rugosum;* also known as *Ageratina altissima*) tends to inspire strong feelings in gardeners: desperate craving in those seeing the rich, dark foliage for the first time and definite exasperation in those who

*Eupatorium rugosum* 'Chocolate'

have made the mistake of letting their plants go to seed. The leaves truly are handsome, particularly when they emerge the deepest brown you can imagine. As the upright stems grow, the older leaves turn purplish brown, but the new growth typically stays dark through most of the summer. Fuzzy-looking clusters of white flowers bloom atop the stems from late summer into fall, by which time the leaves of sun-grown plants are usually a purple-tinged deep green (those

in shade may be solid green). The blossoms are a welcome addition to the late-season garden, but if you're concerned about them self-sowing, cut off the spent flower heads or whack the whole plant to the ground before the seeds form. (Curiously, some gardeners report that their plants rarely or never self-sow, and others in the same hardiness zone get an overabundance of seedlings. If you feel lucky, try leaving the seedheads — they do add winter interest — and see if you end up with any "volunteers.")

**GROWING TIPS:** Snakeroots are normally recommended for shady sites; the leaves will turn green much more quickly, however, if they are in too much shade. A spot with full sun brings out much more of the brownish color in the foliage. Average to moist but well-drained soil is fine. If you decide to let your plants self-sow, keep in mind that not all of the seedlings will have equally dark foliage.

**ALTERNATIVES:** Dark-leaved hardy hibiscus or rose mallow (*Hibiscus*) hybrids thrive in heat and humidity. 'Kopper King' has reddish to coppery green foliage, while 'Plum Crazy' and the more deeply lobed 'Fireball' are purplish green; all three are 3 to 4 feet tall. 'Crown Jewels' is more compact (2 to 3 feet tall), with purplish leaves. Full sun; average to evenly moist or even wet soil. Zones 4 to 10.

# EUPHORBIA
*Euphorbia, spurge*

**Height: Varies**
**Leaf size: Varies**
**Full sun to partial shade**
**Zones vary**

Whether you're looking for hardy border perennials or a splash of single-season color, euphorbias (*Euphorbia*) offer lots of exciting possibilities with purplish to reddish foliage. Purple wood spurge (*E. amygdaloides* 'Purpurea'; also sold as var. *purpurea* and 'Rubra') is showy both in bloom and in leaf, with a clump-forming to slow-spreading habit and upright stems that are about 8 inches tall, clad in whorls of 1- to 3-inch-long, ½-inch-wide leaves. The new foliage is usually deep red, making a great contrast to the bright yellow flowerheads, which bloom another foot or so above the leaves in late spring to early summer. After that, the foliage often turns greenish for the summer, then takes on reddish to purplish shading again in fall and stays that way through the winter. At its best, purple wood spurge is a splendid sight, but unfortunately, the fungal disease powdery mildew will disfigure its foliage in some areas. If that's a problem where you live, consider a mildew-resistant cultivar such as 'Craigieburn' or 'Golden Glory'. All of these are usually hardy in Zones 5 to 8, although they may not stay attractive in winter in the coldest parts of that range. As their blooms fade, cut the flowered stems to the ground to make room for new growth.

E. dulcis 'Chameleon' isn't "ever-purple" like purple wood spurge, but it tends to keep a much stronger reddish purple to deep purple foliage color through the growing season. 'Chameleon' grows in slow-spreading clumps that are 18 to 24 inches tall, with tiny greenish yellow flowers in late spring to early summer. If you cut the plants to the ground around the time the blooms appear, you'll prevent the plants from self-sowing and encourage a flush of deeply colored new foliage for the rest of the growing season. Unfortunately, 'Chameleon', too, is prone to powdery mildew, so it's not a good choice in areas where this fungal disease is a common problem. Zones 5 to 8.

*Euphorbia 'Flame Leaf'*

Tender euphorbias take a little extra work to overwinter, but they definitely repay the effort. *E. cotinifolia* (sometimes called Caribbean copper plant) looks remarkably like a purple-leaved smoke tree (*Cotinus*), and even a small rooted cutting set out after the last frost date can reach 4 to 6 feet tall by the end of the growing season. (Where it's hardy, it may reach 15 feet or more.) The 2-inch, oval to rounded, orangey red to reddish purple leaves hold their rich color from spring until they're touched by frost. The creamy white flowers are interesting, but the foliage is its key feature. Zones 9 to 11. *E.* 'Flame Leaf' is much shorter — usually to about 1 foot — with very slender stems and small, oval to pointed leaves that are deep purple with a narrow, bright green edge. The bushy plants produce tiny flowers that self-sow freely through the growing season, so you're likely to find similarly marked seedlings near the original clump. Zones 9 to 11. Red pencil tree (*E. trucalli* 'Sticks on Fire') is distinctly different, with many-branched, slender, pencil-like stems and a few scattered, tiny, short-lived leaves. The new stems are coppery red in cooler weather (usually more peachy yellow in summer), aging to a mix of pink, peach, yellow, and green shades. If you grow it as an annual, expect it to reach 1 to 2 feet tall; where it's hardy (Zones 10 and 11), it may reach 5 to 10 feet in height.

**GROWING TIPS:** Purple- and red-leaved euphorbias generally produce their best foliage color in full sun, but they will tolerate partial shade. Average to moist but well-drained soil is fine. *Caution:* Wear gloves when working with any euphorbia to protect your skin from the irritating sap (be especially careful not to get it in your eyes).

**ALTERNATIVE:** Purple Japanese honewort or mitsuba (usually sold as *Cryptotaenia japonica* f. *atropurpurea* or 'Atropurpurea') produces dense clumps of chocolate-purple to near-black, three-part foliage. Partial shade brings out the richest color in the leaves, although the plants will tolerate full sun in cooler areas, especially if the soil is evenly moist (but not soggy). Average, well-drained soil is fine in partial shade. Self-sows freely. Zones 4 or 5 to 8.

## HEUCHERA
*Heuchera*

> **Height: 8–12 inches**
> **Leaf size: 4–5 inches long and**
> **wide (for most)**
> **Full sun to partial shade**
> **Zones 3 or 4–8**

The abundance of amazing purple-leaved heucheras (*Heuchera*) has probably done more to lure gardeners to the dark side than any other perennials in this color range. The dense "ever-purple" to "semi-ever-purple" mounds of lobed leaves look great at the edge of a border, walkway, or foundation planting and adapt to life in containers as

well. The sensation started with *H. villosa* f. *purpurea* 'Palace Purple' (also commonly listed under *H. micrantha* var. *diversifolia*), which should have broad, deep purple foliage to about 1 foot tall and tiny white summer flowers in airy clusters on slender stems to about 18 inches tall. Nowadays, the plants sold as 'Palace Purple' are often more greenish than purple, but there are dozens of darker hybrids to choose from, in a range of sizes, leaf colors, and flower colors. New ones appear every year, so here's just a sampling of the options.

For small spaces and planters, consider one of the very compact cultivars, such as 'Petite Pearl Fairy', with tiny reddish to brownish green leaves lightly marbled with silver, along with light pink flowers; it's barely 6 inches tall in leaf and 12 inches tall in bloom. At the other extreme are large-leaved selections such as 'Molly Bush' (reddish purple foliage, with greenish white flowers that are 30 inches tall) and 'Bressingham Bronze' (deep brownish purple leaves, with white flowers that are 2 feet tall). Heucheras with ruffled edges on their leaves provide extra textural interest: purplish brown 'Chocolate Ruffles' and deep purple 'Purple Petticoats' (both about 1 foot tall in leaf and with whitish flowers to 2 feet tall) are two favorites. For a little extra color impact, check out the many selections that have both silver and purple in the leaves, such as 'Amethyst

*Heuchera* 'Palace Purple'

Myst' (with light pink flowers to 2 feet) and 'Ruby Veil' (greenish white flowers to 2 feet). Or go all out with one of the really wild color choices, such as 'Mardi Gras', with orange-red new leaves that are mottled with deep purple to deep green (whitish flowers to 2 feet). 'Peachy Keen' is another multicolored cultivar, with bright reddish to orangey pink new leaves that age to pink-marbled deep green, and the added benefit of bright pink blooms to 2 feet. Several other selections combine showy flowers with deep purple to purple-brown leaves, such as 'Cherries Jubilee' (pinkish red flowers to 18 inches tall), 'Vesuvius' (red blooms to about 2 feet), and 'Ebony and Ivory' (large white flowers to 2 feet).

**GROWING TIPS:** Purple-leaved heucheras produce their richest foliage color in full sun but will also grow well in partial shade. Good drainage is important, because heucheras hate having constantly wet roots (especially in winter), but those in full sun appreciate evenly moist soil. Removing the flowers after they fade (or even as soon as they appear, if the flowers on your plants aren't especially showy) makes the plants look better and promotes rebloom. Clip off any damaged leaves as needed.

**ALTERNATIVES:** For shadier sites, consider foamy bells (× *Heucherella*). 'Burnished Bronze' and lacier 'Chocolate Lace' have deeply lobed leaves aging from deep red to dark chocolate brown; about 6 inches tall in leaf. Or try 'Color Flash' astilbe (*Astilbe*) with bright green new foliage that changes to rich shades of red and deep purple; about 1 foot tall in leaf. Average to moist but well-drained soil. Zones 4 to 8.

## IPOMOEA
*Sweet potato vine*

**Height: 6–12 inches**
**Leaf size: 6–8 inches long;**
 **5–6 inches wide**
**Full sun to partial shade**
**Zones 9 or 10–11**

Sweet potatoes (*Ipomoea batatas*) aren't just for vegetable gardens anymore. These vigorous trailing vines now come in a variety of leaf shapes and colors, making them unusual accents for both borders and containers. Even a small rooted cutting can spread to 10 feet or more by the end of the summer, so the plants make a great single-season ground cover. Their ability to weave among other plants also makes them great fillers for newly planted borders. 'Blackie' was one of the first dark-leaved selections, with deep purple to near-black, lobed foliage. 'Sweet Caroline Purple' is even more deeply lobed, and its growth habit tends to be more restrained, so it's a better choice for container plantings or small gardens. (It's not unusual for this one to produce small pink flowers, too, but they're usually hidden by the foliage.) Plants sold as 'Ace of Spades', 'Black Beauty', and 'Black Heart' have heart-shaped leaves that tend to turn greenish as they age, although the abundance of new growth keeps the plants looking dark overall. 'Sweet Heart Red' is also heart-shaped, but it's deep red instead of deep purple.

**GROWING TIPS:** Full sun produces the darkest and most vigorous growth; vines in partial shade tend to be more greenish purple. Average to moist, well-drained soil is fine. Overwinter sweet potato vines by taking cuttings in fall and growing them as houseplants in a warm, bright spot, or dig up the large tuberous roots and store them in a cool, dry place.

**ALTERNATIVE:** For a much smaller-scale, year-round trailing plant or ground cover, check out the dark-leaved cultivars of *Lysimachia congestiflora*. 'Persian Chocolate' creates 2-inch-tall mats of small, roughly oval leaves that are deep brownish purple; 'Persian Carpet' is similar but its foliage is deep green with dark purple centers. Full sun to light shade; average to moist but well-drained soil. Zones 6 or 7 to 10.

*Ipomoea batatas* 'Sweet Heart Red'

## IRESINE
*Beefsteak plant, bloodleaf*

**Height: 1–3 feet**
**Leaf size: 1–3 inches long;**
   **1–2 inches wide**
**Full sun to partial shade**
**Zones 10 and 11**

In the ground or in containers, as single clumps or in masses, beefsteak plants (*Iresine herbstii*) make fantastic color accents. Their small, greenish white flowers are hardly noticeable, but their foliage is guaranteed to attract attention — not for its size or texture, but instead for its bright markings or rich, deep color. 'Brilliantissima' is a

*Iresine herbstii 'Brilliantissima'*

distinctive selection with roughly oval leaves that are deep purple with bright red to reddish pink veining when young, turning mostly pinkish red with dark purple to dark green marbling. It may reach 3 feet tall but usually stays closer to 2 feet, and you can keep it even smaller with regular pinching. 'Blazin' Rose' seems to be naturally a bit shorter (in the 12- to 18-inch range), with sharply pointed leaves that are mostly light pink to reddish pink with some deep purple mottling, turning a dark purple-green with pink veins. 'Purple Lady' has slightly crinkled leaves that are a solid deep purple throughout. Unlike 'Brilliantissima' and 'Blazin' Rose', which have a bushy, upright form, 'Purple Lady' has more of a trailing habit; it's just 6 to 8 inches tall, but it will spread several feet across over the course of the growing season, because its stems can take root where they touch the soil. *I. lindenii* is also solid-colored, with narrow, deep maroon leaves, but it has the usual bushy, upright habit and is typically 1 to 2 feet tall.

**GROWING TIPS:** Full sun is fine in most areas; in hot climates, however, partial shade helps to keep the leaf color from bleaching to pale pink or near white. Average to evenly moist but well-drained soil is ideal. Snip off the shoot tips a few times from spring to midsummer to promote bushier growth. (These trimmings are easy to root as cuttings and make great fillers for gaps that appear

in your garden during the summer.) For most beefsteak plants, you'll need to start with purchased plants; 'Purple Lady' can be grown from seed, too. Where the plants aren't hardy, bring them indoors in fall and enjoy them as houseplants in winter.

**ALTERNATIVES:** Polka-dot plants (*Hypoestes phyllostachya*; also listed as *H. sanguinolenta*) offer deep green leaves heavily spotted with red, pink, or white. Plants in the Splash Select Series usually stay in the 12- to 18-inch range; those in the Confetti Series stay 6 to 12 inches tall. Morning sun and afternoon shade or light all-day shade; average to evenly moist but well-drained soil. Zones 9 or 10 to 11.

## LACTUCA
*Lettuce*

**Height: 6–12 inches**
**Leaf size: 6–8 inches long;**
   **3–5 inches wide**
**Full sun to partial shade**
**Annual**

Some recommend growing red-leaved lettuces (*Lactuca sativa*) as edible ornamentals, but once you see how beautiful the plants look in beds and borders, you won't want to spoil the effect by harvesting them! Combine the low-growing, glossy-leaved plants with pansies (*Viola*), pot marigolds (*Calendula officinalis*), and other cool-season annuals for spring and fall color, or use them to fill the empty spaces around newly planted tropicals and tender perennials; by the time the

heat-loving plants take off, the lettuces will be on their way out.

Most seed catalogs include at least one or two red-leaved lettuces, and some offer a dozen or more. It seems that each supplier claims that one variety or another is "the reddest around." These claims are often inflated, though, and even photographs can be misleading, so try a few different ones yourself to see which you like best. There are several types of lettuces to choose from. The looseleaf and romaine types seem to blend best into borders, but you can also try heading types (yes, there's even a 'Red Iceberg'). Some lettuces have smooth leaves, while others have a rumpled or puckered leaf surface and/or frilly leaf edges. You also have a choice between red-shaded green leaves ('Cracoviensis', for example); red-spotted green leaves ('Flashy Trout's Back', 'Freckles', and 'Really Red Deer Tongue'); and mostly red leaves. 'Mascara' is great for both color and texture, with medium red leaves that have scalloped to lobed leaf edges. Some varieties with frilly edges and solid-colored leaves are bright red 'Redina' and deep red 'Revolution'; 'Outredgeous' is also deep red, with slightly crinkled foliage. The darkest solid red lettuce to date is probably 'Merlot', with lightly rumpled leaves that hold their color through their life span.

**GROWING TIPS:** Full sun brings out the darkest leaf colors, but afternoon shade will help the plants stay cool, so they'll be slower to bolt (send up a tall flowering stalk). Average to evenly moist but well-drained soil is fine. Sow the seeds directly in the garden in early spring or plant them in cell packs so you can set out the transplants exactly where you want them. For fall fillers, sow again in mid- to late summer. Pull out the plants when they begin to bolt.

**ALTERNATIVES:** The 1-foot-tall leaves of 'Bull's Blood' beets (*Beta vulgaris*) are a rich deep red; 6-inch-tall 'MacGregor's Favorite' has narrower, deep purple-red leaves with a silvery overlay. 'Red Giant' mustard (*Brassica juncea*) has broad, green-veined, purplish red leaves (1 to 2 feet); 'Osaka Purple' is deep purple with pale green veins (8 to 12 inches tall). Full sun to light shade; average, well-drained soil. Sow in the garden in early spring.

## LOBELIA
*Lobelia, cardinal flower*

**Height: 2–4 feet**
**Leaf size: 5–6 inches long;**
**1–2 inches wide**
**Full sun to partial shade**
**Zones vary**

Dark foliage makes a great backdrop for many flower colors, but it's especially striking with rich red blooms — and that's exactly the combination you get with lobelias (*Lobelia*). They grow in dense rosettes of slender, deep red to purple-red leaves at first, then send up equally dark stems topped with spikes of tubular,

lipped, bright to deep red flowers in mid- to late summer. Two- to 4-foot-tall 'Queen Victoria' is one of the best-known selections; you can buy it as started plants or grow your own from seed for flowers the same year. Some vegetatively propagated selections that are usually in the 2- to 3-foot-tall range are 'Crown Royal', 'Dark Crusader', and 'Elmfeuer' ('Elm Fire').

Although it's easy to tell the dark-leaved lobelias from their green-leaved relatives by sight, figuring out their correct names is a lot more complicated. You're likely to find them listed under a variety of species, including *L. fulgens*, *L. × speciosa*, *L. splendens*, and even *L. cardinalis* (which is our native cardinal flower). Their hardiness is also questionable; sometimes you'll see them rated for gardens as far north as Zone 3, while others suggest that Zones 8 to 10 is more realistic. Apparently, these dark-leaved lobelias are the result of crosses between various tender and hardy species, so even though their hardiness can vary, it's probably safe to expect them to act like annuals north of Zone 8. If they do live over in cooler areas, then you get a bonus year of beautiful blooms and fabulous foliage!

**GROWING TIPS:** Full sun with fertile, dependably moist soil usually brings out the best color and vigor, but the plants will also get by with partial shade and average, well-drained soil. Where the plants aren't hardy, pot up the

clumps in fall and overwinter them in a cool but sheltered spot, or stick with 'Queen Victoria' and start it from seed sown indoors in early winter. (Sow the fine seed in early spring in a pot of moist seed-starting medium and just press it into the surface, then enclose the pot in a plastic bag and set it in a warm, bright spot. Leave the bag until the seedlings have several leaves each.)

**ALTERNATIVES:** Don't mistake purple fringed loosestrife (*Lysimachia ciliata* 'Purpurea'; also sold as 'Atropurpurea' and 'Firecracker') with the noxious weed purple loosestrife (*Lythrum salicaria*). Although purple fringed loosestrife can be an aggressive spreader in the garden, it's not a major invasive threat in natural areas. Deep reddish to purplish brown foliage; 2 to 3 feet tall. Full sun to partial shade. Zones 2 or 3 to 8.

*Lactuca sativa* 'Mascara'

*Lobelia* 'Queen Victoria'

*Ocimum basilicum* 'Purple Ruffles'

# OCIMUM
*Basil*

**Height: Varies**
**Leaf size: Varies**
**Full sun**
**Zones 9–11**

If you need an abundance of dark foliage to fill out summer plantings, bushy purple basils (*Ocimum basilicum*) are an excellent option for beds, borders, and container plantings. Most are easy to grow from seed, so you can raise several dozen transplants for the cost of one seed packet. Or buy one well-branched starter plant,

then take cuttings; they root quickly and will give you exact replicas of the original plant. Purple basils produce bushy, upright clumps of spicy-scented, glossy leaves and spikes of small white to pink flowers. Eighteen- to 24-inch-tall 'Dark Opal' (sometimes sold simply as 'Opal') is an old favorite with 2- to 3-inch-long, 1½-inch-wide leaves that should be deep purple, although seed-grown plants range from deep purple to bronzy purple or mostly green. 'Red Rubin' and the slightly smaller-leaved 'Osmin' look similar to 'Dark Opal' but are much more dependable from seed, staying dark through the growing season and rarely if ever producing green seedlings. 'Purple Ruffles' has interestingly puckered foliage that's usually deep purple; like 'Dark Opal', however, it produces many green-leaved seedlings along with the true-to-type ones. And then there's the distinctly different 'Well-Sweep Miniature Purple' (also sold as 'Minimum Purpurascens Well-Sweep'), with compact, 1-foot-tall plants that bear small, purple leaves to 1 inch long and ½ inch wide; this one must be propagated by cuttings.

**GROWING TIPS:** Basils thrive in full sun and average to fertile, well-drained soil. To start them from seed, sow indoors three to four weeks before your last frost date, and wait a week or so after the last frost date to set out the

plants. (Basils hate cold, wet soil, so you won't get a faster start by transplanting them outside any earlier.) If you want to use purple basils as follow-up plants where spring bulbs or early-flowering perennials have gone dormant, direct-sow the seed after the last frost date. Pinch off the shoot tips every few weeks (toss the trimmings into your salads or use them for cooking), and trim off any developing flower spikes to keep the plants producing new foliage. Water during dry spells, but try to avoid wetting the leaves.

**ALTERNATIVES:** For the combination of dark foliage and bright blooms on a hardier perennial, consider cultivars of Arkwright's campion (*Lychnis × arkwrightii*). 'Vesuvius' has deep purple new leaves that age to brown or bronzy green (12 to 18 inches tall); 'Orange Gnome' is shorter (to about 8 inches), with similar foliage. Full sun; average to moist but well-drained soil. Zones 5 or 6 to 8.

# OXALIS
*Oxalis*

**Height: Varies**
**Leaf size: Varies**
**Full sun to partial shade**
**Zones vary**

It's true that some oxalis (*Oxalis*) are pesky weeds; this genus, however, also includes a number of fabulous foliage options for beds, borders, planters, and hanging

baskets. The names tend to be a little mixed up, but it's worth muddling through the confusion. Purple shamrock (listed variously as *O. triangularis* 'Atropurpurea' and *O. regnellii* 'Atropurpurea', 'Triangularis', and var. *triangularis*) is probably the best known of the dark-leaved oxalis, with three-lobed leaves that are 2 to 3 inches long and wide. The triangular leaflets are deep purple on top, with a pinkish to violet-purple shading in the center and reddish purple underneath. 'Mijke' is similar but tends to be solid purple; it may also be a bit slower to come up in spring. 'Charmed Wine' is a rich reddish

*Oxalis triangularis* 'Atropurpurea'

purple, while 'Charmed Velvet' appears practically black. The 6- to 12-inch-tall clumps spread gently and are accented with loose clusters of white to pale pink flowers in summer. These beauties usually prefer morning sun and afternoon shade or light all-day shade and are typically hardy in Zones 7 to 10 (sometimes even into Zone 6).

For a lacier look, consider firefern (*O. hedysaroides* 'Rubra'; also sold as *O. alstonii*). Its 1-inch leaves have rounded, deep red to reddish purple leaflets held on slender, upright stems. It's accented with small but bright yellow flowers through much of the growing season. The spreading clumps typically reach 8 to 12 inches tall in a pot or as first-year garden clumps; where they're hardy, the plants will reach 2 to 3 feet tall. Plants sold as *O. spiralis* var. *vulcanicola* and *O. vulcanicola* 'Zinfandel' look similar but tend to stay 6 to 9 inches tall. Although these oxalis will grow in partial (or even full) shade, their reddish color is deepest in full sun. Zones 9 to 11.

**GROWING TIPS:** Dark-leaved oxalis thrive in evenly moist but well-drained soil. Where they're not hardy, bring them indoors and enjoy them as houseplants for the winter (or let the purple shamrocks go dormant in a frost-free place and barely water them until new growth begins).

**ALTERNATIVES:** If you like the cloverlike foliage of *Oxalis,* then why not give white clover (*Trifolium repens*) a try? Plants sold as 'Purpurascens', 'Atropurpureum', 'Dark Dancer', and 'Purpurascens Quadrifolium' have rounded, green-rimmed leaflets with reddish to brownish centers. Usually 4 to 6 inches tall; spreads widely. Full sun to partial shade; average to moist but well-drained soil. Zones 4 to 8. *Note:* The species is considered invasive in some areas.

## PHYSOCARPUS
*Ninebark*

**Height: Varies**
**Leaf size: 3–4 inches long;**
 **2–3 inches wide**
**Full sun to partial shade**
**Zones 2–7 or 8**

Largely overlooked for many years, ninebarks (*Physocarpus opulifolius*) are now all the rage, thanks mainly to the purple-leaved selections of these marvelous multi-season, deciduous shrubs. All share the usual vase-shaped to fountainlike form, with arching, twiggy branches that develop attractive peeling bark when mature. Rounded clusters of small, white to pale pink flowers appear in late spring to early summer, turning into reddish seed capsules for later summer interest; then the leaves turn shades of orange, red, and purple in fall. Diabolo ('Monlo'; also sold as Diablo) is one of the best-known

cultivars, with deep purple-black new leaves that turn brownish purple in summer (or sometimes purplish green in very hot weather); it typically grows 8 to 12 feet tall and wide. Coppertina ('Mindia') has coppery orange new leaves that turn orangey red in summer; the foliage of 'Center Glow' is reddish purple with yellow-green centers when young, later turning solid deep red. Both are about 8 to 10 feet tall. Summer Wine ('Seward') is more compact than the others (usually 4 to 6 feet tall), with reddish purple, more deeply lobed leaves.

**GROWING TIPS:** Purple-leaved ninebarks usually produce the darkest foliage in full sun, but they will grow well in partial shade too. (In hot-summer areas, a bit of afternoon shade may keep them from turning greenish in summer.) They'll adapt to just about any well-drained conditions, but they're most vigorous in evenly moist, acidic soil. To keep the plants vigorous, prune out a few of the oldest stems at their base each year. Or if the plants are overgrown, cut down all of the stems to about 6 inches in late winter or early spring to get lots of good-looking new shoots (although the plants won't flower that year).

**ALTERNATIVES:** *Prunus cerasifera* 'Newport' is one of the best known purple-leaved plums, with greenish purple new leaves aging to deep reddish purple (15 to 20 feet tall); Zones

*Physocarpus opulifolius* Diabolo

4 to 9. 'Thundercloud' is similar but slightly less hardy, while 'Purple Pony' is more compact (about 10 feet tall); Zones 5 to 9. Purple-leaved sand cherry (*P.* × *cistena*) is usually 4 to 8 feet tall; Zones 3 to 8. Full sun; average to moist but well-drained soil.

## PSEUDERANTHEMUM
*Pseuderanthemum*

**Height: 3–5 feet**
**Leaf size: 4–6 inches long;**
 **2–3 inches wide**
**Full sun to partial shade**
**Zones 8 or 9–11**

If your garden or container combinations need a dash of darkness, pseuderanthemums (*Pseuderanthemum*) could be the perfect choice. Chocolate plant (*P. alatum*) is one stunning option,

with coppery brown foliage that's marked with silver mostly along the midvein, plus purple flowers through most of the summer and into fall, on plants that are usually 12 to 18 inches tall. This one readily self-sows in mild areas unless you deadhead it, and it seems to be a bit hardier than other species (into Zone 8, at least). Make sure it gets plenty of light for the best silver markings.

The names of other pseuderanthemums seem to be rather muddled in the trade, so it's best to buy the plants in person or carefully check catalog descriptions to make sure you're getting the look you want. Plants sold as *P. atropurpureum* and *Eranthemum nigrum* typically grow 2 to 3 feet tall, with green stems and very dark purple-brown leaves. They may also produce white flowers. Those labeled *P. atropurpureum* 'Rubrum' and *P. rubrum* also grow 2 to 3 feet tall, with glossy, deep purplish red leaves on equally dark, usually unbranched stems. Plants sold as *P. atropurpureum* 'Tricolor' and *P. carruthersii* also have red stems and glossy leaves that are deep purple with pink marbling in ample light; in shade, the foliage appears mostly green with white markings. They, too, tend to have a very narrow, vertical effect, growing 3 to 4 feet tall.

**GROWING TIPS:** Pseuderanthemums will grow anywhere from full sun to full shade in cooler areas; in very warm climates, a bit of afternoon shade may be better. Fertile, average to moist but well-drained soil is fine.

**ALTERNATIVES:** Very similar-looking 'Chocolate' caricature plant (*Graptophyllum pictum*) has glossy, deep brown leaves with a light pink center stripe; 'Black Beauty' is similar but without the pink leaf markings. Both usually grow 2 to 3 feet tall. Upright *Zingiber malaysianum* (commonly sold as *Z.* 'Midnight') is a glossy, deep reddish brown; 2 to 5 feet tall. Full sun to light shade; average to moist but well-drained soil. Zones 9 to 11.

*Pseuderanthemum atropurpureum* 'Rubrum'

## SALVIA
*Sage, salvia*

**Height:** Varies
**Leaf size:** Varies
**Full sun**
**Zones vary**

Sages (*Salvia*) come in a diversity of heights, habits, and colors, so it's no surprise that the few with purple foliage look very different from one another. The best known is the one simply called purple sage (*S. officinalis* Purpurascens Group; also sold as 'Purpurascens' and 'Purpurea'). A selection of the common culinary sage, it grows in bushy, 1- to 2-foot-tall clumps of 4-inch-long, 1-inch-wide, aromatic leaves that are deep purple when new, usually aging to grayish purple and then mostly gray-green. It flowers in late spring to early summer, with spikelike clusters of purple-blue flowers. Give this one full sun and average, well-drained soil. Zones 6 or 7 to 9.

Lyreleaf sage (*S. lyrata*) has a completely different growth habit, with rosettes of ever-present, often irregularly lobed leaves that are 6 to 8 inches long and 1 to 2 inches across. Some have purplish markings along the midveins and some are completely reddish purple; you can find the latter under the names 'Burgundy Bliss', 'Purple Knockout', 'Purple Prince', and 'Purple Volcano'. All of these produce leafless 1- to 2-foot-tall flowering stems that emerge from the center of the clumps through most of the growing season. The white to pale pink or purple flowers aren't especially showy, and sometimes they don't appear at all, leaving just a purple-tipped green calyx that eventually turns brown. Some find these seedheads interesting, but others prefer to remove them in favor of the foliage (and to prevent rampant self-sowing). If you decide to snip off the flowering stems, keep in mind that it's a never-ending task because of the long bloom season, and because the deadheading encourages the formation of more stems. In a site with average to moist but well-drained soil where self-sowing isn't a problem, purple lyreleaf sages are useful as an ajuga substitute for full sun, particularly in hot, humid climates. Zones 4 to 10.

Last, there's Sinaloa sage (*S. sinaloensis*) — a gem you'll treasure as much for its intensely blue flowers as for its bronzy, ever-present foliage. The plants spread gently by stolons to form bushy clumps that are typically about 1 foot tall, though they may reach 2 feet or more. The 1-inch-long, ½-inch-wide leaves are deep purple in cool temperatures, usually turning greenish in summer but still with purple-tinged shoot tips. The deep blue, white-marked blooms are most abundant in spring and fall but may also appear in summer. If the plants look a little tattered after the winter, shear them back to promote new growth. Where it's hardy, Sinaloa sage makes a great ground cover; in cooler climates, it looks terrific trailing out of a planter. It thrives in full sun in most areas but appreciates a bit of afternoon shade in hot climates. Average to moist but well-drained soil is ideal. Zones 8 to 11.

**GROWING TIPS:** All three sages differ in their growth needs, but as with most other purple plants, ample sunlight tends to bring out the richest leaf colors.

**ALTERNATIVES:** Many beardtongues (*Penstemon*) have a reputation for being fussy, but not foxglove penstemon (*P. digitalis*). 'Husker Red' (also sold as 'Husker's Red') is by far the best known selection, with low, dense clumps of deep purple leaves that shoot up into leafy, 2- to 3-foot-tall stems. May turn green during hot weather. Full sun to light shade; average, well-drained soil. Zones 3 to 8.

*Salvia lyrata* 'Burgundy Bliss'

---

## SAMBUCUS
*Elderberry, elder*

**Height: 10–15 feet**
**Leaf size: 10–12 inches long;**
    **8–10 inches wide**
**Full sun to partial shade**
**Zones 4–9**

Whether your garden is large or small, you can enjoy the multi-season beauty of purple-leaved elderberries (*Sambucus nigra*). These deciduous, multistemmed shrubs bear attractive, compound leaves throughout the growing season, often with reddish to purplish fall color. The large, flattened clusters of tiny flowers appear in early to midsummer, sometimes with a bonus of black, berrylike fruits later in the season. Left unpruned, elderberries can get large (and they may also spread by suckers), but it's possible to keep them much smaller with yearly pruning. 'Purpurea' and the similar 'Guincho Purple' have deep purple foliage in spring, turning deep green in summer, with pink-tinged white flowers. Newer introductions

*Sambucus nigra* 'Guincho Purple'

Black Beauty ('Gerda') and 'Thundercloud' hold their dark brownish purple to purple-black leaf color during most or all of the growing season, providing a perfect backdrop for their fragrant pink flowers. Black Lace ('Eva') is distinctly different, with deeply cut, purple-black foliage that does look just like black lace, accented with light pink blooms.

**GROWING TIPS:** Purple-leaved elderberries look their best in full sun with evenly moist soil but will grow well in partial shade and average, well-drained soil too. If you want to enjoy seeing the fruits as well as the foliage, plant two cultivars of *S. nigra* (or a cultivar and a seedling). The vigorous plants will tolerate heavy pruning each spring — to a 1- to 2-foot-tall framework or even down to just above the ground —

resulting in larger-leaved but much shorter plants that work well at the back of a mixed border. Remove any unwanted suckers immediately.

**ALTERNATIVE:** Mimosa or silk tree (*Albizia julibrissin*) has many flaws, including serious disease problems and prolific self-sowing. In some areas, in fact, it is classified as a noxious weed. 'Summer Chocolate', though, is beautiful enough to earn a place in the garden (at least in areas where the species isn't invasive). Its many tiny oval leaflets start out deep red to reddish purple and turn reddish brown to near black in summer. It normally forms a 15- to 20-foot-tall tree, but you can prune established plants back hard in late winter or early spring to get shorter new sprouts. Full sun; average, well-drained soil. Zones 6 to 10.

## SEDUM
*Sedum, stonecrop*

**Height: Varies**
**Leaf size: Varies**
**Full sun to partial shade**
**Zones 3–9 (for most)**

Sturdy and dependable, sedums (*Sedum*) come in pretty much every color that leaves can be, as well as a range of heights and habits, so you could easily create an interesting-looking planting filled with them alone. In most cases, though, we end up mixing them into beds and borders, where their colors and textures complement their companions. Sedums come in dozens of dark-leaved forms and new selections appear each year, so it's tough to give more than a sampling of them here. Basically, though, these popular, fleshy-leaved perennials come in two main habits: upright clumpers and carpet-forming creepers.

*Upright sedums.* Among the upright sedums with distinctively dark foliage and late-summer to early-fall flowers are reddish purple to chocolate purple S. 'Lynda Windsor', with deep red blooms, and *S. telephium* 'Bon Bon', with smaller, rounded clusters of rosy pink flowers; both grow about 18 inches tall. 'Purple Emperor' is about the same height, with grayish purple young leaves that turn deep purple and rosy pink flowers in large, flattened heads. *S. telephium* 'Mohrchen' (also sold as 'Morchen') grows about 2 feet tall, with deep red to red-tinged green leaves and rosy pink flowers on deep purple-red stems. The current winner of the "tall, dark, and handsome" category is *S.* 'Black Jack', with black, 18- to 24-inch-tall stems and greenish purple new leaves that quickly turn purple-black, complementing the large clusters of rich pink blooms. (Some gardeners report problems with this selection reverting to its parent 'Matrona', so remove any distinctly lighter purplish gray shoots as soon as you spot them.)

*Creeping sedums.* Selections of two-row sedum (*S. spurium*) aren't nearly as trendy as are the more upright sedums, but their adaptable, easy-care nature, spreading habit, and colorful summer flowers make them great for ground covers. Their small, oval, toothed leaves are present year-round, and they are often shaded with red, especially during cool weather. 'Dragon's Blood' is a classic cultivar with red flowers and red-tinged green summer foliage that turns purplish red for winter. 'Fuldaglut' ('Fulda Glow') and 'Red Carpet' (also sold as 'Elizabeth') have reddish pink flowers and more reddish shading on the leaves during the summer. 'Voodoo' has pinkish red flowers and reddish to deep purple foliage. All of these are 4 to 6 inches tall in bloom. *S. spathulifolium* 'Purpureum' is less hardy than the other sedums discussed here (usually Zones 5 to 9), but it's a good choice if you'd like something a little out of the ordinary: the new foliage is silvery gray, darkening to medium or deep red as it ages (especially in cool conditions). It has yellow summer flowers to about 6 inches tall.

**GROWING TIPS:** Sedums will grow in light shade, but they're most vigorous and produce their deepest leaf colors in full sun. Average to dry, well-drained soil is fine. Some of the taller upright sedums tend to sprawl in rich, moist border soil, so you may need to stake them in spring or cut them back by about half in early summer to encourage lower, bushier growth.

**ALTERNATIVES:** Aeoniums (*Aeonium*) produce short but wide rosettes of glossy, narrow leaves at the tips of thick, leafless gray stems; typically 3 to 5 feet tall. *A. arboreum* 'Atropurpureum' has green foliage shaded with deep purple; *A.* 'Zwartkop' ('Schwartzkopf') is a deeper purple-black. *A.* 'Blushing Beauty' has deep purple-red leaves around a bright green center. Full sun (for best color) to light shade; average, well-drained soil. Zones 9 or 10 to 11.

## SOLENOSTEMON
*Coleus*

**Height: Varies**
**Leaf size: Varies**
**Full sun to partial shade**
**Zones 10 and 11**

Coleus (*Solenostemon scutellarioides;* formerly *Coleus blumei*) have to be some of the best "spokesplants" around for the value of colored foliage in the garden. Sure, they produce flowers, too, but the small, pale blooms are incidental compared to the lovely leaves. Coleus come in an array of heights and habits as well as leaf shapes, colors, and patterns so you're sure to find at least one to complement any combination. With so many cultivars to choose from, though, the

*Sedum spurium* 'Red Carpet'

trick is tracking down the perfect match. It also doesn't help that even a single cultivar can sometimes look very different, depending on the growing conditions. You'll find a sampling of some of the best purple, red, and pink selections here, but the ideal way to choose coleus is to see the plants in person and select those that really catch your eye. Once you've exhausted your favorite local sources, its time to check out some of the mail-order specialty nurseries to expand your collection.

*Solid red or purple.* Coleus are best known for having multiple colors in their leaves; some, however, have fairly uniform coloring. Plants sold as 'Mars' and 'Purple Duckfoot', for example, have small, lobed, reddish purple leaves on plants 12 to 18 inches tall. 'Purple Emperor' produces a much bolder effect, with larger, ruffled, dusty dark purple leaves; it typically grows 24 to 30 inches tall. 'Crimson Velvet', with medium to deep red foliage, usually stays in the 2-foot-tall range. 'Palisandra' is a popular selection that has dark reddish purple to deep purple leaves on 18-inch-tall plants. (You can grow 'Palisandra' from seed, which is a plus if you need lots of plants, but it's also much more apt to produce flower spikes than cutting-grown cultivars are.)

*Red or purple with green.* Coleus with two or more colors in their foliage are great as a "bridge" between companions

with the same colors. If you have a purple-leaved heuchera and a green-leaved ornamental grass, for example, a coleus with both purple and green in the leaves may be the perfect partner. 'Inky Fingers' is a great choice if you'd like something fairly fine-textured, with small, lacy-looking, deep purple leaves that are edged with bright green on 2-foot-tall plants. 'Black Magic' is taller (to 3 feet), and its leaf margins aren't nearly as lobed, but the deep purple centers and scalloped green edges boast a somewhat similar effect. 'Lord Voldemort' is rather more sedate, with fairly simple, reddish purple to deep purple leaves that are edged with green on 12- to 18-inch-tall plants. For a very different effect, check out 2-foot-tall 'Fishnet Stockings'; it has bright green to yellowish green foliage heavily veined with deep purple. 'Kong Red' ('Red Kong') is a seed-grown coleus with exceptionally large leaves that are bright red to reddish pink in the center, shading to purple and then purple-veined green around the edges; to about 18 inches tall.

*Red or purple with pink or scarlet.* Purple foliage always looks great with pink or red flowers, and coleus that contain both colors add even more intensity to the combination. 'Mariposa' is one of the biggest selections, with leaves up to 8 inches long on plants to about 30 inches tall; its foliage has a deep purple center and a wide, rich pink edge.

'Religious Radish' grows about the same height, with 6-inch-long leaves that have a deep purple-brown to purple-black center irregularly edged with scarlet-red. 'Flamingo' has smaller, bright pink foliage with a deep reddish purple edge on 18-inch-tall plants. Or consider 'Trailing Rose', with reddish pink leaf centers edged in reddish purple and rimmed with bright green; it will either trail out of a container (reaching 6 to 12 inches tall that way) or weave up through taller companions.

*Red or pink with yellow.* One of the tallest selections in this group, 30-inch-tall 'Saturn' bears bright yellow to yellow-green leaves with a wide, deep red edge that may also be flecked with yellow. 'Bellingrath Pink' (also known as 'Alabama Sunset', 'Shocking Pink', and 'Texas Parking Lot') is a beauty by any name, with pink-blushed, bright yellow new foliage that ages to shades of orange-pink to deep red; it grows 24 to 30 inches tall. 'Dipt in Wine' (also sold as 'Kona Red') has a bright green to yellow-green heart shading out to bright red and then deep red to purplish red with a thin yellow rim; it's a more compact 18 to 24 inches. Popular, 18-inch-tall 'Bronze Pagoda' combines a medium to deep red center with a wide greenish yellow border on large leaves. 'Kiwi Fern' is about the same height but has a distinctly different look, with narrow, jagged-edged foliage that's deep purple with yellow-

*Solenostemon* 'Purple Emperor'

green edges. And then there's dainty 'India Frills', which grows just 1 foot tall; its small, deeply cut leaves have light yellow edges and pink or reddish purple centers (depending on whether you buy the "light form" or the "dark form").

**GROWING TIPS:** Long recommended mostly for shady gardens, newer coleus cultivars tend to produce their most vibrant leaf colors in full sun with moist but well-drained soil. Pinch or trim off the shoot tips every few weeks to promote bushy growth and discourage flowering. To keep your favorite coleus from year to year, take cuttings in late summer or fall, then keep them in a sunny spot or under plant lights through the winter. Wait until after the last frost date, when the weather is warm and settled, to set them back outside; these heat-loving plants *hate* to get chilled.

**ALTERNATIVES:** Coleus-like *Perilla* 'Magilla' has deep purple leaves with a magenta center, aging to purple-tinged green with a light pink center; 18 to 24 inches tall. Purple perilla, shiso, or beefsteak plant (*P. frutescens* var. *purpurascens*) is the "classic" perilla, with glossy, deep reddish purple, aromatic foliage; 18 to 36 inches tall. 'Crispa' has deeply scalloped, somewhat rumpled leaves. Self-sows rampantly. Full sun to partial shade; average, well-drained soil. Annual.

## STROBILANTHES
*Persian shield*

**Height:** 3–4 feet
**Leaf size:** 4–7 inches long;
   2–3 inches wide
**Full sun to partial shade**
**Zones 9–11**

In the garden or in container plantings, Persian shield (*Strobilanthes dyerianus*) is sure to

*Strobilanthes dyerianus*

attract attention. The shrubby clumps produce an abundance of elliptical leaves that are an iridescent violet-purple with dark green veins when new, often turning pinkish green before aging to silver-tinged deep green. In some conditions, you may see short spikes of small, pale purple to blue flowers in summer, but they're of little interest compared to the spectacular foliage. Where Persian shield is hardy, it looks great all year long; elsewhere, treat it as an annual or bring it indoors for the winter. (Some Zone 8 gardeners find that the plants lose their top growth over winter but come back from the roots in spring.) It's not the easiest houseplant to keep happy — it likes lots of light, plenty of warmth, and high humidity, too — but it's worth trying to overwinter if you can't easily find replacement plants locally in the spring.

## TRADESCANTIA
*Tradescantia, spiderwort*

**Height:** Varies
**Leaf size:** Varies
**Full sun to partial shade**
**Zones vary**

Unlike the typical border spiderworts (*Tradescantia* Andersoniana Group), which are grown for their flowers, these tradescantias are prized primarily for their foliage. Show off their trailing habit by letting them cascade out of a hanging basket or planter, or enjoy them as ground covers (in sites where they can't take over your whole yard); either way, they're guaranteed to attract

**GROWING TIPS:** Persian shield usually produces its best color in full sun and warm weather; in southern gardens, however, it may perform better with some afternoon shade. Rich, evenly moist but well-drained soil is ideal. Pinch off the stem tips a few times in spring and summer to encourage branching and more colorful new shoots.

**ALTERNATIVES:** 'Red Dragon' and the very similar 'Chocolate Dragon' persicaria (*Persicaria microcephala*) produce arching red stems clad in pointed, deep green leaves marked with a silvery V pattern and heavily blushed with red when new, aging to mostly green with a red-tinged center; usually 3 to 4 feet tall. Full sun to partial shade; average to moist but well-drained soil. Zones 6 to 9; may be hardier.

attention. *Caution:* The sap in their succulent stems and leaves may irritate sensitive skin, so wear gloves when handling them.

Purple heart (*T. pallida* 'Purpurea' and 'Purple Heart'; also sold as *Setcreasea pallida* and *S. purpurea*) grows 8 to 10 inches tall, with upright to trailing, thick but brittle stems. Their 4- to 5-inch-long, 1- to 1½-inch-wide leaves tend to be folded or curved upward from the midrib. The new foliage is pinkish purple aging to rich purple, often with a slight grayish cast. Short-lived, small pink flowers appear occasionally at the tips but aren't especially showy compared to the foliage. 'Kartuz Giant' (also sold as 'Giant Purple Heart') looks just like 'Purpurea' but is about twice the size. Purple heart is typically rated for Zones 8 or 9 to 11, but surprisingly, some gardeners as far north as Zone 6 have had luck overwintering it outdoors. (The plants tend to die back to the ground when touched by frost; otherwise, they are "ever-purple.")

*Tradescantia zebrina* is well known as a houseplant, but it's a beauty in the garden too. It's typically about 6 inches tall, but its stems can trail for several feet, and they can take root anywhere they touch the soil. The lance-shaped leaves are about 3 inches long and 1 inch wide, with bright purple undersides and purplish green to deep green tops that are boldly striped with silver.

*Tradescantia pallida* 'Purpurea'

Keep in mind that both species are naturally well suited to be ground covers, and they are fantastic single-season space-fillers in areas where they aren't hardy. In mild regions, though, they can spread aggressively, so think twice about planting them in the ground where they aren't surrounded by paving or some other hard surface.

**GROWING TIPS:** Purple heart looks best in full sun but will take light shade, while *Tradescantia zebrina* looks best in partial shade. (It will have more purple in the leaves with more light, but then the silvery stripes aren't

as distinct.) The plants thrive in moist but well-drained soil, although they can also be quite drought-tolerant — especially purple heart. Regularly pinching the shoot tips encourages the stems to branch, thus producing a denser clump. They root easily, so use the trimmings to start new plants. Where these tradescantias aren't dependably hardy, bring them indoors in fall and enjoy them as winter houseplants.

**ALTERNATIVES:** Velvet plants (*Gynura*) typically have jagged-edged or toothed, dull green leaves covered with fine, bright purple hairs. Plants labeled *G. sarmentosa* tend to be upright to sprawling (2 to 3 feet tall), while those sold as *G. aurantiaca* 'Purple Passion', *G. × sarmentosa*, and *G. aurantiaca* var. *sarmentosa* usually have a more distinctly spreading or trailing habit. Full sun (for best color) to partial shade; average to moist but well-drained soil. Zones 9 to 11.

---

## VITIS
*Grape*

**Height: To 30 feet**
**Leaf size: 4–6 inches long and wide**
**Full sun to partial shade**
**Zones 6–9**

If you're looking for a purple-leaved climber, claret vine (*Vitis vinifera* 'Purpurea') is one of your only options — but it's not something you'll simply have to settle for. Also known as teinturier grape, this deciduous, woody-stemmed climber is a beauty in

its own right, with deeply lobed leaves that are silvery green when new, turning pinkish to reddish purple and then deep purple. Barely noticeable greenish flowers mature into clusters of deep purple fruits in late summer; they're not good for eating, but they add a wonderful decorative feature that's most apparent when the leaves turn shades of red in autumn. Claret vine may grow to 30 feet, but you can keep it in the 10- to 15-foot-tall range fairly easily with regular pruning. Train it onto a fence or trellis panel (help the vines hold on by tying them to the support with natural twine), or let it scramble into a tree. Pair claret vine with a clematis vine to enjoy an abundance of beautiful blooms and fabulous foliage from the same amount of garden space.

**GROWING TIPS:** Claret vine produces its richest leaf colors in full sun, but it will get by with partial shade as well. Because you're not growing this grape for its fruits, you don't need to worry about exactly how to prune it; just trim off whatever's necessary in late winter to keep it the shape and size you want.

**ALTERNATIVE:** Claret vine isn't especially common, but 'Blue Northern Brewer' hops (*Humulus lupulus*) is even more elusive; still, it's worth hunting for if you'd like something truly different. This deciduous twining vine has broad, lobed leaves that emerge practically black, turning deep green with a purplish tinge; grows from ground level to 15 feet or more by midsummer. Full sun to partial shade; average, well-drained soil. Zones 4 to 8.

*Vitis vinifera* 'Purpurea'

## WEIGELA
*Weigela*

**Height:** Varies
**Leaf size:** 3–4 inches long;
  1–2 inches wide
**Full sun to partial shade**
**Zones 4 or 5–8**

Weigelas (*Weigela*) used to be dismissed as single-season flowering shrubs, but now they're among the most popular garden shrubs, due in large part to the abundance of beautiful dark-leaved selections. Instead of being the main feature, the deep pink, funnel-shaped, late-spring to early-summer blooms are secondary to the reddish or brownish purple leaves, which are wonderful for supplying spring-to-fall color in mixed borders and foundation plantings. These deciduous shrubs have arching branches that create

*Weigela florida* Wine and Roses

a handsome, mounded form, and they come in a range of sizes to fit just about any site. Wine and Roses (*W. florida* 'Alexandra') typically reaches 4 to 6 feet tall. *W.* 'Ruby Queen' is slightly shorter (usually 3 to 4 feet). The most compact cultivars include 2- to 3-foot-tall *W.* 'Dark Horse', *W. florida* Midnight Wine ('Elvera'), and *W.* 'Tango'. Besides fitting easily into flower gardens, these lower-growing selections also look great planted in masses as an out-of-the-ordinary ground cover.

**GROWING TIPS:** Dark-leaved weigelas produce their deepest color in full sun; they'll be closer to purple-tinged green in partial shade. Average, well-drained soil is fine. If needed, trim lightly right after the main flush of flowers fades to maintain a neat, mounded shape. (It's not unusual for scattered flowers to appear later on in the growing season.) On established plants, removing a few of the oldest stems at their base before new growth starts each spring will help keep the shrubs vigorous.

**ALTERNATIVE:** 'Albury Purple' St.-John's-wort (*Hypericum androsaemum*) is a compact deciduous shrub with slender, arching stems clad in deep purple leaves that age to mostly green; 18 to 24 inches tall. Full sun; average to moist but well-drained soil. Zones 6 to 9. *Note:* In some climates (particularly the Pacific Northwest), this plant is very prone to disfiguring fungal rusts; in these areas, consider another option for purple foliage.

*Alternanthera ficoidea* 'Red Threads'

## ALTERNANTHERA
*Alternanthera*

**Height:** Varies
**Leaf size:** Varies
**Full sun**
**Zones 9–11**

Purple-leaved alternantheras (*Alternanthera*) are a great option for adding deep dark foliage to border and container combinations. And now that there's been a resurgence of interest in these versatile, easy-to-grow tender perennials, there's also an abundance of new selections to give foliage aficionados even more options to choose from. Classic Christmas clover or blood leaf (*A. dentata*) comes in a number of dark-leaved cultivars, with 2- to 3-inch-long, 1-inch-wide, glossy leaves held on sturdy stems that tend to be more horizontal than upright, forming spreading mounds. It gets the common name Christmas clover from the clustered, off-white blooms that appear in the wintertime. 'Rubiginosa' (also sold as 'Ruby' and 'Wave Hill') usually grows 24 to 30 inches tall, with deep red to reddish purple foliage; 'Purple Knight' is similar but typically a little shorter (18 to 24 inches), and its seedlings tend to be more uniformly dark than those of 'Rubiginosa'. Several other lesser-known cultivars have similarly dark foliage: 'Gail's Choice' is about the same size as 'Purple Knight'; 'Ruby Red' reportedly has a more open habit and narrower leaves; and 'Red Marble' is splashed or streaked with red to pink.

If you like the solid, dark color of 'Rubiginosa' and its relatives but need a smaller-scale plant, consider water amaranth (sold under a variety of names, including *A. polygonoides* 'Purple Select' and 'Purple Selection', *A.* 'Red Runner', and *A. reineckii*). Its leaves are about 2 inches long and ⅓ to ½ inch wide; the plants themselves are about 1 foot tall but will spread several feet. It may self-sow prolifically.

Cultivars of parrot leaf (*A. ficoidea*) also offer a number of top-notch choices. 'Red Threads' ('Red Thread') and 'New Burgundy' have very narrow, upward-folded leaves that are medium red when new, with deep red older leaves and stems on 6- to 12-inch-tall plants. 'Broadleaf Red', as you might guess, has wider leaves that are brownish red to deep red when new and red-tinged green when older; it's about 1 foot tall. In the 18-inch-tall range are 'Cognac', with medium to deep reddish purple leaves, and 'Grenadine', which is also deep reddish purple but with bright pink veins (very much like *Iresine herbstii* 'Brilliantissima'). If you'd like pink combined with more green than purple, look for 'Purpurea' (also sold under *A. purpurea*) or 'Party Time' (also sold as 'Partytime').

**GROWING TIPS:** Alternantheras normally perform well in full sun to partial shade, with fertile, evenly moist but well-drained soil. Pinching off their shoot tips helps to shape the plants and promotes bushier growth.

**ALTERNATIVES:** Want to really spice up your garden — literally? Hot peppers (*Capsicum annuum*) offer some of the best deep purple foliage you can find, and they're easy to grow from seed, so you can have plenty of plants to work with for the price of just one seed packet. 'Explosive Embers' has small, pointed deep purple leaves; 6 to 12 inches tall. 'Little Nubian', 'Peruvian Purple', 'Pretty in Purple', and 'Royal Black' are 18 to 24 inches tall. Stunning 'Black Pearl' has broader, near-black leaves; 1 to 2 feet tall. Full sun to light shade; average, well-drained soil. Zones 9 to 11; grow as annuals or bring indoors for the winter elsewhere.

## ASTER
*Aster*

**Height:** Varies
**Leaf size:** Varies
**Full sun to partial shade**
**Zones 4 or 5–8**

Asters (*Aster*) have long been popular border perennials for their flowers; their foliage normally isn't much to speak of. In the case of some calico asters (*A. lateriflorus;* also known as *Symphyotrichum lateriflorum*), though, the leaves are an eye-catching feature in their own right, extending the plants' season of interest past a few weeks of bloom time to span the entire growing season. These asters form shrubby clumps of upright main stems with horizontal side stems clad in small, narrow leaves that are deep purple-black in sun and purple-green in partial shade. In early to mid-fall, the side stems are lined with hundreds of flowers with white to palest pink "petals" and purplish pink centers. The individual blooms are small, but they are so abundant that they practically smother the foliage, and they're a great favorite with both bees and butterflies. 'Prince' has 2- to 3-inch-long, ¼- to ½-inch-wide leaves and usually grows about 2 feet tall; 'Lady in Black' has 3- to 5-inch-long, ½- to ¾-inch wide leaves and is typically 3 to 4 feet tall. Both show off best when set in front of brighter-leaved companions.

**GROWING TIPS:** Sturdy and dependable, calico asters produce their darkest foliage and most abundant flowers in full sun, but they will also grow in partial shade. Evenly moist but well-drained soil is ideal. The plants are drought-tolerant when established, but they tend to drop their lower leaves during dry spells.

**ALTERNATIVES:** Seed-grown plants of herbaceous *Clematis recta* labeled 'Purpurea' have purple new leaves that typically turn green by early summer; the intensity and persistence of their purple coloring varies. For more consistent leaf color, consider a vegetatively propagated selection, such as Serious Black ('Lime Close') or 'Velvet Night'. Their 3- to 6-foot stems are upright at first, then sprawling. Full sun to light shade; average to moist but well-drained soil. Zones 3 to 9.

*Aster lateriflorus* 'Lady in Black'

## GAURA
*Gaura, bee blossom, wand flower*

**Height:** 2 to 3 feet
**Leaf size:** 2–3 inches long; about ½ inch wide
**Full sun**
**Zones 5 or 6–9**

With a perennial that blooms as abundantly as gaura (*Gaura lindheimeri*) does, it's almost superfluous to look for selections that also have colorful foliage. But since it does take a few weeks to start flowering in spring, why not have some reddish foliage there to bridge the gap? 'Siskiyou Pink', which grows in loose 2-foot-tall clumps, has deep red foliage in spring, but it typically turns mostly green in summer. Pink Fountains ('Walgaupf') is about the same height and has similar foliage traits but is much fuller-looking. Three-foot-tall 'Passionate Pink' and 12- to 18-inch-tall 'Crimson Butterflies' tend to keep most or all of their deep red leaf color throughout the year. 'Bijou Butterflies' is similar to 'Crimson Butterflies' but with variegated foliage; due to the overall red blush, though, the leaf edges usually appear light pink instead of creamy white. These selections all have maroon buds and medium to light pink flowers fading to lighter pink or white.

**GROWING TIPS:** Full sun brings out the best leaf color and most abundant bloom display. Well-drained soil is important, too, especially in winter. (In fact, with

good drainage and dependable snow cover, gauras can be winter-hardy as far north as Zone 3.) If your soil is on the heavy side, try growing your gauras in raised beds or in containers. When flowering slows in mid- to late summer, shear off the flower stems to promote new reddish growth and another flush of flowers for fall. The plants often self-sow, but the seedlings will probably have mostly green foliage. Keep in mind that gauras may be short-lived, fizzling out after three or four years, so be prepared to replace them with younger plants as needed.

**ALTERNATIVE:** 'Black Prince' snapdragon (*Antirrhinum majus*) produces a somewhat similar foliage effect to the red-leaved gauras, with small, narrow, dark red to red-tinged green leaves on 12- to 18-inch-tall stems. The foliage color is most intense in cool weather. To grow snapdragons as annuals, sow indoors in mid- to late winter; plant out only the darkest-leaved seedlings. May be perennial in Zones 6 or 7 to 10. Full sun; average, well-drained soil.

*Haloragis erecta* 'Wellington Bronze'

*Gaura lindheimeri* 'Passionate Pink'

## HALORAGIS
*Haloragis, toatoa*

**Height:** 1–3 feet
**Leaf size:** 1–2 inches long; ½ inch wide
**Full sun to partial shade**
**Zones 6 or 7–11**

For gardeners on the lookout for exciting new foliage plants, haloragis (*Haloragis erecta*) is quickly

becoming a hot favorite. Its small, toothed foliage is a rich coppery brown to bronzy green that provides all kinds of possibilities for eye-catching combinations in borders, planters, and even hanging baskets. Tiny brownish flowers bloom along the upper parts of the stems in summer, but you'll barely notice them. The compact, bushy plants are "ever-brown" to "semi-ever-brown" where they're hardy; elsewhere, treat them as annuals or bring them indoors for the winter. Seeds or plants sold as 'Wellington Bronze' typically grow 2 to 3 feet tall.

**GROWING TIPS:** Full sun brings out the truest brown in the foliage; in partial shade, the leaves will be a bit greener, but still with brown shading. Average to evenly moist but well-drained soil is ideal. Sow the seed indoors

in late winter to early spring; wait until all danger of frost has passed to set out the seedlings. After the first year, you may also find self-sown seedlings. If you don't want these volunteers in the future, pinch off the shoot tips several times during the summer to remove the flowers, with the added benefit of encouraging even bushier growth.

**ALTERNATIVES:** 'Copper Carpet' New Zealand bur (*Acaena microphylla* 'Copper Carpet' or 'Kupferteppich') grows in wide-spreading carpets of small, rounded, toothed leaflets that are coppery bronze, often with a light grayish cast; 2 to 3 inches tall. Purple goose leaf (*A. inermis* 'Purpurea') has grayish purple to reddish purple foliage; 3 to 4 inches tall. Full sun to light shade; average to dry, well-drained soil. Zones 6 or 7 to 10.

## ACER
*Maple*

**Height:** Varies
**Leaf size:** 2–4 inches long
and wide for most
**Full sun to full shade**
**Zones 5 or 6–8**

Japanese maples (*Acer palmatum*) offer an abundance of fabulous foliage colors, but the cultivars with reddish to purplish leaves are probably the best known. They have long been treasured by gardeners for their lacy texture, upright or weeping growth habit, and stunning fall colors, as well as for their often changeable spring and summer appearance. There are many dozens of cultivars to choose from; below is a brief overview of some that tend to stay in the red-to-purple range through most or all of the growing season. The compact selections look great in small spaces, foundation plantings, and containers; enjoy the larger ones in bigger mixed borders or as specimens. If possible, site them where you can see the sun shining through the foliage; the stained-glass effect is amazing. *Note:* This species is considered invasive in some areas.

*Tall, upright Japanese maples* (*15 feet or more*). The names *A. palmatum* f. *atropurpureum*, Atropurpureum Group, and 'Atropurpureum' refer to seed-grown plants that have red to purplish, palmately lobed leaves about 3 inches long and wide on upright trees in the range of 20 to 25 feet tall. These maples produce many seedlings, which vary in the depth and persistence of their foliage colors. If you'd like an upright, reddish-leaved Japanese maple and aren't particular about the exact color or height, some seed-grown maples are very pretty, and relatively inexpensive. Most gardeners like to know what to expect from their investment, though, so they choose a named cultivar.

'Bloodgood' is a classic selection with large leaves that are deep red to reddish purple in spring and summer and bright red in fall; it's usually 15 to 20 feet tall. 'Fireglow' and 'Red Emperor' are similar to 'Bloodgood' but seem to be more sun- and heat-tolerant, so they're better choices for southern gardens. 'Iijima-sunago' is in the 15- to 25-foot-tall range, with orange-red spring foliage that turns bronzy green in summer and shades of red, orange, and yellow in fall. 'Kasagiyama' has bright reddish pink, purple-veined leaves in spring, turning pink to greenish with deeper green veins and edges in summer, then shades of red, orange, and yellow in fall. It eventually reaches about 20 feet tall. 'Nuresagi', with dark purple new leaves that usually age to reddish purple in summer, then turn bright red in fall, is 15 to 18 feet tall when mature. 'Beni-otake' has purplish red spring and summer foliage and bright red fall color, with very narrow lobes that give this elegant tree a lacy appearance. It can grow 20 to 25 feet tall.

*Medium-tall, upright Japanese maples* (*usually 8 to 15 feet tall*). 'Ô-kagami' is a handsome, vase-shaped smaller tree (usually 12 to 15 feet tall) that's a purplish red early in the season, turning a glossy, deep reddish purple for most of the summer and then orangey red in fall. 'Tsukushi-gata' ('Tsukushigata'), in the same height range, is even darker in spring and holds its purplish red well through the summer, turning brilliant red in autumn. Shrubby 'Beni-fushigi' will reach 8 to 10 feet tall, with small, somewhat crinkled leaves that are bright red in spring, pinkish red in summer, and red again in fall. 'Pixie', with rich red new leaves, deep purple-red older foliage, and bright red autumn color, is usually in the 6- to 10-foot-tall range. Tiny-leaved 'Shaina' has bright red new growth that ages to deep purplish red in summer and bright red in fall. It tends to be upright at first, later developing more of a rounded form. You'll often see it described as growing 4 to 6 feet tall, but it can eventually reach 10 or even 15 feet when mature.

*Compact, upright Japanese maples* (*to about 8 feet tall*). Even if space is limited, your options aren't. 'Red Pygmy' is just one splendid selection in this group, with exceptionally slender-lobed foliage that's deep red in spring, turning purple in summer and bright red in fall; it's usually 5 to 8 feet tall. 'Aratama' is one of the smallest selections (just 3 to 5 feet when mature); it's rich red to purplish red from spring into summer, taking on some greenish tinges later and usually turning shades of red and orange in fall.

*Cutleaf Japanese maples.* "Regular" Japanese maples are elegant in their own right, but the "cutleaf" types look even lacier, due to their even greater number of leaf lobes and the fact that each of those lobes is also toothed. *A. palmatum* var. *dissectum* Dissectum Atropurpureum Group or 'Dissectum Atropurpureum' refers to seed-grown plants with the typical lacy, reddish to purplish leaves and twisted, cascading branches that produce an overall mounded form. The plants grow 6 to 8 feet tall and wide but may reach 10 feet or more after many years. 'Dissectum Nigrum'

*Acer palmatum* 'Shaina'

(often sold as 'Ever Red' and 'Everred') is a well-known selection with a similar height and habit; its foliage is silvery when just opening, turning purple-red to red-tinged green in summer and glowing red in fall. 'Crimson Queen' tends to hold its reddish color through most or all of the summer. 'Tamukeyama' isn't quite as lacy as the others but is an even darker red-purple during the summer, with better heat tolerance than many other selections in this group. 'Orangeola' shares the usual cascading habit but with orange-red spring growth, reddish shoot tips against greenish older growth in summer, and bright orange to scarlet foliage in fall. **GROWING TIPS:** These Japanese maples need ample light to produce their richest summer colors, but too much strong sun will scorch the leaves. In hot-summer areas, light all-day shade or morning sun with afternoon shade usually works well; in cooler areas, full sun to light shade is fine. Evenly moist but well-drained soil is ideal. **ALTERNATIVES:** Selections of African rose mallow or cranberry hibiscus (*Hibiscus acetosella;* also known as *H. eetveldianus*) have palmately lobed, deep red leaves. 'Red Shield' ('Coppertone') has rounded lobes, while plants sold as 'Jungle Red' and 'Maple Sugar' have pointed lobes; 8 to 10 feet tall where hardy, shorter elsewhere. Full sun to light shade; average to moist but well-drained soil. Zones 8 to 11. *Note:* This species is considered invasive in some areas.

## ANTHRISCUS
*Cow parsley,*
*wild chervil*

**Height: 12–18 inches**
**Leaf size: 6–12 inches long;**
   **6–8 inches wide**
**Full sun to partial shade**
**Zones 5–9**

Lacy foliage is a pretty addition to almost any combination, but when it's dressed up in basic black, the effect can be absolutely decadent. Maybe that's why gardeners have a difficult time resisting 'Ravenswing' cow parsley (*Anthriscus sylvestris;* also listed as 'Raven's Wing'), with its dense mounds of finely cut, fernlike leaves that emerge greenish and quickly turn deep brownish purple to near-black. 'Ravenswing' blooms, too, sending up 2- to 3-foot-tall, branched stems topped with clusters of pinkish buds and tiny white to palest pink flowers, usually in late spring to early or midsummer. Although

the flowers are attractive, it's a good idea to cut off most or all of them before they set seed. The plants are usually biennial, but if you stop them from producing seed, they may return and flower for a few more years. At some point, let one or two flower clusters ripen and drop seed so you'll have a few replacement plants coming along, but don't let more than that set seed; otherwise, you'll likely have seedlings coming up everywhere. *Note:* This species is considered invasive in several states. **GROWING TIPS:** 'Ravenswing' cow parsley grows in full sun or partial shade with evenly moist but well-drained soil. It can be a little tricky to get established; small seedlings often settle in better than do larger plants. If you want to start 'Ravenswing' (or the similar 'Moonlit Night') from seed, sow it as soon as possible after it ripens — ideally in late summer

to late fall — and leave the pots outdoors for the winter. The seedlings are usually dark-leaved, but there may be some green ones if the regular wild chervil is growing nearby; weed out the off-type seedlings. One other recommendation: if you don't care about the flowers, cut down the stems as soon as you see them form. That way, your plants will stay better-looking through the summer, and you'll never have unwanted seedlings to deal with. **ALTERNATIVES:** Plants sold as *Angelica sylvestris* 'Vicar's Mead' and 'Purpurea' produce broad mounds of compound, purplish green to deep purple-black foliage; *A. stricta* var. *purpurea* ('Purpurea') is similar in leaf. Both are 2 to 3 feet tall in leaf. Deadhead to extend the life of your original plants or let some of the seeds ripen for replacement seedlings. Full sun to light shade; evenly moist but well-drained soil. Zones 4 to 8.

*Anthriscus sylvestris* 'Ravenswing'

## CIMICIFUGA
*Black snakeroot, black cohosh,*
*bugbane*

**Height: Varies**
**Leaf size: 2–3 inches long; 1–2**
   **inches wide (individual leaflets)**
**Full sun to full shade**
**Zones 3–7**

If you prefer perennials with immediate impact, black snakeroots (*Cimicifuga*) probably aren't a good choice for you. But if you can be patient enough to wait a few years for them to settle in and fill out, they'll repay you with

*Cimicifuga simplex* 'Brunette'

handsome clumps of fine-textured foliage and fuzzy-looking, spikelike clusters of white flowers for many years to come. The most difficult thing about growing them is keeping up with their various name changes! You'll also see black snakeroots listed under the genus *Actaea*, and you're likely to find the stunning dark-leaved selections sold under several species names, such as *C. simplex* (*A. simplex*), *C. racemosa* (*A. racemosa*), and *C. ramosa* (*A. ramosa*).

To gardeners, the names of these plants don't matter nearly as much as their looks — and their price. Because of their slow-growing nature, black snakeroots can be costly, so you want to be a smart shopper. Those sold as Atropurpurea Group and 'Atropurpurea' are grown from seed, so they tend to be the least

expensive, but their leaves and stems are mostly a purple-tinged green. Selections with foliage and stems that are dependably a deep brownish to purplish black cost more at first, but they're a worthwhile investment if you're fanatical about dark foliage. It seems like new cultivars are released each year, each claiming to be darker than the rest, but they're all quite beautiful if you give them plenty of moisture and plenty of light. 'James Compton' reaches about 3 feet tall in bloom, while 'Brunette' and 'Black Negligee' are usually 3 to 5 feet tall and 'Hillside Black Beauty' can reach 5 to 7 feet. All of these have purplish or pinkish buds that open to fragrant white flowers in late summer to early or mid-fall. Four- to 6-foot-tall 'Pink Spike' is billed as having pink blooms, although the pinkish cast isn't always noticeable. Keep in mind that the dark-leaved snakeroots sometimes look greenish when their new foliage appears, but they usually darken quickly.

**GROWING TIPS:** Full sun brings out the richest leaf colors, but it may also cause the foliage to scorch and shrivel if the soil isn't constantly moist. In full shade, the plants will survive quite well, but they'll look more greenish than usual, and they probably won't flower. A site with morning sun and afternoon shade or light all-day shade with humus-rich, evenly moist but well-drained soil is usually ideal. Regular watering is particularly important for the

first few years. Established plants will tolerate short dry spells but may be much shorter in dry years. Generally speaking, black snakeroots perform best in cool climates; in hot-summer areas, their foliage tends to be more greenish than purplish, and the plants themselves may grow even more slowly than usual.

**ALTERNATIVE:** A much faster-growing, late-flowering option for the middle or back of a border is purple-leaved white mugwort or ghost plant (*Artemisia lactiflora* Guizhou Group; also sold as 'Guizhou' and 'Guizho'). This clump-forming perennial produces deeply cut foliage that's typically deep purple when new, gradually turning purple-tinged green to deep green; 4 to 6 feet tall. Full sun to light shade; average to evenly moist but well-drained soil. Zones 3 to 8.

---

## DAHLIA
*Dahlias*

**Height: Varies**
**Leaf size: 6–12 inches long**
    **and wide**
**Full sun**
**Zones 8–10**

Dahlias (*Dahlia*) have long been prized by some gardeners for their big, bold blooms — and overlooked by others who dismissed them as being simply too gaudy. With the abundance of lovely dark-leaved cultivars coming on the market, though, their popularity has skyrocketed. They still have beautiful blooms, but now boast lacy deep purple to

brownish purple leaves that add welcome color from planting to frost. Enjoy the medium-height to tall selections near the middle of a mixed border or in a large planter; the compact cultivars work well near the edge of beds and borders or in mixed containers. Dahlias are especially useful as follow-up plants for spring bulbs and early-blooming perennials. Start them in pots and enjoy them as mobile accents for a few weeks, then tuck them in wherever gaps appear in your garden in mid- to late summer. Dahlias will flower any time during the summer or fall, but blooms are usually most abundant in early summer and in autumn, when the air temperature is on the cool side.

One of the best-known dark-leaved dahlias is 'Bishop of Llandaff', with single to semi-double, orange-red flowers over near-black, lacy foliage on plants about 3 feet tall. It has given rise to a number of equally beautiful dark-leaved cultivars that are about the same height: some of these are the deep red 'Bishop of Auckland', reddish purple 'Bishop of Canterbury', pink 'Bishop of Leicester', yellow 'Bishop of Oxford', and light orange 'Bishop of York'. If you're not particular about the flower colors you get, look for 'Bishop's Children' as seed or seedlings: they produce single or semi-double blooms in a wide array of solid colors and bicolors. Many of these are just as beautiful as the named

*Dahlia* 'Roxy'

Series (such as semi-double yellow 'Classic Summertime' and creamy white 'Classic Swanlake') and the Happy Single Series (including peachy orange 'Happy Single First Love', purplish pink 'Happy Single Juliet', yellow 'Happy Single Party', and deep red 'Happy Single Romeo').

Some dark-leaved dahlias in the 12- to 18-inch-tall range are single yellow 'Chic', rich pink 'Roxy', and red to reddish orange 'Ellen Huston' (also sold as 'Ellen Houston'). For a range of flower colors, grow semi-double to double 'Redskin Mixed' or mostly double 'Diablo Mixed' from seed.

**GROWING TIPS:** Dark-leaved dahlias produce their richest leaf colors and bloom most abundantly in full sun with fertile, well-drained soil. To start them from seed, sow indoors in mid- to late winter. If you buy them as bare tuberous roots, give them a jumpstart by planting them in pots indoors four to six weeks before your last frost date, or plant them directly in the garden in late spring to early summer. If you're able to buy already growing potted dahlias, wait until all danger of frost has passed to set them outdoors. Pinching or snipping off the shoot tips once or twice in early to midsummer encourages bushier growth and reduces the need for staking on the taller types. (You can use these trimmings as cuttings to make more dahlias, by the way.) To keep your favorites from year to year, dig

selections, and it's easy to keep your favorites from year to year.

Options are equally abundant among more-compact cultivars (those roughly 2 feet tall). Semi-double 'Bednall Beauty' is deep red; semi-double 'Moonfire' is yellow and red; single 'Yellow Hammer' is orangey yellow; and double 'David Howard' is light to deep orange. 'Terracotta' has both orange and yellow in each single bloom, while semi-double 'Fascination' is a rich purplish pink. Other dark-leaved dahlias in this height range are the Classic

them up after the first frost, cut off the tops, and store the roots in a cool but frost-free place for the winter.

**ALTERNATIVE:** Bronze fennel (*Foeniculum vulgare* 'Purpureum'; also sold as 'Bronze', 'Rubrum', and 'Smokey') starts out as a dense clump of feathery, aromatic foliage, then shoots up to 4 to 6 feet tall in mid- to late summer. The deep brown new foliage ages to a brown-tinged gray-green. Self-sows enthusiastically. Full sun to light shade; average, well-drained soil. Zones 4 to 9. *Note: F. vulgare* is considered invasive in some areas.

## GERANIUM
*Geranium, cranesbill*

**Height: Varies**
**Leaf size: Varies**
**Full sun to partial shade**
**Zones vary**

Hardy geraniums (*Geranium*) are well-known for their abundant blooms, but they also sport some of the best foliage textures and colors around. While the variegated and golden-leaved geraniums offer a number of exciting options, it's the dark-leaved cultivars that have really grabbed the spotlight. There are currently well over a dozen to choose from, and new selections appear on the market every year, each one more mouthwatering than the last. Here's a sampling of some of the best to inspire your creativity; you'll find endless ways to enjoy them in border combinations,

as ground covers, and even in containers.

One main group of dark-leaved hardy geraniums includes the selections of meadow cranesbill (*G. pratense*). These sun-loving border beauties grow in dense mounds of deeply cut, lacy-looking leaves that are usually 4 to 6 inches long and wide. Their saucer-shaped, purple-blue flowers are most abundant in late spring to early summer, with rebloom possible later in the season. Plants sold as 'Victor Reiter', 'Victor Reiter Jr.', and similar names are 18 to 24 inches tall, with deep purple spring foliage that ages to purple-tinged green or deep green by early summer. The plants are often propagated by seed (correctly called the Victor Reiter Junior strain), so they will be somewhat variable. Some of the best have been selected and named, and they've given rise to other cultivars, including the 2- to 3-foot-tall 'Purple Haze' and its 12- to 18-inch-tall seedlings 'Okey Dokey' and 'Hocus Pocus'. 'Black Beauty', to about 1 foot tall, is supposed to hold its deep purple foliage color through most, if not all, of the growing season. 'Midnight Reiter' tends to be even more compact (to about 8 inches), and it, too, holds its purple leaf color well into summer. Zones 4 to 8.

Wild geranium (*G. maculatum*) grows best in partial shade, but it will also perform well in full sun where the soil is evenly moist.

'Elizabeth Ann' and 'Espresso' produce dense, 12- to 18-inch-tall clumps of deeply lobed, medium to dark brown leaves that are 4 to 5 inches long and wide. They're accented with purplish pink flowers on 18- to 24-inch-tall stems in mid- to late spring. Zones 5 to 9.

Plants in the third main group of dark-leaved geraniums are short but wide-spreading, with 1- to 2-inch-wide and -long, shallowly lobed leaves that have scalloped edges and an overall rounded outline. Ground-hugging *G. sessiliflorum* subsp. *novae-zelandiae* 'Nigricans' (also sold as *G. sessiliflorum* 'Nigricans' or 'Nigrescens') is barely 3 inches tall but a foot or more wide, forming carpets of small, dark brown leaves sprinkled with tiny pale pink to white flowers from spring to fall. It's been crossed with other species to produce hybrids with slightly larger, brownish foliage and equally long-blooming flowers. 'Chocolate Candy', for instance, is a cross between 'Nigricans' and *G. traversii* 'Elegans' (these hybrids are usually listed under *G. × antipodeum*). It's more of a mound-former — 6 to 12 inches tall and 1 foot wide — with medium to dark brown foliage and light pink flowers with darker pink veins. In cool climates, it will bloom from late spring to frost; in hot areas, it often takes a break in summer. 'Bertie Crug', 'Dusky Crug', 'Foie Gras', 'Kahlua', and 'Tanya Rendall' are just a few of the many other lovely cultivars with similar characteristics. Hardiness recommendations vary widely for this group: anywhere from Zones 4 to 10 to Zones 8 to 10. Where winters tend to be cold and rainy, the plants demand good drainage and still may not succeed; gardeners in areas with mild winters or dependable snow cover instead of rain are likely to have better results. Enjoy these sun-loving low growers at the front of a border, along a path, or trailing over the edge of a planter.

**GROWING TIPS:** Dark-leaved geraniums usually produce their richest leaf colors in full sun. Cultivars of *G. maculatum* also look good with morning sun and afternoon shade or light all-day shade. Average, well-drained soil is usually fine. Cutting back plants of *G. pratense* and *G. maculatum* to a few inches above the ground as soon as the blossoms fade encourages a flush of deeply colored new leaves and possible rebloom; it also prevents self-sowing.

**ALTERNATIVES:** The ferny, mounded foliage of 'Purple Rain' Jacob's ladder (*Polemonium yezoense*) appears deep purple in spring and fall, turning greenish in summer; it's about 10 inches tall in leaf. *P.* 'Bressingham Purple' is a bit more compact — it typically reaches about 8 inches tall in leaf — and its cool-season leaves are usually even darker. Full sun (for best leaf color) to partial shade; evenly moist but well-drained soil. Zones 3 to 8.

*Geranium maculatum* 'Espresso'

# 4 STUNNING SILVER, GRAY, AND BLUE

ABOVE: **Simply elegant.** For cool color and dramatic texture, too, it's tough to beat the leaves of *Hosta sieboldiana* 'Elegans'.

RIGHT: **Summertime blues.** While evergreens are particularly prized for their winter presence, those with icy blue foliage — such as this blue spruce (*Picea pungens*) — have a strong visual impact during the growing season as well.

When it comes to anything-but-green foliage, plants with silver, gray, and blue leaves are by far the most popular offerings out there, and with good cause: they're widely available, and they make a lovely complement to just about any companion. Whether you garden in sun or shade, you have lots of options to choose from for beds, borders, ground covers, and containers.

Silvers, grays, and blues harmonize beautifully with an array of soft colors, looking particularly good with lighter shades of blue, purple, and pink. They're absolutely elegant when paired with white flowers, and undeniably dramatic when contrasted with burgundy and black. Bright silvers can match vibrant magenta, reds, and purples in intensity, while dusty blues and grays impart a cooling touch to hot-colored groupings. This adaptability makes silvers, grays, and blues a safe choice if you're just getting started with colored foliage. Their close affinity to green also makes them appealing partners if leaf colors like yellow and purple are too gaudy for your taste. Simply put, it's almost impossible to create *bad* partnerships with silvers, grays, and blues!

## GETTING STARTED WITH SILVERS, GRAYS, AND BLUES

Beyond being simply pretty, silver, gray, and blue foliage can serve a practical function, too: as a sign of where a plant would best like to grow. Silvers and grays, in particular — on artemisias, lavenders, and the like — tend to shine in sites with excellent drainage and lots of sun, and there's a reason. Over time, they have evolved to cope with hot, dry climates by covering their green leaves with tiny hairs. These hairs protect the foliage from intense sunlight and help block drying winds, thereby reducing moisture loss through the leaf pores. The length, thickness, and density of these hairs influence how silvery a leaf appears.

Knowing why silvery plants are the way they are will help you decide where to put them in your garden. Although some will tolerate evenly moist soil during the growing season, most perform best where the soil is on the dry side, especially in wintertime. Sloping sites are particularly good for many silver- and gray-leaved plants, as there's little chance of the soil staying soggy. Full sun is usually necessary, too. In shady sites, moisture tends to cling to the leaf hairs, providing perfect conditions for rots and other disease problems. In areas with high summer humidity, even full sun and good air circulation may not be enough to keep diseases at bay; here, you'll need to experiment with different cultivars or different species if you really want the silver effect.

Now, what about pulmonarias, spotted dead nettle (*Lamium maculatum*), hardy cyclamen, and other silvery, shade-loving beauties? No, they're not simply exceptions to the "sun and dry" rule; they're in a class

by themselves. Their coloration is not due to hairs, but rather to blisters or air pockets just below the leaf surface. These reflect light and produce the silvery appearance. This can occur between the leaf veins, along the veins, or at random, producing the variety of silvering patterns available. Plants with particularly metallic-looking leaves, such as many begonias, create a dramatic, modern effect when combined with silvery, coppery, or black containers or ornaments.

LEFT: **Just to be different.** Unlike most silver-leaved plants, silver willow (*Salix alba* var. *sericea*) actually prefers evenly moist soil.

RIGHT: **A bright idea.** Shade-loving silvers, such as heart-shaped Chinese wild ginger (*Asarum splendens*) and lacy Japanese painted fern (*Athyrium niponicum* var. *pictum*), are super for brightening up dark, dreary areas. Like their sun-loving counterparts, they're also effective for outlining pathways to make the edges easier to see. (Chanticleer, PA)

In the case of blue, blue-green, and some gray-leaved plants, the coloration comes from a waxy or powdery coating (sometimes referred to as a "bloom") on the leaf surface. Like the hairs on silver foliage, this coating helps reflect intense light and reduces moisture loss. But unlike plants with hairy leaves, which usually prefer dry, sunny sites, those with "glaucous" foliage run the gamut from sun to shade and moist to dry. Options for glaucous foliage also come in a wide range of heights and habits, although they're especially abundant among low-growing succulents and rock-garden-type plants. Their smooth, matte appearance makes them ideal choices for many garden spaces, whether you're looking for elegant color harmonies or eye-popping textural contrasts.

LEFT: **A study in blue.** Their colors are strikingly similar, but the very different textures of rosette-forming echeverias and spiky blue chalk sticks (usually sold as *Senecio mandraliscae*) give each a very distinctive appearance. (Hobbs garden, Vancouver, BC)

## SILVERS, GRAYS, AND BLUES FOR SHADE

*Aquilegia flabellata*, *A. viridiflora*

*Asarum shuttleworthii*, *A. splendens*, others

*Athyrium niponicum* var. *pictum*

*Begonia* 'Escargot', 'Looking Glass', others

*Brunnera macrophylla* 'Jack Frost', 'Looking Glass', others

*Carex flacca*, *C. platyphylla*

*Cyclamen coum*, *C. hederifolium*, others

*Dicentra* 'King of Hearts', 'Pearl Drops', others

*Fothergilla* 'Blue Mist', 'Blue Shadow'

× *Heucherella* 'Quicksilver', 'Silver Streak'

*Hosta* 'Hadspen Blue', 'Halcyon', others

*Lamiastrum galeobdolon* 'Hermann's Pride'

*Lamium maculatum* 'Shell Pink', 'White Nancy', others

*Lonicera caerulea* var. *edulis* 'Blue Velvet'

*Pulmonaria* 'Cotton Cool', 'Silver Streamers', others

*Schizophragma hydrangeoides* 'Moonlight'

*Viola grypoceras* var. *exilis* 'Sylettas'

## SILVERS, GRAYS, AND BLUES FOR SUN

*Agave americana*

*Artemisia abrotanum*, *A. absinthium*, others

*Brachyglottis* Dunedin Group 'Sunshine', others

*Cedrus atlantica* 'Glauca Pendula', others

*Centaurea gymnocarpa* 'Colchester White'

*Cerastium tomentosum*

*Chamaecyparis pisifera* 'Baby Blue', 'Boulevard', others

*Cistus* 'Brilliancy', 'Victor Reiter', others

*Cynara cardunculus*

*Dianthus* 'Bath's Pink', 'Bewitched', others

*Dichondra argentea* 'Silver Falls'

*Echeveria glauca*, *E. secunda*, others

*Elymus magellanicus*

*Eucalyptus cinerea*, *E. gunnii*, others

*Festuca glauca* 'Elijah Blue', 'Meerblau', others

*Helichrysum italicum*, *H. petiolare*, others

*Helictotrichon sempervirens*

*Juniperus horizontalis* 'Wiltonii', 'Bar Harbor', others

*Lavandula angustifolia*, *L.* × *intermedia*, others

*Lotus berthelotii*

*Lychnis coronaria*, *L. flos-jovis*, others

*Melianthus major*

*Panicum virgatum* 'Cloud Nine', 'Heavy Metal', others

*Perovskia* 'Filigran', 'Little Spire', others

*Picea pungens* 'Glauca Prostrata', 'Sander's Blue', others

*Plectranthus argentatus*

*Rudbeckia maxima*

*Ruta graveolens*

*Salvia argentea*, *S. officinalis*, others

*Santolina chamaecyparissus*

*Schizachyrium scoparium* 'The Blues'

*Sedum sieboldii*, *S. spectabile*, others

*Senecio cineraria*, *S. viravira*

*Stachys byzantina*

*Verbascum bombyciferum*, *V. olympicum*, others

TOP: **Neat and petite.** White-flowered fan columbine (*Aquilegia flabellata* 'Nana Alba') is a dainty beauty for lightly shaded gardens.

BOTTOM: **Easy to please.** Fuzzy silver *Plectranthus argentatus* is a dependable and adaptable foliage accent for beds, borders, and containers too.

LAMIUM MACULATUM
'WHITE NANCY'

DICENTRA 'KING OF
HEARTS'

PICEA PUNGENS
'HOOPSII'

SCHIZOPHRAGMA
HYDRANGEOIDES 'MOONLIGHT'

OPUNTIA

HELIANTHEMUM
'RHODANTHE CARNEUM'

BRUNNERA MACROPHYLLA
'JACK FROST'

MELIANTHUS MAJOR

SALIX ALBA VAR. SERICEA

SENECIO VIRAVIRA

## WHAT'S IN A NAME?

When you see a plant in person or in a photograph, it's immediately obvious if the foliage falls in the silver, gray, or blue range. But if you're skimming through books or catalogs that don't have pictures, you may need to rely on a plant's name for clues to the foliage color. Here are some words that may indicate leaves in this color range.

*alba, -um, -us* (white, pale)

*albescens* (turning white)

*albicans* (almost or turning white)

*albida, -um, -us* (whitish)

*albifolia, -um, -us* (with white leaves)

*argentata, -um, -us* (silver)

*argentea, -um, -us* (silvery)

*argophylla, -um, -us* (shining or whitish)

*argyrophylla, -um, -us* (with silvery leaves)

blue

*cana, -um, -us* (gray due to hairs)

*candicans* (turning white)

*candida, -um, -us* (very white)

*candidula, -um, -us* (somewhat white)

*canescens* (grayed)

*cinerea, -um, -us* (ash gray)

*farinacea, -um, -us* (with a floury covering)

frost, frosted, frosty

ghost, ghostly

*glauca, -um, -us* (grayish or blue-green)

*glaucescens* (turning glaucous)

*glaucifolia, -um, -us* (with glaucous leaves)

*glaucophylla, -um, -us* (with glaucous leaves)

glaucous (developing a whitish covering)

gray, grey

haze, hazy

ice, icy

*incana, -um, -us* (gray)

*leucophaea, -um, -us* (grayish white)

*leucophylla, -um, -us* (with white leaves)

*livida, -um, -us* (lead-colored)

mercury

*metallica, -um, -us* (with metallic appearance)

mist, misty

*nivea, -um, -us* (snow white)

pale

*pallida, -um, -us* (pale)

pewter

*pruinosa, -um, -us* (frosted)

quicksilver

*senescens* (graying)

silver, silber

slate

smoke, smoky

snow, snowy

steel

white

ABOVE: **A rose to know.** When it comes to roses, attractive foliage isn't an attribute you hear mentioned often. But blueleaf rose (*Rosa glauca*) is an exception: it's better known for its pink-tinged gray leaves than for its small pink flowers.

LEFT: **Quick silver.** Cascading over a wall, spilling out of a container, or spreading over the ground like a shimmering pool, fast-growing silver ponyfoot (*Dichondra argentea* 'Silver Falls') is invaluable for adding an abundance of foliage in a short amount of time.

## SILVERS, GRAYS, AND BLUES IN THE GARDEN

With so many wonderful silver-, gray-, and blue-leaved plants to choose from, the possibilities for creating pleasing combinations are almost unlimited. If you enjoy soothing, harmonious plantings, soft grays and blues are the perfect complements to pastel flowers. For a bit more drama, pair rich, jewel-toned blooms with sparkling silvers and cool grays. There's great potential for pure shock value, too, if you're willing to try out-of-the-ordinary combinations as well.

ABOVE: **Summer shimmer.** Lovely enough to grow for its foliage alone, silverbush (*Convolvulus cneorum*) also produces pretty pinkish buds and beautiful white flowers.

RIGHT: **A serene reflection.** Blue foliage forms a perfect complement to a pool, pond, or other water feature. (Meadowbrook Farm, PA)

As with other non-green leaves, silvers, grays, and blues are great in moderation but overwhelming in excess. Smaller-scale plants such as annuals and perennials with these leaf colors are easiest to use effectively as accents or in combinations. With trees and large shrubs, bright silver or blue foliage can be overpowering in masses; gray is much less intense and easier to use in the landscape.

### Silver, Gray, and Blue as a Group

A garden based on primarily silver, gray, and blue foliage can be bold and dramatic in sun or cool and soothing in shade. Mix in some blue and purple-blue blossoms to add a bit of richness, and the results are guaranteed to please! Using roughly equal amounts of silver and blue, silver and gray, or all three colors together provides the most satisfying results. Going too heavy on silver and silvery white foliage may make the planting glaringly bright and unpleasant to look at; too much blue and gray may appear hazy and unfocused (although that might be fine in a small space, or in a garden area you'd like to use for relaxing).

### Silver, Gray, and Blue with Green Companions

Masses of a single blue-leaved plant can form an eye-catching accent, but mixing several different ones in a small area may create a dusty-looking or washed-out effect unless you tuck in some intense greens or other colors to provide some contrast. Silver and gray leaves also look terrific with bright or dark green companions: think of silvery 'Berggarten' sage (*Salvia officinalis*) against a carpet of rich green thyme, for example. If you find other foliage colors, such as chartreuse and burgundy, to be "unnatural-looking," a garden based on silvers, grays, blues, and greens might be right up your alley. There are so many possible plants to choose from that you can create dramatic foliage combinations based on texture and still enjoy the subtle natural color variations too. Pairing any of these colors with green flowers will produce interesting effects, but blue leaves combined with green flowers — such as the yellow-green trumpets of *Nicotiana langsdorffii* paired with deep-blue 'Love Pat' hosta — are particularly pleasing, especially in shady sites.

## Silver, Gray, and Blue with Yellow and Orange

Bright silver foliage acts rather like white, so it can hold its own with bright yellow and orange flowers (and gold-variegated foliage) if you're looking for an out-of-the-ordinary accent. Grays and blues tend to appear somewhat dingy next to bright yellow and orange, but they can be very pretty with more-pastel shades of those colors. (Tossing in a few silver-leaved plants, by the way, peps up pastel plantings that are a little too soft-looking.) Pairings of bright silver or blue foliage with clear yellow leaves can be very dramatic. Greenish yellow partners also work just fine with blue but tend to look somewhat sickly next to strong silvers. Gray leaves with bright yellow or greenish yellow leaves may also appear a little "off."

LEFT: **Silver chic.** If you enjoy strong contrasts, combining bright silvery white foliage with glowing orange blooms could provide all the drama you desire. This combination features spiky Scotch thistle (*Onopordum acanthium*), which seeds around readily and is considered invasive in some areas; you may want to substitute cardoon (*Cynara cardunculus*) for a somewhat similar effect.

## Silver, Gray, and Blue with White

Perhaps the very best use of silver foliage is with white flowers. The effect is crisp and pure, especially when you include a bit of deep green foliage to add depth and contrast. Plus, these pale beauties will pick up even the faintest hint of light, making them a must-have for any evening garden. Lining a path or walkway with silver leaves is another great idea. Besides clearly marking the way, many silvery plants have aromatic foliage, so you can enjoy their scents as well as their color while you stroll. Blue leaves are also lovely with white flowers and white-variegated foliage. Gray leaves, too, have a place in "white" gardens, although sometimes they make white blooms look a little dull. Arranging the plants so the white flowers aren't directly against gray foliage will help avoid this problem.

RIGHT: **Feel the chill.** Snow-in-summer (*Cerastium tomentosum*) gets its common name from the abundance of snowy white flowers in late spring to early summer, but its silver-frosted foliage adds a cooling touch to combinations throughout the other seasons as well.

## Silver, Gray, and Blue with Red and Pink

When you're working with bright red and hot pink flowers (and clear red foliage), silver-leaved partners provide a dramatic contrast, while gray foliage softens the shocking colors a bit. Silvers and grays also mix beautifully with purplish pink, bluish pink, and clear pink blooms, as well as soft pastel pink. Blue foliage isn't quite as versatile — it usually doesn't offer much when paired with red foliage or flowers, and it may or may not appear pleasing with purplish pink blooms — but it too can help tone down hot pink or complement clear pinks, bluish pinks, or light pinks. Silver, gray, and blue leaves all work well with deep maroon foliage, whether you're looking for drama (try bright silver partners) or more-subtle contrasts (use grays or blues).

LEFT: **Expect the unexpected.** Left to their own devices, your plants may create eye-catching combinations you wouldn't have thought of. Here, the brilliant red blooms of 'Jacob Cline' bee balm (*Monarda*) have sprawled onto a fuzzy cushion of 'Big Ears' lamb's ears (*Stachys byzantina*).

RIGHT: **A soothing scene.** With its elegant pairing of light pink flowers and gray-green foliage, 'Mountain Mist' dianthus adds a touch of softness and romance to the garden.

## *Silver, Gray, and Blue with Purple, Black, and Brown*

Silvers look great with the whole range of purples in flowers and foliage, from bright violet-purple to basic blue-purple and practically black. Grays work with the same color range, but while silvers make purple pairings "pop," grays have a softening influence on adjacent colors. Blue leaves also have a cooling effect on purple-flowered companions. Pale lavender blooms may be lost against blue leaves, but bright purples and purple-blues hold up well, as do deep purple-black blooms and foliage. Silver, gray, and blue foliage can all be interesting with brown-leaved companions, such as the New Zealand sedges (*Carex buchananii*, for example), but these unusual combinations definitely don't appeal to everyone. Still, it's fun to experiment in small spaces with foliage colors like bright silver and bronzy brown in metallic containers or with metal garden ornaments tucked in among the leaves.

### MORE PLANNING POINTERS

The intensity of the blue in foliage varies widely depending on a number of factors, including the amount of the waxy coating on the leaf, the age of the leaf, and the overall vigor of the plant. On some plants, you can actually wipe off the "bloom" with the oil on your fingers or with a spray of pest-controlling horticultural oils (which is why these sprays are not recommended for plants that have blue leaves). On other plants, the blue is more a part of the leaf surface, so it tends to be more persistent. Strong sun and rain sometimes damage the coating, but actively growing foliage typically replaces it as needed. Young leaves are the best at keeping their bright color; more-mature leaves may turn nearly all green as they age.

*Elymus magellanicus*

## ASTELIA
*Astelia, silver spear*

**Height:** Varies
**Leaf size:** Varies
**Full sun to full shade**
**Zones 9–11**

Looking for something dramatically different to add height and texture to your container plantings? Then "ever-silver" astelias (*Astelia*) are a great option. These clump-forming perennials look something like yuccas but are a bit softer in outline, with stiffly upright new leaves that gradually arch outward to cover an area several feet across. The sword-shaped foliage is light green with a covering of silvery scales (especially on the undersides), giving the whole plant a pale silver-green sheen. The species you're most likely to find is *A. chatham-*

*ica* (also sold as *A. nervosa* var. *chathamica* and *A.* 'Silver Spear'); it typically reaches 4 to 6 feet tall and wide, with 3- to 6-foot-long, 2- to 4-inch-wide leaves. Greenish to yellowish flowers sometimes appear in spring, but they're tucked down into the foliage and not especially showy. If you have both male and female plants, the female flower heads may ripen into clusters of orange berries by late summer to early fall. *A. banksii* is similar, but its leaves are narrower and the overall height is closer to about 3 feet.

**GROWING TIPS:** Astelias are amazingly adaptable, thriving in anything from full sun to full shade and moist to dry soil, and they're quite drought-tolerant once established. Usually, though, they perform best in full sun to light shade with average to evenly moist but well-drained soil. A site that's sheltered from strong wind is ideal. Regularly trim off the oldest foliage to keep the plants looking their best, but avoid handling the younger leaves, because it's easy to rub off their silvery covering.

**ALTERNATIVE:** Hardier San Diego sedge (*Carex spissa*) offers spiky gray to gray-blue foliage in slow-spreading clumps that are 3 to 5 feet tall and about as wide. Full sun to full shade, but looks best in partial shade with evenly moist soil. Zones 6 or 7 to 10. Dalmatian iris (*Iris pallida*) is another option for sturdy, swordlike, gray-green foliage in a variety of climates. Full sun; average, well-drained soil. Zones 4 to 8.

*Astelia chathamica*

## DIANTHUS
*Dianthus, pinks*

**Height:** 4–6 inches
**Leaf size:** 2–3 inches long;
¼ inch wide
**Full sun**
**Zones 3–9**

Also commonly called pinks, dianthus (*Dianthus*) are best known for their beautiful flowers, but their attractive foliage deserves attention too. Some dianthus have green leaves, but several species and many hybrids have blue-green to silvery blue foliage that typically looks great year-round. These low-growing perennials produce tight mounds or spreading mats perfectly suited for edging borders and pathways, cascading over low walls, or serving as gorgeous ground covers for sunny sites. There are already dozens of delightful dianthus to choose from and new ones are released each year, so options abound. If possible, buy plants from a local source, so you can see the foliage for yourself and select the effect that most appeals to you. Catalog photos usually show the flowers, not the foliage, but many mention the leaf color in the plant description if it's especially blue or silvery.

It used to be that dianthus weren't recommended for southern gardens, because the heat

*Dianthus* 'Mountain Mist'

and humidity would cause them to "melt out." Many modern selections, however, have proved far more adaptable to these tough conditions while still providing beautiful foliage and wonderfully fragrant flowers. 'Bath's Pink', for instance, is a popular and dependable selection that's 8 to 12 inches tall in bloom, with light pink flowers held a few inches above spreading carpets of gray-green leaves. It flowers mostly in late spring, with some rebloom possible later in the season. 'Mountain Mist' is very similar. 'Bewitched' is also light pink but flowers over a longer period — late spring through early summer, with scattered rebloom through the rest of the growing season. It's 6 to 8 inches tall in flower, over silvery blue leaves. If you'd prefer white flowers, check out 'Greystone'; for a more brilliant pink bloom over exceptionally blue foliage, choose 'Feuerhexe' ('Firewitch'). 'Frosty Fire' is a rich reddish pink to red. This is just a sampling of the best blue-leaved dianthus; there are many other garden-worthy cultivars out there.

**GROWING TIPS:** Dianthus will grow in light shade, but they look best in full sun with neutral to slightly alkaline soil. Good drainage is a must, especially in winter. The plants also suffer in bone-dry conditions, so be prepared to water them during prolonged dry spells. Removing the faded flowers encourages rebloom on most dianthus; shear off the spent flowering stems just above the foliage.

**ALTERNATIVES:** Corkscrew chives (sold as *Allium senescens* subsp. *montanum* var. *glaucum*, *A. senescens* subsp. *glaucum*, or *A. senescens* 'Glaucum') form clumps of slender, twisted, blue-gray leaves; 6 inches tall. Full sun; average, well-drained soil. Zones 4 to 8. Blue chalk sticks (*Senecio mandraliscae* or *Kleinia mandraliscae*) is a succulent with slender, cylindrical, powder blue leaves; 12 to 18 inches tall. Full sun to light shade; average to dry soil. Zones 9 to 11.

# FESTUCA
*Fescue*

**Height: Varies**
**Leaf size: 4–8 inches long;**
   ⅛ inch wide
**Full sun**
**Zones 3 or 4–8**

For spiky foliage on a small scale, blue fescues (*Festuca*) are tough to beat. These compact perennial grasses grow in dense, rounded mounds of slender leaves that often have a blue-green, gray-blue, or silvery blue cast. In early summer, taller stems topped with airy greenish to tan flowers extend 6 to 8 inches above the foliage, giving the plants a much different appearance. It's easy to reclaim the spiky effect, though: shear off the flowering stems just above the leaves to shape the plants (and prevent self-sowing as well). Fescues are cool-season grasses, which means you can expect them to look best from fall through spring. In many areas, they still look respectable during

the summer, but in warm climates, they may look rather dull during the hottest weather. These low growers typically look best planted in groups: at least three together at the front of a border or along a path or in larger masses as a ground cover.

There are dozens of blue fescues to choose from, but many are very similar, differing only slightly in their leaf color or the fineness of their foliage. 'Elijah Blue' blue fescue (*F. glauca*; sometimes listed as *F. cinerea* and *F. ovina* var. *glauca*) is one of the most popular cultivars, for its durable nature and silvery blue foliage; it's usually 8 to 10 inches tall in leaf. Some other cultivars in the same height range are silvery blue 'Blaufuchs' ('Blue Fox'), bright blue 'Blauglut' ('Blue Glow'), and distinctly silvery 'Blausilber' ('Blue Silver'). 'Meerblau' ('Ocean Blue') is a good blue to blue-green through most of the year, sometimes taking on reddish to orange tinges during the summer. Bright powdery blue 'Boulder Blue' tends to be a bit more compact (6 to 8 inches in leaf), with better-than-average heat tolerance. 'Siskiyou Blue' Idaho fescue (*F. idahoensis*) has equally narrow but much longer silvery blue foliage (it's about 18 inches tall in leaf). Keep in mind that seed-grown fescues sold under any cultivar name can vary quite a bit in their colors, so if it's important that they be uniform, shop locally to see the plants for yourself, or seek out sources that

*Festuca glauca* 'Elijah Blue'

guarantee vegetatively propagated plants.

**GROWING TIPS:** Blue fescues normally look their best in full sun, but they appreciate a little afternoon shade in warmer areas. Average, well-drained soil is fine. Overall, fescues prefer a relatively cool, dry climate. In early spring, comb through the clumps with your fingers to pull out any dead leaves, or cut back the plants to 2 to 3 inches if there are a lot of winter-damaged tips. Dividing the clumps every three or four years (or whenever they start to die out in the center) will help to keep them vigorous and good-looking.

**ALTERNATIVES:** For spiky blue foliage that's better suited to some shade, check out some of the sedges (*Carex*). 'Blue Zinger' blue sedge (*C. flacca*; also sold as *C. glauca*) has silvery blue foliage in steadily spreading clumps that make a great ground cover; Zones 4 to 8. Silver sedge (*C. platyphylla*) has wider blue-gray leaves; Zones 3 to 8. Both are 6 to 12 inches tall. Best in partial shade; average, well-drained soil.

SPIKY

## JUNCUS
*Rush*

**Height: Varies**
**Leaf size: 1–2 feet long;**
**⅛–¼ inch wide**
**Full sun to partial shade**
**Zones vary**

Rushes (*Juncus*) are excellent choices for adding both color and texture to moist- and wet-soil sites. These striking perennials grow in slowly spreading clumps of slender, cylindrical stems that are "ever-blue" in mild climates. You'll hardly notice the leaves, which are reduced to brownish

*Juncus inflexus*

sheaths at the base of the stems. For a very vertical effect, check out California gray rush (*J. patens*), with stiffly upright, gray-blue to gray-green, leaflike stems to about 2 feet tall and reddish brown flower clusters throughout the summer. 'Carman's Gray' (often listed as 'Carmen's Gray') is dependably grayish green; 'Elk Blue' and 'Occidental Blue' are more of a blue-gray. California gray rush and its cultivars are usually recommended for Zones 7 to 9.

Hard rush (*J. inflexus*) typically has very upright green stems, but its cultivars offer some fantastically textured blue foliage. 'Afro' (also known as 'Blue Medusa' and blue Medusa rush) grows in dense clumps that are 12 to 18 inches tall, with blue-green stems that are tangled and twisted into loose spirals. Weeping 'Lovesick Blues' has arching, gray-blue stems that form graceful mounds just a foot or so tall but up to 3 feet across. Both of these rushes produce small clusters of not-especially-showy brown flowers near the stem tips in summer. Zones 3 or 4 to 10.

**GROWING TIPS:** Rushes generally grow best in full sun with evenly moist soil (a few inches of standing water is also fine), but they usually adapt to drier conditions if you give them some afternoon shade. They seldom need any special care; simply cut them back in early spring to remove the dead stems and make room for fresh new growth.

**ALTERNATIVE:** For a vertical look in average to dry soil, 'The Blues' little bluestem (*Schizachyrium scoparium*; also known as *Andropogon scoparius*) is a worthy possibility. This narrowly upright, clump-forming perennial grass grows 2 to 4 feet tall (occasionally to 5 feet), with slender pink stems and narrow gray-blue leaves that typically turn reddish orange in fall. Full sun; best in low-fertility soil. Zones 3 to 9.

## LEYMUS
*Wild rye, lyme grass*

**Height: Varies**
**Leaf size: Varies**
**Full sun to partial shade**
**Zones vary**

Wild ryes (*Leymus*) produce some of the best blue foliage you can find, but you must do your homework before you decide to add them to your garden. The various species differ in their needs and — even more importantly — in their tendency to spread, so you'll want to choose carefully. The most widely available one is commonly called lyme grass, blue lyme grass, and European dune grass, and you'll see it sold under several names, including *L. arenarius*, *L. arenarius* 'Glaucus', *Elymus arenarius*, and *E. glaucus*. This cool-season grass is a beauty, with arching, blue-gray leaves that are about 2 feet long and about ½ inch wide, and it's amazingly tolerant of difficult growing conditions, including drought and salty soil. It's also an aggressive spreader,

*(Elymus) Leymus magellanicus*

however: a plus if you want it to stabilize sandy slopes or to fill the planting strip between a street and a sidewalk but a serious potential problem if you let it run loose in a mixed border. *Note:* This species is classified as invasive in some states. Narrow, blue-green flower spikes appear atop 3- to 5-foot-tall stems in summer. If you cut the plants to the ground when the spikes start to turn brown, you'll encourage a flush of fresh new foliage that will stay attractive all through the winter in mild climates. Seed-grown plants vary somewhat in leaf color. 'Blue Dune' is a selection that should have very silvery blue foliage. 'Findhorn' is a somewhat more compact cultivar (usually about 18 inches tall in leaf). *L. racemosus* (*E. racemosus*) is a separate species, but it looks virtually identical to *L. arenarius*. Zones 4 to 10. 'Canyon

Prince' wild rye (*L. condensatus;* also sold as *E. condensatus*) is also about the same size but usually spreads more slowly than the others. Zones 7 to 9.

Blue wheat grass or blue Magellan grass (usually sold as *Elymus magellanicus* but sometimes as *L. magellanicus* or *Agropyron magellanicum*) is one of the very bluest of the blue-leaved grasses. Unlike its wild rye relatives, it basically stays in one place, forming fountainlike clumps of upright-then-arching, bright silvery blue leaves that are 1 to 2 feet long and ¼ to ½ inch wide. Its slender, late-spring to early-summer flower spikes are the same color as the foliage at first, later turning tan; they usually reach 24 to 30 inches tall. 'Blue Tango' tends to have even-more-arching foliage, with a somewhat more compact overall height (to about 18 inches). Blue wheat grasses are undeniably eye-catching, but they aren't the easiest grasses to please. They sulk in hot climates and dislike wet or humid conditions, but they also don't perform well where the soil dries out. Try them in a sunny site with good air circulation and evenly moist but well-drained soil in Zones 4 or 5 to 8.

**GROWING TIPS:** Wild ryes generally grow best in full sun and average, well-drained soil, but they usually tolerate light shade as well. If you can't plant the spreading types in a site that's surrounded by paving or some other hard surface to contain them, try growing them in a planter.

**ALTERNATIVE:** Blue oat grass (*Helictotrichon sempervirens*) grows in dense, rounded, 12- to 18-inch-tall mounds of stiff, narrow, blue-gray leaves that look good through the growing season and most, if not all, of the winter. 'Saphirsprudel' ('Sapphire Fountain') is a bright blue-gray and is reportedly more resistant to rust, a disfiguring fungal disease prevalent in humid conditions. Full sun; average to moist soil, but good drainage is a must. Zones 4 to 8.

## PANICUM
*Switchgrass*

**Height: Varies**
**Leaf size: 2 feet long;**
    **½ inch wide**
**Full sun**
**Zones 4–9**

Dependable, adaptable, and colorful, switchgrasses (*Panicum*) are invaluable for bringing height, texture, and year-round interest to gardens and landscapes in a range of climates. The plants spread slowly but are distinctly clump-forming, and they seldom need much more care than an annual trim. Although the spring and summer foliage color of the species ranges from green to bluish or grayish green, there are several selections with dependably blue-tinged leaves. *P. virgatum* 'Cloud Nine' is one of the tallest — reaching 6 to 8 feet by bloom time in late summer — with vase-shaped clumps of blue-green foliage and long-lasting, airy flowerheads about the same color. Blue-gray 'Heavy Metal' is more narrowly upright and 4 to 5 feet tall in bloom, and 'Prairie Sky' is an even brighter silvery blue, in rather loose 3- to 5-foot-tall clumps that tend to sprawl a bit by fall. 'Dallas Blues' is distinctly different, with wider-than-usual powder blue foliage and showy pinkish plumes that are 6 to 7 feet tall. Zones 4 to 9. *P. amarum* 'Dewey Blue' is bright blue-gray, reaching 3 to 4 feet tall with a fountainlike form and gracefully arching flower clusters in early fall. Zones 3 to 9.

**GROWING TIPS:** Switchgrasses thrive in full sun. Selections of *P. virgatum* will grow in anything from evenly moist to dry soil, but average to dry soil is best for *P. amarum.* Fertile soil encourages lush, vigorous growth but produces taller, weaker stems that may need staking. Switchgrasses turn yellow to tan in fall, then stay good-looking through most or all of the winter; cut down the top growth to a few inches above the ground in late winter to early spring.

**ALTERNATIVE:** Indian grass (*Sorghastrum nutans*) is another warm-season perennial grass with blue-green to blue-gray leaves; 3 to 4 feet tall in leaf. 'Bluebird' is greenish blue, 'Indian Steel' is blue-gray, and 'Sioux Blue' is bright powder blue. Full sun is best. Will grow in anything from evenly moist to dry soil; the more moisture they get, the taller they'll be (and the more likely they'll be to sprawl). Zones 4 to 9.

*Panicum virgatum* 'Dallas Blues'

## YUCCA
*Yucca, Adam's needle*

**Height: Varies**
**Leaf size: 1–3 feet long;**
    **1–3 inches wide**
**Full sun to partial shade**
**Zones vary**

Yuccas (*Yucca*) are a classic part of southwestern landscapes, but many are hardy enough to bring year-round color, texture, and structure to plantings in much colder climates as well. They grow in rosettes of sword-shaped leaves, sometimes at ground level and sometimes atop tall branched or unbranched stems. When the rosettes are several years old, they produce tall flowering stems topped with clusters

*Yucca filamentosa*

of white bells in summer. The rosettes usually die after flowering, but they produce several or many offsets to take their place. Yucca leaves tend to be stiff and spiny, so they're not an ideal choice for planting right next to a path, but they're terrific for mixed borders and superb on slopes.

There are many yucca species to choose from, and the foliage of most of them is in shades of blue-green to gray-green. Soap-weed (*Y. glauca*) is one of the hardiest yuccas (Zones 3 to 10), with stemless or short-stemmed, 2- to 3-foot-tall rosettes of stiff, 18- to 24-inch-long, ½-inch-wide, gray-green leaves; it's 4 to 5 feet tall in flower. Adam's needle (*Y. filamentosa;* also sold as *Y. flaccida*) is another hardy species (Zones 4 to 10), with 18-inch-long, 1-inch-wide, gray-green leaves in usually stemless rosettes that are 2 to 3 feet tall; it's about 10 feet tall in bloom. Beaked yucca (*Y. rostrata*),

also known as big bend yucca, grows in rounded rosettes of 2-foot-long, ½-inch-wide, blue-gray foliage atop a 5- to 10-foot-tall, woody trunk; 'Sapphire Skies' has particularly showy powder blue leaves. Zones 5 or 6 to 10. Some other species to look for are stemmed, blue-gray Schott's or mountain yucca (*Y. schottii*), Zones 6 to 10; stemless, silvery blue to blue-gray pale yucca (*Y. pallida*), Zones 7 to 10; and stemmed, bright blue-gray blue yucca (*Y. rigida*), Zones 7 or 8 to 10.

**GROWING TIPS:** Yuccas thrive in full sun and average, well-drained soil; most will tolerate partial shade as well. Good drainage is especially important in winter, particularly in colder climates. Cut off the flower stems when the blooms fade, and pull off dead leaves to keep the plants looking their best.

**ALTERNATIVES:** Agaves or century plants (*Agave*) produce "ever-blue" rosettes of spiny-edged and -tipped leaves. *A. americana,* with wide, blue- to gray-green leaves to 6 feet long, is rated for Zones 8 or 9 to 11; the blue-gray variety or subspecies *protoamericana* is hardy into Zone 7. Rattlesnake master (*Eryngium yuccifolium*) grows in clumps of lance-shaped, upright-to-arching, gray-green leaves; 2 to 3 feet tall. Zones 3 or 4 to 9. Full sun; average, well-drained soil.

## BRUNNERA
*Hardy forget-me-not,
Siberian bugloss*

**Height: 12–18 inches
Leaf size: 6–8 inches long and wide
Partial to full shade
Zones 3–7**

It's easy to find silver foliage for sunny sites, but options for shady gardens are more limited — and that's where hardy forget-me-not (*Brunnera macrophylla*) really shines. This slow-spreading perennial offers several silvery selections, all with the usual small leaves and sprays of sky blue flowers in spring, followed by a fresh set of large leaves that emerge in early summer and last through the rest of the growing season. 'Langtrees' (also sold as 'Aluminum Spot') has deep green foliage with a V-shaped pattern of silvery spots. 'Silver Wings' has silvery mottling all over the leaf, with a silvery white edge.

'Jack Frost' is frosted with silver over the whole leaf, with green visible only along the veins. And then there's 'Looking Glass', with green-veined silver leaves in spring and solid-silver summer and fall foliage.

**GROWING TIPS:** Hardy forget-me-nots thrive in sites that are sunny in spring and partly to mostly shady in summer. Humus-rich, average to evenly moist but well-drained soil is ideal. Overall, the plants perform best in cooler climates. Hardy forget-me-nots self-sow abundantly if you don't remove the faded flowers. Seedlings of 'Langtrees' often have the silver spotting of their parents, but the seedlings of other selections are seldom as silvery as the original plants.

**ALTERNATIVES:** There are several types and dozens of cultivars of begonias (*Begonia*) with silvery leaves. 'Escargot' rex begonia is a

*Brunnera macrophylla* 'Jack Frost'

classic, with a deep gray to green center and edge and a wide, bright silver-gray ring; about 1 foot tall. 'Looking Glass' cane begonia has wavy-edged silver foliage with deep gray-green veining; can eventually reach 8 feet tall. Light all-day shade; average to moist but well-drained soil. Zones 9 to 11.

## CRAMBE
*Sea kale*

**Height:** 12–18 inches
**Leaf size:** 10–12 inches long;
about 6 inches wide
**Full sun to partial shade**
**Zones 4 or 5–8**

If you're searching for something out of the ordinary to add beautiful foliage *and* flowers to your garden, sea kale (*Crambe maritima*) might be just the thing. Each spring, its thick taproot sends up tightly curled, often purple foliage that expands into thick, wavy-edged, somewhat twisted leaves in shades of blue-gray to blue-green with paler gray veining. Two- to 4-foot-tall bloom stalks topped with clusters of small, sweetly scented white flowers appear in late spring or early summer, followed by small, rounded seedpods. 'Lily White' is a seed strain that tends to lack the purplish color on its new foliage.

**GROWING TIPS:** Sea kale grows best in full sun but tolerates partial shade (especially in the warmer parts of its range). Neutral to slightly alkaline soil is ideal. Established clumps will withstand drought well (and salty condi-

tions, too), but they generally perform best with evenly moist soil. Good drainage is very important, though, especially in winter.

**ALTERNATIVE:** Horned poppy (*Glaucium flavum*) grows in clumps of deeply lobed, curled, silvery gray, hairy leaves; about 1 foot tall in leaf. Although it is usually a short-lived perennial, it can bloom the first year from seed, so grow it as an annual if desired. Full sun to light shade; average, well-drained to dry soil. Zones 5 or 6 to 10. *Note:* This species is considered invasive in some areas.

## CYNARA
*Cardoon, artichoke*

**Height:** 5–6 feet
**Leaf size:** 3–4 feet long;
1 foot wide
**Full sun**
**Zones 6 or 7–10**

Looking something like a gigantic silvery fern, cardoon (*Cynara cardunculus*) and artichokes (*C. cardunculus* Scolymus Group; also known as *C. scolymus*) make unusual and dramatic additions to sun-drenched borders. Both grow from a thick taproot that starts producing new growth very early in the season, sending up masses of arching, deeply lobed leaves that are silvery gray to gray-green on top and silvery white underneath. The thick, white to pale green leafstalks are often spiny on the edges, although there are spineless types too (such as the cardoon cultivar 'Pleine Blanc Inerme'). In hot climates, 6- to 8-foot-tall

flower stalks usually appear from early spring to midsummer (after which the plants may go dormant for a while); in most other areas, they bloom from midsummer into early fall. The oval to rounded flower buds are 3 to 4 inches across and enclosed in leathery scales that are very spiny on cardoon and usually less spiny or spineless on artichokes. They open into brushy-looking, purplish to blue blooms up to 6 inches across, then turn into fluffy seedheads. Cardoon, in particular, self-sows prolifically and is considered invasive in some areas.

If you don't have enough space for cardoon or artichokes, consider *C. baetica* subsp. *maroccana* (*C. hystrix*), with narrow, very spiny, gray-green leaves, and flower stems to only 18 inches tall. Typically hardy in Zones 8 to 10, it's especially eye-catching just before bloom, with its dramatically spiny, purplish pink flower buds.

**GROWING TIPS:** Cardoon and artichokes thrive in full sun with deep, fertile, evenly moist soil that's also well drained, especially in winter. They're most likely to overwinter successfully in Zones 7 to 10, but you can enjoy them in colder climates as foliage annuals; sow the seeds indoors in late winter or early spring and set them outdoors around your last frost date. If you want to try them as perennials north of Zone 7, look for artichoke cultivars that are billed as being especially hardy, such as 'Violetta'. A single

*Crambe maritima*

*Cynara cardunculus*

packet of cardoon seeds will produce very mixed results as far as plant hardiness, so if possible, set out several seedlings; one or more of them may overwinter in Zone 6 or sometimes even Zone 5 conditions.

**ALTERNATIVE:** Matilija poppy (*Romneya coulteri*) isn't suited to every garden, but it's quite beautiful in the right site. It produces jagged, blue-green to gray-green leaves on stems that can be anywhere from 4 to 8 feet tall. It may be a little difficult to get established, but once it settles in, it spreads rampantly by rhizomes. Full sun; average, well-drained to dry soil. Zones 7 or 8 to 10.

*Hosta sieboldiana* 'Elegans'

## HOSTA
*Hosta, plantain lily*

**Height: Varies**
**Leaf size: Varies**
**Full sun to full shade**
**Zones 3–8**

When it comes to fantastic foliage, hostas (*Hosta*) boast some of the best colors and textures around. The greens, golds, and variegates are all great, but the blues are in a class by themselves — maybe because there are so few other options for bold foliage in this color for shady sites. Blue hostas actually have green leaves, but they're covered with a thin waxy coating that makes them appear blue or gray, especially when they emerge in spring. Over the course of the growing season, this coating may wash off in a heavy rain or melt away if the plants get too much sun in hot weather. Though actively growing leaves keep producing a fresh layer of wax, mature foliage is likely to look green by mid- to late summer. Choosing the planting site carefully helps keep the blue effect as long as possible; also, seek out cultivars that have been selected for their durable color.

There are dozens of beautiful blue hostas to choose from, in a wide range of sizes. One of the tiniest is 'Blue Mouse Ears', with smooth, rounded, blue-gray leaves in mounds barely 6 inches tall and 1 foot across. The Tardiana Group — based on a cross between blue-leaved *H. sieboldiana* 'Elegans' and green-leaved

*H.* 'Tardiflora' (*H. tardiflora*) — includes a number of small to medium-sized hostas with usually smooth, particularly good blue foliage. Some of the best are 'Hadspen Heron' or 'Blue Heron' (about 8 inches tall in leaf) and 'Blue Wedgwood' ('Blue Wedgewood'), 'Halcyon', and 'Hadspen Blue' (14 to 18 inches tall).

For more small to medium-sized hostas, the Tokudama Group supplies some excellent options. They tend to have rounded, cupped leaves that are distinctly ribbed and/or puckered, producing an intriguing corrugated or "seersucker" effect. Besides adding extra textural interest, their thick leaves are less prone to slug damage than are the thin-leaved types. *H.* 'Tokudama' (*H. tokudama*) itself, as well as hybrids 'Abiqua Drinking Gourd', 'Blue Cadet', and 'Love Pat', to name just a few, are eventually 12 to 18 inches tall in leaf, although they will take many years to reach that size. ('Love Pat' tends to fill out a bit more quickly than the others.)

The Elegans Group, based on *H. sieboldiana* 'Elegans', includes some of the largest hostas you'll find. They, too, tend to be rather slow-growing, with thick, heavily textured, blue-green foliage. Clumps of 'Elegans' and 'Big Daddy' can eventually reach 2 to 3 feet tall and 4 to 5 feet across; 'Blue Angel' will get even bigger (to about 3 feet tall and as much as 6 feet across). 'Krossa Regal' isn't part of this group, but it also

gets quite large (about 3 feet tall and to 6 feet wide), with a distinctive vase-shaped habit and narrower blue-gray leaves.

**GROWING TIPS:** You'll often hear that blue hostas belong in shade; that's not always the case, however. They certainly tolerate partial to full shade everywhere, and they in fact prefer light shade in hot climates, but ample sunlight is important for keeping the plants vigorous (and, in turn, keeping them as blue as possible for as long as possible). Soil moisture is another key factor: the more sun they get, the more moisture they need to thrive. When in doubt, try a site that gets morning sun and afternoon shade or light all-day shade, with fertile, evenly moist but well-drained soil. Blue-leaved hostas sport light purple to white blossoms that usually complement the foliage; wait until they fade to cut off the spent flowering spikes, or snip them off as soon as they appear if you want only the leaves.

**ALTERNATIVES:** Set out transplants of garden cabbage (*Brassica oleracea*) in mid-spring, and by early summer the broad, flat outer leaves and inner rounded head will fill a space 18 to 30 inches across and about 1 foot tall. Ordinary cabbage has blue-green outer leaves and pale green heads; "red" types (such as 'Ruby Ball') have silvery blue outer leaves and reddish purple heads. Full sun to light shade; average, well-drained soil.

## MELIANTHUS
*Melianthus, honey bush*

**Height: 8–12 feet**
**Leaf size: 12–18 inches long;**
**about 1 foot wide**
**Full sun to partial shade**
**Zones 8–11**

Honey bush (*Melianthus major*) gets its common name from the honeylike nectar that drips from its brownish red flowers, but to most gardeners, the flowers are far less interesting than the fabulous foliage. This large shrub spreads by suckers to form broad clumps of thick, upright stems clad in deeply lobed, blue-green leaves that have jagged edges. When you brush the leaves, you'll notice their strong scent, which some describe as peanut-butter-like and others describe as bitter or unpleasant. The long flowering spikes usually appear in spring atop the previous year's stems. 'Antonow's Blue' is a selection with distinctly silvery blue foliage. Two other species you might find are *M. comosus* and *M. villosus*; they look similar to *M. major* but tend to be more compact. Any of these is guaranteed to be an attention-grabber in a container planting or in a mixed border. Even where they're not hardy, melianthus grow quickly enough to make a good show in just one season.

**GROWING TIPS:** Honey bush grows best in full sun to light shade with rich, evenly moist but well-drained soil, but it will adapt to less-than-ideal conditions. In mild climates, the foliage usually looks good year-round, but if it gets winter-damaged, feel free to cut back the stems to about 6 inches in spring. In the cooler parts of its hardiness range, the top growth often dies back completely, but the plant will usually resprout from the roots, so trim off all the dead growth in spring. In either case, the plant won't flower that year, but it will produce plenty of good-looking new growth, and it will be shorter, too (typically in the 4- to 6-foot-tall range). In marginal areas, setting the crown a few inches deeper than usual at planting time will increase the chance that your plant will resprout if the top growth is winter-killed. *Caution:* Handling honey bush may irritate sensitive skin, so wear gloves and long sleeves when you do the yearly pruning.

**ALTERNATIVES:** Plume poppies (*Macleaya cordata* and *M. micro-carpa*) are another excellent option for bold foliage on a grand scale — if you don't mind its tendency to spread far and wide. Stout, pale stems reach 6 to 8 feet tall by mid-summer, with large, lobed leaves that are gray-green on top and grayish white underneath. Full sun to partial shade; average to moist but well-drained soil. Zones 3 to 10.

*Melianthus major*

*Rudbeckia maxima*

## RUDBECKIA
*Coneflower, black-eyed Susan*

**Height: 1–2 feet (leaves only)**
**Leaf size: 12–18 inches long;**
**4–6 inches wide**
**Full sun**
**Zones 4 or 5–9**

In a genus best known for its bright blooms, giant coneflower (*Rudbeckia maxima*) is definitely out of the ordinary. But it's more than just a curiosity: it's a stunning perennial in its own right, even if it never flowers!

Giant coneflower grows in broad, spreading clumps of roughly oval, blue-gray leaves that look great all through the growing season. During the summer (early in the South; mid- to late in the North), the plants go into flowering mode, sending up 6- to 7-foot-tall stems topped with blooms to about 3 inches across. Each flower is composed of a dark, raised center cone surrounded by a ring of drooping yellow "petals." Even after the yellow parts drop, the seedheads remain attractive into winter (or until demolished by hungry birds).

The most difficult part of growing giant coneflower is figuring out how to use it. Its overall height makes it best suited to the back of a border, but then you see very little of the foliage. Try it in a narrow bed along a fence or around a post; another option is to place it near the front or middle of a border and clip off the flowering stems to have just the foliage effect.

**GROWING TIPS:** Full sun is best. As you might guess from another of this plant's common names, swamp sunflower, it enjoys evenly moist but well-drained soil. Established clumps will tolerate a fair bit of drought.

**ALTERNATIVES:** For an annual option, consider some of the beautiful gray- to blue-leaved kales (*Brassica oleracea*). Those sold as 'Red Russian', 'Russian Red', and 'Ragged Jack' have broad, deeply lobed, gray-green leaves with pinkish purple veining. 'Nero di Toscana'

(also known as 'Lacinato' and dinosaur kale) has narrow, deeply veined leaves. Sow indoors or outdoors in mid-spring or mid- to late summer. Full sun to light shade; average, well-drained soil.

## VERBASCUM
*Mullein*

**Height: 1–2 feet (foliage only)**
**Leaf size: 8–12 inches long;**
**    4–6 inches wide**
**Full sun**
**Zones 4 or 5–8**

Mulleins (*Verbascum*) provide two distinctly different effects from just a single plant. In their

first year, they produce low but wide rosettes of broad, felted foliage that can be anything from grayish green to strongly silver. In their second summer, the rosettes send up a stout, upright stalk topped with small but abundant single blooms that are usually bright yellow. It's a bit challenging to find a site where you can admire both the foliage and the flower spikes. The foliage usually shows off best near the front of the border, but the tall flower spikes may look out of place there. A mid-border position is a good compromise.

Common mullein (*V. thapsus*) produces nice-looking rosettes of grayish green leaves and 5- to 10-foot-tall flower spikes. *Note:* This species is considered invasive in some areas, and it can self-sow enthusiastically in the garden; still, you might choose to enjoy it as a foliage plant and keep the flower stalks clipped off. Greek or Olympic mullein (*V. olympicum*) has silvery gray foliage and is about 6 feet tall in bloom. Turkish or silver mullein (*V. bombyciferum*) is even more beautiful from a foliage standpoint, with stunning bright silver leaves and 6- to 8-foot-tall flower stems. You'll often find the seeds sold under the names 'Polar Summer', 'Polarsommer', and 'Arctic Summer'; 'Silver Lining' is said to have even more silvery foliage. These species and seed strains all have yellow blossoms.

There are also a number of mullein hybrids that are clad in

gray-green leaves with a wider range of heights and flower colors. 'Jackie', for instance, has pale peach flowers and is only 12 to 18 inches tall in bloom; 'Helen Johnson' usually reaches 3 to 4 feet tall in flower, with peachy pink-to-orange blossoms. Four-foot-tall 'Caribbean Crush' has yellow, peach, and pink flowers on the same spike. These and other short-lived perennial hybrids tend to be slightly less hardy than the species (usually Zones 5 to 8). Their more compact height makes it easier to blend them into beds and borders. As a bonus, they usually don't set seed, so they bloom over a much longer period, and you won't have to worry about unwanted seedlings.

**GROWING TIPS:** A site with full sun and average to dry soil suits mulleins. Good drainage is critical, especially in winter. Removing the flower spikes as soon as most of the blossoms fade prevents self-sowing and also encourages the plants to return the following year.

**ALTERNATIVE:** Silver sage (*Salvia argentea*) is another beautiful biennial or short-lived perennial for silvery foliage, with dense rosettes of hairy, wavy-edged, 6- to 8-inch-long leaves that are silvery white throughout their first growing season. In the second year, the leaves are more of a pale grayish green. Prone to rot in hot, humid conditions and in wet areas, especially in winter. Full sun; average, well-drained soil. Zones 5 to 10.

*Verbascum thapsus*

# AQUILEGIA
*Columbine*

**Height:** Varies
**Leaf size:** ½–1½ inches long and
  wide (individual leaflets)
**Partial shade**
**Zones 3–8**

When columbines (*Aquilegia*) come up in conversation, you'll usually hear all about their beautiful late-spring to early-summer flowers, but that's not all these perennials have to recommend them. Their foliage is around for the entire growing season, so why not look at the leaves as well as the flowers when you choose your columbines? Most have compound leaves with leaflets that are light green, but there are some with blue-green or gray-green foliage that makes a pleasing accent for both color and texture. You're best off buying

*Aquilegia* 'Nana Alba'

the plants in person, if possible, because catalog descriptions seldom mention the foliage color, and it may vary even within a single seed strain. One species that's fairly dependable for blue-green to gray-blue leaves is fan columbine (*A. flabellata;* also sold as *A. akitensis*). Its dense foliage clumps are anywhere from 4 to 12 inches tall, with pale to deep blue-and-white flowers on stems 6 to 18 inches tall. *A. flabellata* var. *pumila* ('Nana') is reliably compact (6 to 9 inches in bloom). Some other 6- to 9-inch-tall selections are 'Blue Angel', with deep blue-and-white flowers; 'Ministar', with lighter blue-and-white blooms; and 'Nana Alba', with all-white flowers. Chocolate columbine (*A. viridiflora*) is another species that usually produces lacy, blue-green leaves, along with its distinctive purple-brown-and-yellow-green blooms to about 1 foot tall.

**GROWING TIPS:** Columbines thrive in light shade with average to moist but well-drained soil. They can tolerate dry shade but won't look as lush. If you snip off the faded flowers, the plants may rebloom. It's a good idea to let a few seeds form, though, because the plants tend to be short-lived, and allowing a little self-sowing will ensure that you have some replacements on hand. (Pull out any with foliage that is more greenish than blue.) Tiny insects called leaf miners often attack the foliage, chewing tunnels just below the surface. If you notice

this problem, or if the leaves look a little tattered after bloom, cut back the whole plant to the crown. A fresh set of leaves usually appears within a few weeks, although sometimes it may wait until fall or even the following spring to resprout.

**ALTERNATIVES:** *Oxalis triangularis* (commonly called shamrock or oxalis and also sold as *O. depressa* and *O. regnellii*) produces a very similar foliage effect, with 6- to 12-inch-tall clumps of three-part leaves with triangular leaflets. 'Fanny' has light to medium green leaflets centered with silver-gray; 'Dorothy Chao' and 'Charmed Jade' are solid gray-green. Full sun to partial shade; average to moist but well-drained soil. Zones 7 or 8 to 10.

# ARABIS
*Wall rock cress*

**Height:** 4–6 inches
**Leaf size:** 1 inch long;
  ½ inch wide
**Full sun**
**Zones 3–7**

If you're looking to carpet the ground with grayish foliage, wall rock cress (*Arabis alpina* var. *caucasica;* also known as *A. caucasica* and *A. albida*) is a great easy-care plant. It grows in low but wide mounds of toothed, felted, gray-green leaves that are handsome all year long. In early spring, you'll enjoy the abundance of sweetly scented, four-petaled white flowers that usually reach 8 to 12 inches tall. 'Flore Pleno' (also sold as 'Flore

*Arabis alpina* subsp. *caucasica*

Plena' or simply 'Plena') has double flowers that don't set seed, so their spring show lasts several weeks longer. For a more compact plant, look for 'Snowcap', with single white flowers to about 6 inches tall. Plants sold as 'Rosea' and 'La Fraîcheur' (the latter is often listed under *A. × arendsii*) have pink flowers. Any of these are excellent as a ground cover (especially on slopes); they also work well for edging paths, beds, and borders.

**GROWING TIPS:** Wall rock cress thrives with full sun and average, well-drained soil; it will tolerate light shade, too, especially in the warmer parts of its hardiness range. The plants perform best in relatively cool, dry areas; the combination of heat and humidity is usually fatal. Once the blooms fade, shear back the plants by about half to remove the spent flowers and encourage fresh, dense growth.

MEDIUM

**ALTERNATIVE:** The upright, branching stems of Pacific or silver-and-gold chrysanthemum (*Ajania pacifica*; also known as *Chrysanthemum pacificum* and *Dendranthema pacifica*) carry shallowly lobed leaves that are gray-green with a silver rim on top and solid silver underneath. The 1- to 2-foot-tall mounds spread by short rhizomes. Full sun (or morning sun and light afternoon shade in hot-summer areas); average, well-drained to dry soil. Zones 5 to 9.

## ASARUM
*Wild ginger*

**Height: Varies**
**Leaf size: Varies**
**Partial to full shade**
**Zones vary**

Whether you grow them as accents, as ground covers, or in containers, wild gingers (*Asarum*

*Asarum splendens*

or *Hexastylis*) are made for the shade. Their leathery, rounded to heart-shaped leaves are often solid green, but there are also a number of species and selections that are spotted or mottled with various amounts of silver, adding texture and color through most, if not all, of the year. Wild gingers usually spread slowly but steadily by rhizomes, forming eye-catching carpets. They produce flowers, too, but the blooms are normally hidden by the foliage and typically a brownish or deep purple, so most of the species are prized primarily for their foliage.

Options for silver- and gray-marked wild gingers abound. Some are vegetatively propagated named selections, so their markings are consistent from plant to plant. Seed-grown plants vary in their patterns and colors; buy them from a local source, if possible, so you can choose those you find most appealing. Six- to 8-inch-tall, mottled wild ginger (*A. shuttleworthii* or *H. shuttleworthii*) is one of the most readily available of the silver-marbled wild gingers. Its glossy leaves are usually 3 to 4 inches long and wide but may be larger. 'Callaway' is more compact (3 to 4 inches tall), with particularly striking silver mottling. Silver-marked *A. naniflorum* (*H. naniflora*) 'Eco Decor' and *A. takaoi* 'Galaxy' have even smaller leaves and are barely 3 inches tall. Zones 5 or 6 to 9. For a larger ginger, consider Chinese wild ginger (*A. splendens* or *H. splendens*), with broadly

heart-shaped to arrowhead-shaped, silver-marbled leaves that are 6 to 8 inches tall (usually Zones 6 to 9). Alabama wild ginger (*A. speciosum* or *H. speciosa*) is even larger — typically 8 to 12 inches tall — and hardy in Zones 5 to 9; 'Woodlanders Select' and extra-large-leaved 'Buxom Beauty' are two selections with exceptionally good patterning. Specialty nurseries offer many other lovely silvery species and selections in a range of leaf sizes, patterns, and hardiness ranges.

**GROWING TIPS:** Wild gingers thrive in partial to full shade with acidic, humus-rich, evenly moist but well-drained soil. Water new plantings regularly for the first year or two; after that, they rarely need any special care.

**ALTERNATIVE:** Ivy-leaved cyclamen (*Cyclamen hederifolium*; also known as *C. neapolitanum*) sends up its solid green or gray- to silver-mottled leaves in mid-fall; they look good in winter and spring, then disappear by midsummer; 4 to 6 inches tall. Partial to full shade; light, humus-rich soil that's on the dry side in summer and moist but well-drained while the leaves are present. Zones 5 to 8 or 9.

## BRACHYGLOTTIS
*Brachyglottis, senecio*

**Height: 2 to 5 feet**
**Leaf size: 2–3 inches long;**
  **1–2 inches wide**
**Full sun**
**Zones 8 or 9–10**

The name *Brachyglottis* may not roll trippingly off the tongue,

but if you're a fan of silvery foliage, it's a name you need to know. These furry-foliaged tender shrubs are developing a devoted following in the Pacific Northwest, and they're starting to show up in cutting-edge container plantings elsewhere too. The one you're most likely to find travels under several names, including *B.* Dunedin Group 'Sunshine', *Senecio* 'Sunshine', and *S. greyi*. This "ever-silver" shrub grows in somewhat sprawling mounds that will reach 3 to 5 feet tall and 5 to 6 feet wide, although you can easily keep it smaller with pruning. As the silver-gray new growth matures, the stems and leaf undersides keep their fuzzy white felt, while the tops of the oval to oblong leaves turn grayish green and finally deep green. Loose clusters of small, bright yellow daisies bloom in early to midsummer; some gardeners enjoy them but others remove them in favor of the foliage. *B. compacta* (*S. compactus*) looks similar, as does *B. monroi* (*S. monroi*), although the latter is distinctive for its wavy leaf edges. Hybrid Walberton's Silver Dormouse ('Walbrach'; also sold as 'Silver Dormouse') tends to have a denser, less sprawling habit with slightly larger, more silvery new foliage.

**GROWING TIPS:** A site with full sun and average, well-drained soil is ideal. These plants are particularly suited to growing in coastal areas, because they can withstand strong winds and salt

*Brachyglottis* 'Sunshine'

spray, but they will grow elsewhere too. To keep the plants from sprawling open and dying out in the center, cut them back to 6 to 12 inches in mid-spring. (This hard pruning usually prevents them from flowering that year.) Shearing the plants lightly before or just after bloom also helps maintain their mounded form and controls their size.

**ALTERNATIVE:** Jerusalem sage (*Phlomis fruticosa*) has lance-shaped, grayish green leaves that curl upward along the edges to reveal the white woolly undersides; about 2 feet tall in leaf. The spreading clumps keep their grayish foliage through the winter in Zones 8 and 9; in Zones 4 to 7, they die back to the ground each winter. Full sun to light shade; average to dry soil with excellent drainage (especially in winter).

## BUDDLEIA
### Butterfly bush

**Height:** Varies
**Leaf size:** 3–5 inches long;
   1–2 inches wide
**Full sun**
**Zones vary**

Butterfly bushes (*Buddleia* or *Buddleja*) are best known for their abundance of colorful and fragrant flowers, so it's not surprising that you don't hear much about their foliage. Quite a few of them, though, have narrow, silvery to gray-green leaves that make a particularly beautiful backdrop for the purplish, pinkish, or white blooms. Silver fountain butterfly bush (*B. alternifolia* 'Argentea'), for example, has especially silvery, 3-inch-long foliage on slender, arching stems. It blooms in mid- to late spring on the previous year's shoots, with rounded clusters of tiny purple flowers. The plants usually grow 10 to 12 feet tall. Zones 4 or 5 to 9. *B. nivea* subsp. *yunnanensis* is less hardy (Zones 6 or 7 to 9), but it's even showier for foliage interest, with leaves that can be up to 1 foot long. The tops of the older leaves are usually deep green, but the white woolly undersides, young shoots, and flower buds give the plant an overall grayish appearance. Long, slender clusters of small, pale purple blooms show up in late summer to early fall. The plants can easily reach 10 or more feet tall and wide in one season, even if pruned in spring.

Among the more common summer-to-fall-flowering butterfly bushes (including *B. davidii, B. fallowiana,* and various hybrids), there are a number of selections with distinctly grayish green foliage. 'Attraction', for instance, has reddish purple flowers, while 'Lochinch' is purple-blue and 'Ellen's Blue' is light blue; they can grow 6 to 8 feet tall. If you'd prefer something a bit more compact (in the 3- to 5-foot-tall range), consider white-flowered 'Silver Frost' or 'White Ball', clear pink 'Pink Delight', purple-blue 'Dwarf Indigo', and violet-purple 'Nanho Purple'. The leaves of all of these are typically 5 to 8 inches long and 1 to 3 inches across. *Note:* Although these and other cultivars add a long season of foliage and flower color to the garden, butterfly bushes are considered invasive in some areas.

**GROWING TIPS:** A site with full sun and average, well-drained soil is ideal for butterfly bushes. In the cooler parts of their hardiness range, most of them die back to the ground by spring; elsewhere, cut back the stems to about 1 foot in early spring to keep the plants more compact, bushy, and free-flowering. Remember that *B. alternifolia* flowers on older stems, so don't prune it until just after the blooms fade, and trim just enough to maintain its elegant arching form. Regular, thorough deadheading prevents self-sowing and encourages rebloom on the summer-flowering kinds.

**ALTERNATIVE:** Need something shorter? Hummingbird bush (*Dicliptera suberecta*; also listed as *Jacobina suberecta* or *Justicia suberecta*) grows in bushy, upright clumps about 2 feet tall, with small, rounded leaves densely covered with silvery gray hairs. Frequent pinching encourages the plants to stay in low, dense mounds. A great accent for both borders and containers. Full sun to partial shade; average, well-drained soil. Zones 7 or 8 to 10.

*Buddleia* 'Lochinch'

*Eucalyptus cinerea*

## EUCALYPTUS
*Eucalyptus*

**Height:** Varies
**Leaf size:** Usually 1–2 inches long
    and wide (juvenile leaves)
**Full sun**
**Zones vary**

Unless you live in a mild coastal climate, you may never have considered growing eucalyptus (*Eucalyptus*) in your garden. But there are many hundreds of species, and some of them are surprisingly hardy, even as far north as Zones 5 and 6. In warmer areas, eucalyptus usually grow into large trees that are prized for their beautiful, smooth bark as much as for their aromatic foliage. Cold winter temperatures can kill the shoot tips or all of the aboveground growth, but the very hardiest species will resprout from their roots, so they act essentially like perennials. Besides keeping the plants much more compact — a bushy 6 to 9 feet tall, rather than a towering 50 feet or more — this promotes the vigorous "juvenile" growth that most of us associate with eucalyptus. (These juvenile leaves tend to be rounded and held in opposite pairs, and they are typically silvery gray, gray-green, or blue-green. "Adult" leaves are usually longer, narrower, and greenish, and they're held alternately along the stems.) Even where eucalyptus don't die back to the ground, cut them back hard every year or two to maintain this fresh, colorful growth.

To improve the odds of eucalyptus overwintering north of Zone 8, start with the hardiest species, and, if possible, buy plants propagated from trees that have overwintered in your area or an even colder climate. One of the best-known species is silver dollar tree or Argyle apple (*E. cinerea*), with oval to heart-shaped, silvery gray juvenile leaves on white stems. Cider gum (*E. gunnii*) is also quite root-hardy; its oval to rounded juvenile foliage is blue-gray to grayish green. Other particularly hardy species are alpine cider gum (*E. archeri*), with rounded, gray-green juvenile leaves; alpine snow gum (*E. pauciflora* subsp. *nipophila* or *E. nipophila*), with oval, silvery to grayish green juvenile foliage; and New England peppermint (*E. nova-anglica*), with roughly triangular, blue-green juvenile leaves. Specialty nurseries offer many other options. As northern gardeners become more adventurous about trying eucalyptus, these species are likely to become more readily available, but their striking colors and textures will keep them from ever being ordinary! *Note:* Other species of eucalyptus are considered invasive in some areas, so check lists of local problem species before planting any eucalyptus.

**GROWING TIPS:** Eucalyptus grow best in full sun and average, well-drained soil. Choose their planting site carefully, as they often don't recover well from transplanting. Spring planting increases the likelihood that the plants will overwinter in cooler areas. If the ground isn't dependably covered by snow through the winter, protect the roots with a thick mulch, particularly for the first few years. To enjoy eucalyptus as cut-back shrubs in areas where the top growth isn't winter-killed, let the plants grow undisturbed for two or three years, then prune them to a foot or two above the ground in spring.

**ALTERNATIVE:** Blue honeywort (*Cerinthe major* 'Purpurascens') also offers beautiful blue-tinged foliage, and you can grow it anywhere — as a perennial in mild areas and as an annual everywhere else. Spoon-shaped to oval, cream-dotted, gray-green to blue-green leaves grow on upright to somewhat sprawling stems; 2 to 4 feet tall. Oblong, leaf-like bracts at the shoot tips are an intense purple-blue. Full sun to light shade; humus-rich, moist but well-drained soil.

## EUPHORBIA
*Euphorbia, spurge*

**Height:** Varies
**Leaf size:** Varies
**Full sun**
**Zones vary**

With a genus as large and diverse as *Euphorbia*, it's hardly surprising to find species and selections with a variety of foliage colors. Its blue-leaved options are particularly attractive, and they come in a range of heights and habits to fit into a wide array of eye-catching combinations. Along with their "ever-blue" foliage, euphorbias produce blooms: typically insignificant true flowers surrounded by much showier, bright yellow to yellow-green, petal-like bracts that are especially striking against the icy blue leaves.

Myrtle euphorbia or donkey-tail spurge (*E. myrsinites*) looks as if it belongs in a desert setting, but it's hardy enough to add a touch of the Southwest to beds and borders in many parts of the country. It grows in 4- to 6-inch-tall clumps of trailing stems up to 12 inches long, with closely packed, pointed-oval, gray-blue foliage that's usually 2 to 4 inches long and 1 to 2 inches wide. In late winter, the stem tips turn upward, then produce rounded bloom clusters that are showy through the spring. Myrtle euphorbia makes an interesting ground cover or front-of-the-border plant but shows off best on a slope or atop a low wall. In mild areas, it looks great year-round; in the colder parts of its range, the foliage tends to shrivel if it is not protected by snow cover. Zones 5 to 9. *Note:* This species is considered invasive in some areas, particularly in the western states. *E. rigida* looks similar but tends to be more upright (1 to 2 feet tall), although it, too, gradually sprawls to cover a space up to 3 feet across. Its gray-green to blue-green foliage often takes on a reddish purple tinge from fall to spring. Zones 7 or 8 to 11.

If you prefer plants that form bushier mounds, check out the hybrid *E.* 'Blue Haze'. It's usually 1 to 2 feet tall, with reddish stems that are quite upright in spring and slightly more sprawling as the summer progresses. The very narrow, 2-inch-long leaves are powder blue through most of the growing season, often taking on a pinkish tint in the colder months. Flowers typically appear in mid-summer but may be earlier or later. Zones 5 or 6 to 9. *E.* 'Blue

Lagoon' is another beauty, with slightly longer and wider, blue-green foliage that's reddish when new and held in dense whorls around the upright stems. The plants reach about 2 feet when the frothy flower clusters appear in late spring; they last well into summer. Zones 6 or 7 to 10. *E. nicaeensis* isn't quite as densely leafy, but it's rather quite attractive, with blue-green foliage, pinkish stems, and abundant summer flowers in rounded, 2-foot-tall mounds. Zones 5 or 6 to 9.

Shrubby Mediterranean spurge (*E. characias*) and its various subspecies and selections are also fantastic foliage plants, forming rounded, 3- to 4-foot-tall mounds of upright, unbranched stems bearing narrow gray-green to bluish green, 4- to 5-inch-long leaves. In spring, second-year stems are topped with large, cylindrical flower clusters, adding another 6 to 12 inches to the overall height. Gray-green 'Portuguese Velvet' is about half the size of the species (18 to 24 inches); there are many other cultivars as well. *Note:* These spurges can self-sow prolifically if you don't deadhead them and may be considered invasive in some areas. Zones 7 to 10.

**GROWING TIPS:** Blue-leaved euphorbias grow in full sun or light shade with average to dry, well-drained soil. It's a good idea to deadhead your euphorbias to prevent self-sowing. *Caution:* Wear gloves when working with

the plants to protect your skin from the irritating sap, and be especially careful not to get it in your eyes.

**ALTERNATIVE:** For a medium-sized perennial that suits moist sites, check out *Persicaria microcephala* 'Silver Dragon'. Its bushy clumps of reddish stems carry pointed leaves that are reddish when new, quickly turning silvery green. Typically 3 to 4 feet tall but may reach 5 to 6 feet in ideal conditions. Full sun to partial shade; average to moist but well-drained soil. Usually Zones 6 to 9; may survive in colder areas.

*Euphorbia myrsinites*

## FOTHERGILLA
*Fothergilla, witch alder*

**Height: Varies**
**Leaf size: 2–3 inches long and wide**
**Full sun to full shade**
**Zones 5–8**

Gardeners with shady yards don't have many options for blue-leaved shrubs, but there are a few — including some lovely selections of fothergilla (*Fothergilla*). These dense, bushy, deciduous shrubs tend to be fairly compact, so it's easy to work them into woodland gardens and mixed borders for multi-season interest. Short, brushy clusters of small,

*Fothergilla gardenii* 'Blue Shadow'

white, fragrant flowers bloom at the stem tips in spring. The foliage is typically bluish green in summer, usually turning shades of yellow, orange, red, and/or purple in autumn. The classic cultivar *F. gardenii* 'Blue Mist' has bright silvery blue to blue-gray summer leaves and orange to yellow fall color on plants 2 to 4 feet tall and about as wide. (It can also spread by suckers to form broader patches over time.) 'Blue Shadow' is a sport from the larger-growing, green-leaved 'Mount Airy', which is classified either as a hybrid between *F. gardenii* and *F. major* or as a selection of *F. major*. It has distinctly blue-green foliage on plants 5 to 6 feet tall and about 5 feet wide. Its fall color is often more vibrant than that of 'Blue Mist'.

**GROWING TIPS:** Fothergillas are commonly associated with partly shaded areas, but they'll grow in full sun or full shade too. (They usually bloom best and produce the brightest fall colors in sun; on the downside, their summer foliage may look greenish without some shade.) Humus-rich, acidic, evenly moist but well-drained soil is ideal; fothergillas in shadier sites typically tolerate average to dry conditions.

**ALTERNATIVES:** 'Blue Velvet' blueleaf honeysuckle (*Lonicera korolkowii* var. *floribunda*) has an open, spreading form with small, oval to rounded, blue-gray leaves; 10 to 12 feet tall. Full sun to partial shade; average, well-drained soil.

Zones 3 to 7. 'Blue Velvet' honey-berry or sweetberry, usually listed under *L. caerulea* var. *edulis*, *L. kamchatika*, or *L. kamtschatica*, has grayish green foliage; about 4 feet tall. Partial shade; moist but well-drained soil. Zones 2 or 3 to 7.

## HEUCHERA
*Heuchera, coral bells, alumroot*

**Height: 8–12 inches**
**Leaf size: 4–5 inches long and wide**
**Full sun to partial shade**
**Zones 3 or 4–8**

Silver-marked heucheras (*Heuchera*) sure don't get the same attention as the purple, yellow, and multicolored heucheras do, even though they make equally great garden plants. Perhaps it's because silvery to grayish foliage isn't all that unusual in some species. American alumroot (*H. americana*), for instance, shows varying amounts of grayish to silvery shading on its leaves. Sharp-eyed breeders have taken these subtle beginnings and turned them into some spectacular selections, and more appear on the market each year, so it's not possible to give more than a sampling of them here.

If you're looking for only foliage interest, plant cultivars that have not-especially-showy blooms, then clip off the flower spikes as soon as they appear. *H. americana* 'Dale's Strain' (also sold as 'Silver Selection') is a seed strain that produces smooth, gray-green leaves that are lightly shaded

*Heuchera* 'Raspberry Ice'

with silver. *H.* 'Eco-Magnififolia' leaves are light gray with light green edges and purple veining when new, aging to deep green with some silvery gray marbling; 'Eco-Improved' is even brighter silver. 'Mint Frost' is bright silver with darker gray-green veining, while 'Pewter Veil' and 'Silver Scrolls' have purplish foliage that's heavily silvered between the veins on the upper side.

Interested in flowers as well as foliage? Several hybrids produce an abundance of small, bell-shaped blooms in spikelike clusters usually 18 to 24 inches tall, as well as showy leaves. 'Venus' has large silvery leaves veined with purple-gray to gray-green, plus white flowers. 'Gypsy Dancer' foliage is pinkish when new, aging to silver with grayish purple veining and an overall purplish appearance; the flowers are light pink. 'Raspberry Ice' is silvery green with darker green to purple veining. And then there's 'Strawberry Candy', with medium green leaves marbled with silver-gray and accented with larger-than-usual, bright reddish pink flowers.

**GROWING TIPS:** Silvery-leaved heucheras will grow in full sun or partial shade with average to moist but well-drained soil. Remove the flowers after they fade to tidy the plants and possibly promote rebloom. Clip off any damaged leaves as needed.

**ALTERNATIVES:** The heuchera relative known as foamy bells (× *Heucherella*) also offers some silver-marked selections, including 'Quicksilver' (with purplish leaves that are marked with silver between the veins) and 'Silver Streak' (deep purple foliage shaded with silver-gray); both are about 6 inches tall in leaf. In hot-summer areas, foamy bells may die back during the warmest months. 'Forest Frost' fringe cups (*Tellima grandiflora*) also looks much like a heuchera in leaf, with dense clumps of silver-shaded green leaves that darken to purple-green in winter. Great for woodland gardens. Partial shade; average to moist but well-drained soil. Zones 4 to 8.

## LYCHNIS
*Campion*

**Height: Varies**
**Leaf size: 4–6 inches long;**
    **1–2 inches wide**
**Full sun**
**Zones 4–8**

Colorful campions (*Lychnis*) have long been favorites for cottage gardens for their tendency to seed around and pop up in unlikely places, but they're also useful fillers for perennial beds and borders. Rose campion (*L. coronaria*) grows in rosettes of hairy, silvery gray leaves that look great all through the growing season, with the bonus of 2- to 3-foot-tall, branching flower stems topped with flat-faced, vibrant magenta flowers mostly in late spring or early summer to midsummer. *L.* × *walkeri* 'Abbotswood Rose' is a slightly less intense magenta and is usually somewhat shorter (to about 2 feet). If you prefer softer colors, consider plants or seeds sold as *L. coronaria* 'Angel's Blush' or Oculata Group (their blooms are white with a pink center) and 'Alba' (pure white). *L. coronaria* 'Dancing Ladies' is a seed strain that includes an array of colors (white, white-and-pink, bright pink, and even near-red). *L. coronaria* 'Gardeners' World' is distinctive for its deep pinkish red double blooms. It doesn't set seed, so it blooms much longer into the summer, and it doesn't produce any unwanted seedlings. Flower-of-Jove (*L. flos-jovis*) isn't

quite as silvery as rose campion; instead, it's more of a light grayish green that's a perfect complement to the rosy pink summer flowers. The species can grow up to 2 feet tall in bloom; 'Peggy' is only 10 to 12 inches tall.

**GROWING TIPS:** Campions thrive in full sun and average to moist but well-drained soil; light shade is fine, too, especially in the afternoon in the warmer parts of their hardiness range. It's usually best to cut off the flowering stems when the blooms have faded to minimize self-sowing. Allow a few seeds to form, though; the

clumps may be short-lived, so it's good to have some replacement plants coming along to carry on when older plants die out.

**ALTERNATIVES:** Pearly everlastings (*Anaphalis*) produce spreading clumps of upright, branching stems with felted gray-green leaves. *A. margaritacea* grows anywhere from 1 to 3 feet tall with narrow leaves; it's an aggressive spreader in ideal conditions. *A. triplinervis* is usually much more restrained, with broader foliage on 12- to 18-inch-tall stems. Best in relatively cool, dry regions. Full sun to light shade; dry to moist but well-drained soil. Zones 3 to 8.

*Lychnis coronaria*

Lysimachia atropurpurea 'Beaujolais'

## LYSIMACHIA
*Loosestrife*

**Height:** 2–3 feet
**Leaf size:** 4–6 inches long;
   2–3 inches wide
**Full sun**
**Zones vary**

Loosestrifes (*Lysimachia*) include some splendid foliage plants, but many gardeners hesitate to plant them because of their reputation for being aggressive spreaders. That's certainly a concern with some species; however, those with blue or gray foliage tend to be much more restrained clump-formers. They aren't exactly common, but it's worth hunting for them or growing them from seed to enjoy them in your garden. One that isn't too difficult to find is *L. ephemerum,* with dense basal clumps of lance-shaped, blue-gray to blue-green foliage and upright stems topped with narrow, spikelike clusters of small, milky white flowers through the summer. It can be a little tricky to please this perennial: it dislikes hot, dry conditions but doesn't seem especially cold-tolerant, either. It's usually rated for Zones 6 or 7 to 8 or 9.

   *L. atropurpurea* (not to be confused with the purple-leaved *L. ciliata* 'Atropurpurea') is an even better-kept secret. It's usually biennial but may be a short-lived perennial. The leafy basal clumps are light gray to gray-green; the narrower, wavy-edged stem leaves tend to be even brighter gray. Throughout the summer, arching to upright spikes of deep purple buds open to purple-red, blackberry-scented flowers. You'll occasionally see plants or seeds sold under the cultivar names 'Beaujolais' and 'Geronimo', but they don't seem to be significantly different from the species. Zones 3 or 4 to 9. *L. minoricensis* and *L. lichiangensis* have gray-green leaves that are veined with silvery gray. Their pink-stemmed flower spikes tend to be shorter than those of the other species

(usually 12 to 18 inches tall), with creamy white to pinkish flowers that aren't especially showy. You may decide to snip off the flower stems to enjoy these just as foliage plants, but consider letting one or two stems flower and set seed so the plants can self-sow lightly. They're usually hardy in Zones 7 to 9; in cooler climates, grow them as annuals.

**GROWING TIPS:** These loosestrifes thrive in full sun to light shade with average to evenly moist but well-drained soil. Snipping off the spent flower spikes will extend the bloom season.

**ALTERNATIVES:** Silver speedwell (*Veronica spicata* subsp. *incana* or *V. incana*) forms 6-inch-tall carpets of silver-haired, oblong leaves that look good from spring well into winter. Cultivars vary in flower height and color: some to look for include 'Minuet', 'Saraband', 'Silbersee', 'Silver Carpet', 'Silver Slippers', and 'Wendy'. Full sun with average to dry soil; good drainage is critical, especially in winter. Zones 4 to 7 (or Zone 9 where summers aren't especially humid).

## MARRUBIUM
*Horehound*

**Height:** Varies
**Leaf size:** 1–2 inches long;
   1 inch wide
**Full sun**
**Zones vary**

Horehounds (*Marrubium*) are well-known to herb gardeners, but they're also interesting additions to ornamental plantings. There are many silvery to grayish species, but only a few seem to be available. White or common horehound (*M. vulgare*) is one option, growing in creeping clumps of upright, 1- to 3-foot-tall, silky white stems clad in rounded to oval, deeply veined leaves that are grayish green on top and woolly white underneath. Tiny white flowers bloom in clusters along the upper parts of the stems in summer, but they aren't especially showy. Zones 3 to 10. White horehound is easy to find, but it's not one of the showiest species. It also self-sows abundantly in the garden and is

*Marrubium vulgare*

considered invasive in some areas. If you'd like to use it simply as a short-term filler, grow it from seed and pull out the plants before the following spring (they generally don't flower until the second year). Or track down some of the other species, such as silver horehound (*M. incanum*; also known as *M. candidissimum*); its oval to oblong leaves are gray-green on top and heavily felted with white underneath, on white-haired, 18- to 24-inch-tall stems with near white flowers in early summer. Zones 3 to 10. Or consider silver-edged horehound (*M. rotundifolium*), which grows in 6- to 10-inch-tall mounds of felted green leaves that are rimmed and backed with silvery white hairs. Zones 5 to 9.

**GROWING TIPS:** Horehounds grow best in full sun to light shade with lean, average, well-drained to dry soil. Shearing off the flowering tips helps keep the clumps dense and bushy and prevents self-sowing.

**ALTERNATIVES:** Dittany-of-Crete (*Origanum dictamnus*) grows in 6- to 10-inch-tall mounds of slender, arching stems clad in rounded, white-felted foliage. Zones 7 or 8 to 11; protection from winter wet is essential. False dittany (*Ballota pseudodictamnus*) is upright, with 18- to 24-inch, furry white stems and rounded, silvery gray new leaves that age to grayish green. Zones 6 to 9. Both perform best in dry climates. Full sun; average, well-drained to dry soil.

*Plectranthus* 'Silver Shield'

## PLECTRANTHUS
*Plectranthus, spurflower*

**Height: Usually 1–2 feet**
**Leaf size: Varies**
**Full sun to full shade**
**Zones 10 and 11**

In borders or in containers, the foliage of plectranthus (*Plectranthus*) adds color and texture to combinations throughout the growing season. Silver plectranthus or silver spurflower (*P. argentatus*) is especially useful, because it's one of the few fuzzy-leaved silvers that will thrive in areas with hot and humid summers. This tender perennial grows quickly early in the season but stays relatively compact, producing bushy clumps 2 to 3 feet tall and 4 to 5 feet wide, with pinkish, well-branched stems. The 3- to 5-inch-long, 3-inch-wide, scalloped-edged oval leaves are silvery white when new, aging to silvery

green. 'Silver Shield' and 'Longwood Silver' are two particularly silvery selections. Spikes of purple buds open to purplish flowers, appearing mostly in late summer to fall but at other times too. If you'd like silvery foliage on a low, mounded plant instead of an upright one, look for *P.* 'Nicoletta'. It's usually only 6 to 8 inches tall, but its vigorous, trailing stems can spread to cover an area 3 to 4 feet across, so it's great as a ground cover or cascading out of a large planter or hanging basket. Candle plant (*P. oertendahlii*) has a similar size and growth habit, but its smaller leaves are medium to deep green with gray veins on top and purplish underneath. 'Uvongo' has very silvery veining; 'Silver Star' is solid silver-gray on top.

**GROWING TIPS:** These plectranthus grow in full sun in cool

areas; elsewhere, they tend to perform best with morning sun and afternoon shade or light all-day shade. Average, well-drained soil is fine. Pinching or clipping off the stem tips several times during the growing season encourages bushier growth. (Plectranthus cuttings root readily, so you can use those shoot tips to make more plants.)

**ALTERNATIVES:** Velvet leaf (*Kalanchoe beharensis*) typically has triangular, 6- to 12-inch-long, light green leaves covered with fine grayish felt. About 3 feet tall in pots; 10 to 12 feet where hardy. Panda plant (*K. tomentosa*) has 3- to 4-inch-long, gray-green to blue-green leaves covered with whitish fuzz and spotted with rusty brown on the edges; 12 to 18 inches tall. Full sun to partial shade; average, well-drained to dry soil. Zones 10 to 11.

## PULMONARIA
*Pulmonaria, lungwort*

**Height: 8–12 inches**
**Leaf size: 8–12 inches long;**
**    4–5 inches wide**
**Partial to full shade**
**Zones 4–8**

You'll often hear that silvery foliage needs full sun to thrive, and that's usually true, but pulmonarias (*Pulmonaria*) are one wonderful exception to that rule. While their clustered, bell-shaped, blue, pink, or white blooms are a welcome addition to the early-spring garden, it's their handsome mounded forms and long-lasting foliage that make them such a

delight in shady beds and borders. Pulmonarias are best known for their silver leaf spots, which occur naturally in several species, such as the narrow-leaved *P. longifolia* and the broader-leaved *P. saccharata*. These and others have given rise to many dozens of stunning selections and hybrids. 'Bertram Anderson', with deep blue flowers, and 'Roy Davidson', with baby blue flowers, are two classic *P. longifolia* cultivars that are still popular. 'Sissinghurst White', another older cultivar, often attributed to *P. officinalis,* has white flowers over broad, spotted foliage. More-recent hybrids come in an array of silvering patterns

*Pulmonaria* hybrid

and flowers colors. 'Berries and Cream', for example, has heavily silver-mottled, wavy-edged foliage and rosy pink to purplish pink flowers, while 'Victorian Brooch' has distinct silver spotting on its deep green leaves, plus pinkish red blooms. For extreme silvering, consider 'Excalibur', which is mostly solid silver with a narrow, silver-spotted margin, and 'Silver Streamers', with narrow, ruffled-edged leaves that are almost entirely silver.

To be honest, the leaf markings of many pulmonarias look very much alike in a garden setting, so you may want to pay more attention to other traits when selecting them. These woodland plants often don't perform well in hot-summer areas, for instance, so southern gardeners should look for those that have shown better-than-average heat tolerance, such as 'High Contrast', 'Little Blue', and 'Milky Way' (all with pink flowers that turn blue). Another problem to consider is the fungal disease powdery mildew, which produces a dusty gray covering on the leaves and weakens the plants. Along with choosing a planting site with good air circulation and keeping the soil evenly moist, starting with resistant cultivars is an important step in preventing this disease from getting a foothold. Some pulmonarias that have shown good to excellent resistance are narrow-leaved *P. longifolia* subsp. *cevennensis* and hybrid 'Cotton Cool' (both with blue flowers); 'Apple Frost'

and 'Dark Vader' (with both pink to blue flowers); and 'Ice Ballet' (with white flowers). The Gaelic Series is also reported to have excellent mildew resistance.

**GROWING TIPS:** Pulmonarias thrive in partial shade with humus-rich, moist but well-drained soil. Snip off the spent flower clusters to tidy the plants and prevent self-sowing. (The seedlings usually have silver markings, too, but won't be identical to the parents.) If the leaves are damaged or discolored, then cut down the whole plant to just above the ground — and water thoroughly if the ground is dry — to get a flush of fresh new foliage.

**ALTERNATIVES:** Pulmonaria relative *Mertensia sibirica* (*M. pterocarpa*) offers distinctly blue leaves (especially on new growth); usually 18 to 24 inches tall. Plants sold as *P. pterocarpa* var. *yezoensis* are similar but 6 to 12 inches tall. Partial shade; evenly moist but well-drained soil. Zones 3 to 8. For exceptional blue-gray foliage in full-sun sites with excellent drainage, look for plants sold as *M. asiatica, M. maritima,* and *M. simplicissima.* Zones 4 to 8.

---

## ROSA
*Rose*

**Height:** Varies
**Leaf size:** 1–1½ inches long;
   1 inch wide
**Full sun to partial shade**
**Zones vary**

You won't often see roses (*Rosa*) touted as foliage plants; their showy blooms inevitably attract

most of the attention. With a little investigating, though, you can find a number of surprising foliage features on roses. Some have wonderful fragrance, others have a distinctly ferny look, a fascinating "mossy" covering, evergreen interest, or showy fall color — or even beautiful gray to blue foliage throughout the growing season.

Blueleaf rose (*R. glauca;* also known as redleaf rose, or *R. rubrifolia*) is one of the best-known roses for foliage interest. Its new spring growth is richly shaded with red, gradually turning gray-blue to gray-green but usually keeping a pinkish to purplish blush in full-sun sites. Small, single pink flowers appear briefly in late spring or early summer on the previous year's growth, followed by rounded to oblong, orange-red to deep red fruits (called hips) that last through most or all of the winter. The canes are upright at first, then arch under the weight of the ripening hips, creating an overall fountainlike form that is typically 6 to 8 feet tall and wide, although it may reach to 10 feet or more in some areas. Don't be surprised if you find some self-sown seedlings; they usually aren't abundant enough to be a problem, though. Zones 2 to 8.

Alba roses (*R.* × *alba*) are beloved by gardeners for their delicate-looking blooms, great fragrance, and adaptable, easy-care nature. One might say that their only drawbacks are their rather large form and their once-

*Rosa glauca*

blooming habit — but when you're of a mind to admire their blue-green to grayish green foliage, those traits simply mean that you have more leaves to enjoy when the plants aren't in flower. Their foliage isn't as eye-catching as that of blueleaf rose, but it makes a beautiful background for the white or pink, single or double blooms in early summer. (Consider pairing an alba rose with a pink or white hybrid clematis to repeat the effect a little later in the season.) Albas produce long, slender, arching stems that create a fountainlike shrub 6 to 8 feet tall; you can also train them against a wall or arbor or let them scramble up into a tree. This class includes a number of popular "old garden roses," such as 'Alba-semiplena', with semi-double white flowers; 'Céleste' (also known as 'Celestial'), with double, clear pink blooms; and 'Great Maiden's Blush', with very full, light pink flowers. Zones 3 or 4 to 9.

**GROWING TIPS:** Roses are well known as sun-lovers, but these will also tolerate a site that's shaded for part of the day. Average to moist but well-drained soil

is fine. Both blueleaf and alba roses tend to have better-than-average pest and disease resistance and perform nicely with a minimum of fuss. On blueleaf rose, you can prune the whole plant lightly after flowering or cut out a third of the oldest stems right at ground level. Another option is to cut the entire plant to the ground each spring; you'll give up the flowers and fruits, but you'll get a more compact, bushy foliage clump to enjoy. With alba roses, trim lightly after flowering to shape the plants; if you'd like to reduce the size a bit, cut out a quarter to a third of the oldest stems and trim the rest back by about a third.

**ALTERNATIVES:** Dusty zenobia (*Zenobia pulverulenta*) bears toothed, oblong leaves that can range from deep green to blue-green; 'Woodlander's Blue' has particularly bright blue-green leaves. Fall color can be bright shades of yellow to red. This 3- to 6-foot-tall shrub is usually deciduous but may hang on to its leaves well into winter. Full sun to light shade; acidic, average to moist but well-drained soil. Zones 5 to 8.

---

## SALVIA
*Sage, salvia*

**Height:** Varies
**Leaf size:** Varies
**Full sun to partial shade**
**Zones vary**

Medium-textured silvery sages (*Salvia*) are invaluable for adding sparkle to sunny-site combinations. Some produce pretty flowers and some are strongly scented, but it's their waxy or felted leaves that really make them favorites of foliage-appreciating gardeners. Common or culinary sage (*S. officinalis*) is the most readily available option, with 3-inch-long, 1-inch-wide, grayish green leaves that are both fragrant and flavorful. It grows in dense, shrubby clumps that are 2 to 3 feet tall with purple-blue summer flowers. 'Compacta' ('Nana') is about half the size, so it's great for smaller spaces or containers. Zones 4 to 9. 'Berggarten' is distinctly different, with shorter, more oval, bright

silver-gray leaves on 18-inch-tall plants; it's recommended for Zones 5 to 9. Rose sage (*S. pachyphylla*) has the same suggested hardiness range, but it must have excellent drainage to survive in the cooler zones. Even where you can't enjoy the "ever-gray" foliage from year to year, it's worth growing for both the aromatic, gray-white to gray-green leaves and the dense, summer-into-fall spikes of purple-blue flowers surrounded by bright rosy pink bracts. Its rather loose clumps usually reach 2 to 3 feet tall.

There are also some excellent sages among the less hardy species. White sage or bee sage (*S. apiana*), for instance, is 2 to 3 feet tall in leaf and 5 to 6 feet tall when the spikes of white flowers emerge in late spring to early summer. Its slender, very aromatic foliage starts out gray-green and matures to bright gray. As with culinary sage, the white sage cultivar 'Compacta' is half the size of

*Salvia officinalis* 'Berggarten'

the species. Excellent drainage is a must for white sage. Zones 8 to 11. Canary Island sage (S. canariensis) is a larger shrub, growing 8 feet tall and wide, with spikes of purple flowers in summer. Its arrowhead-shaped leaves are light green on top, but their silvery undersides and stems give the whole plant a grayish appearance. Andean silverleaf sage (S. discolor) also has pale green leaf surfaces, with silvery undersides and sticky, silvery stems that make the plants look silvery gray overall. From early or midsummer to frost, the 2- to 3-foot-tall clumps carry abundant spikes of deep purple-black flowers,

which make an amazing contrast to the light foliage. These two species are hardy in Zones 9 to 11. If you're a sucker for fragrance, you must try Cleveland sage (S. clevelandii). It grows 3 to 5 feet tall, with intensely aromatic gray-green leaves and purple-blue summer flowers. Zones 8 or 9 to 11.

**GROWING TIPS:** Silvery and gray sages thrive with average to dry, well-drained soil in full sun but may appreciate a bit of afternoon shade in hot-summer areas. They usually perform best and live longest where there is relatively low humidity, although you can enjoy them as annuals just about anywhere. Trimming off the spent flower spikes neatens the plants and encourages rebloom.

**ALTERNATIVES:** In warm climates, kohuhu or pittosporums (Pittosporum tenuifolium) are popular hedging and screen plants for their evergreen foliage and ability to tolerate regular clipping. 'Silver Sheen' has silvery green leaves on near-black stems, with a loosely conical habit to about 20 feet tall. Shorty ('Argentea Nana') forms dense, rounded, 4- to 5-foot-tall mounds of small, silver-gray foliage. Full sun to partial shade; average, well-drained soil. Zones 8 or 9 to 10.

*Schizophragma hydrangeoides* 'Moonlight'

## SCHIZOPHRAGMA
*Japanese hydrangea vine*

**Height: 20–30 feet**
**Leaf size: 2–4 inches long and wide**
**Partial to full shade**
**Zones 5–9**

If you'd like some vertical interest in a shady site, you can't do better than 'Moonlight' Japanese hydrangea vine (Schizophragma hydrangeoides). This deciduous, woody-stemmed climber bears an abundance of broadly heart-shaped leaves that are usually blue-gray with deep green veins in spring and a deeper grayish green in summer, turning yellow in autumn. In mid- to late summer, the established vines produce lacy-looking bloom clusters up to 10 inches across, made up of tiny, greenish cream-colored true flowers surrounded by a ring of larger, heart-shaped, creamy white bracts. Japanese hydrangea vine's reddish brown stems cling to tree trunks, walls, and fences with rootlike "holdfasts," but they don't *have* to climb; you can also let them sprawl to cover a large slope or rocky area.

**GROWING TIPS:** A site with morning sun and afternoon or light all-day shade usually encourages the most vigorous and flowering, but the plants will grow in full shade as well. Acidic, moist but well-drained soil is ideal. Established vines rarely need any attention.

**ALTERNATIVES:** Silver-leaved grapevine (Vitis vinifera 'Incana') is especially silvery-woolly on its new foliage and stems, aging to grayish green; to about 20 feet tall; Zones 6 or 7 to 10. 'Walker Ridge' California grape (V. californica) and desert wild grape (V. girdiana) also tend to have a grayish overall appearance. To 30 feet; Zones 8 to 10. All of these have woody stems that climb by tendrils. Full sun to light shade; average, well-drained soil.

## SEDUM
*Sedum, stonecrop*

**Height: Varies**
**Leaf size: Varies**
**Full sun to partial shade**
**Zones vary**

The adaptable nature and dependable performance of sedums (Sedum) make them ideal choices for beginning gardeners, and the exciting diversity of sizes, habits, and colors makes them intriguing to more-experienced gardeners too. Blue- to gray-leaved species and selections are particularly abundant, providing ample opportunities for eye-catching combinations in beds and borders and handsome ground-covering carpets, as well. Here's a sampling of some of the more readily available options; specialty nurseries — particularly those that focus on rock-garden plants or ground covers — offer many others.

*Upright to trailing sedums.* Typically growing in distinct clumps or mounds and blooming in late summer to early fall, these sedums usually adapt happily to life in beds and borders in full sun to light shade with average to moist but well-drained soil. This group includes the popular showy stonecrop (S. spectabile or Hylotelephium spectabile), which bears 3-inch-long, oval, grayish green leaves on upright, 18- to 24-inch-tall stems topped with clusters of pink flowers. You can choose from a number of cultivars, which vary mainly in flower color; among them are bright pink 'Brilliant', rosy pink 'Carmen', reddish 'Meteor', and white 'Iceberg'. The popular hybrid 'Autumn Joy' ('Herbstfreude') and the newer 'Autumn Fire', both with deep pink flowers, offer oblong, even larger, grayish green leaves to about 5 inches long.

Sedums with purple-tinged blue or gray leaves don't fall neatly into either the "blue foliage" or "purple foliage" category, especially because they often have purplish or deep red stems. This unusual mix of features makes them handy for unifying companions that have distinctly blue or gray foliage with those that have purple leaves — silvery artemisias with purple heucheras, for example.

*Sedum cauticola* 'Lidakense' is one of the shortest (to about 6 inches), with rounded, blue-green leaves that are tinged with reddish purple, and pink flowers. The rounded foliage of October daphne (*S. sieboldii*) is mostly bright blue-gray, but its leaf rims and arching stems are pinkish to reddish, with pink flowers in mid- to late fall. The mounded plants are usually 6 to 8 inches tall, but 'Nana' is about half that size. Some slightly taller sedums (in the range of 8 to 12 inches) with purplish gray or blue leaves and reddish pink flower clusters on arching to trailing stems are the old standards 'Vera Jameson' and 'Ruby Glow' (also sold as 'Rosy Glow') and the newer 'Bertram Anderson' and 'Sunset Cloud'. 'Hab Grey' orpine (*S. telephium* subsp. *ruprechtii;* also listed as

'Hab Gray') is a bit taller (usually 18 to 24 inches), with pink-tinged, blue-gray leaves and pinkish flower buds that open creamy yellow. 'Matrona' grows significantly taller (2 to 3 feet), with purple-tinged gray-blue foliage and light pink flower clusters. All of these sedums are usually hardy in Zones 3 or 4 to 9.

*Ground-hugging sedums.* Low-growing sedums show off best where you can see them up close: right next to a path, for instance, or in a pot or raised planter. One of their favorite haunts, though, is a dry, rocky site, which makes them an ideal choice for stony slopes or flat sites where digging is practically impossible. Like the more upright border-type sedums, these produce flowers (often through the summer), but they're better known for their usually "ever-blue" foliage. One of the most readily available sedums is sold under a variety of names, including *S. rupestre* var. *glaucum, S. reflexum* 'Blue Spruce', and *S. pinifolium* 'Blue Spruce'. Commonly called blue spruce sedum, it gets its name from its very short, upright stems clad in blue-green, needlelike leaves; the spreading, 4-inch-tall mats do resemble forests of miniature blue spruce (*Picea pungens*) trees, if you use your imagination. The flowers are yellow. Zones 4 to 9. Plants sold as *S. pachyclados* and *S. pachycladus* (correctly known as *Rhodiola pachyclados*) grow in spreading carpets of 2-inch-tall rosettes of tiny, blue-gray leaves,

*Sedum dasyphyllum*

with pale yellow flowers to about 4 inches tall. Zones 4 or 5 to 9. Little blue Spanish stonecrop (*S. hispanicum* var. *minus*) and Corsican stonecrop (*S. dasyphyllum*) are even shorter, reaching barely 1 inch in height; they have tiny blue-green leaves and very pale pink flowers. They're usually recommended for Zones 5 or 6 to 9, but like the other sedums in this group, they may survive the winters a zone or two farther north; they are likely to drop their leaves in winter there, however. *S. spathulifolium* 'Cape Blanco' is a distinctly different possibility, with bright grayish white foliage during the growing season and reddish to pinkish leaves in winter. The plants are 4 inches tall in leaf and about 6 inches tall when the yellow flowers appear. Zones 5 to 9.

**GROWING TIPS:** Sedums will grow in light shade, but they are most vigorous and produce their

brightest blue to gray leaf colors in full sun. Average to dry, well-drained soil is ideal. Good winter drainage is especially important for the very low-growing species and selections. Although the taller upright sedums can adapt to the fertile, humus-rich soil of pampered perennial borders, they're likely to sprawl there, so you may need to stake them in spring or cut them back by about half in early summer to encourage lower, bushier growth.

**ALTERNATIVE:** 'Dragon's Blood' white clover (*Trifolium repens*) has compound leaves composed of three small, rounded, silvery gray leaflets that are green near their base with an irregular splash of purple-red through the center. Usually 4 to 6 inches tall; can spread widely if not contained. Full sun to partial shade; average to moist but well-drained soil. Zones 4 to 8. *Note:* The species *T. repens* is considered invasive in some areas.

*Stachys byzantina* 'Big Ears'

## STACHYS
*Lamb's ears*

**Height: 6–12 inches**
**Leaf size: Varies**
**Full sun to partial shade**
**Zones vary**

The fuzzy foliage of lamb's ears (*Stachys byzantina*; also known as *S. lanata* and *S. olympica*) has endeared it to generations of gardeners. The "please-touch" leaves aren't the only reason to grow it, though; it's also one of the most sturdy and adaptable silver-leaved plants around — at least where the weather isn't especially humid. "Ever-silver" in mild climates, lamb's ears forms creeping carpets of 4-inch-long, 2-inch-wide, oblong to lance-shaped leaves that are densely covered with silvery white wool. In early to midsummer, they produce upright, equally woolly, 1- to 3-foot-tall flowering stems that bear whorls of small purplish pink blooms. Some gardeners find

the flowers appealing, but others prefer to clip them off as they form to better feature the foliage. Growing the cultivar 'Silver Carpet', which is much less likely to produce flowering stems, is one way to keep the clipping to a minimum. If you like the spiky look of the upright stems but don't want self-sown seedlings, look for 'Cotton Boll' (also sold as 'Cotton Ball', 'Silver Ball', and 'Sheila Macqueen'); it looks like it's going to bloom, but the flowers never actually open. 'Big Ears' (also known as 'Helene von Stein') is about twice the size in leaf and seldom produces flower stalks. Its leaves aren't quite as hairy, so it's more grayish green than silvery, but it's also somewhat less likely to rot in humid conditions. Zones 3 or 4 to 8.

For silvery foliage *and* showy flowers, consider woundwort (*S. albotomentosa*; reportedly the same as *S. coccinea* 'Hidalgo').

It's also known as 7-Up plant because the 2- to 4-inch-long, 1- to 2-inch-wide, gray-green leaves release a fruity fragrance when you rub them. From late spring into fall, it sends up slender 1- to 2-foot-tall stems with clusters of small orange-pink flowers that age to coral red. The leafy clumps eventually spread several feet across, making a great ground cover for a slope or a dry-soil border; it also looks excellent in a container. Zones 7 or 8 to 10.

**GROWING TIPS:** A site with full sun to partial shade and average, well-drained soil suits both species. Lamb's ears will even take dry shade. Be aware that in the moist, rich soil of a perennial border, it can spread aggressively; you're better off using it alone as a ground cover or combined with equally vigorous spreaders. Both species may self-sow if you don't remove the spent flowering spikes. Where summers are humid, cut back the whole clump to an inch or two above the ground after flowering (or any time the foliage gets discolored) for a flush of fresh new leaves.

**ALTERNATIVE:** As you might guess from its common names — white gossamer and white velvet — *Tradescantia sillamontana* has a cobwebby white covering over its gray-green leaves. The stems are upright at first, then trailing. Ideal for cascading out of a container, or as a temporary ground cover in cool climates. Full sun to light shade; average to dry, well-drained soil. Usually Zones 10 to 11; may be hardier.

## BOLTONIA
*Boltonia, false aster, doll's daisy*

**Height: Varies**
**Leaf size: 4–6 inches long;**
   **½ inch wide**
**Full sun**
**Zones 3–9**

Boltonia (*Boltonia asteroides*) is best known for its abundance of small, daisylike flowers from mid- or late summer into fall, but it can add foliage interest earlier in the growing season as well. It grows in slowly spreading clumps of upright, branching stems with slender, blue-green to gray-green leaves that contribute both texture and color to borders through

*Boltonia asteroides*

the spring and much of the summer, up until the flowers virtually smother the foliage. *B. asteroides* var. *latisquama* 'Snowbank' has pure white flowers and *P. asteroides* 'Pink Beauty' has light pink blooms; both are in the 4- to 5-foot-tall range. If you'd prefer a more compact plant, consider pink-flowered *B. asteroides* var. *latisquama* 'Nana'; it's typically 2 to 3 feet tall.

**GROWING TIPS:** Full sun is usually best, but the plants may appreciate some light shade in hot climates. Boltonias can take some drought but prefer average to moist soil; they'll even withstand seasonally wet conditions. The full-size cultivars may flop by bloom time in rich, moist soil; to avoid the need for staking, cut back the plants by about half in late spring or early summer to promote lower, bushier growth.

**ALTERNATIVES:** False indigos (*Baptisia*) bloom, too, but the bushy clumps of three-part leaves are their main feature for most of the summer and fall. Blue false indigo (*B. australis*), for Zones 3 to 9, and white wild indigo (*B. alba*), for Zones 4 or 5 to 9, both grow 2 to 4 feet tall. Yellow wild indigo (*B. sphaerocarpa*) is 2 to 3 feet tall; Zones 5 to 9. Full sun to partial shade; average, well-drained soil. Lead plant (*Amorpha canescens*) grows as a shrub or a perennial in 2- to 4-foot-tall, moderately spreading clumps. Its compound leaves have tiny oval leaflets that are gray-green to silver-gray. Full sun to light shade; average, well-drained to dry soil. Zones 2 to 8.

## CERASTIUM
*Snow-in-summer*

**Height: 4–6 inches**
**Leaf size: ½–1 inch long;**
   **⅛–¼ inch wide**
**Full sun**
**Zones 2–7**

The crisp, cool combination of silvery foliage and white flowers makes snow-in-summer (*Cerastium tomentosum*) an elegant ground cover for sun-drenched sites. This low-growing perennial spreads quickly to form carpets of small, slender, silver-gray leaves. In late spring to early summer, the plants are covered with small but abundant, bright white blooms held a few inches above the foliage for a total height of 6 to 12 inches.

The cultivar 'Yo Yo' tends to be denser and a somewhat less vigorous spreader. You may also find plants labeled 'Silberteppich' ('Silver Carpet') and *C. biebersteinii*. They have minor differences from *C. tomentosum*, but from a gardener's perspective, they all look similar.

Besides making an attractive "ever-gray" ground cover, snow-in-summer shows off well on slopes, planted atop a low wall, or tucked into pockets of soil among rocks. *Note: C. biebersteinii* is considered invasive in some areas of the country.

**GROWING TIPS:** A site with full sun and average, well-drained soil is usually ideal; in the warmer parts of its hardiness range, this plant may appreciate light shade, especially in the afternoon. Snow-in-summer thrives in cool, dry climates and is prone to rotting in areas with wet, rainy winters or hot, humid summers. Shearing back the plants by about half as soon as the flowers finish blooming prevents self-sowing, neatens the plants, and encourages dense regrowth that looks good for the rest of the season.

**ALTERNATIVE:** Edelweiss (*Leontopodium alpinum*) is another furry-foliaged plant perfectly suited to cool climates. It grows in 6- to 8-inch-tall mounds of unbranched stems clad in slender, gray-green leaves and tipped with a whorl of longer, leaflike, woolly white bracts. Edelweiss prefers full sun with evenly moist soil; excellent drainage is critical, though, especially in winter. Zones 3 to 7.

*Cerastium tomentosum*

## CONVOLVULUS
*Convolvulus, morning glory*

**Height: Varies**
**Leaf size: Varies**
**Full sun**
**Zones vary**

At first glance, you'd probably never guess that *Convolvulus cneorum* is closely related to the classic vining morning glories (*Ipomoea*). It grows in shrubby mounds 2 to 3 feet tall and wide, with small, lance-shaped, silvery gray leaves that are about 2½ inches long and 1 to 1½ inches wide. When the pink buds open to 1- to 2-inch-wide, funnel-shaped white flowers, it's much easier to see the morning glory resemblance. Commonly called

*Convolvulus cneorum*

silverbush or bush morning glory, the "ever-silver" plants usually bloom from late spring through the summer. Grow silverbush in masses as a ground cover, on slopes, or in dry perennial borders where the plants are hardy (Zones 8 to 10); in cooler areas, enjoy it in containers or as an annual color accent in beds and mixed plantings.

Ground morning glory (*C. sabatius;* also sold as *C. mauritanicus*) isn't nearly as silvery as silverbush; its oval to rounded, 1-inch-long and -wide, furry leaves are more of a light grayish green. The small, spring-to-fall, purple-blue blooms are quite showy, though, on trailing stems that mound up 6 to 12 inches (occasionally to 2 feet) in height and spread to about 3 feet across. 'Blue Casbah' (also sold as 'Moroccan Beauty') has an especially dense, well-branched habit. Ground morning glory makes a handsome "ever-grayish" ground cover in Zones 7 or 8 to 10; it's also a fantastic addition to hanging baskets, window boxes, and planters in any area of the country.

**GROWING TIPS:** Both species thrive in full-sun sites with average, well-drained to dry soil; light shade is acceptable. Those growing in containers usually appreciate regular watering, as do new in-ground plantings; established garden plantings are normally quite drought-tolerant. Shear back the plants by about half after flowering to shape them and encourage bushy regrowth.

**ALTERNATIVES:** Also known as shrubby or bush germander, silver germander (*Teucrium fruticans*) bears small, oval, aromatic leaves that are green to gray-green on top and white underneath, on white-felted stems. The "ever-silver" plants can eventually reach to 6 feet tall and twice as wide; regular trimming will keep them smaller and bushier. Full sun to light shade; neutral to alkaline, average, well-drained to dry soil. Zones 8 to 10.

## DICHONDRA
*Dichondra*

**Height: 3 inches**
**Leaf size: ½–¾ inch long;**
**     1 inch wide**
**Full sun to partial shade**
**Zones 9–11**

You need a silvery ground cover that'll spread far, wide, and fast? That calls for *Dichondra argentea* 'Silver Falls'! The common names silver ponyfoot and silver nickel vine do a good job describing

*Dichondra argentea* 'Silver Falls'

its appearance: velvety, silver-white to gray-green, kidney-shaped leaves on slender, vinelike stems that can trail or creep to 6 feet long. The ground-hugging stems will take root all along their length, so their eventual spread is essentially unlimited. Even where they're not hardy, the plants grow quickly enough to create an extensive ground cover by mid- to late summer. The vining stems can also weave among taller companions without crowding them out, making them great fillers among perennials, shrubs, and slower-growing ground covers in newly planted gardens. Silver ponyfoot also looks smashing when allowed to cascade over a wall or out of a hanging basket, window box, or large container planting. Tiny, creamy white flowers appear throughout the summer, but you'll barely notice them.

**GROWING TIPS:** Full sun brings out the most silvery appearance, but the plants will still be a quite attractive gray-green in some shade. Average, well-drained to dry soil is fine; silver ponyfoot appreciates some irrigation in very dry conditions, though. Clip the shoot tips as needed to keep the plants where you want them. Silver ponyfoot self-sows freely.

**ALTERNATIVES:** For a lacier-looking foliage carpet, consider blue goose leaf (*Acaena saccaticupula*). It grows about 4 inches tall (or taller if it can scramble up through larger companions), with small, toothed, blue-gray leaves on slender, trailing stems. 'Blue Haze' is a selection with bright silvery blue foliage. Full sun to light shade; average to dry, well-drained soil. Zones 6 or 7 to 10.

## ECHEVERIA
*Echeveria, hens-and-chicks*

**Height: 4–8 inches**
**Leaf size: 2–4 inches long;**
 **½–1 inch wide**
**Full sun to partial shade**
**Zones 10 and 11**

Echeverias (*Echeveria*) share the common name hens-and-chicks with the genus *Sempervivum*: both grow from central rosettes (the "hens") that readily produce smaller offsets (the "chicks"). Echeverias are much less cold-hardy than their relatives, but they produce such exquisitely beautiful plants that they're worth bringing indoors for the winter in frost-prone areas; keeping them in pots makes this a snap. Outdoors, echeverias are excellent on slopes, tucked among rocks, or combined with other low-growing succulents as a ground-covering carpet.

There are dozens of species and hybrids to choose from; the tricky part is *finding* them. Local or mail-order nurseries that specialize in cacti and succulents are a good place to start. Among the species to look for are painted lady (*E. derenbergii*), blue echeveria (*E. glauca;* also known as *E. secunda* var. *glauca*), and *E. secunda,* with blue-gray to blue-green leaves that may be edged in pink. Plush plant (*E. pulvinata*) has plump green leaves

*Echeveria* hybrid

that are covered with a fine gray-white fuzz. *E. runyonii* 'Topsy Turvy' has blue-green leaves that are cylindrical near the base and flattened toward the tips; hybrid 'Perle von Nürnberg' bears broad rosettes of blue-gray leaves that may be shaded with pink. This is just a sampling of the many options available in a range of sizes, leaf shapes, and shadings. Echeverias also produce flowers, by the way: upright to arching stems tipped with small, bell-shaped blooms that are typically shades of yellow, rosy pink, or red, often with contrasting tips. Flowering times vary widely. Two other, very similar options for beautiful blue-green rosettes are plump-leaved *Pachyphytum* species and × *Pachyveria glauca*, a hybrid resulting from *Pachyphytum* crossed with *Echeveria*.

**GROWING TIPS:** Echeverias usually thrive in full sun with average, well-drained soil; many also perform well in morning sun and afternoon shade or light all-day shade. They tolerate dry conditions but appreciate occasional watering during dry spells. Remove dead or discolored leaves from the base of the rosettes in spring to keep the plants looking tidy. Feel free to pick off the "chicks" and plant them elsewhere to expand your collection.

**ALTERNATIVES:** Duncecaps (*Orostachys iwarenge*) produce succulent, 1-inch-tall, blue-gray rosettes often tinged with pink. Zones 5 to 9. Live-forevers (*Dudleya*) are much larger, with long, narrow, flattened leaves in rosettes that grow to about 1 foot tall. Powdery live-forever (*D. farinosa*) has powdery white new leaves and light gray older foliage; chalk live-forever (*D. pulverulenta*) ranges from grayish white to bright blue-gray. Zones 10 to 11. Full sun; average, well-drained to dry soil.

*Helianthemum* 'Rhodanthe
Carneum'

## HELIANTHEMUM
*Rock rose, sun rose*

**Height: 8–12 inches**
**Leaf size: 1–2 inches long;**
**⅓–½ inch wide**
**Full sun**
**Zones 5 or 6–8**

Those of you who garden in sandy, fast-draining soil may find it challenging to grow many of the classic humus- and moisture-loving border plants, but you have a distinct advantage when it comes to rock roses (*Helian-themum*). These compact, bushy plants are often sold with perennials but are technically shrubs; their low, spreading habit also earns them a place in the ground cover category. Some rock roses have solid green leaves, but quite a few have fuzzy gray to silvery

foliage, which provides a beautiful backdrop for the 1-inch-wide, five-petaled flowers and looks good on its own for the rest of the year. The blooms come in an array of bright and pastel colors with a cluster of yellow stamens in the middle and appear mainly in late spring to early summer, occasionally with light rebloom in late summer to early fall. Rock roses are sometimes sold as cultivars of *H. nummularium,* but most are hybrids. If you enjoy bright flower colors, look for orange-red 'Fire Dragon', deep orange 'Henfield Brilliant', or brick red 'Stoplight'. 'Raspberry Ripple' has varying amounts of rich purplish pink and white in each bloom; 'Wisley White' is white with a yellow center. For a pretty pastel, consider light yellow 'Wisley Primrose' or yellow-centered, light pink 'Rhodanthe Carneum' (also sold as 'Wisley Pink').

**GROWING TIPS:** Rock roses prefer full sun but appreciate afternoon shade in the warmer parts of their hardiness range. Neutral to alkaline soil is best, and excellent drainage is critical, particularly in winter. These plants are usually recommended for Zones 6 to 8, but gardeners have reported success with them as far north as Zone 3. In Zones 5 and north, a lightweight mulch such as evergreen boughs will increase the odds of winter survival. Trim the plants lightly in early spring, if needed, or shear them back by about a third after the main flush of bloom fades; this will help to

keep them dense and possibly encourage rebloom.

**ALTERNATIVES:** Also commonly known as rock roses, *Cistus* hybrids are typically taller as well as far more heat-tolerant than those of *Helianthemum.* A few of the many selections with grayish green foliage include 2-foot-tall *C. × pulverulentus* 'Sunset' (also sold as *C.* 'Sunset' and *C. crispus* 'Sunset'); the similar, if not identical, *C.* 'Brilliancy'; and 3- to 4-foot-tall *C.* 'Victor Reiter'. Full sun; average, well-drained soil. Zones 8 to 10.

## HELICHRYSUM
*Helichrysum*

**Height: Varies**
**Leaf size: Varies**
**Full sun**
**Zones vary**

In the garden or in containers, helichrysums (*Helichrysum*) offer some of the best-looking silvery foliage around. Probably the best known of the many species is *H. petiolare* (also sold as *H. petiolatum*), commonly known as licorice plant. You'll usually see it sold as an annual, but where it's hardy (Zones 9 or 10 to 11), it's actually an "ever-gray" shrub. Both the long, trailing stems and 1- to 1½-inch-long and -wide, oval to heart-shaped leaves are covered with a velvety white felt. Small clusters of tiny, cream-colored flowers may appear in summer, but they're not very showy. Licorice plant grows in low carpets that are usually 12 to 18 inches tall (to 4 feet or more in

mild areas) and easily spread or trail 4 feet or more across. The stems will take root where they rest on the soil, extending the spread even farther. Planted in masses, it makes a striking ground cover; in borders, it likes to weave among and creep up through taller companions. Selections with smaller leaves are sold under various names, including 'Dwarf Licorice', 'Petite Licorice', 'Minus', and 'Nana'. *Note:* The species appears to be invasive in some areas (mostly in very mild coastal regions).

Helichrysums also come in a number of upright, bushy forms equally well suited for use in borders and planters. Curry plant (*H. italicum;* also sold as *H. angustifolium*) grows about 2 feet tall and 3 feet wide, with bright silvery gray, 1½-inch-long, linear leaves that have a strong, spicy-warm, currylike aroma. Clusters of deep yellow flowers bloom at the stem tips from summer into fall. Zones 7 to 10. Silver spike (*H. thianschanicum;* also sold as *H. thianschanicum* 'Icicles' and *H.* 'Icicles') looks similar, but its silvery white, needlelike leaves are up to 4 inches long, so it has an even finer appearance. The plants are also more compact (about 1 foot tall and 18 to 24 inches wide), occasionally with yellow summer flowers. Its hardiness range still seems to be in question — some sources claim it's hardy as far north as Zone 5 but it's usually rated for Zones 9 to 11 — so don't

*Juniperus squamata* 'Blue Star'

depend on it being perennial until you've tried it for yourself.

*H.* 'Ruby Cluster' (sometimes sold as *H. amorginum*) is distinctly different from all of these, growing in low rosettes of narrowly oblong, soft, silvery green to gray-green leaves to about 8 inches tall. Through the summer, upright, 8- to 10-inch-tall flowering stems are topped with clusters of pink buds that open into white, papery-petaled blooms with large yellow centers. Zones 8 or 9 to 11.

**GROWING TIPS:** Helichrysums thrive in full sun and average, well-drained soil; licorice plant may appreciate light afternoon shade in hot-summer areas.

The leaves of a few species are a favorite food of some butterfly larvae, which can defoliate a whole plant; avoid spraying, if possible, because the plants will usually recover quickly once the larvae are done feeding.

**ALTERNATIVES:** For the look of licorice plant on a smaller scale, consider *Plecostachys serpyllifolia* (also sold as *Helichrysum petiolare* var. *microphyllum,* among other names), with tiny, silvery gray leaves on woolly, trailing stems; 1 to 2 feet tall. Zones 9 or 10 to 11. *Hebe pimeleoides* 'Quicksilver' has slender, arching, near-black stems clad in tiny, gray-blue leaves; about 1 foot tall. Zones 8 or 9 to 11. Full sun; average, well-drained soil.

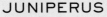

# JUNIPERUS
*Juniper*

**Height: Varies**
**Leaf size: ¼–½ inch long; about ⅛ inch wide**
**Full sun**
**Zones vary**

Durable and dependable junipers (*Juniperus*) are a classic choice for year-round interest in landscapes across the country. The fact that they're common doesn't mean they have to look ordinary, though; this genus offers some exceptional options for "ever-blue" foliage in a range of plant forms, from low-growing carpets to larger mounds and distinctly upright accents. They're especially welcome for adding winter color to cold-climate landscapes, either planted alone in masses or

*Helichrysum* 'Petite Licorice'

combined with other conifers and with deciduous shrubs that have bright berries or showy bark. There are several species and dozens of selections to choose from; here's a sampling of the offerings.

*Ground-cover junipers.* If you have lots of space to fill, blue-needled junipers can do the job in style. Selections of creeping juniper (*J. horizontalis*) are great for ground-hugging carpets: 'Wiltonii' (also sold as 'Wiltoni' and 'Blue Rug' and commonly called blue rug juniper) is a popular cultivar with bright blue-gray needles that take on purple tints in winter; it grows about 6 inches tall and 6 to 8 feet across. Zones 3 to 9. 'Bar Harbor' is similar but usually slightly taller. Zones 3 or 4 to 9. 'Blue Carpet' flaky or singleseed juniper (*J. squamata*) is bright blue-gray, growing to about 1 foot tall and spreading to 6 feet or more over time. Zones 4 to 8. 'Silver Mist' shore juniper (*J. conferta*; also listed under *J. rigida* subsp. *conferta*) is about the same size, with short, dense needles that are bright silvery blue during the growing season

and purplish in winter. Zones 5 or 6 to 9.

*Mound-forming junipers.* For both width and height, there are plenty of mounding selections. 'New Blue' tamarix juniper or savin juniper (*J. sabina;* also sold as 'Tamariscifolia New Blue' and 'Tam No Blight') has blue-green needles on layered stems mounding 18 to 30 inches tall and spreading 6 to 10 feet. Zones 3 to 7. *J. squamata* 'Blue Star' is an exceptionally bright blue-gray on plants about 3 feet tall and 4 feet wide. Zones 4 to 8. Bushier 'Blue Vase' (listed under either *J. chinensis* or *J. × media*) is a light silvery blue; it reaches 6 to 8 feet tall and 4 to 6 feet across. Zones 4 to 9. 'Blue Alps' (usually listed under either *J. chinensis* or *J. squamata*) is a similar color but gets rather larger — 8 to 12 feet tall and about 6 feet wide after many years. Zones 4 to 8.

*Strongly upright junipers.* Need a vertical accent? Consider blue-green 'Blue Point' Chinese juniper (*J. chinensis*), with a pyramidal form that's 10 to 12 feet tall and about 8 feet across. Zones 4 to 9. Rocky Mountain juniper (*J. scopulorum*) offers some even taller, silvery blue cultivars, including 'Moonglow' — to about 20 feet tall and 5 feet wide — and 'Skyrocket' (also listed under *J. virginiana*) — 15 to 20 feet tall but only 1 to 2 feet across. Zones 3 or 4 to 8.

**GROWING TIPS:** Blue junipers prefer fun sun and average, well-drained soil but can tolerate light shade for part of the day. Established plants seldom need any care; simply trim off any wayward shoots as desired.

**ALTERNATIVES:** Among the many foliage colors of Scotch heather (*Calluna vulgaris*) are some superb "ever-silvers." One is 'Silver Queen', with bright silver-gray foliage in broad mounds; 12 to 18 inches tall. 'Silver Knight' is more upright (about 2 feet tall); its silvery gray leaves turn purplish in winter. Specialty nurseries offer many other options. Full sun; acidic, well-drained soil. Zones 4 to 7. *Note: C. vulgaris* is considered invasive in some areas.

*Lamium maculatum* 'White Nancy'

## LAMIUM
*Dead nettle*

**Height: 6–8 inches**
**Leaf size: 1–2 inches long;**
    **about 1 inch wide**
**Partial to full shade**
**Zones 3 or 4–9**

As ground covers, border accents, or container plants, spotted dead nettle (*Lamium maculatum*) and its various selections are a real treasure for silver-seeking shade gardeners. These low-growing perennials create sparkling carpets of small, toothed leaves that may be lightly or heavily marked with silver. The new shoots are upright at first; later they trail along the ground and take root where they touch the soil. The plants also spread outward by creeping underground stems. As a bonus, clustered flowers bloom just above the leaves in late spring to early summer. The leaves of white-flowered 'Album' are green with a silvery white center stripe. 'Chequers' has a slightly narrower silver stripe and deep pink flowers; 'Shell Pink' has similar markings and light pink flowers. 'Beacon Silver' ('Silbergroshen') also has deep pink to purplish pink blooms, over nearly solid silver, green-edged leaves that may be tinged with a bit of purple. Other mostly silver selections are 'Red Nancy', with reddish pink flowers; 'Purple Dragon', with deep pinkish purple blooms; 'Orchid Frost', with lighter purplish pink flowers; and light pink 'Pink Chablis' and 'Pink Pewter'. If you'd prefer white flowers, look for 'White Nancy'. *Note: L. maculatum* is considered invasive in some areas.

**GROWING TIPS:** Spotted dead nettles thrive with morning sun and afternoon shade or light all-day shade; they will also grow in full shade but may not be as dense. Evenly moist but well-drained, humus-rich soil is ideal. If you use dead nettles in a border setting, keep an eye on their spread, and be prepared to trim their shoots or dig out some of them if they threaten to crowd more-delicate companions. Mow or shear the plants to an inch or two above the ground just after the blossoms fade, and they'll send up fresh new growth that looks good well into winter. As an added benefit, this will prevent self-sown seedlings, which vary in their silvering patterns and flower colors. If you don't trim your plants in midsummer, then do it in early spring before new growth begins.

**ALTERNATIVE:** Yellow archangel (*Lamiastrum galeobdolon*; also sold as *Lamium galeobdolon* or *Galeobdolon luteum*) also has silver-mottled green leaves, but its creeping stems spread far and wide, and the species is considered invasive in some areas. The selection 'Hermann's Pride' ('Herman's Pride'), however, stays in tight, well-behaved clumps about 1 foot tall and wide, with silver-marked foliage. Partial to full shade; dry to average or moist but well-drained soil. Zones 4 to 9.

## LAVANDULA
*Lavender, lavandin*

**Height: Varies**
**Leaf size: 1–2 inches long;**
    **¼ inch wide**
**Full sun**
**Zones vary**

Lavenders (*Lavandula*) aren't always the easiest plants to keep from year to year, but they're such a delight in the garden that it's worth growing them as annuals if you have to. These aromatic, upright, shrubby plants have woody-based stems with narrow leaves that range from grayish green to bright silvery white. The spikes of small flowers can be white, pink, or any shade of purple-blue. If you're just getting started with lavenders, pick up some locally available plants or grow your own from seed and see how they perform for you; as you gain experience with them, explore some of the less common selections available from herb growers and specialty nurseries.

*Lavandula stoechas* 'Otto Quast'

English lavender (*L. angustifolia*) is a good plant to try if you're not sure you'll have luck overwintering lavenders in your area. In sandy or gravelly soil with dependable winter snow cover, it may survive as far north as Zone 4; in heavier soils with less than perfect drainage, Zone 6 is more likely its northern limit. English lavender typically grows 2 to 3 feet tall and wide and blooms in early to midsummer, with relatively short spikes of purple-blue flowers. Its new shoots tend to be light green, turning gray-green to silvery gray as the leaves mature. There are numerous cultivars, selected mostly for their flower color — such as white 'Alba' and pale pink 'Jean Davis' — or for their size, like compact, blue-flowered Blue Cushion ('Lavandula Schola'), which grows to about 18 inches tall in full bloom.

If you want to grow lavender as an annual, consider the seed strains 'Lady' ('Lavender Lady'), with purple-blue blooms, and 'Lacy Frills', with white flowers. The seedlings usually flower the same year if you start the seeds indoors in late winter to early spring.

Lavandin or Provence lavender (*L. × intermedia*) is slightly less hardy than English lavender (usually Zones 6 to 9) and blooms a bit later (in mid- to late summer), with longer purple-blue flower spikes held well above the exceptionally fragrant gray-green foliage. Most of the selections are prized for their blooms; 'Fred Boutin', though, has especially silver-gray foliage. 'Seal' ('Seal Seven Oaks') is also a bit more silvery than usual, with deeper purple blue flowers that can reach 4 feet tall.

The more tender lavenders — those normally hardy in Zones 8 to 9 or 10 — also boast some exceptionally beautiful foliage. Woolly lavender (*L. lanata*), for example, is distinctive for the silvery white hairs on its leaves (a perfect backdrop for the deep purple, 3-foot-tall, late-summer blooms). Some of its slightly hardier hybrid offspring, which you may find listed under either *L. × chaytorae* or *L. × hybrida*, are 'Richard Gray' and 'Sawyers'. Tender 'Goodwin Creek Grey' (listed under *L. × ginginsii* or *L. × hybrida*) resulted from a different *L. lanata* cross; it has large, fuzzy, slightly toothed leaves that are a bright silver-gray, with purple blooms that can reach 2 to 3 feet tall. 'Otto Quast' Spanish lavender (*L. stoechas*) is slightly shorter, with grayish green foliage. These represent just a small fraction of the many available gray- to silver-leaved lavenders; there are countless others.

**GROWING TIPS:** Lavenders perform best in full sun and average to dry, neutral to slightly alkaline soil. Good drainage is critical, especially in winter. If your soil isn't naturally free-draining, try growing hardy lavenders in raised beds or atop individual mounds of sandy soil to improve their odds of winter survival. Mulching with ½ inch to 1 inch of gravel also helps to keep the crown dry and minimizes the chance of rot. Cut back lavenders by a third to a half to shape them and encourage a dense, bushy form. Some gardeners like to do this in mid-spring, *after* new growth appears; others prefer to wait until after the first flush of flowers fades. Shearing off the faded flower stems encourages rebloom.

**ALTERNATIVES:** Lavender cotton (*Santolina chamaecyparissus*; also known as *S. incana*) grows in 2-foot-tall and 3- to 4-foot-wide mounds of aromatic, feathery foliage that's such a bright silver-gray it can appear nearly white. 'Pretty Carol' ('Pretty Carroll') grows 12 to 18 inches tall and wide; the variety *nana* ('Nana') is about 1 foot tall and wide. Full sun to light shade (in hot-summer areas); average, well-drained to dry soil. Zones 6 or 7 to 10.

## LOTUS
*Parrot's beak, lotus vine*

**Height: 6–8 inches**
**Leaf size: ½–¾ inch long;**
  **¹⁄₁₆ inch wide**
**Full sun to partial shade**
**Zones 9 or 10–11**

The silver-gray, needlelike leaves of parrot's beak (*Lotus berthelotii* or *L. bertholetii*) may look sharp and spiny, but that couldn't be further from the truth. This tender perennial is a fantastic textural accent that's soft to the touch *and* easy on the eye, creating an elegant complement to pastel flowers and a stunning setting for jewel-toned blooms in borders, baskets, window boxes,

*Lotus berthelotii*

and planters. Its trailing stems spread several feet in all directions, so it also makes a great ground cover (permanent in frost-free areas and single-season elsewhere). In mild areas, clusters of 1-inch-long, clawlike, orange-red blooms appear along the stems in late spring to early summer and sometimes again in fall; they look much like flames flickering against the ash-gray foliage. 'Red Flash' has red flowers; 'Gold Flash' (usually listed under either *L. maculatus* or *L. maculata*) has orange-shaded yellow blooms. Hybrid 'Amazon Sunset' produces red-shaded orange flowers longer into the summer.

**GROWING TIPS:** In most areas, parrot's beak thrives in full sun or light shade; where it's hardy, it may perform better with morning sun and afternoon shade or light all-day shade. Average to moist but well-drained soil is usually ideal; container plants in particular appreciate regular watering and fertilization. Pinching or trimming off the shoot tips encourages bushier growth.

**ALTERNATIVES:** Cushion bush (*Leucophyta brownii* or *Calocephalus brownii*) forms airy mounds of interlaced, slender stems with tiny, scale-like leaves and silvery white hairs; 3 feet tall. 'Silver Bush' grows 8 to 12 inches tall. Zones 10 to 11. Pearl bluebush (*Maireana sedifolia*) has 3-foot-tall upright stems with tiny, fleshy, oblong, gray-blue leaves; from a distance, it looks much like a silvery conifer. Zones 9 to 11. Full sun; average, well-drained to dry soil.

## NEPETA
*Catmint*

**Height: Varies**
**Leaf size: ¾–1½ inches long;**
   **½–¾ inch wide**
**Full sun to partial shade**
**Zones 3 or 4–8**

Catmints (*Nepeta*) are a classic border favorite for their beautiful blue to purple-blue flowers, but their foliage can be an attractive color accent in its own right. Quite a few species and selections have a covering of tiny hairs on their aromatic, oval to lance-shaped, toothed-edged leaves, so their foliage has an overall gray-green appearance. Growing catmints is easy, but straightening out their botanical names can be tricky; selections listed under *N. mussinii*, for example, often belong to *N. × faassenii*, while what was *N. mussinii* is currently known as *N. racemosa*. The key is to pay attention to the cultivar name when you shop; that way, you're likely to get the traits you want regardless of what species it's listed under.

If you're looking for gray-green in a ground-covering carpet, several compact cultivars (mostly of *N. racemosa*) are good candidates. Try 'Little Titch' (with blue flowers to 10 inches tall), 'Snowflake' (with white blooms to 1 foot tall), 'Superba' (with medium purple-blue flowers to about 15 inches tall), or 'Blue Wonder' (with blue flowers to about 18 inches tall). In the 18- to 24-inch-tall range, consider 'Walker's Low', with rich purple-blue

*Nepeta racemosa* 'Walker's Low'

blooms, or the larger-flowered *N.* 'Dropmore'. Purple-blue *N.* 'Six Hills Giant' grows 2 to 3 feet tall with a fairly open habit; *N. grandiflora* 'Pool Bank' also reaches about 3 feet tall but has a bushier, more upright form. *N. parnassica* is one of the biggest in the bunch, typically growing to 4 or even 5 feet tall and 3 or more feet wide. Its purple-blue flowers start to appear later than those of the other catmints (usually in mid-summer). These and other gray-green-leaved catmints make a particularly pleasing complement for pastel-flowered companions in borders, along pathways, and even in container plantings from early spring well into autumn.

**GROWING TIPS:** Catmints thrive in full sun and average, well-drained to dry soil; in hot climates, morning sun and afternoon shade or light all-day shade may provide better results. Most selections start flowering in late spring to early summer; shear them back by about half in mid- to late summer to promote bushier growth, encourage rebloom, and prevent self-sowing.

**ALTERNATIVES:** Grayleaf geranium (*G. cinereum*) and its cultivars have 2-inch, deeply lobed, gray-green leaves in mounds usually 6 to 12 inches tall; Zones 4 or 5 to 8. The lobed leaves of *G. harveyi* are even more strongly silvered, on a wide-spreading (and self-sowing) mound to about 1 foot tall and up to 4 feet across. Zones 7 to 9; may be hardier. Full sun to light shade; average, very well-drained soil.

## PICEA
*Spruce*

**Height:** Varies
**Leaf size:** ½–1 inch long;
⅛ inch wide
**Full sun**
**Zones vary**

When you're thinking of sprucing up your garden with some "ever-blue" foliage, you need to give blue-needled spruces (*Picea*) a good look. With several species and dozens of cultivars to choose from, you'll have plenty of options, whether you want a vertical accent, a mid-border space-filler, or even a large-scale ground cover. Here's a sampling of smaller-scale selections that are well suited to the average home garden; there are many others that mature into large trees over time.

*Spreading spruces.* For a spruce that will carpet the ground or cascade over a wall, choose selections such as blue-gray 'Glauca Prostrata' and 'Glauca Procumbens' Colorado spruce or blue spruce (*P. pungens*). Left to sprawl, they'll typically reach 18 to 24 inches tall and spread to 6 feet or more; if any upright shoots appear, clip them off to maintain the low growth. Another option is to stake them up to a few feet to get a bit of height, then let their branches sweep down to create a graceful "skirt." Zones 2 or 3 to 8.

*Mounding spruces.* Compact, rounded to mounded spruces make great year-round foliage accents in mixed borders or foundation plantings. 'Cecilia' white spruce (*P. glauca*) is one of the smallest, with short, silver-blue needles and a globe-shaped form eventually reaching about 2 feet tall after many years. Zones 2 or 3 to 6. *P. pungens* 'St. Mary's Broom' gets slightly larger, growing slowly to reach 2 to 3 feet tall and 3 to 4 feet across. Blue-green 'Kellerman's Blue Cameo' Norway spruce (*P. abies*) is about the same size. Plants sold as *P. pungens* 'Glauca Globosa' ('Globosa') grow in a dense, bright blue-gray mound usually 3 to 4 feet tall and wide; 'R. H. Montgomery' ('Montgomery') is practically identical but eventually develops a more upright center reaching about 5 feet tall. Zones 2 or 3 to 7. Silvery green 'Papoose' Sitka spruce (*P. sitchensis*) also starts out with a rounded form, but it turns into a plump pyramid to about 6 feet tall. Zones 7 and 8.

*Upright spruces.* If you're interested in blue-needled spruces for a more distinctly vertical accent, there are several options here too. Blue-green *P. glauca* 'Sander's Blue', for instance, forms tight, symmetrical cones that grow slowly to about 6 feet tall. Zones 2 or 3 to 6. Bright blue-gray *P. pungens* 'Fat Albert' is a very popular option for a larger, broadly pyramidal tree 10 to 15 feet tall. If you'd prefer a narrower accent, consider *P. pungens* 'Fastigiata', which grows in tight, 10- to 15-foot-tall pillars. Zones 2 or 3 to 7.

**GROWING TIPS:** Spruces thrive in full sun and average, well-drained soil. Most rarely need pruning, but a little light trimming in spring will help shape the mounded forms, if desired.

**ALTERNATIVES:** One compact blue-gray pine (*Pinus*) is mounded, 3- to 4-foot-tall 'Blue Mound' Swiss stone pine (*P. cembra*); Zones 3 to 7. Blue-gray to blue-green, 1- to 2-foot-tall 'Sea Urchin' and blue-green, 3- to 5-foot-tall 'Blue Shag' are two compact Eastern white pines (*P. strobus*); Zones 3 or 4 to 8. Taller, pyramidal limber pines (*P. flexilis*) include blue-gray 'Cesarini Blue' and blue-green 'Vanderwolf's Pyramid'; 20 to 25 feet. Zones 4 to 8. Full sun; average, well-drained soil.

*Picea pungens* 'R. H. Montgomery'

## SALIX
*Willow*

**Height:** Varies
**Leaf size:** Varies
**Full sun**
**Zones vary**

Deciduous willows (*Salix*) aren't among the best-known plants for silver, gray, or blue foliage, but some of the smaller species are quite lovely for both texture and color in cooler-climate mixed borders and shrub plantings.

One of the most beautiful — and most readily available — is commonly known as either dwarf arctic willow or purple osier willow (*S. purpurea* 'Nana'). This fast-growing shrub reaches 3 to 5 feet tall and wide but will grow even taller if left unpruned. The slender, deep purple-red stems carry narrow leaves that are 1 to 1½ inches long and about ¼ inch wide. The foliage is light green to gray-green on top with bluish undersides, giving the whole plant a blue-green appearance. 'Canyon Blue' is even more distinctly blue. Let dwarf arctic

*Salix alba* var. *sericea*

willow grow naturally in a graceful, fine-textured mound or shear it into a more formal shape. Zones 3 or 4 to 8.

Coyote willow (*S. exigua*), also known as sandbar willow, grows 6 to 20 feet tall and tends to spread by suckers to form broad thickets. Regular pruning, though, keeps the stems shorter and bushier. Its leaves are 3 to 6 inches long and about ½ inch across. They emerge bright silvery gray and age to light green to gray-green. Zones 2 or 3 to 6. Similar-looking

silver willow (*S. alba* var. *sericea*) can grow to 60 feet but also stays much smaller with regular pruning. Zones 2 or 3 to 8.

Several willow species grow as ground covers or very compact mounds instead of shrubs, and some of these have exceptionally beautiful silvery leaves; unfortunately, they're not often available commercially. One you may find in the trade is known as silver creeping willow (*S. repens* var. *argentea;* also sold as *S. arenaria*). It grows 2 to 3 feet tall and spreads to 6 feet or more across, with 1½-inch-long, 1-inch-wide, silvery gray leaves. Zones 5 to 7. **GROWING TIPS:** Willows thrive in full sun with average to evenly moist soil, but they will usually tolerate light shade and drier conditions too. Regular pruning helps to control the size of the upright, shrubby willows; dwarf arctic willow, in particular, benefits from hard pruning (to about 4 inches above the ground if you really want to keep it shorter; to 1 to 2 feet if you'd like it to stay a bit larger).
**ALTERNATIVE:** It's easy to fall in love with weeping willowleaf pear (*Pyrus salicifolia* 'Pendula'), with its slender, willowlike leaves that are bright silver-gray in spring, turning a softer shade of gray-green by summer; eventually to 20 feet tall and wide. This elegant tree won't thrive everywhere, though; it suffers in hot conditions and is susceptible to fireblight, a bacterial disease. Full sun; average, well-drained soil. Zones 4 or 5 to 7.

## ACHILLEA
*Yarrow*

**Height: Varies**
**Leaf size: Varies**
**Full sun**
**Zones vary**

Grow yarrows (*Achillea*) for their foliage? Well, you probably won't want to cut off the colorful flowers just to show off the lacy leaves, but the foliage does provide an attractive color and textural accent when the plants aren't in bloom. Quite a few of the many dozens of yarrow species and hybrids have silvery to gray foliage, so you have lots of options to choose from. Among the better-known border hybrids are the clump-formers 'Coronation Gold', with gray-green leaves and large, flat-topped clusters of golden yellow blooms atop 3-foot-tall stems; 'Schwellenburg', which is similar but with brighter gray foliage; and clear yellow 'Moonshine' and softer yellow 'Anthea', with silvery gray leaves and 1- to 2-foot-tall flowering stems. *A. clypeolata* reaches 18 to 24 inches tall in bloom, with bright yellow flowers over silvery green leaves.

*Achillea* 'Schwellenburg'

These yarrows bloom from early or midsummer to early fall and should perform well in Zones 2 or 3 to 9.

There are also a number of low-growing, carpeting yarrows suited for use as ground covers, along pathways, or on rocky slopes. For ferny, silvery foliage combined with white summer flowers, look for 3- to 4-inch tall *A. jaborneggii;* 4- to 8-inch-tall Greek yarrow (*A. ageratifolia*); and 6- to 8-inch-tall *A. clavennae* (sometimes sold as *A. argentea*), *A. × kellereri,* and *A. umbellata.* These vary in hardiness but are usually rated for Zones 4 or 5 to 8 or 9. If you'd prefer yellow flowers, look for 4-inch-tall *A. × lewisii* and its pale yellow selection 'King Edward' or the faster-spreading woolly yarrow (*A. tomentosa*), with clear yellow flowers reaching 6 to 12 inches tall. Zones 3 to 8.

**GROWING TIPS:** Full sun and average, well-drained soil suits most yarrows just fine. (Excellent drainage is especially important for the low-growing, silvery species.) Don't be too generous with compost, fertilizer, or water, because rich, moist soil can lead to floppy stems. Snip off faded flower heads just above a lower bud to encourage rebloom, or cut back the whole flowering stem to the foliage clump.

**ALTERNATIVES:** Monarch-of-the-veldt (*Arctotis fastuosa;* also known as *Venidium fastuosum*) and African daisy (*A. venusta;* also known as *A.*

*stoechadifolia*) form low mounds of 4- to 5-inch-long, deeply lobed, silvery green to silvery gray leaves. Hybrid treasure flowers (*Gazania*) that look very similar in leaf include the Talent Series, 'Sundrop', and 'Christopher Lloyd'. Full sun; average, well-drained soil. All can be perennial in mild areas but are usually grown as annuals.

## ANTHEMIS
*Marguerite*

**Height:** Varies
**Leaf size:** About 3 inches long;
   ½–1 inch wide
**Full sun**
**Zones vary**

Daisy-form flowers are always welcome in the garden, and when you combine them with silvery foliage, you know you have a winner on your hands! Perennial marguerites (*Anthemis*) are marvelous for sunny sites with excellent drainage — in a border, in a container, or in masses as a colorful ground cover. Though none of them is exactly common, hybrid 'Susanna Mitchell' is becoming more widely sold for its relaxed, 18- to 30-inch-tall mounds of deeply cut, gray-green foliage and abundance of pale yellow to creamy white, golden-centered daisies in early to midsummer (and again later if you remove the faded flowers). Plants sold as *A. tinctoria* 'Kelwayi' or 'Kelway's' are similar in size but tend to be variable, with either grayish or green foliage and bright yellow

flowers. Zones 3 or 4 to 7. Golden marguerite or St. John's chamomile (*A. sancti-johannis*) is also fairly available; it grows in somewhat short-lived, 2- to 3-foot-tall clumps of ferny grayish foliage topped during most of the summer with bright blooms that have large, domed golden centers surrounded by short orange-yellow "petals." Zones 3 or 4 to 8. Among the lesser-known marguerites are some species with even more silvery foliage, such as *A. marschalliana* (also sold as *A. biebersteiniana*). The 8- to 12-inch-tall, bright yellow daisies appear mostly in late spring to early summer over mats of feathery, silver-gray leaves that spread 18 to 24 inches across. Zones 7 to 9. *A. punctata* var. *cupaniana* is similar but sports white daisies. Zones 6 to 9. *A. carpatica*, also sold as *A. cretica* subsp. *carpatica* and usually seen as the cultivar 'Karpatenschnee' ('Carpathian Snow' or 'Snow Carpet'), offers 6-inch-tall white daisies through much of the summer over carpets of finely divided, gray-green foliage. Zones 4 to 8.

**GROWING TIPS:** Marguerites perform best with full sun and well-drained soil that's not especially fertile. Pinching back the bushy types in spring will produce denser growth that's less prone to sprawling. Regular deadheading promotes rebloom and prevents self-sowing; shear the plants lightly after each set of flowers fades.

**ALTERNATIVES:** Also known as marguerite or marguerite daisy, *Argyranthemum* offers several cultivars with finely cut, blue-green to gray-green foliage. *A. gracile* 'Chelsea Girl', with nearly threadlike, blue-gray leaves on 2-foot plants, is one classic favorite; new selections appear each year. Zones 9 to 11. For deeply cut, silver-gray foliage on a larger scale, consider yellow bush daisy (*Euryops pectinatus*); 3 to 5 feet tall and wide. Zones 10 to 11. Full sun; average, well-drained soil.

*Anthemis tinctoria* 'Kelwayi'

## ARTEMISIA
*Artemisia, wormwood*

**Height:** Varies
**Leaf size:** 1–4 inches long; width varies
**Full sun**
**Zones vary**

Artemisias (*Artemisia*) offer some of the most beautiful silvery foliage available, but many of them have a reputation for being garden thugs. The trick to getting the best out of these perennials is choosing carefully to match the plants to your site and your needs. There are a number of species and selections, so you have lots of options. Below is a sampling of some of the most readily available artemisias;

*Artemisia* 'Powis Castle'

specialty nurseries are starting to offer some lovely lesser-known native species too. Besides their showy color and texture, many artemisias are also quite aromatic. They flower as well, but the yellowish blossoms are usually tiny and not very showy; in fact, many gardeners cut back the plants hard when the plants flower to encourage better-looking foliage.

*Spreading artemisias.* One of the most readily available artemisias is commonly called silvermound (usually sold as *A. schmidtiana* and 'Silver Mound'). It grows about 1 foot tall and 2 to 3 feet across, with very finely cut, silky silver-gray foliage. At its best, silvermound is a gorgeous garden plant, but keeping it in peak form can take some effort. At the very least, it usually needs a hard cut (down to about 2 inches above the ground) in late spring or early summer to prevent it from flopping open. In some areas, you may need to trim back the plants partway every few weeks to keep them looking good. Silvermound performs best in Zones 3 (with excellent drainage) to 7 or 8.

If you like the fine texture of silvermound but don't want to bother with such frequent trimming, consider 6- to 12-inch-tall *A. versicolor* 'Sea Foam' (also sold simply as *A. versicolor*) or 12- to 18-inch-tall Roman wormwood (*A. pontica*). They're rather more upright and not quite as feathery in appearance; they also

spread much more vigorously. Zones 4 or 5 to 8. 'Silver Brocade' beach wormwood (*A. stelleriana;* also known as 'Boughton Silver') has broader but still deeply cut, gray-white leaves in rhizomatous clumps usually 6 to 8 inches tall and 1 to 2 feet across. Zones 3 to 7.

Creeping artemisias also come in some more strongly upright forms, including several selections of white sage or western mugwort (*A. ludoviciana*). 'Silver King', with jagged-edged, lanced-shaped, silvery gray leaves on 2- to 3-foot-tall stems, is one of the best known. There's also a 'Silver Queen'; it's fairly similar, but the plants sold under this name vary in height and leaf form. 'Valerie Finnis' is the boldest of the bunch, with broader, finely toothed foliage in dense clumps to about 18 inches tall. Zones 3 or 4 to 8.

*Clump-forming artemisias.* If you prefer plants that tend to stay right where you put them, options abound for you too. One of the most popular choices is the hybrid 'Powis Castle', which grows in woody-based clumps of deeply cut, silvery gray foliage that can reach anywhere from 2 to 4 feet tall and 3 to 4 feet wide. Zones 5 or 6 to 9. *A. arborescens*, with ferny, silvery white foliage, is about the same size but somewhat less hardy (usually Zones 8 and 9). Southernwood (*A. abrotanum*) is usually 3 to 4 feet tall and wide, with feathery, gray-green leaves. Zones 5

to 8. Wormwood (*A. absinthium*) typically reaches 2 to 3 feet tall, with silvery gray, lacy foliage; the cultivar 'Lambrook Silver' is usually about 2 feet tall. Zones 3 or 4 to 8. Four- to 6-foot-tall 'Huntingdon' is often listed under *A. absinthium* but is less hardy (usually Zones 5 to 8). *Note: A. absinthium* is considered invasive in some areas.

To enjoy shrubby clumps of silvery foliage on a smaller scale, consider the hybrid 'Beth Chatto' (about 18 inches tall and wide) and *A. pycnocephala* 'David's Choice' (about 1 foot tall and 3 feet wide) for Zones 6 to 9. *A. alba* 'Canescens' (also sold as *A. canescens* and *A. vulgaris* 'Canescens') grows 12 to 18 inches tall and wide, with more finely cut, silver-gray foliage. Zones 4 to 8.

**GROWING TIPS:** Artemisias need full sun and thrive in average, well-drained soil that's not especially fertile. Most of them don't appreciate hot, humid conditions; they tend to flop and/or drop their lower leaves. Cutting down affected plants to a few inches above the ground encourages fresh, bushy regrowth. There are several ways to keep creeping artemisias from getting out of hand. In a border setting, you could surround them with some kind of buried root barrier, or divide the clumps every year or two to prevent them from getting too settled in. Other options are planting in a container, giving them a tough site (such as a dry slope) where few other plants will thrive, and putting them in a place where they can't escape (such as a spot surrounded by paving).

**ALTERNATIVES:** *Tanacetum argenteum* (also sold as *Achillea argentea*) forms ground-hugging carpets of deeply cut, near white leaves; Zones 5 to 7. *T. ptarmiciflorum* (also known as *Chrysanthemum ptarmiciflorum* and *Pyrethrum ptarmiciflorum* and often sold as 'Silver Feather' or 'Silver Lace' dusty miller) is rated for Zones 8 to 10 but usually grown as an annual for its lacy gray leaves; 2 to 3 feet tall. Full sun; average to dry soil.

*Athyrium niponicum* var. *pictum*

## ATHYRIUM
*Painted fern*

**Height: 12–18 inches**
**Leaf size: 12–18 inches long;**
    **4–5 inches wide**
**Partial to full shade**
**Zones 3 or 4–8**

Fern fanciers appreciate the differences among the many available species and selections, but to other gardeners, most ferns look pretty much alike. Japanese painted fern (*Athyrium niponicum* var. *pictum;* also known as *A. goeringianum* var. *pictum*), though, is one that even beginning gardeners can readily identify, thanks to its silvery gray foliage. This deciduous beauty bears narrowly triangular, deeply cut fronds that have reddish purple central stems. The burgundy stem color often shades into the base of the leaflets; they typically show some blue-green to light green areas as well. Plants sold simply

as *A. niponicum* var. *pictum* and *A. niponicum* 'Pictum' vary in color from plant to plant; other named selections are more consistent, although they, too, can vary in color depending on the growing conditions and the age of the fronds. (New fronds growing in cool temperatures and ample light tend to be brightest.) 'Apple Court' is a fairly tall selection (1 to 2 feet) with mostly silver-gray fronds that have frilly tips. Similarly colored 'Wildwood Twist', with slightly twisted fronds, is about 18 inches tall. The long, arching fronds of 'Silver Falls' tend to be even brighter silver, and it's typically 12 to 15 inches tall. If you'd like a bit more color, consider 'Pewter Lace' or 'Burgundy Lace', both to about 1 foot tall, or 'Ursula's Red', to about 18 inches tall; their fronds have a broad, deep gray-green to

purplish gray center stripe and bright silver along the edges. There are also several hybrids between Japanese painted fern and lady fern (*A. filix-femina*), including 1- to 2-foot-tall 'Branford Beauty' and 2- to 3-foot-tall 'Ghost'. These produce more-upright clumps with dark-stemmed, gray-green fronds.

**GROWING TIPS:** Painted ferns will grow in full shade, but tend to produce their brightest leaf markings with lots of light, so a site with morning sun and afternoon shade is best. Humus-rich, evenly moist but well-drained soil is ideal, encouraging the plants to produce colorful new fronds through much of the growing season. Clip off the dead foliage in late winter or early spring.

**ALTERNATIVES:** *Viola grypoceras* var. *exilis* 'Sylettas' (also sold as 'Syletta', *V. koreana*, and *V. coreana*)

is also strongly veined with silver, but its deep green leaves are rounded (very much like cyclamen foliage). *V.* 'Sylvia Hart' is similar but has pointed leaf tips. Both grow 2 to 4 inches tall. Partial shade (full sun is fine in cool areas); humus-rich, evenly moist but well-drained soil. Zones 4 to 8.

## CHAMAECYPARIS
*False cypress*

**Height: Varies**
**Leaf size: ¼ inch or less (individual**
    **needlelike or scalelike leaves)**
**Full sun**
**Zones 4 or 5–8**

If you're looking for "ever-blue" foliage for your borders or landscape, false cypresses (*Chamaecyparis*) are definitely worth considering. These conifers come in a wide range of shapes and sizes, are usually quite adaptable, and seldom need any special care. There are many species and selections to choose from; below is an overview of some smaller-scale cultivars that you might run across in local nurseries and mail-order catalogs. Specialty nurseries, of course, offer many more. Be aware that the genus name is likely to change — some experts are inclined to combine both false and true cypresses into the genus *Cupressus*, for instance, while others have suggested other genus names — but you'll probably still find these species sold as *Chamaecyparis* for many years to come.

The best known of the blue false cypresses is probably 'Boulevard' Sawara false cypress (*Chamaecyparis pisifera* or *Cupressus pisifera*). The upright silvery blue to gray-blue plants are typically pyramidal when young (especially with regular pruning), gradually developing a broader conical shape to about 10 feet tall. Bright gray-blue 'Baby Blue' is similar but usually more compact (to about 6 feet tall). Silvery blue 'Curly Tops' ('Curley Tops'), with twisted shoot tips, is somewhat rounded when young, turning pyramidal to conical with age. Curiously enough, some gardeners report

this selection to be slow-growing to about 4 feet tall, while others claim it grows quickly to 10 feet or more. If you want to give it a try — and you likely will if you get the chance to see it in person — check with local gardeners or an arboretum to find out how it usually performs in your area before you choose a planting site. All three of these have short, needlelike leaves that are surprisingly soft to the touch. They belong to a category known as the Squarrosa Group and are sometimes referred to as moss false cypresses.

Hinoki false cypress (*Chamaecyparis obtusa* or *Cupressus obtusa*) also offers several notable "ever-blue" selections. 'Split Rock' ('Splitrock') is one of the bluest in the group, with a pyramidal shape that grows slowly to about 6 feet tall. Blue-gray to blue-green 'Blue Feathers' (also known as 'Ivan's Column') has a rather rounded form when young but develops a more narrow, upright shape to about 6 feet tall over time. If you'd prefer a cultivar that's very narrowly upright even when young, there's blue-green 'Elwood's Pillar' Lawson cypress or Port Orford cedar (*Chamaecyparis lawsoniana* or *Cupressus lawsoniana*). It grows very slowly to about 6 feet tall.

'Heatherbun' Eastern white cedar (*Chamaecyparis thyoides* or *Cupressus thyoides*) is another noteworthy cultivar. Its rounded, 3-foot mounds are

blue-green in summer but turn a lovely deep purple color in winter.

**GROWING TIPS:** False cypresses thrive in full sun with humus-rich, evenly moist but well-drained soil; light shade is fine too. Water during dry spells for the first few years to help young plants get established. A bit of judicious spring pruning will help them develop a more symmetrical form, if desired.

**ALTERNATIVES:** Looking for more "ever-blue" conifers? Among the many cedars (*Cedrus*) are weeping blue Atlas cedar (*C. atlantica* 'Glauca Pendula') and narrowly upright 'Glauca Fastigiata'; 10 to 15 feet tall. Zones 6 to 9. Full sun to light shade; average to moist but well-drained soil. 'Blue Ice' Arizona cypress (*Cupressus arizonica* var. *glauca*) forms a bright silvery blue column eventually to 30 feet tall. Full sun; average, well-drained to dry soil. Zones 6 or 7 to 9.

## DICENTRA
*Bleeding heart*

**Height: 8–12 inches for most**
**Leaf size: 6–12 inches long;**
   **4–6 inches wide**
**Full sun to partial shade**
**Zones 3–9**

Bleeding hearts (*Dicentra*) offer the best of both worlds: ferny foliage and beautiful blooms too. The classic common bleeding heart (*D. spectabilis*) has green leaves, but many of the compact, smaller-flowered forms have a distinct bluish cast to their deeply

divided, mound-forming foliage. Most of these are hybrids between fringed bleeding heart (*D. eximia*) and western bleeding heart (*D. formosa* subsp. *oregana*) — occasionally *D. peregrina* as well — but you'll often see them listed under one species or the other; just go by the cultivar name to get the particular traits you're interested in. Besides the feathery foliage, these hybrids boast sprays of nodding reddish, pink, or white blooms over a very long period: usually starting in late spring to early summer and often continuing into autumn if you give them dependably moist soil and remove the spent flowers regularly.

There are lots of options to choose from, differing mostly in flower color. If you'd like reddish to deep rosy pink flowers, look for 'Adrian Bloom', 'Bacchanal', 'Bountiful', and 'Zestful'. 'Luxuriant' is in the same color range but tends to be taller than usual (up to about 18 inches). 'Candy Hearts' is a medium pink, as are 'King of Hearts' and 'Stuart Boothman'; the latter two have particularly striking blue-green to blue-gray foliage. ('King of Hearts' also tends to be quite compact — usually 6 to 8 inches tall — and it doesn't set seed, so it blooms over a long period even without deadheading.) 'Langtrees' and 'Pearl Drops' have white flowers slightly tinged with pink; *D. formosa* 'Aurora', 'Ivory Hearts', *D. eximia* 'Snowdrift', and 'Snowflakes' are white.

*Chamaecyparis pisifera* 'Curly Tops'

*Dicentra* 'King of Hearts'

**GROWING TIPS:** In the cooler parts of their hardiness range, bleeding hearts will grow in full sun; in warmer areas, morning sun and afternoon shade or light all-day shade bring better results. A steady supply of moisture produces the most vigorous growth and flowering. The plants tolerate drier conditions but usually stop flowering in summer; they may even die back to the ground and not reappear until the following spring. Even though moisture is important, good drainage is also a must, especially in winter.

**ALTERNATIVES:** Yellow corydalis (*Corydalis lutea*) and the similar *C. ochroleuca* grow in dense, 1-foot-tall mounds of lacy, blue-green to grayish green leaves; may go partially or

totally summer-dormant. Zones 5 to 9. Dusty meadow rue (*Thalictrum flavum* subsp. *glaucum*; also known as *T. speciosissimum*) is taller — usually 4 to 6 feet — with bright gray-blue, fernlike foliage. Zones 4 to 8. Full sun to light shade; average to moist but well-drained soil.

---

## PEROVSKIA
*Russian sage*

**Height: Varies**
**Leaf size: 2 inches long;**
    **1 inch wide**
**Full sun**
**Zones 4 or 5–9**

Russian sages (*Perovskia*) are a real boon for gardeners looking for late-summer flowers, but their finely cut foliage, woolly white stems, and handsome habit make them a welcome addition during the rest of the year too. They show off beautifully in mass plantings if you have a lot of space to fill; single clumps or small groupings are a great addition to mixed borders.

Russian sages are rather mixed up as far as names are concerned. Most sold simply as *P. atriplicifolia* and *P. abrotanoides* are actually hybrids of the two species. They vary in height, in the exact color of their flowers, and in the fineness of their foliage; in general, though, they grow in shrubby clumps that can reach anywhere from 3 to 6 feet tall and about as wide. Their slender stems carry toothed to deeply cut, aromatic, gray-green leaves and are topped with long, airy,

spiky-looking clusters of small blue flowers. In the warmest parts of their range, they may start blooming in early summer; in most areas, expect flowers from mid- or late summer into early fall or even later. From a foliage standpoint, the various named selections are pretty much alike except for 'Filigran', which has particularly lacy leaves. There's also 'Little Spire', which tends to be more compact (closer to 2 to 3 feet tall). Other full-size cultivars you're apt to run across are 'Blue Haze' and 'Blue Mist', which have slightly lighter-than-usual blue flowers, and 'Blue Spire' (which some say is the same as 'Longin'), with darker-than-usual purple-blue flowers.

**GROWING TIPS:** Full sun with average soil is fine, and good drainage is essential, especially in winter. Salt and drought don't bother Russian sage much, so it's a good choice for seaside gardens and for areas next to paved surfaces that are treated with deicing salt in winter. The leafless stems hold their form even through ice and snow, so don't be in a hurry to cut them down after frost; instead, wait until early spring, then trim the entire plant to a few inches above the ground to encourage dense new growth that's less likely to sprawl. Russian sage may self-sow in some areas, so if you find seedlings, you may prefer to snip off the spent flower clusters as soon as the blooms fade. Keep in mind that it may also spread by

creeping roots in some conditions (mostly in mild climates).

**ALTERNATIVE:** Ghost bramble (*Rubus thibetanus*; also listed as *R. tibetanus* and sometimes with the cultivar name 'Silver Fern') is an out-of-the-ordinary shrub that grows in spreading, multistemmed, 3- to 6-foot-tall clumps of spiny, arching canes. The young stems are covered with a bright white "bloom," providing interest even after the finely cut, gray-green leaves drop in autumn. Full sun to partial shade; average, well-drained soil. Zones 6 to 9.

*Perovskia* 'Little Spire'

*Ruta graveolens*

## RUTA
*Rue*

**Height: 2–3 feet**
**Leaf size: 3–6 inches long;**
  **2–3 inches wide**
**Full sun**
**Zones 4–9**

Rue (*Ruta graveolens*) has long been a welcome addition to herb gardens for its beautiful "ever-blue" to "semi-ever-blue" foliage, but it works just as well in ornamental plantings. The dense, shrubby clumps of upright stems carry an abundance of dissected, blue-green to blue-gray leaves that have a strong, bitter scent. They're topped with clusters of yellow flowers for most of the summer. 'Jackman's Blue' has particularly blue-gray foliage and typically grows about 2 feet tall; 'Blue

Mound' is also intensely blue and usually 12 to 18 inches tall.

**GROWING TIPS:** Rue grows best in full sun (light shade is acceptable too) and thrives in lean, average, well-drained to dry soil. It may self-sow but is seldom a problem. Cut back the plants by about half in spring to promote lush new growth; if desired, trim them again a few times during the growing season to shape them and control their size. *Caution:* Handling rue may irritate sensitive skin that's exposed to sunlight, so wear gloves.

**ALTERNATIVE:** Imagine lacy carrot leaves in a bright silvery blue, and you'll have some idea what to expect from moon carrot (*Seseli gummiferum*). In its first year, you'll enjoy this unusual biennial's dense

foliage rosettes; in the second year, they shoot up into sparsely leafy, 3- to 4-foot-tall flowering stems. Moon carrot typically dies after flowering but usually self-sows. Full sun; average, well-drained soil. Zones 4 or 5 to 9.

## SENECIO
*Dusty miller*

**Height: 1–2 feet**
**Leaf size: 3–6 inches long;**
  **1–1½ inches wide**
**Full sun to partial shade**
**Zones 5 or 6–10**

When it comes to dusty millers, gardeners who like to use common names have an advantage over those who insist on knowing the exact botanical names of the plants they're growing. The dusty millers sold as annual bedding plants are usually listed under *Senecio cineraria*, but you may also find them under *Centaurea cineraria* and *C. maritima*. By any name, dusty millers are fantastic foliage accents for all but the shadiest gardens, with shallowly lobed to distinctly lacy, velvety leaves in shades of bright silver-gray to nearly white. Their compact size (8 to 12 inches tall in one year) and adaptable nature make it easy to tuck them into even small spaces, and they thrive with practically no care. Among the more readily available selections are 'Cirrus' and 'Diamond', with fairly broad, shallowly lobed leaves, and the much more deeply lobed 'Silver Dust'

('Silverdust'). Tender *S. viravira* (also listed as *S. vira-vira* and *S. leucostachys*) has finely divided, bright grayish white leaves, but it gets taller (2 to 3 feet tall and wide in one season) and its overall effect is a bit more delicate-looking than that of the usual dusty millers.

**GROWING TIPS:** Dusty millers prefer full sun but will tolerate partial shade (and may, in fact, perform better there in hot-summer areas). Average, well-drained soil is fine; once settled in, the plants sail through most dry spells with little or no watering. You'll usually see dusty millers rated as

*Senecio viravira*

hardy only in Zones 9 and 10, but they may surprise you by making a return appearance as far north as Zone 5. Second-year plants usually want to flower, and tend to get somewhat leggy-looking. Unless you really like the small, buttonlike yellow blossoms, it's best to cut back the plants hard when they bloom (or even before then) to encourage bushier regrowth and more foliage.

**ALTERNATIVE:** Another lacy-leaved dusty miller that's on the taller side is *Centaurea gymnocarpa* 'Colchester White' (also sold under *C. maritima*). It can reach about 30 inches in one season, with upright stems clad in arching, feathery, silvery white foliage. It thrives in the same growing conditions as other dusty millers but seems to be even more tolerant of hot and humid weather. Zones 7 or 8 to 10.

RIGHT: **A pleasant surprise.** The blue-gray juvenile foliage of many eucalyptus species adds a touch of the unexpected to borders and containers, particularly when paired with darker-leaved partners. (Longwood Gardens, PA)

# 5 MARVELOUS MULTICOLORS

ABOVE: **Getting an edge.** The addition of pink and white markings can turn even an ordinary perennial such as cushion spurge (*Euphorbia polychroma*) into something special — like the selection 'First Blush'.

OPPOSITE: **Multicolor magic.** This breath-taking pairing of 'Brother Stephan' hosta and 'Burgundy Lace' painted fern (*Athyrium*) would grace any shady border. (Plant Delights, NC)

What is it that attracts so many gardeners to variegated plants? For some, it's the thrill of the hunt — seeking out the newest introductions and rarest selections, regardless of cost or garden-worthiness. Others appreciate variegated plants for the design opportunities they offer. Used singly as an accent, in groups for beds and borders, or in masses as ground covers, these undeniably eye-catching plants are invaluable for supplying visual interest and creating exciting color effects.

The science behind the causes and kinds of variegation is a fascinating study, but you don't need to understand the difference between streaking and stippling to enjoy growing variegated plants. You can simply look at them and decide whether they appeal to you. Don't be dissuaded by spoilsports who dismiss all variegates as being sickly, with dire threats of nasty viruses infecting your entire garden. Admittedly, irregular or streaky variegation *is* a classic symptom of some viruses, and sometimes it's difficult to tell perfectly healthy variegated plants from infected ones. But in the vast majority of variegates, the foliage patterns are caused by natural changes within the plants themselves, and you can grow them with no fear (or hope) of their variegation "spreading" to other plants in your garden.

## GETTING STARTED WITH MULTICOLOR PLANTS

Ask several gardeners to define *variegated foliage,* and you'll probably get several different answers. Some consider that a leaf with any two or more colors qualifies as variegated; others define it more specifically as a green leaf with any other color. In this chapter, I'm using the broadest definition — leaves with two or more colors, with or without green — with two exceptions: we've discussed silver markings on green leaves in chapter 4 (Stunning Silver, Gray, and Blue, starting on page 140) and purple or red markings on green leaves in chapter 3 (Rousing Red to Basic Black, starting on page 88).

So, what causes green leaves to develop other colors? Leaf cells normally contain structures called *chloroplasts,* which hold the chlorophyll pigments that plants need to carry out photosynthesis. These chlorophyll pigments make plants look green. If chloroplasts are absent altogether, the leaf tissue will be white; if they are present but can't produce chlorophyll, those tissues may instead be yellow, pink, red, purple, or other hues, due to the presence of other (nongreen) pigments.

Cells that lack chlorophyll don't contribute much, if anything, to producing energy; that's why a variegated form of a particular plant tends to be less vigorous than the all-green version. When the variegation is slight, you may not notice the difference, but when there's a lot of variegation, the effect on the plant's vigor is usually quite distinct. If most or all of its leaves lack chlorophyll, the plant will be very weak. Weak plants tend to be difficult to propagate; that's why

dramatically variegated plants are frequently rare and expensive. Or they may die before anyone gets a chance to propagate them, so they're lost completely. Fortunately, there are plenty of plants that are attractively variegated but still strong enough to perform well in our gardens — and are readily available for purchase without maxing out our credit cards.

LEFT: **Fine lines.** The crisp, distinctive variegation of *Sanchezia speciosa* makes it an appealing addition to the garden, either alone as an accent or paired with equally striking flowering and foliage partners.

OPPOSITE: **Stripes are stars.** Long touted for its textural interest, spiky iris foliage can also provide season-long color to your combinations. Shown here is variegated Dalmatian iris (*Iris pallida* 'Variegata') with 'Worcester Gold' caryopteris (*Caryopteris* × *clandonensis*) and variegated fragrant Solomon's seal (*Polygonatum falcatum* 'Variegatum').

### The Origins of Variegation

Understanding how plants become variegated in the first place can help you decide if you want to grow them, as well as how to care for them if you do choose to include them in your garden. The most common cause of variegation is genetic changes that occur in cells on the growing tip of a shoot. If the mutation occurs right at the growing tip, the resulting growth is apt to be evenly variegated. If the mutated cell is to the side of the growing tip, the new growth may have only one variegated leaf; or variegated leaves on one side and green on the other; or some variegated shoots and some plain ones.

Variegated growth that appears on a normally green plant is commonly called a *sport*. This term also applies to different variegation patterns that appear on an already variegated plant. To preserve these sports, you can attempt to propagate them by stem cuttings, budding, grafting, or division. (Root cuttings and leaf cuttings typically produce all-green plants.) If some parts of a plant are

LEFT: **Seeing patterns.** When you look closely at variegated foliage, you'll often notice varying shades of green along with the brighter markings, as on this leaf of 'Meehanii' rose-of-Sharon (*Hibiscus syriacus*).

more strongly variegated than others, repeatedly propagating from the most colorful parts may help to stabilize the markings and lead to more-uniform variegation. Sometimes, variegated plants start producing all-green shoots. These reversions tend to grow more vigorously than the variegated parts, so if you don't remove them quickly, you may end up with a plain green plant. Usually, it's enough to snip off a reverted shoot back to the variegated part. If the reverted parts grow directly from the ground, you're better off digging up the whole plant, dividing it, and replanting only the variegated parts of the clump.

Some variegated plants can also be reproduced by seed. These variegates tend to have speckled or streaky markings throughout their leaves; don't expect crisp margins or uniform stripes. If all of its seedlings tend to be variegated, a plant is said to come true from seed. It's more usual that a plant comes "mostly true" or "partly true"; in these cases, you'll want to remove the green seedlings and leave the variegated ones, a process called *rogueing out*. Just keep in mind that some seed-grown plants take a while to show their variegation — variegated corn (*Zea mays* var. *japonica*) is one example. So if you expect some variegation but the seedlings

---

### VARIEGATES FOR SUNNY GARDENS

*Abelia* × *grandiflora* 'Francis Mason', others

*Abutilon pictum* 'Thompsonii', others

*Arundo donax* 'Variegata'

*Brugmansia* 'Miner's Claim', 'Snowbank', others

*Buddleia davidii* 'Harlequin', 'Santana', others

*Canna* 'Bangkok', 'Pretoria', others

*Capsicum annuum* 'Fish', 'Shu', others

*Caryopteris divaricata* 'Snow Fairy'

*Cornus alba* 'Elegantissima', 'Gouchaultii', others

*Cortaderia selloana* 'Albolineata', 'Aureolineata', others

*Euphorbia polychroma* 'First Blush', others

*Forsythia* × *intermedia* 'Fiesta', 'Golden Times', others

*Hebe speciosa* 'Tricolor', 'Variegata'

*Heliopsis helianthoides* 'Loraine Sunshine'

*Hemerocallis fulva* 'Kwanzo Variegata'

*Iris pallida* 'Argentea Variegata', 'Variegata'

*Liriope muscari* 'Variegata', 'Silvery Sunproof', others

*Lysimachia punctata* 'Alexander', others

*Miscanthus sinensis* 'Morning Light', 'Variegatus', others

*Nerium oleander* 'Variegatum', others

*Phlox paniculata* 'Becky Towe', 'Harlequin', others

*Physostegia virginiana* 'Variegata'

*Rhamnus alaternus* 'Variegata'

*Rosa wichurana* 'Variegata'

*Salix integra* 'Hakuro-nishiki', others

*Sedum* 'Frosty Morn', others

*Tropaeolum majus* 'Alaska', 'Jewel of Africa'

*Weigela* 'Gold Rush', 'Sunny Princess', others

*Yucca filamentosa* 'Bright Edge', 'Golden Sword', others

## VARIEGATES FOR SHADY SPOTS

*Alpinia zerumbet* 'Variegata', others

*Arum italicum* 'Pictum'

*Aucuba japonica* 'Gold Dust', 'Picturata', others

*Brunnera macrophylla* 'Hadspen Cream', 'Variegata'

*Caladium bicolor* 'Miss Muffet', 'White Christmas', others

*Carex siderosticha* 'Variegata', others

*Cleyera japonica* 'Variegata'

*Eleutherococcus sieboldianus* 'Variegatus'

*Farfugium tussilaginea* 'Argenteum', 'Aureomaculatum', others

× *Fatshedera lizei* 'Anna Mikkels', 'Variegata'

*Fatsia japonica* 'Spider's Web', 'Variegata'

*Geranium phaeum* 'Margaret Wilson', 'Variegatum', others

*Hakonechloa macra* 'Albovariegata', 'Aureola'

*Hedera colchica* 'Dentata Variegata', 'Sulphur Heart'

*Hosta* 'Ginkgo Craig', 'Great Expectations', others

*Iris tectorum* 'Variegata'

*Kadsura japonica* 'Variegata', others

*Kerria japonica* 'Picta'

*Lamium maculatum* 'Elizabeth de Haas', others

*Leucothoe fontanesiana* 'Rainbow', others

*Liriope muscari* 'Gold Band', 'Silver Midget', others

*Pachysandra terminalis* 'Silveredge'

*Philadelphus coronarius* 'Variegatus'

*Phlox stolonifera* 'Variegata'

*Pieris japonica* 'Little Heath', 'White Rim', others

*Polemonium reptans* 'Stairway to Heaven'

*Polygonatum falcatum* 'Variegatum'

*Tricyrtis hirta* 'Albomarginata', 'Miyazaki Gold'

come up all green, give them a few more days or weeks to see if the markings appear. It's also possible for some seedlings to be all white, but these will die soon after they sprout, because they can't carry out photosynthesis to feed themselves.

Viruses, too, can cause leaves to be variegated in a speckled, streaked, or stippled pattern. Some mosaic viruses can severely weaken a plant; others, such as the kind that infects flowering maples (*Abutilon*), have little effect on the plant's vigor. Harmful viruses may spread by tools or insects, and they attack a wide variety of plants. Those that produce "ornamental" effects are transmitted mainly by grafting and are usually much more specific about the plants they affect. That's why it's generally safe to grow virus-induced ornamental variegates in your garden with little fear that your other plants will be harmed. (Viris-infected hostas, such as 'Break Dance', are one exception.)

Sometimes leaf markings are the result of nutrient imbalances, rather than genetic or viral changes. Iron or magnesium deficiency, for example, can result in yellow leaves with green veins; other imbalances can produce yellow or whitish spots. If you have existing plants that appear to become variegated, or if you spot a plant in a nursery that seems to be variegated when you'd normally expect it to be solid green, the effect may be only temporary. Try fertilizing with a product that contains trace minerals (micronutrients), such as iron, manganese, and molybdenum, as well as nitrogen and other macronutrients, then wait a week or two. If the discoloration disappears, then nutrient deficiency was the problem; if the variegation pattern is still present on the new growth, the markings are probably permanent.

LEFT: **All in vein.** In a genus of shrubs normally grown for their flowers, the intricately marked leaves of 'Kumson' forsythia make it a standout.

RIGHT: **The lure of the rings.** With lovely leaves like these, 'Mr. Henry Cox' zonal geranium (*Pelargonium* × *hortorum*) doesn't even need to bloom to be beautiful.

# PATTERNS OF VARIEGATION

*MISCANTHUS SINENSIS*
'ZEBRINUS'

*LONICERA NITIDA*
'LEMON BEAUTY'

*ACER* 'KALLIOPE'

*CALAMINTHA*
*GRANDIFLORA* 'VARIEGATA'

*HEMEROCALLIS FULVA*
'KWANZO VARIEGATA'

*CORNUS KOUSA*
'GOLD STAR'

*FORSYTHIA* 'KUMSON'

*WISTERIA FLORIBUNDA*
'MON NISHIKI'

*ALPINIA ZERUMBET*
'VARIEGATA'

*TSUGA CANADENSIS*
'GENTSCH WHITE'

## Siting Variegated Plants

Most variegated garden plants perform perfectly well with average care. You simply need to keep their somewhat reduced vigor in mind when you use them in designs, and set them at slightly closer spacings than you'd use for the all-green forms. Their slower growth rate can be a benefit if the plain-green version grows quickly enough to be considered a pest — as with gooseneck loosestrife (*Lysimachia clethroides*), for example. The variegated selection 'Geisha' tends to be shorter and doesn't spread as quickly, although it can still be too aggressive by many gardeners' standards. The lesson here is that even less vigorous variegated selections can still grow more quickly than many other plants, so don't count on variegation to slow down true thugs too much.

The main consideration for placing variegated plants is the amount of light they require. In general, the more white or yellow areas a leaf has, the more sun it needs to produce the same amount of food as an all-green leaf. That isn't always an option, though, because strong sunlight may actually damage highly variegated leaves. The trick is to give enough light for the plant to thrive but not so much that the leaves get scorched. Start with a site that provides about the same amount or a little less light than the all-green version thrives in; then, if it isn't as vigorous as you'd like, or if its variegation isn't as dramatic as you expected, move it to a brighter spot. (Supplying extra moisture reduces the chance of leaf damage in strong sun.) Fortunately, most plants are very forgiving if you don't get the site quite right at first; just don't move them *too* frequently. Often, they'll settle in just fine after a few weeks or months, even if the growing conditions in that spot aren't exactly optimal.

RIGHT: **A careful balance.** Variegated selections of Japanese maple (*Acer palmatum*) usually produce their best markings with morning sun and afternoon shade, or with light all-day shade.

OPPOSITE: **Captivating companions.** Who says shade gardens can't be filled with color? Choosing an assortment of fantastic foliage plants ensures excitement all through the growing season. (Jabco-Henderson garden, PA)

LEFT: **Banding together.** There's nothing delicate about this vibrant combination of Tropicanna canna and zebra grass (*Miscanthus sinensis* 'Zebrinus'). It will thrive in all the sun you can give it!

## WHAT'S IN A NAME?

Many plants come in at least one variegated form, and some (such as hostas) have hundreds of multicolored selections. Often, you can tell that a plant has some kind of variegation without ever seeing it; just look at its name! If you see one or more of the words below in a plant's botanical or common name, there's a good chance it has out-of-the-ordinary foliage.

*albomaculata, -um, -us* (spotted with white)

*albomarginata, -um, -us* (edged with white)

*albopicta, -um, -us* (splashed with white)

*albopunctata, -um, -us* (spotted with white)

*albostriata, -um, -us* (striped with white)

*albovariegata, -um, -us* (variegated with white)

*argenteomarginata, -um, -us* (edged with silver or silvery white)

*argenteovariegata, -um, -us* (variegated with gold)

*aureomarginata, -um, -us* (edged with gold)

*aureoreticulata, -um, -us* (netted or veined with gold)

*aureostriata, -um, -us* (striped with gold)

*aureovariegata, -um, -us* (variegated with gold)

band, banded

bicolor (with two colors)

chameleon

*commixta* (mixed)

*commutata, -um, -us* (changeable)

dapple, dappled

*discolor* (with different colors)

dot, dotted

edge, edged

flamingo

freckle, freckled

gold dust

*goshiki* (with five colors)

*guttata, -um, -us* (spotted)

harlequin

Joseph's coat

kaleidoscope

leopard

line, lined

*maculata, -um, -us* (spotted)

marble, marbled

*marginata, -um, -us* (margined)

*marmorata, -um, -us* (marbled)

*mediopicta, -um, -us* (painted in the middle)

*mediovariegata, -um, -us* (variegated in the middle)

medley

montage

mosaic

multicolor

*multistriata, -um, -us* (with many stripes)

*nishiki* (brocade [patterned fabric])

peacock

*picta, -um, -us* (painted or splashed)

*picturata, -um, -us* (variegated)

*punctata, -um, -us*

*quadricolor* (with four colors)

rainbow

*reticulata, -um, -us* (netted)

silver dust

snow, snowstorm

spangled

speckle, speckled

splash, splashed

spot, spotted, spotty

stained glass

stipple, stippled

streaked

*striata, -um, -us* (striped)

striped

sunspot

swirl

Taff's (for Stephen Taffler, a variegated-plant expert)

tapestry

tiger

*tricolor* (with three colors)

*variegata, -um, -us* (variegated)

*variifolia, -um, -us* (variegated leaves)

*varia, -um, -us* (variegated)

*versicolor* (with various colors, or changing color)

*viridistriata, -um, -us* (striped with green)

*vittata, -um, -us* (striped)

zebra

*zebrina, -um, -us* (striped)

# MULTICOLORED PLANTS IN THE GARDEN

Variegated plants are more than just garden oddities — they're also quite useful from a design standpoint. Their eye-catching foliage makes them ideal as accents or focal points, and their lighter colors are great for brightening up shady sites. Multicolors may be just what you need to "break up" large groupings of all-green foliage in a border or an expanse of ground covers. Those with particularly bold markings can add as much or even more color than typical flowering plants, and they look good for longer than most blooming plants too. Because their leaves contain multiple colors, variegated plants are also invaluable as building blocks for creating elegant or dramatic combinations.

In most cases, variegates work best in sites where you see them up close. And the more subtle the markings, the closer they need to be! Seen from a distance, even strongly marked white-variegated plants may have an overall grayish or pale green cast; those with gold markings appear yellowish. That's not necessarily a bad thing; it's just something to keep in mind when considering variegates for a particular area. To really make the most of these patterned plants, keep them nearby — along a path, in a foundation planting, or at the front of a large bed or border, for example. Multicolors are excellent in containers, too, because you can easily admire even subtle markings without having to stoop. Large trees, conversely, are probably the least effective choices for

LEFT: **Connect the dots.** When pairing strongly variegated partners, it's helpful to toss in some solid-colored foliage. (Beds and Borders, NY)

showcasing variegation: their brightly patterned leaves may be overwhelming in an average landscape, or their leaves may be so far above that the individual markings are indistinct.

## Multicolors Paired with Plain Green

Of all the colors you can combine variegated plants with, greens are both safe and satisfying choices. Pairing the all-green and variegated versions of a particular plant (such as green and variegated hostas) provides a contrast of color, at the same time keeping the visual harmony of consistent form and texture. Foliage of all sorts in shades of deep to bright green is ideal for setting off yellow- or white-marked leaves, providing a solid background that really makes brightly striped or spotted leaves stand out. Green flowers make subtle but elegant companions, too; because they often have a yellowish green cast, they're intriguing partners for yellow-variegated plants.

ABOVE: **Rim shot.** The bright bordering on 'Axminster Gold' comfrey (*Symphytum × uplandicum*) is a standout even from a distance.

## Combining Multicolored Plants

You'll often hear that you shouldn't put two or more variegated plants right next to each other. Like all other design rules, this one is made to be broken! It's true that a mixture of many different variegates may look a little too "busy," but it's certainly possible to use a variety of multicolors even in a small area without creating an ugly jumble. One way is to combine plants that show their markings in different seasons, such as spring-colorful 'Sunningdale Variegated' masterwort (*Astrantia major*) planted under 'Pulverulenta' elderberry (*Sambucus nigra*), which usually doesn't develop its showy spotting until early summer. Another option is to pair plants that are variegated with different amounts of the same two colors: one that's mostly green with a little yellow combined with one that's mostly yellow with a little green, for example. Variegated partners with distinctly different forms or textures can work well together too. If you'd like to use many different multicolors in one garden, adding in some solid green companions should supply enough uniformity to offset the dramatic patterns.

## Multicolors with White and Silver Companions

Few pairings are as pleasing as white-and-green leaves with white flowers. In shady sites, the look is cool and elegant; in sun, it's bold and dramatic. Crisp white blooms and bright silver leaves usually work best with pure white variegation. In a partly shaded site, for instance, try the strappy, white-striped foliage of 'Kwanzo Variegata' daylily (*Hemerocallis fulva*) with the broad silver leaves of 'Looking Glass' hardy forget-me-not (*Brunnera macrophylla*); the contrast of forms is dramatic, but the equally intense silver and white markings provide pleasing harmony.

Creamy variegation can make clear white flowers look "dirty" but will complement similarly cream-colored blooms. The most challenging combination is yellow-marked leaves with white flowers or silver foliage. You can easily create contrast with different forms and textures, but it takes some effort to find harmony as well. One trick here is to use white flowers with yellow centers: the centers echo the yellow foliage markings, while the white petals provide variation of form and color. One of my favorites of this type of partnership is the white-petaled, yellow-centered blooms of 'Becky' Shasta daisy (*Leucanthemum*) in front of the yellow-banded foliage of porcupine grass (*Miscanthus sinensis* 'Strictus').

If you're working with foliage that includes white plus two or more other colors, pairing it with white flowers or bright silvery white foliage can provide a visual link to tie them together. Multicolors that don't include white (pink-and-yellow coleus, for instance, or peach-and-green phormiums) produce a strong contrast with those same white or silvery partners. With gray bedmates, there is still some contrast, but the overall visual effect is much softer.

RIGHT: **Out of the ordinary.** Distinctly dissimilar in color and texture, variegated phormium and silvery white dusty miller create a traffic-stopping contrast. (Minter Gardens, Rosedale, BC)

OPPOSITE: **Make the connection.** 'Schwarzwalder' calla lily (*Zantedeschia*) and 'Summer Sorbet' caryopteris have very different leaf sizes and variegation patterns, but the green they share makes for a harmonious pairing. (Plant Delights Nursery, NC)

## Multicolors with Blue and Gray

If softer pairings are more to your taste, combining variegates with blue or gray partners is ideal. Blue flowers of all shades, as well as blue leaves, look great with either white- or yellow-marked foliage. Gray leaves usually work nicely with white variegates (especially when mixed with silver leaves and white flowers in "white" or evening gardens) but may look dull next to yellow-variegated companions.

## Multicolors with Yellow and Orange Partners

Just as white variegates combine beautifully with white flowers, yellow-marked leaves look wonderful with yellow and orange flowers, and with all-yellow foliage too. If you'll see the combination up close, matching the intensity of the colors (pale yellow flowers with pale yellow leaf markings, for instance) adds an extra touch of harmony to the pairing. But if you're using the pairings as part of a larger bed or border, you can get away with a variety of yellows, golds, and oranges in both the flowers and the foliage. Yellow flowers and yellow-variegated leaves also produce a very cheerful effect with white variegates.

TOP: **Toning things down.** Worried about variegated foliage looking too busy? Cool blue foliage, such as that of 'Blue Hawaii' hosta, can provide a calming backdrop.

LEFT: **Fall for it.** Strongly contrasting in form and color through most of the season, striped Hakone grass (*Hakonechloa macra* 'Aureola') develops a reddish autumn blush that beautifully complements the lacy darkness of 'Raven-swing' cow parsley (*Anthriscus sylvestris*).

OPPOSITE: **Please repeat.** The yellow bloom center makes an elegant echo to the sunny leaf markings on 'First Lady' flowering dogwood (*Cornus florida*).

Abutilon pictum 'Thompsonii'

## Multicolors with Purple, Red, and Odd Colors

Because variegated leaves tend to be bright and eye-catching, they're ideal for drawing attention to purple, deep red, and near black flowers, fruits, and foliage. Rusty orange and coppery brown blooms and leaves associate particularly well with yellow variegates, while pinks of all shades look equally good with white- and yellow-marked foliage. For those of you who enjoy experimenting with truly over-the-top combinations, flamboyantly variegated plants can be absolutely invaluable, particularly when paired with other out-of-the-ordinary foliage colors. You might site a brightly striped grass in front of a deep purple shrub, for instance, or have it rise out of a pool of near-black foliage. So much contrast can get overwhelming on a large scale, but in small doses, it's a fun way to add some shock value to an otherwise ordinary-looking area.

### MORE PLANNING POINTERS

Like other types of colorful foliage, multicolors are showy through much, if not all, of the growing season. When using variegates in combinations, however, be aware that the intensity of variegation may vary throughout the year. With some plants — variegated yellow flag iris (*Iris pseudacorus* 'Variegata'), for example — the variegation is most pronounced in spring and fades or disappears as the season goes on. (With some variegated perennials, cutting back the faded shoots by half or more in early to midsummer encourages a flush of brightly marked new growth.) In a few cases, such as 'Pineapple Upside Down Cake' hosta and 'Nancy's Revenge' colocasia, the reverse happens: their leaves start out totally or mostly green and develop more variegation as the season progresses. Colors can also change: yellow markings, for instance, may age to cream or white, as with 'Marginata' elderberry (*Sambucus nigra*) and 'Paul's Glory' hosta.

If you want a specific color for a combination, then, don't depend on photographs of variegated plants, because they show only one point in time. Instead, read their descriptions carefully and, if possible, talk to other gardeners who have grown them, to find out if and how they might change over time in your own garden.

RIGHT: **Quite a splash.** Though not to everyone's taste, the dramatic variegation on this 'Spotted Tiger' yucca is sure to attract attention. (Brookside Gardens, MD)

## ARRHENATHERUM
*Oat grass*

**Height: 8–12 inches**
**Leaf size: 8–12 inches long;**
**¼ inch wide**
**Full sun to partial shade**
**Zones 4–8**

The brightly striped foliage of variegated bulbous or tuberous oat grass (*Arrhenatherum elatius* subsp. *bulbosum* 'Variegatum') makes quite a splash in the spring garden. This eye-catching clump-former grows in compact mounds of slender foliage that's bright white with a very thin green center stripe. The plants may also produce pale green to tan flowerheads in midsummer, but these aren't especially showy. This cool-season grass starts growing very early in spring, so it's an excellent companion for spring bulbs and early-flowering perennials, and it keeps its good looks well into summer where temperatures don't get too high. Where hot, humid weather is the norm, the plants often look tired or die back to the ground, but new growth appears when cooler weather returns in fall, and it will stay attractive for most or all of the winter in mild areas.

**GROWING TIPS:** Variegated bulbous oat grass grows nicely with average to evenly moist but well-drained soil in either full sun or partial shade in cool-summer areas; elsewhere, summer shade may help to keep the plant from going dormant during hot weather. If the leaves still look droopy and discolored, cut back the whole clump to the ground to clear the way for the fresh fall foliage. Dividing the clumps every other year in spring or fall helps to keep them dense and vigorous. Remove any solid green growth right away.

**ALTERNATIVE:** If you like the effect of variegated bulbous oat grass but want it to last throughout the growing season, consider variegated society garlic (*Tulbaghia violacea* 'Variegata'; also sold as 'Silver Lace'). It grows in 1-foot-tall, semievergreen clumps of narrow, gray-green leaves edged with creamy white. 'Tricolor' has a pinkish tinge to the foliage in spring. Full sun; average to moist but well-drained soil. Zones 7 or 8 to 10.

*Arrhenatherum elatius*
subsp. *bulbosum* 'Variegatum'

## ARUNDO
*Giant reed*

**Height: 6–15 feet**
**Leaf size: 24–30 inches long;**
**2–3 inches wide**
**Full sun to partial shade**
**Zones 6 or 7–10**

Giant reed (*Arundo donax*) has sturdy, upright stems that can reach 15 feet tall in a single growing season, and thick creeping rhizomes that create substantial clumps just as wide. The stems may be topped with fluffy purplish pink to tan flower plumes in late summer to early fall, but the real feature is the arching, straplike leaves, which are spectacular in the variegated cultivars. *Note:* This species is considered invasive in some areas.

The most commonly available selection — usually sold under the name 'Variegata' or *A. donax* var. *variegata* — is edged and striped with white to cream on the new growth; the older growth may have yellow-green markings or be solid gray-green. Although a few growers list 'Variegata' and 'Versicolor' (*A. donax* var. *versicolor*) separately, most sources consider these names to be interchangeable. The stripes of smaller *A. formosana* 'Oriental Gold' are light yellow to greenish yellow.

**GROWING TIPS:** Variegated giant reeds love warmth and are most brightly colored in full sun, but they will tolerate partial shade. They adapt to a range of soil conditions but are most vigorous with a steady supply of moisture. Cut to the ground in early spring.

**ALTERNATIVES:** Variegated corn (*Zea mays* var. *japonica*; also sold as 'Variegata' and 'Quadricolor') lets you enjoy colorful, strappy foliage on easy-to-manage annual plants. The upright stalks are clad in long, arching bright green leaves that are striped with cream, white, and pink; 5 to 6 feet tall. Green-and-white-striped 'Tiger Cub' grows about 3 to 4 feet tall. Direct-sow in late spring. Full sun; average, well-drained soil.

*Arundo donax* 'Variegata'

## CAREX
*Sedge*

**Height:** Varies
**Leaf size:** Varies
**Full sun to full shade**
**Zones vary**

You'll often see sedges (*Carex*) lumped in with ornamental grasses, even though they belong to a different family, because both sedges and true grasses have similar habits and foliage textures. Another similarity is that sedges typically have interesting but not especially showy flowers. Generally speaking, though, sedges tend to perform better than grasses in shadier sites, providing welcome contrast to the bold or ferny textures of many other shade-garden favorites. There are hundreds of species and thousands of selections, with many variegates among them. Below is a small sampling of some of the best in a variety of heights, habits, and color combinations. As with other groups of plants with very similar-looking selections, some sedges that look nearly identical are sold under different names, so it's a good idea to select plants in person to make sure you're getting the look you want.

**Green with white to cream markings.** Mounded *C. conica* 'Snowline' (also sold as 'Marginata') grows in 6- to 12-inch-tall clumps of arching, 6- to 12-inch-long, ¼-inch-wide, deep green leaves narrowly edged with creamy white. Plants sold as *C. morrowii* 'Variegata' and 'Gilt' are similar. *C. morrowii*

var. *temnolepis* 'Silk Tassel' also grows in mounds, but its ⅛-inch wide, arching leaves are white with green edges; unless you're right next to it, the plant appears an overall pale green. *C. morrowii* 'Ice Dance' has wider green leaves (½ inch across) rimmed with white; instead of staying in a tight clump, it spreads moderately by rhizomes to create a carpetlike effect to about 1 foot tall. *C.* 'Silver Scepter' (sometimes listed under *C. morrowii*) is very similar but spreads more slowly. All of these are evergreen (in mild climates) to semievergreen and grow in Zones 5 to 8.

Eight-inch-tall *C. siderosticha* 'Spring Snow' is another spreading carpet-former, but its deciduous, white-centered, green-edged leaves are much broader (about 1 inch across) and more upright, creating a spikier effect. 'Variegata' has white edges and stripes. Zones 6 to 9. Three- to 6-inch-tall *C. ciliatomarginata* 'Treasure Island' looks like a miniature version of *C. siderosticha* 'Variegata'. Zones 5 to 8.

Slow-spreading, usually deciduous palm sedge (*C. muskingumensis*) has a decidedly different habit, with slender, upright, 2-foot-tall stems clad in horizontal, bright green leaves that are 6 to 8 inches long and ¼ inch wide; on 'Ice Fountains', each leaf has a white center stripe that's brightest in spring. Zones 4 to 9. Evergreen *C. phyllocephala* 'Sparkler' supplies the most dramatic impact for both bright color and

spiky texture. Its sturdy, upright, 1- to 2-foot-tall stems are densely topped by 6- to 8-inch-long, ¾-inch-wide green leaves broadly bordered with creamy white. Zones 7 or 8 to 10.

**Green with yellow to cream markings.** Among the mound-formers in this color range is *C. dolichostachya* 'Kaga-nishiki' (also sold as 'Gold Fountains'), with arching, 8- to 12-inch-long, ¼-inch-wide, bright green leaves edged with bright to light yellow. Its clumps are about 1 foot tall and are evergreen to semievergreen. *C. oshimensis* 'Evergold' (also listed under *C. hachijoensis* or *C. morrowii*) is similar but with reverse variegation: light yellow to cream leaf centers and deep green edges. *C. oshimensis* 'Gold Strike' has cream to light yellow edges and green centers on somewhat taller plants (12 to 18 inches). All of these are usually hardy in Zones 5 to 9.

*C. siderosticha* has much broader (to 1 inch wide), more upright, deciduous leaves on spreading plants that create spiky-looking, 8- to 12-inch-tall carpets. Its cultivar 'Island Brocade' has light green leaves bordered with light yellow to cream; 'Banana Boat' has wide, bright to light yellow centers with green edges. Zones 6 to 9.

'Oehme' palm sedge (*C. muskingumensis*) is distinctly upright, with 2-foot-tall stems holding horizontal, narrow, bright green leaves narrowly edged with light to bright yellow. The slow-

*Carex phyllocephala* 'Sparkler'

spreading plants are usually deciduous; hardy in Zones 4 to 9.
**GROWING TIPS:** Sedges generally tolerate full sun if the soil is dependably moist, but most perform best with morning sun and afternoon shade or light, all-day shade with average to moist but well-drained soil. If evergreen species look tattered by spring, trim off the dead leaf tips, or cut back all of the top growth to an inch or two above the crown.
**ALTERNATIVES:** Monkey or mondo grasses (*Ophiopogon*) spread slowly but steadily to create evergreen carpets of grasslike, deep green, arching foliage. Variegated cultivars that typically reach only 6 inches tall include *O. planiscapus* 'Little Tabby', with cream to white striping; *O. japonicus* 'Shiroshima-ryu' and 'Silver Mist', with bright white striping; and *O. japonicus* 'Torafu', with yellow to creamy white banding across the leaves. Partial to full shade; average, well-drained soil. Zones 6 to 10.

## HAKONECHLOA
*Hakone grass*

**Height:** Varies
**Leaf size:** 8–12 inches long;
   about ½ inch wide
**Partial to full shade**
**Zones 5–8**

Although shady-site gardeners don't have a wide variety of ornamental grasses to choose from, they can lay claim to one of the most graceful options: namely, Hakone grass (*Hakonechloa macra*). The all-green species is gaining in popularity, but the variegated versions are much more readily available, adding both color and texture to borders, foundation plantings, pathway edges, woodland gardens, and even pots. Their slowly expanding clumps of slender leaves start out spiky in spring, then gradually arch outward to form fountain-like mounds. Grown singly or in small groups, they make striking accents; in masses, they are great as a ground cover. 'Aureola' has thin green stripes on bright yellow leaves that age to pale yellow or yellowish green (often with reddish tints in fall) on 12- to 18-inch-tall plants. 'Alboaurea' is supposed to have both white and yellow stripes in its leaves, but plants sold under this name usually look like 'Aureola'. 'Albovariegata' (also sold as 'Albostriata') tends to be taller — usually 2 feet, but up to 3 feet — with green leaves that are striped with white. All of these also bloom, with loose, yellow-green to tan flower heads in mid- to late summer, but their foliage is the key feature.

**GROWING TIPS:** Morning sun and afternoon shade, or light all-day shade, with evenly moist but well-drained, humus-rich soil usually brings out the best color and vigor on variegated Hakone grasses. They'll tolerate full sun in the cooler parts of the hardiness range if their soil doesn't dry out; in full shade, the foliage tends to be mostly greenish by midsummer. Pluck out the occasional all-green shoots. Cut down any remaining top growth in early spring.

**ALTERNATIVES:** Variegated spider plants (*Chlorophytum comosum*) make great single-season fillers in garden or container combinations. The long, arching leaves grow in 1-foot-tall mounds. 'Variegatum' has green centers with white edges; 'Vittatum' has cream to white centers with green stripes and green edges. Compact 'Mandianum' has light yellow leaf centers and green edges. Partial shade is ideal; evenly moist but well-drained soil. Zones 9 to 11; may be root-hardy into Zone 7.

*Hakonechloa macra* 'Aureola'

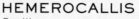

*Hemerocallis fulva* 'Kwanzo Variegata'

## HEMEROCALLIS
*Daylily*

**Height:** Varies
**Leaf size:** Varies
**Full sun to partial shade**
**Zones 3 or 4–9**

Grow daylilies (*Hemerocallis*) for their foliage instead of their flowers? You bet! When you're raising the variegated-leaf forms in the garden, you probably won't care if they ever bloom at all. In fact, some gardeners go so far as to cut off the flowers so they don't detract from the leaves.

The best-known selection in this group is *H. fulva* 'Kwanzo Variegata' (also sold as 'Kwanso Variegata' and 'Variegated Kwanso'), a vigorously spreading perennial with semievergreen, straplike leaves that are 1 to 3 feet long and 1 to 1½ inches wide. The arching foliage and upright, 3-foot-tall flowering stems are green striped with varying amounts of cream to white; the large, double, mid- to late-summer flowers are orange with reddish center markings. It may take the plants a few years to settle in, but after that, their rhizomes begin to creep, creating patches several feet across and often popping up through border companions. Growing them in large planters is one way to control the spread; dividing every two or three years is another option. Zones 3 to 9. Note: The species *H. fulva* is considered invasive in some areas. Deciduous Golden Zebra ('Malja') is more compact, with clumps of 1-foot-long, ½- to ¾-inch-wide green leaves edged and striped with light yellow aging to cream. Its smaller, single orange-yellow flowers appear mostly in midsummer atop

18-inch-tall stems, but they may bloom sporadically through the rest of the growing season as well. Its smaller size and less rampant spreading habit makes it a better choice for pots and easier to manage in borders. Zones 4 to 9.

**GROWING TIPS:** Daylilies thrive in full sun, but the variegated-leaf selections will also grow well in morning sun and afternoon shade or light all-day shade. Average, well-drained soil is fine; humus-rich, evenly moist (but not water-logged) soil is even better. Dig out and discard any all-green pieces of 'Kwanzo Variegata' as soon as you spot them.

**ALTERNATIVES:** Like daylilies, African lilies (*Agapanthus africanus*) normally get attention for their beautiful summer blooms, but several selections offer the bonus of variegation on their straplike leaves to complement their blue flowers. Summer Gold ('Hinag') has 15-inch-long, light green leaves bordered with light yellow; *A.* 'Tinkerbell' is about half the size, with cream-edged foliage. Full sun to partial shade; average to moist but well-drained soil. Zones 8 to 10.

## IRIS
*Iris*

**Height: Varies**
**Leaf size: Length varies; usually**
**    1–1½ inches wide**
**Full sun to full shade**
**Zones vary**

Adding variegated foliage to the exquisite flowers of this classic garden perennial is almost a matter of gilding the lily — or in this case, the iris! Irises (*Iris*) are favorites for adding pretty blooms and spiky foliage to sunny, well-drained beds and borders, but there are species suited for use as ground covers, in wet-soil sites, and even in shade. Selections with variegated leaves extend the color contribution from their short spring to early-summer bloom period through the rest of the growing season, making these dependable perennials work even harder with no extra effort on your part.

*Green with white to cream markings.* Looking much like a hybrid bearded iris in bloom, 'Argentea Variegata' Dalmatian iris (*I. pallida;* also known as 'Albovariegata' and 'Argenteovariegata') grows in flattened "fans" of 1- to 2-foot-tall foliage. Each leaf is partly blue-green and partly white; the proportions vary from leaf to leaf. Large purple-blue flowers bloom atop sturdy 2- to 3-foot-tall stems in early summer. Zones 4 to 8.

Variegated Japanese iris (*I. ensata* 'Variegata'; also listed under *I. kaempferi*) is a splendid choice for average to moist-soil borders as well as wet areas, with 2- to 3-foot-long leaves that are light green and cream to white. The showy late-spring to early-summer flowers are reddish purple to purple-blue on stems to about 3 feet tall. Zones 5 to 9. Variegated Japanese crested iris (*I. japonica* 'Variegata') adapts to the same soil conditions but usually prefers partial shade. Its mostly evergreen leaves are similar but only 18 to 24 inches tall, spreading by surface rhizomes into patches. Pale blue to white flowers bloom in late spring to early summer. Zones 7 to 10.

For sites that have full sun and dependably wet soil, consider variegated Japanese water iris (*I. laevigata* 'Variegata'). It grows 3 to 5 feet tall, with creamy white striped green leaves and deep purple blue flowers in early to midsummer. Zones 4 to 9.

Variegated Gladwyn iris (*I. foetidissima* 'Variegata') will adapt to full sun or full shade, but it generally prefers partial shade and average, well-drained soil. Its deep green, cream-striped leaves are evergreen, so you can admire them year-round. (A site protected from wind will help prevent them from getting tattered in winter.) The 18- to 24-inch-tall, clump-forming plants seldom bloom, but if they do, the pale purple, early-summer flowers are followed by pods that split open to reveal orange-red seeds in fall. Zones 5 to 9. Variegated Japanese roof iris (*I. tectorum* 'Variegata') is another beautiful choice for partly shaded beds and borders with average to evenly moist but well-drained soil. Its 1-foot-tall green leaves are striped with creamy white in spring, usually turning mostly green after the blue flowers appear in late spring or early summer. Zones 5 to 8.

*Green with yellow to cream markings.* If you want yellow

*Iris pallida* 'Variegata'

variegation, your best bet is variegated Dalmatian iris (*I. pallida* 'Variegata'; also sold as 'Aureovariegata' and 'Aurea Variegata'). It grows like its white-variegated relative described above, but its broad, flat leaves are blue-green with a light yellow stripe. Zones 4 to 8.

The 3- to 5-foot-tall green leaves of variegated yellow flag iris (*I. pseudacorus* 'Variegata') are striped with bright yellow when young, fading to yellow green or light green by midsummer. Bright yellow flowers bloom in early to midsummer. This iris likes full sun and will grow in anything from average garden soil to standing water. It spreads vigorously by creeping rhizomes and may also self-sow. Hardy in Zones 3 to 9. *Note:* The species is considered invasive in many areas.

**GROWING TIPS:** Irises vary in their light and moisture preferences (described above), so keep

in mind what your garden has to offer when you're choosing which ones you want to grow. Remove any all-green parts that appear. Snipping off the spent flowers helps to keep plants looking tidy.

**ALTERNATIVES:** Variegated sweet flag (*Acorus calamus* 'Variegatus') looks much like an iris, with deciduous, cream- to white-striped green leaves that spread by rhizomes to form large patches; 2 to 4 feet tall. Zones 5 to 10. Grassy-leaved sweet flag (*A. gramineus*) offers a number of 6- to 10-inch-tall cultivars with narrow, variegated, evergreen to semievergreen foliage. Zones 6 to 10. Full sun to partial shade; best in moist soil or even standing water.

*Liriope spicata* 'Silver Dragon'

# LIRIOPE
*Lilyturf, liriope*

**Height: 12–18 inches**
**Leaf size: 8–18 inches long;**
   **¼–½ inch wide**
**Full sun to full shade**
**Zones 5 or 6–10**

Lilyturfs (*Liriope*) are popular ground covers in warmer areas, and with good reason. They adapt readily to a wide range of growing conditions; their arching, evergreen foliage looks great all year long; and they produce pretty clusters of purple-blue to white summer flowers.

Big blue lilyturf (*L. muscari*) grows in dense tufts that spread by slow-creeping rhizomes. On the classic cultivar 'Variegata', the deep green leaves are edged with light yellow to cream. Slightly taller 'Silvery Sunproof' (also sold as 'Ariaka-janshige' and under *L. exiliflora*) is similar, but its yellow stripes tend to age to white by midsummer. Plants sold as 'John Burch' ('John Birch') and 'Gold Band' ('Gold Banded') have slightly wider leaves (to ¾ inch) that are narrowly bordered with creamy yellow. 'Silver Midget' ('Silvery Midget') is a more compact selection — to about 10 inches tall — with light yellow to creamy white stripes. For something different from the usual striping, check out 'Hawk's Feather' ('Hawk Feathers'), with pale yellow to cream mottling throughout the leaves, or 'Okina', with mostly white spring leaves that gradually turn solid green by fall. Besides serving as

ground covers, these variegated selections are usually restrained enough to work well in mixed borders; they make eye-catching container plants as well.

Creeping or spike lilyturf (*L. spicata*) spreads much more rapidly than big blue lilyturf does, forming carpets of glossy, deep green leaves that are terrific for filling space under trees and shrubs and for covering shady slopes. 'Silver Dragon' (also known as 'Gin-ryu') is a striking selection with bright white stripes on its narrow, deep green leaves. *Note: L. spicata* is considered invasive in some areas.

**GROWING TIPS:** Lilyturfs can take anything from full sun to full shade. Evenly moist but well-drained soil is ideal, although established plants tolerate drier conditions. A site that's sheltered from strong winds will minimize leaf browning in winter. In early spring, set your mower's blade at its highest possible position and mow your lilyturf plants (or trim small patches by hand) to remove the old leaves and make room for fresh new growth.

**ALTERNATIVE:** Liriope look-alike Aztec grass shares the tufted habit but is much taller — to about 2 feet — with light yellow to creamy white leaf striping. You can find it sold under a variety of names, including *Liriope muscari* 'Aztec' and 'Mexican Giant'; *Ophiopogon intermedius* 'Argenteomarginatus'; and *O. jaburan* 'Argenteovittatus', 'Variegatus', and 'Vittatus'. Full sun to full shade; average to moist but well-drained soil. Zones 7 to 10.

# MISCANTHUS
*Miscanthus, eulalia,*
*Japanese silver grass*

**Height: Varies**
**Leaf size: 2–4 feet long;**
   **½–1 inch wide**
**Full sun to partial shade**
**Zones 5 or 6–9**

When it comes to variegated ornamental grasses, miscanthus (*Miscanthus sinensis*) offers the most extensive range of heights, textures, colors, and patterns, all on sturdy plants that seldom need special maintenance. Along with their striking summer foliage, they contribute attractive late-summer to fall flower- and seed-heads, changeable fall leaf colors, and a dependable winter presence, making them valuable for adding multi-season interest to sun-drenched borders, foundation plantings, and even containers.

*Note:* This species is now considered invasive in many areas, due to self-seeding into natural areas. Late-flowering variegated cultivars, such as 'Cosmopolitan', 'Morning Light', and 'Zebrinus', are usually safe to grow (at least in northern areas), as they tend to bloom too late to set seed. If you can bear to do it, cutting off all of the flowerheads on any cultivar is a good way to ensure that it won't be a problem. In any case, it's smart to investigate the potential invasiveness of miscanthus in your area before you plant, and if there's any uncertainty, choose another option for spiky variegated foliage.

*Miscanthus sinensis* 'Zebrinus'

If you want to give variegated miscanthus a try, you have lots to choose from. Here's an overview of some time-tested favorites; newer cultivars appear each year. The heights given below refer to the foliage; the flowerheads may add 1 to 3 feet to the total height.

*Green with white to cream markings.* The classic cultivar 'Variegatus' is so heavily striped that the leaves appear more white than green. It's very showy, but its loose, 6-foot-tall clumps tend to flop open after a few years. 'Silberpfeil' (also sold as 'Silver Arrow') is very similar. Equally striped 'Dixieland' and 'Rigoletto' grow only 3 to 4 feet tall and are much less apt to sprawl. If you like the bold effect and height of 'Variegatus' but don't want to deal

with staking, consider 'Cabaret' or 'Cosmopolitan' (both selections of *M. sinensis* var. *condensatus*). 'Cabaret' has deep green leaf edges with creamy white centers; 'Cosmopolitan' has creamy white edges and a thin white center stripe on a mostly deep green leaf center. They're about 6 feet tall in leaf. *M. sinensis* 'Morning Light' is distinctly different from all of these, with very narrow green leaves neatly edged with white. Its 4- to 6-foot-tall, fine-textured clumps are fountainlike when young, turning into rounded mounds after a few years.

*Green with yellow to cream markings.* 'Goldfeder' ('Gold Feather') is the main option in this color range if you want a grass striped along the length of each leaf. Its loose clumps grow about 6 feet tall, with medium green leaf blades that have light yellow edges and a thin white center stripe. *M. sacchariflorus* 'Gotemba Gold' is more showily striped with yellow, but it's a rampant spreader, so it's better in a container than in a border.

Many more yellow-variegated miscanthus are available with narrow to wide bands of yellow and green across each leaf. Sometimes it takes a while for the bands to appear, so don't be alarmed if the new shoots are solid green. Zebra grass (*M. sinensis* 'Zebrinus') is an old favorite with loose, 6-foot-tall clumps of arching foliage; porcupine grass ('Strictus') is about the same height but decidedly more

upright and rarely needs staking. Some compact (3- to 4-foot-tall) versions of zebra grass are 'Kirk Alexander', Little Nicky ('Hinjo'), and 'Little Zebra'. For the upright, spiky habit of porcupine grass on a shorter plant (3 to 4 feet tall), check out 'Puenktchen' ('Little Dot') and 'Gold Bar'.

**GROWING TIPS:** Full sun with average to evenly moist soil is best for miscanthus. The plants will grow in partial shade but are less upright there. Even in full sun, old clumps may die out in the center and sprawl around the edges. Dividing the clumps every three years in spring is a good way to keep your miscanthus vigorous and sturdy. (Dividing them this frequently also makes the job easier, because long-established clumps are a major ordeal to dig up!) In late winter, cut any remaining top growth a few inches above the crown to make room for new growth. *Caution:* Wear gloves when working with miscanthus at any time of year, because the leaf edges are very sharp.

**ALTERNATIVES:** Pampas grass (*Cortaderia selloana*) is another large-scale, clump-forming perennial. 'Albolineata' ('Silver Stripe') has narrow white stripes; 4 to 5 feet tall in leaf. 'Silver Comet' has wider white stripes; 4 to 6 feet in leaf. For yellow stripes, check out 5- to 7-foot-tall 'Aureolineata' ('Gold Band') or 4- to 5-foot-tall Sun Stripe ('Monvin'). Full sun and average, well-drained soil. Zones 8 to 10. *Note:* The species is considered invasive in some areas.

## MOLINIA
*Purple moor grass*

**Height: 12–18 inches
Leaf size: 10–12 inches long;
 ¼ inch wide
Full sun to partial shade
Zones 4–9**

If you're looking for a compact, easy-to-manage grass with extended color interest, variegated purple moor grass (*Molinia caerulea* 'Variegata') is a great candidate. This perennial grows in distinct clumps, so you'll never have to worry about it taking over your garden. Plus, it looks terrific from spring through fall, with

*Molinia caerulea* 'Variegata'

arching, narrow green leaves that are striped with light yellow aging to cream, then turning all-yellow in autumn. In cooler areas, the plants produce wispy yellowish to tan flower heads to about 30 inches tall in mid- to late summer; they're somewhat interesting but not a key feature. Variegated purple moor grass grows quite slowly, so you if you can find only small plants to start with, plant three or more together to enjoy the immediate effect of a good-looking clump.

**GROWING TIPS:** Variegated purple moor grass will grow in full sun in cool climates, as well as in warmer areas with dependably moist soil; in most regions, light shade with acidic, average to evenly moist but well-drained soil is fine. The top growth usually breaks down on its own by early winter, so cleanup is minimal; simply snip or pull off any remaining dead leaves in early spring.

**ALTERNATIVES:** 'Northern Lights' tufted hair grass (*Deschampsia cespitosa*) is pale yellow-striped and pink-tinged in spring, cream-striped in summer, and orange-pink in fall; 8 to 16 inches in leaf. Full sun (in cool areas) to partial shade. Zones 4 to 8. Tightly tufted 'Little Honey' fountain grass (*Pennisetum alopecuroides*) has white-centered green blades; about 8 inches tall. Full sun. Zones 5 or 6 to 9. Average to moist but well-drained soil for both.

*Phalaris arundinacea var. picta*

## PHALARIS
*Ribbon grass, gardener's garters*

**Height: 2–3 feet for most**
**Leaf size: 12–18 inches long;**
**¾ inch wide**
**Full sun to partial shade**
**Zones 3–9**

Don't be fooled by how cute and bushy these gorgeous grasses look in a nursery pot. Commonly known as ribbon grasses or gardener's garters, selections of *Phalaris arundinacea* var. *picta* can be true thugs, spreading far and wide by rhizomes that quickly take over a bed or border. They occasionally revert to solid green, too, and those plants may self-sow. *Note:* Ribbon grasses definitely qualify as aggressive in the garden, and the species (which is known as reed canary grass in its all-green form) is considered seriously invasive

in many areas. So why even talk about these grasses? Well, you'll see the variegates for sale just about everywhere in spring, and if you really can't resist buying them, then you need to know how to make the best of them.

Like other plants that are vigorous spreaders, variegated ribbon grasses are useful as ground covers in tough sites where few other plants will survive. They also work well planted by themselves in good-sized containers, or in areas surrounded by paving so they can't escape. If you're prepared to keep them under control, there are several kinds to choose from. Those sold simply as 'Picta' usually have medium green leaves variably striped with cream to white; 'Wood's Dwarf' is similar but more compact (to about 1 foot tall). 'Tricolor' includes a

pink blush in cool weather. Plants sold as 'Feesey', 'Feesey's Form', 'Mervyn Feesey', and 'Strawberries and Cream' typically have wider white to cream stripes as well as a pink tinge in spring and fall; 'Dwarf Garters' has the same colors on 1-foot-tall plants. 'Luteopicta' ('Aureovariegata') has light yellow spring stripes that typically fade to cream or light green in summer.

**GROWING TIPS:** Ribbon grasses grow in full sun to partial shade and adapt to just about any soil conditions, although they prefer ample moisture. Cut down the remaining top growth in late winter, then cut again in midsummer (when the flowers appear) to prevent self-sowing and encourage a flush of bright new growth for fall. Remove and destroy all-green parts immediately. Container plantings need frequent division.

**ALTERNATIVES:** Variegated feather reed grasses (*Calamagrostis × acutiflora*) create a somewhat similar spring show, but on distinctly clump-forming plants; 2 to 3 feet tall. 'Overdam' has white stripes on the leaf edges and a green center; 'Avalanche' has a white center stripe and narrow green edges; and 'Eldorado' has a light yellow center stripe that ages to greenish yellow. Feather reed grasses may be discolored by fungal rusts in humid conditions; a site with good air circulation may help to prevent the problem. Full sun to light shade; average, well-drained soil. Zones 3 or 4 to 9.

*Phormium* 'Yellow Wave'

## PHORMIUM
*Phormium*

**Height: 3–5 feet**
**Leaf size: 3–5 feet long;**
**1½–3 inches wide**
**Full sun to full shade**
**Zones 8 or 9–11**

Formerly limited mostly to mild climates, phormiums (*Phormium*) have developed a following all across the country as a striking textural addition to both borders and container plantings. Granted, you need to bring them indoors for the winter in many areas, but most gardeners consider them worth the effort. The plants can be pricey even for single crowns, and they may take a bit of work to track down, so holding them over from year to year ensures that you'll have good-sized clumps of your favorites every year without blowing your plant-buying budget each spring.

Phormiums produce strap-like evergreen leaves that may be solid green or burgundy or striped with a wide range of colors. Below is a sampling of those that are green with yellow to cream; those that are primarily red, pink, or bronze are covered on page 110. The sizes are the approximate heights they can eventually reach in containers; in the ground, some may grow several feet taller.

Selections of mountain flax (*P. cookianum* subsp. *hookeri*; also sold as *P. colensoi*) have wide, dramatically arching foliage. 'Cream Delight' has a broad pale yellow center and narrow green edges rimmed with red; 2 to 3 feet tall. 'Tricolor' is rich green with variable yellow striping often rimmed with red (and sometimes blushed with pink) in cool weather; about 4 feet tall.

Hybrid phormiums and selections of New Zealand flax (*P. tenax*) tend to produce more-upright, spikier-looking clumps. Two- to 3-foot-tall *P. tenax* 'Variegatum' ('Variegata') and *P.* 'Wings of Gold' are edged with light yellow to cream; the latter may also be rimmed with red. *P.* 'Tiny Tiger' ('Aurea Nana') and *P.* 'Duet' are similar but only 2 feet tall. *P.* 'Gold Sword' (2 to 3 feet) and *P.* 'Yellow Wave' (3 to 4 feet) have medium to light yellow centers and narrow green edges; *P.* 'Apricot Queen' (3 to 5 feet) is similar but is often blushed with pink in fall to create a light peachy effect.

Three-foot-tall *P. tenax* 'Radiance' has green leaves striped with cream and pale yellow throughout.

**GROWING TIPS:** Variegated phormiums grow well in full sun but may appreciate light shade (especially in the afternoon) or even full shade in hot climates. Established plants are somewhat drought-tolerant but usually perform best with evenly moist but well-drained soil. Shelter from strong wind is beneficial, especially in winter. Remove all-green leaves or shoots at their base. Removing some of the older, faded leaves during the season helps maintain a brightly variegated look overall. Although some phormiums are hardy in the ground in Zone 8 and even parts of Zone 7, the variegates are usually a little more cold-tender, especially in containers. It's safest to bring them indoors in most areas north of Zone 9; give them a cool, bright spot and keep their soil on the dry side.

**ALTERNATIVES:** Closely related flax lilies (*Dianella tasmanica*) are evergreen or semievergreen, with upright-then-arching, straplike leaves; 2 to 3 feet tall. 'Variegata' is edged with bright white; 'Yellow Stripe' ('Gold Stripe') is striped with yellow to cream. They spread by rhizomes to form dense patches in a bed or planter. Can grow in full sun but usually best in partial to full shade with evenly moist but well-drained soil. Zones 8 to 10.

## PLEIOBLASTUS
*Bamboo*

**Height: Varies**
**Leaf size: Varies**
**Partial shade**
**Zones vary**

It seems that few gardeners are on the fence about bamboo: they either love it passionately, or they immediately reject the idea of planting it anywhere on their property. While it's true that some species of bamboo can be ultra-aggressive spreaders, it's also possible to enjoy others safely and responsibly. And once you've seen how stunning they can look

*Pleioblastus variegatus*

in the right spot, you'll know it's worth a little extra care in choosing just the right site for them.

Dwarf greenstripe bamboo (*Pleioblastus auricomus*; also known as *P. viridistriatus*, *Arundinaria auricoma*, and *A. viridistriata*) creates a spectacular show from spring to early summer, when the 4- to 8-inch-long, 1-inch-wide, bright yellow leaves are narrowly striped with green; later on, they turn light green with deep green stripes. In mild climates, the foliage is usually evergreen; in colder areas, it is deciduous. The slender, upright stems grow 2 to 4 feet tall and several feet outward by creeping underground stems (rhizomes). This species is classified as a running bamboo, but it's one of the more restrained spreaders. Faster-creeping dwarf whitestripe bamboo (*P. variegatus*; also known as *P. fortunei* and *A. variegata*) normally grows to 2 feet tall, with 4- to 6-inch-long, 1-inch-wide deep green leaves that are striped with bright cream to white. Both of these bamboos are typically recommended for Zones 7 to 11, but they can often survive in much colder areas (even into Zone 4). Nurseries that specialize in bamboo offer many other variegates in a range of heights.

**GROWING TIPS:** Dwarf greenstripe bamboo can grow in full sun to full shade, but a site with morning sun and afternoon shade or light all-day shade tends to bring

out the best color. Partial shade is also ideal for dwarf whitestripe bamboo. Both species grow most vigorously in humus-rich, fertile, evenly moist but well-drained soil; drier, less fertile conditions can slow them down a bit, but don't depend on that completely. To keep them contained, plant them along a road or next to a large pond or stream, or in a site where you can mow a 15- to 20-foot-wide strip around them at least once a year (in spring). They can also make great groundcovers on slopes or other tough sites where other plants can't grow, and they are perfect candidates for containers. Where the leaves drop in winter, cut all of the stems to the ground before new growth appears in spring; elsewhere, cut out individual dead stems as needed and cut down the whole clump every two or three years.

**ALTERNATIVES:** Silver-edge bamboo (*Sasa veitchii*) has large, deep green leaves during the growing season; in fall, they develop wide tan to creamy white borders for a dramatic variegated effect in winter. Relatively slow-spreading; 3 to 4 feet tall. Zones 5 to 10. *Sasaella masamuneana* 'Albostriata' (*S. masamuneana* f. *albostriata*) has narrower foliage with deep green stripes against a bright white to creamy yellow background; 3 to 5 feet tall. Zones 6 to 10. Partial shade; average, well-drained soil.

## SETARIA
*Foxtail grass, variegated palm grass*

**Height: 18–36 inches**
**Leaf size: 6–12 inches long; 3–4 inches wide**
**Full sun to partial shade**
**Zones 9 or 10–11**

Foxtails (*Setaria*) typically aren't something you'd deliberately add to your garden; mostly they are unwanted weedy grasses that you'd be more likely to curse at than to lust after. But few foliage fanatics would turn down the opportunity to grow variegated palm grass (*S. palmifolia* 'Variegata'), a tender perennial prized for its long, broad, pleated leaves elegantly edged and center-striped with white. The outward-arching stems, which are thick and burgundy-colored near the base of the plant, hold the evergreen foliage almost horizontally, creating a broad clump. Variegated palm grass shows off beautifully in a pot by itself or in a large mixed planter, and it makes an eye-catching accent for a bed or mixed border. The species may be invasive in tropical areas, so if you have any concerns that it might self-sow in your area, simply cut off the flower stems; the blooms aren't the main feature anyway.

**GROWING TIPS:** Variegated palm grass grows well in partial shade (especially in hot climates) but typically prefers full sun and average to moist but well-drained soil. In most parts of the country, you'll want to bring the clumps

*Setaria palmifolia* 'Variegata'

indoors before frost and keep them in a bright spot for the winter; water sparingly. Don't be too quick to move them back outside; wait at least a week or two after your last frost date, or until nights are dependably above 45°F or so.

**ALTERNATIVES:** Variegated Chinese ground orchids (*Bletilla striata*) are an elegant addition to shady borders and woodland gardens, with upright to arching, pleated, 6- to 12-inch-tall leaves through the growing season. They spread by rhizomes to form handsome patches. Plants sold as 'Albostriata', 'Marginata', or 'Variegata' all have narrow white leaf edges. Morning sun and afternoon shade or light all-day shade; humus-rich, evenly moist but well-drained soil. Zones 6 to 9.

## STENOTAPHRUM
*St. Augustine grass*

**Height: 6–8 inches**
**Leaf size: 6 inches long;**
**⅓ inch wide**
**Full sun to partial shade**
**Zones 9–11**

Gardeners with limited space are always on the lookout for ways to shoehorn more plants into already crammed beds and borders, so it's almost inevitable that they'll start eyeing all that "wasted" lawn space. Wouldn't it be great to jazz it up with something more colorful? Believe it or not, there's actually a variegated turf grass: specifically, variegated St. Augustine grass (*Stenotaphrum secundatum* 'Variegatum'). Its flat or folded blades are light green boldly striped with creamy white, on creeping horizontal stems that send out roots as they travel across the soil. Although you probably wouldn't want to replace your whole lawn with this tender perennial grass, it makes an interesting ground cover for smaller areas. Its trailing stems also look terrific cascading out of a planter, window box, or hanging basket. *Note:* The species is considered invasive in some areas.

**GROWING TIPS:** Variegated St. Augustine grass thrives in full sun but also performs well in partial shade (though it tends to grow a few inches taller there). Average to evenly moist but well-drained soil is fine. Stringy flowerheads usually appear in late summer to early fall; shear them off to keep the planting looking tidy. Where this grass isn't hardy, pot up a few plants in early fall and bring them indoors before frost to enjoy as houseplants in a bright spot. Wait until all danger of frost has passed to set them outdoors the following spring.

**ALTERNATIVE:** Variegated manna grass (*Glyceria maxima* 'Variegata'; also listed under *G. aquatica*) grows 2 to 3 feet tall, with long, arching, bright green leaves that are heavily marked with pale yellow to cream stripes (often pink-blushed in cool weather and turning tan for winter). It's an aggressive spreader that thrives in full sun with constantly moist soil to several inches of standing water. Zones 5 to 10. *Note:* The species is considered invasive in some areas.

## YUCCA
*Yucca, Adam's needle*

**Height: Varies**
**Leaf size: 1–3 feet long;**
**1–3 inches wide**
**Full sun to partial shade**
**Zones vary**

Beds and borders planned for flowers instead of foliage are usually pretty, but they may not be completely satisfying. Often, what's lacking is a definite focal point — a plant or feature with a strong textural presence to counterbalance the wispiness of dainty, delicate blooms. Yuccas (*Yucca*) are ideal for adding this kind of impact, thanks to their spiky, sword-shaped, evergreen foliage. Selections with yellow- or white-marked leaves are even more dramatic, contributing extra color that's eye-catching from spring through fall and particularly welcome during the winter. Older clumps produce flowers, too, with equally bold, creamy white bells on tall stalks in summer.

Yuccas come in a range of sizes and variegation patterns to fit just about any site or color combination. Below is an overview of some of the best. Mix them with annuals, perennials, and shrubs in beds, borders, and containers, or pair them with lower-growing

*Stenotaphrum secundatum* 'Variegatum'

*Yucca flaccida* 'Golden Sword'

ground covers on a dry slope or in an open, sun-drenched site. Just keep in mind that the leaf tips of some yuccas are rather sharp, so avoid planting them right next to a path, patio, bench, or doorway. The sizes given here are the approximate height of the foliage; the flower spikes are usually several feet taller.

**Green with white to cream markings.** Plants sold as *Y. filamentosa* 'Variegata' generally reach 18 to 30 inches tall, with grayish green leaves brightly bordered with cream to white. As with other selections of *Y. filamentosa*, its foliage is edged with long, thin, curly fibers that provide another element of interest when you see the plants up close. Zones 5 to 9.

**Green with yellow to cream.** This color range offers many options, most of which take on a pinkish blush in winter. Those with grayish green centers and light yellow edges include narrow-leaved, 2-foot-tall *Y. filamentosa* 'Bright Edge' (sometimes listed under *Y. flaccida*) — usually hardy in Zones 5 to 9 — and broader-leaved *Y. gloriosa* 'Variegata', which grows on stems to about 4 feet tall (Zones 6 or 7 to 10). Those two have very spiky foliage overall, while the leaves of *Y. recurvifolia* 'Marginata' (sometimes sold as 'Variegata') are upright when new and arching when older.

Some with yellow centers and gray-green edges are *Y. flaccida* 'Golden Sword' ('Gold Sword';

also listed under *Y. filamentosa*) and *Y. filamentosa* 'Color Guard', both with very rigid leaves. *Y. flaccida* 'Garland Gold' ('Garland's Gold', 'Gold Garland', 'Golden Garlands'; also listed under *Y. filamentosa* and *Y. filifera*) has yellow-centered leaves that arch as they age. All of these are about 3 feet tall and usually hardy in Zones 5 to 9. *Y. recurvifolia* Banana Split ('Monca') and 'Gold Ribbons' are also yellow-centered, but with arching leaves on trunklike stems that eventually reach 4 to 6 feet tall. 'Tiny Star' (usually listed under *Y. recurvifolia*) is a very compact selection (to barely 6 inches tall), with light yellow leaves very thinly striped with green. Zones 7 to 10.

**GROWING TIPS:** Yuccas thrive in full sun and dry soil, but most will tolerate partial shade and average to moist garden soil. Good drainage is a must, though, especially in winter. Cut off the flower stems when the blooms fade. Cut out all-green leaves or rosettes as soon as you see them.

**ALTERNATIVES:** Century plant (*Agave americana*) forms evergreen rosettes of broad, spiky, blue-green leaves. Those sold as 'Marginata' and 'Variegata' have yellow to cream leaf edges; 'Mediopicta' has light yellow centers. About 6 feet in leaf. Zones 8 or 9 to 11. *Furcraea foetida* 'Mediopicta' (*F. gigantea* 'Mediopicta') has glossy, deep green leaves with broad, light yellow to creamy white centers brushed with pale green; to 5 feet. Zones 10 to 11. Full sun; dry, well-drained soil.

## ALPINIA
*Ginger*

> **Height:** Varies
> **Leaf size:** 1–2 feet long; to 6 inches wide
> **Sun to partial shade**
> **Zones 8–11**

Variegated gingers (*Alpinia*) add a tropical touch to gardens in any climate. Plant them directly in the ground or enjoy them in containers; even if they don't bloom, their foliage provides a dramatic accent all through the growing season.

The most widely available selection is variegated shell ginger (*A. zerumbet* 'Variegata'; also sold as *A. speciosa* 'Variegata'), with thin stripes to bold blocks of yellow with rich green in between; to about 6 feet tall. *A. intermedia* 'Sun Spice' is even more heavily marked with yellow stripes and blocks; 18 to 24 inches tall. Formosan or pinstripe ginger (*A. formosana*; also sold as *A. formosana* 'Pinstripe' and 'Waimanalo') has deep green leaves marked with many thin white stripes; usually 4 to 6 feet tall. *A. japonica* 'Extra Spicy' has showier white stripes and blocks with green in between; 2 to 3 feet tall.

**GROWING TIPS:** Keep the soil evenly moist but not soggy. Gingers generally prefer partial shade, but they'll usually adapt to full sun in cooler areas, especially if the soil doesn't dry out. Rich soil and regular feeding encourage lush growth. Where the plants aren't winter-hardy, bring

them indoors before the first frost and give them a bright spot for the winter.

**ALTERNATIVES:** *Zingiber* includes a number of white-variegated selections, including 'Dancing Crane', 'Nakafu', 'White Feather', and 'Variegata' Japanese or myoga gingers (*Z. mioga*; 2 to 3 feet tall), as well as variegated shampoo or pinecone ginger (*Z. zerumbet* 'Darceyi'; also sold as 'Darcyi', *Z. darceyi*, and *Z. darcyi*), which grows 3 to 5 feet tall. Full sun (in cooler areas) to partial shade; moist but well-drained soil. Zones 7 or 8 to 11.

*Alpinia zerumbet* 'Variegata'

*Arum italicum* 'Pictum'

## ARUM
*Arum, lords-and-ladies*

**Height: 12–18 inches**
**Leaf size: 8–12 inches long;**
    **2–4 inches wide**
**Partial to full shade**
**Zones 6–10**

Talk about turning the seasons upside down! Instead of putting on most of its growth in spring, Italian arum or Italian lords-and-ladies (*Arum italicum*) sends up its arrow-shaped leaves in early to mid-fall. Hard freezes can leave them limp, but new leaves appear in milder weather. Greenish white, hooded flowers are hidden among the leaves in late spring. Soon after that, the leaves disappear, but stalks of green berries remain to turn bright red in late summer to early fall.

Forms of Italian or painted arum that have creamy white to greenish white veining are sold under a number of names, including *A. italicum* 'Pictum', *A. italicum* 'Marmoratum', and *A. italicum* ssp. *italicum* var.

*marmoratum.* If possible, buy a plant already in leaf so you can see what you're getting. (Keep in mind that it may take young plants a year or two to show their markings.) Or look for 'Winter White', which reliably offers showy white veining and marbling. *Note: A. italicum* is considered invasive in some areas.

**GROWING TIPS:** Italian arum prefers partial to full shade with average to evenly moist but well-drained soil. Pair it with other plants that will fill in during the summer but be gone in winter.

**ALTERNATIVES:** For a similarly bold splash of green and white that you can enjoy in summer and fall, seek out the stunning *Pinellia tripartita* 'Silver Dragon'. It's about 18 inches tall and thrives in the same conditions as does Italian arum. Underwood's trillium or long-bract wakerobin (*Trillium underwoodii*), another shade lover, has dainty green leaves with a white center streak and speckling; to about 8 inches tall. Zones 5 to 9.

## BRUGMANSIA
*Brugmansia, angel's trumpet*

**Height: 10–15 feet where hardy;**
    **4–6 feet elsewhere**
**Leaf size: Usually 6–8 inches long;**
    **4–6 inches wide**
**Full sun to light shade**
**Zones 7 or 8–10**

When big and bold is what you need, brugmansias (*Brugmansia*) definitely fill the bill. The plants themselves easily reach shrub-size stature and the pendant, trumpet-shaped, fragrant flowers are nearly a foot long. But for foliage fanatics, it's the large, velvety leaves that draw the eye.

By far the best of the bunch for fantastic variegation are 'Snowbank', with a wide, irregular, creamy white edge and a gray-green to deep green center (plus light peach flowers); and 'Miner's Claim', with irregular yellow to cream leaf edges and pink flowers. Brugmansias with thinner cream to white edges are available under a variety of names, such as 'Maya', 'Sunset', *B.* × *candida* 'Variegata', and *B. suaveolens* 'Variegata'. The names are quite mixed up in the trade, so if you collect variegates and want to be sure a potential purchase is different from what you already have, you're best off seeing the plant in person before you buy.

**GROWING TIPS:** Although full sun promotes best flowering, afternoon shade or light all-day shade is fine if you're more interested in admiring the foliage. Evenly moist (but not waterlogged) soil is ideal; if the ground is dry, the leaves

tend to wilt dramatically. In Zone 9 and south, expect brugmansias to grow as shrubs; in Zone 8 (and sometimes in Zone 7), they normally die back to the ground but resprout from the roots each spring. Elsewhere, buy new plants each spring, or bring them indoors for the winter.

**ALTERNATIVES:** 'Pink Diamond' glorybower (*Clerodendrum bungei*) has deep green leaves edged and marbled with cream and white; 3 to 4 feet tall. *Note:* This species spreads aggressively by suckers and is considered invasive in some areas. *C. trichotomum* 'Carnival' ('Harlequin', 'Variegatum') has an irregular cream-yellow leaf edge that ages to white; to about 6 feet. Both are usually root-hardy from Zone 7 south. Full sun to partial shade; average, well-drained soil.

*Brugmansia* 'Sunset'

**BOLD**

*Brunnera macrophylla* 'Variegata'

## BRUNNERA
*Hardy forget-me-not,*
*Siberian bugloss*

**Height: 12–18 inches**
**Leaf size: 6–8 inches long and wide**
**Partial to full shade**
**Zones 3–7**

Love the broad foliage of hostas but need the bold effect sooner in the growing season? Hardy forget-me-not (*Brunnera macrophylla*) forms dense, mounded plants that make a great textural contrast to dainty foliage, such as that of ferns and bleeding hearts (*Dicentra*). They also boast showy sprays of bright blue flowers in spring, making them a handsome companion for many other early-blooming perennials and bulbs.

Several variegated selections are available, all with similar markings. 'Variegata' has light green leaves with wide, creamy white to pure white edges. Many

sources say that 'Dawson's White' is the same as 'Variegata', but a few claim that 'Dawson's White' is less prone to leaf browning during the summer. The edges of 'Hadspen Cream' are yellowish cream in spring, aging to creamy white by summer.

**GROWING TIPS:** Variegated hardy forget-me-nots aren't the easiest plants to please, but when you find the right spot, they are spectacular. Partial to full shade with consistently moist soil is best. A bit of morning sun is fine, but any afternoon sun is likely to cause browned leaf edges. Cutting damaged leaves back to the ground encourages fresh new foliage to form. Remove any all-green leaves as soon as you notice them; if more appear from the same spot, divide the clump, remove the plain green part, and replant the variegated part.

**ALTERNATIVES:** Gardeners in hot climates (Zones 7 or 8 to 10) can enjoy similar bold foliage for moist, shady sites with leopard plant (*Farfugium tussilaginea*, formerly *Ligularia tussilaginea*). 'Argenteum' (also known as 'Albovariegatum' and 'Variegatum') has dramatically white-splashed leaf edges. 'Kinkan' ('Kin Kan') has a thin white edge; 'Gold Ring' has a narrow yellow edge. Yellow-spotted selections include 'Aureomaculatum', 'Kin-botan', and 'Kagami-jishi' (which also has crinkled leaf edges).

## CALADIUM
*Caladium, angel wings*

**Height: 1–3 feet**
**Leaf size: 6–12 inches long;**
**6–8 inches wide**
**Partial to full shade**
**Zones 9–11**

For big, bold leaves in a hurry, it's tough to beat caladiums (*Caladium bicolor;* also known as *C. × hortulanum*). Plant tubers in spring and just add heat and moisture: within a few weeks, you'll enjoy large clumps of lush leaves in an array of shapes, sizes, and colors until frost. "Fancy-leaved" selections have large, shield-shaped foliage; "lance-leaved" types are sharply pointed with ruffled edges; and "strap-leaved" types have narrower foliage. Mail-order caladium specialists stock dozens of selections; here's an overview of some of the best.

*Mostly white with green.* 'Aaron' (wide green edges, 1 to 2 feet tall,

fancy); 'Candidum' (narrow green veining, 1 to 2 feet, fancy; 'Candidum Jr.' is half the size); 'Jackie Suthers' (narrow green edges, 6 to 12 inches, lance); 'Gray Ghost' (narrow green edges, 1 to 2 feet, fancy); 'White Christmas' (wide green veining, 1 to 2 feet, fancy).

*Mostly white with green and pink.* 'Gingerland' (green edges and deep pink spots, 10 to 14 inches, lance); 'Pink Gem' (green edges and heavy pink veining, 6 to 12 inches, strap); 'White Queen' (green veining with pink near the center, 1 to 2 feet, fancy).

*Mostly pale green to chartreuse with pink.* 'Miss Muffet' (pink center and dark pink speckling, 10 to 14 inches, fancy); 'Scarlet Pimpernell' (deep pink center starburst, 18 to 30 inches, fancy).

*Caladium* 'Gray Ghost'

**GROWING TIPS:** Caladiums are traditionally shade plants; some, however, such as 'White Queen', will tolerate quite a bit of sun. Compost-enriched soil that's evenly moist but not soggy is ideal. Regular fertilizing encourages lush growth, but it can also bring out more green in the leaves (so will heavy shade). Where they're not hardy, lift the tubers in fall and store them indoors for the winter, or buy new tubers or started plants each spring.

**ALTERNATIVES:** *Xanthosoma atrovirens* 'Albomarginata' (also listed as *X. atrovirens* var. *albomarginata*, *X. albomarginata,* and *X.* 'Albo Marginata') has broad, deep green foliage boldly splashed with light green, cream, and white. The light- to deep green leaves of *X. lindenii* 'Magnificum' (also listed under *Alocasia lindenii* and *Caladium lindenii*) are veined with bright cream to white. Both can reach 3 to 5 feet tall. Partial shade; moist soil. Zones 8 to 10.

---

# CANNA
*Canna*

> **Height:** 4–7 feet
> **Leaf size:** 18–30 inches long;
>   8–12 inches wide
> **Full sun**
> **Zones 7 or 8–10**

It's easy to find bold foliage for shade, but sunny spots really show off spectacular leaves to advantage, and cannas (*Canna*) are tailor-made for bright sites. Hybrid cannas have long been prized for their large, colorful flowers, and those with vibrantly variegated foliage add even more interest to summer beds and borders.

Most variegated cannas are marked with narrow, parallel stripes that angle upward from the midrib toward the edges of the paddle-shaped leaves. 'Pretoria' (also known as 'Aureostriata', 'Bengal Tiger', and 'Imperialis') is a popular selection with green leaves striped with bright yellow and thinly edged with red, plus orange flowers; about 6 feet tall. Tropicanna Gold ('Mactro') is similar but usually a little shorter (4 to 5 feet), with orange-yellow flowers. 'Bangkok' (also sold as 'Bankok', 'Bangkok Yellow', 'Christ's Light', 'King of Siam', 'Minerva', 'Nirvana', and 'Striped Beauty') is a classic with white leaf stripes and yellow flowers; 4 to 6 feet. Looking for even more color? Try 'Pink Sunburst', with yellow stripes and an overall pinkish cast plus pink blooms to about 4 feet tall, or Tropicanna ('Phasion' or 'Phaison') with purple leaves that have reddish pink, salmon, and yellow stripes and orange flowers on 6- to 7-foot stems. Plants sold as 'African Sunset' look identical. 'Durban' is very similar and often confused with 'Phasion' but is supposed to have red flowers. 'Stuttgart' is distinctly different from all of these, with stripes and blocks of white; it's very showy but tends to scorch. The orange flowers bloom atop 6- to 8-foot-tall stems.

**GROWING TIPS:** All cannas thrive in rich, fertile soil that's dependably moist; in fact, most will grow even in standing water. Full sun is best, but you can get away with partial shade if you want mainly foliage. Fertilize often for lush growth. Remove individual damaged leaves as needed, or to promote new growth, cut whole stems to the ground if their leaves look dull. Where they aren't hardy, dig them up in fall and store indoors for the winter, or buy new rhizomes each spring.

**ALTERNATIVES:** Crotons (*Codiaeum variegatum* var. *pictum* and hybrids) bear large, leathery leaves marked with combinations of green, red, orange, pink, and yellow; 3 to 6 feet tall. Sun to partial shade; evenly moist but well-drained soil. Variegated banana (*Musa* 'Ae Ae') has spectacular leaves marked with stripes and blocks of bright green, pale green, and white; eventually 10 to 18 feet tall. It's not the easiest plant to grow well, but it can be worth the effort. Light shade; average to moist but well-drained soil. Zone 10.

*Canna* Tropicanna

## COLOCASIA
*Colocasia, elephant's ears, taro, coco yam, dasheen*

**Height: 3–6 feet**
**Leaf size: 2–3 feet long;**
 **1–2 feet wide**
**Sun to partial shade**
**Zones 8–10**

In a pot or in a pond, in a bed or in a border, the gigantic, heart-to shield-shaped leaves of colocasia (*Colocasia esculenta*) are guaranteed to catch the eye. Add in white or yellow markings, and these fast-growing, shrub-sized tropicals make amazing color accents wherever you use them. Among the several outstanding variegated selections, 'Nancy's Revenge' (also sold as 'Nancyana' and *C. nancyana*) is the most readily available. Its huge leaves start out a solid light green, then gradually develop a bright creamy white to yellow center patch that spreads out along the veins toward the leaf edges. 'Elepaio' is about half the size (to about 3 feet tall), but it also offers dramatic markings, in the form of bright white to gray-green flecks and splashes. 'Yellow Splash' is intermediate in size (to about 4 feet), with each leaf variegated with varying amounts of bright yellow, yellow-green, and green. The leaves of 'Chicago Harlequin' are only subtly mottled with shades of green, but its leafstalks are showily striped with white. *Note:* The species *C. esculenta* is considered to be invasive in southern coastal areas.

**GROWING TIPS:** Colocasias generally prefer partial shade in hot climates, but they'll take more sun if they have plenty of moisture; these heat-lovers thrive in full sun in more-temperate climates. Evenly moist to wet soil (or even standing water) and ample fertilizer encourage fast growth and large leaves. Where the plants are not hardy, dig up the corms or bring potted plants indoors for the winter.

**ALTERNATIVES:** Alocasias (*Alocasia*) produce similarly striking foliage and usually thrive in the same areas and growing conditions. Variegated giant taro (*A. macrorrhiza* 'Variegata') has extra-large, deep green leaves with creamy white and gray-green splashes. *A. odora* 'Okinawa Silver' is more compact, with a dramatic mixture of green, gray-green, and white in the leaves. Hybrid 'Hilo Beauty' has medium green leaves splashed heavily with pale green and white; to 3 feet tall.

*Colocasia esculenta* 'Yellow Splash'

## FATSIA
*Japanese aralia*

**Height: 4–6 feet**
**Leaf size: 8–12 inches long**
 **and wide**
**Full sun to full shade**
**Zones 8–10**

Long prized as an evergreen shrub in hot climates, Japanese aralia (*Fatsia japonica*) also makes a splendid, large-scale container specimen in northern gardens. The all-green versions are handsome year-round (with the bonus of large, branching clusters of tiny, creamy white flowers in fall), but the variegated selections really show off the "fingers" of each deeply lobed leaf. 'Spider's Web' is the most readily available variegate, with white edges and heavy white speckling over each leaf. The newest leaves have a greenish yellow or light green base color; the older leaves are deep green below the speckling. The edges of 'Variegata' (also sold as 'Marginata') are irregularly lined and splashed with white.

**GROWING TIPS:** Where it's hardy, Japanese aralia grows best in partial to full shade; in cooler areas, you may be able to get away with more sun if the soil is dependably moist (but not waterlogged). A spot that's sheltered from wind and the strong afternoon sun is ideal in most areas. Japanese aralia may overwinter in Zone 7 with protection, but generally you're best off keeping it in a pot and enjoying it as a houseplant during the winter in Zone 7 and north.

**ALTERNATIVES:** Bush or tree ivy (× *Fatshedera lizei*), with glossy, less deeply lobed leaves and a more sprawling or vining habit to about 6 feet tall, is a cross between *Fatsia japonica* 'Moseri' and Atlantic or Irish ivy (*Hedera hibernica*). 'Variegata' is narrowly edged with creamy white; 'Anna Mikkels' ('Annemieke', 'Aureomaculata', 'Aureovariegata', 'Maculata') has an irregular yellow-green to creamy yellow leaf center. Bush ivies thrive in the same conditions as Japanese aralia.

*Fatsia japonica* 'Spider's Web'

*Hedera canariensis* 'Gloire de Marengo'

## HEDERA
*Ivy*

**Height: To 40 feet or more as a
climber; about 6 inches tall
as a ground cover**
**Leaf size: 4–10 inches long and
wide**
**Partial to full shade**
**Zones vary**

Grow them as ground covers or
let them climb up walls and trees:
either way, variegated selections
of large-leaved ivies (*Hedera*) are
superb for their bold texture and
year-round interest in shady sites.
'Gloire de Marengo' Algerian ivy
(*H. canariensis*; also known as *H.
algeriensis*) has medium green
leaf centers that are marbled
with gray and irregularly edged
with cream to white. Its heart-
shaped to slightly lobed foliage is
5 to 8 inches wide and long. It's
sometimes listed as being hardy
to Zone 7 but is usually recommended for Zones 9 to 11; it
makes an interesting addition to
large containers in cooler areas.
Persian or colchis ivy (*H. colchica*) comes in two commonly
available variegated cultivars with
heart-shaped leaves. 'Dentata
Variegata' has deep green foliage
with subtle to heavy, grayish

green marbling and a wide border
of light yellow aging to creamy
white; the leaves are 3 to 8 inches
long and wide. 'Sulphur Heart'
(also known as 'Paddy's Pride')
has deep green leaves with a
bright yellow to greenish yellow center. The amount of yellow
varies widely, even on the same
plant, from nearly solid to a small
center splash or veining. Its foliage is 3 to 8 inches wide and up
to 10 inches long. Persian ivy is
usually best suited to Zones 7 to
11 but may perform well in parts
of Zone 6 with protection from
winter sun and wind. *Note:* Both
*H. canariensis* and *H. colchica*
are considered invasive in some
areas.

**GROWING TIPS:** Both Algerian and
Persian ivies grow in partial to full
shade with average to moist, well-
drained soil. If you use them as
ground covers, give them a good
trim every few years in spring
with hedge shears or with a lawn
mower on its highest blade setting to keep the planting looking fresh. *Caution:* Wear gloves,
because the plants may cause
skin irritation if you touch them.

**ALTERNATIVE:** For a bold climber
that's suited to a brighter site,

consider variegated grape (*Vitis
vinifera* 'Variegata'). Its broad, deciduous, medium green leaves are randomly splashed with light yellow
to creamy white (often with a pink
tinge when young); to 30 feet tall.
Full sun to partial shade; average,
well-drained soil. Zones 6 to 9. *Note:
V. vinifera* is considered invasive in
some areas.

## HOSTA
*Hosta, plantain lily*

**Height: Varies**
**Leaf size: Varies**
**Full sun to full shade**
**Zones 3–8**

Variegated hostas (*Hosta*) may
be an obvious choice for bold foliage in shady gardens, but that
doesn't mean they have to be a
boring one. They come in such a
wide array of sizes, leaf shapes,
and variegation patterns that they
are invaluable for creating combinations with other flowering and
foliage favorites anywhere from
the front of a border to the back.
They're also spectacular alone as
an accent in the ground or in a
container, or in groups as masses
or ground covers.

With so many hundreds of hostas to choose from and new ones
coming out every year, it's impossible to cover them all here. In
most cases, you're best off buying them in person, or from reli-
able mail-order nurseries with
lots of photographs in their catalog or on their Web site, to get
the specific colors and sizes you
need. Keep in mind that plants

of the newest selections tend to
be fairly small and very expensive, so if you're more interested
in particular colors than in having the latest introductions, older
cultivars are a better buy. To get
you started, here's an overview of
a few time-tested favorites in the
most common variegation patterns, with their approximate foliage height:

*Green center, white edge:*
'Ginkgo Craig' (1 foot); 'Francee'
(18 inches); 'Antioch' (2 feet).

*White center, green edge:* 'Fire
and Ice' and 'Remember Me'
(1 foot); 'Loyalist' and 'Night
Before Christmas' (18 inches).

*Hosta* 'June'

*Green center, yellow edge:* 'Golden Tiara' (16 inches); 'Abba Dabba Do' and *H. montana* 'Aureomarginata' (2 feet).

*Yellow center, green edge:* 'Geisha' (8 inches); 'Stained Glass' (14 inches); 'Captain Kirk' and 'Guacamole' (18 inches).

*Blue center, white to yellow edge:* 'El Niño' (white edge, 18 inches); 'Regal Splendor' (cream edge, 3 feet); 'Parky's Prize' and 'Tokudama Flavocircinalis' (yellow edge, 18 inches).

*White to yellow center, blue edge:* 'Moonstruck' (white center, 1 foot); 'Great Expectations' (cream center, 2 feet); 'June' (yellow center, 1 foot); 'Tokudama Aureonebulosa' (yellow center, 18 inches).

**GROWING TIPS:** Although hostas adapt to a number of light conditions, they typically thrive in morning sun and afternoon shade or light all-day shade. Variegated selections tend to need more sun than all-green ones, but too much sun will cause the paler parts of the leaves to turn brown. Established plants can tolerate dry soil; however, young plants — and even older plants getting lots of sun — benefit from watering during dry spells. Humus-rich soil and regular fertilizing encourage strong, lush foliage. Be aware that a virus, known as Hosta Virus X, has been spreading through the hosta population. It can produce a variety of symptoms, including leaf mottling and distorted growth, although sometimes the plants show no symptoms. Avoid buying any hostas with visible symptoms, and destroy (do not compost) any of those in your garden that you suspect might be infected.

**ALTERNATIVES:** Variegated horseradish (*Armoracia rusticana* 'Variegata') has wide, 2- to 3-foot-long, medium green leaves streaked and splashed with white, most obviously in spring and on established plants. Spreads moderately. Zones 3 to 8. For a quick fix of supersized variegated foliage, try flowering cabbages (*Brassica oleracea*). These low-growing annuals have smooth- or frilly-edged, pale green leaves that gradually develop more and more white; 12 to 18 inches tall. Full sun; average, well-drained soil.

## PHYTOLACCA
*Pokeweed, pokeberry, poke*

**Height: 4–6 feet**
**Leaf size: 6–8 inches long;**
 **4–6 inches wide**
**Full sun to partial shade**
**Zones 5–9**

Long dismissed as merely a weed, pokeweed (*Phytolacca americana*) is developing a following among gardeners who appreciate its handsome foliage, white summer flowers, and nodding clusters of deep purple berries in fall. Its sturdy, pinkish red stems grow straight upward, then branch at the top, producing a large, spreading clump that looks great near the middle or back of a border. Although the species itself has plenty to offer, foliage lovers flip over the stunning selection called 'Silberstein' (also known as 'Steve Silberstein' and 'Variegata'), with cream speckling so heavy that some leaves have almost no green at all.

**GROWING TIPS:** Pokeweed grows equally well in sun or partial shade. Average, well-drained soil is fine, although dependable moisture is a plus in full-sun sites. Like the species, 'Silberstein' produces many seedlings; most, if not all, will also be variegated.

**ALTERNATIVE:** Variegated kiss-me-over-the-garden-gate (*Persicaria orientalis* 'Shiro-gane-nishiki' or 'Variegata', also listed under *Polygonum orientale*) grows quickly to about 6 feet tall, with upright-then-arching stems clad in heart-shaped, medium green leaves irregularly splashed with cream. This showy annual self-sows prolifically, and the seedlings are variegated too. Full sun to partial shade; average soil. *Note:* The species is considered invasive in some areas.

*Phytolacca americana* 'Variegata'

## SANCHEZIA
*Sanchezia, shrubby whitevein*

**Height:** 4–8 feet
**Leaf size:** 6–12 inches long;
   3–5 inches wide
**Full sun to partial shade**
**Zones 9 and 10**

If you prefer your variegation in tidy lines instead of random splashes and speckles, you'll appreciate the bold, gold- to cream-veined foliage of *Sanchezia speciosa* (also known as *S. nobilis*). The intensity of the veining varies from leaf to leaf; the overall effect, however, is absolutely smashing, and reddish stems add even more color to the mix. Grown as a shrub or border perennial where it's hardy, this eye-catching tropical makes a stunning large-container specimen or summer and fall border plant in cooler climates too.

The species itself is most commonly available, but you may be able to find a few selections, including the more compact 'Nana' and 'Ecuador Gold' (also sold as 'Equador Gold'), which reportedly has even brighter veining.

**GROWING TIPS:** Sanchezia leaves produce their most dramatic coloring when they get plenty of light, but they tend to wilt when exposed to too much strong sun. As a compromise, try a site with morning sun and afternoon shade or light all-day shade. Humus-rich, evenly moist (but not water-logged) soil is ideal. Where sanchezia is not hardy, enjoy it indoors as a houseplant during the winter.

**ALTERNATIVE:** Fast-growing variegated tapioca (*Manihot esculenta* 'Variegata') forms shrubby clumps of large, pink-stalked, rich green leaves with prominent creamy yellow centers that extend into the deeply cut lobes; 3 to 6 feet tall in pots (taller where hardy). This heat-loving euphorbia relative thrives in full sun (and keeps its best color there) but will also take partial shade; average to moist soil. Zone 10 and parts of Zone 9.

## SYMPHYTUM
*Comfrey*

**Height:** Varies
**Leaf size:** Varies
**Full sun to full shade**
**Zones 4–8**

Comfreys aren't just for the herb garden anymore. These vigorous perennials produce an abundance of big, bold foliage without much fussing from you; an occasional trim is all they need to stay in good shape. Just be sure to give them plenty of room, because their wide-spreading leaves will quickly smother more-delicate companions.

For a low-growing, ground-cover-type comfrey, consider the hybrid 'Goldsmith' (often listed as 'Jubilee' and 'Variegatum' and under *S. ibericum* or *S. grandiflorum*). In spring it looks rather like a fuzzy-leaved hosta, with 6- to 10-inch-long, rich green leaves widely but irregularly edged with yellow aging to cream; 8 to 12 inches tall. 'Hidcote Variegated' looks similar in leaf but is said to have light blue flowers instead of whitish ones. Several larger-scale selections of Russian comfrey (*S. × uplandicum*) are available, with wide clumps of broad, gray-green leaves that are up to 2 feet long. 'Axminster Gold' has wide yellow edges. 'Denford Variegated' (also sold as 'Densford Variegated') has very heavy yellow speckling, to the point that some leaves are practically all yellow. 'Variegatum' has bright creamy white edges. All three are 18 to 24 inches tall in leaf and 3 to 5 feet in bloom.

**GROWING TIPS:** Comfreys will adapt to a range of growing conditions, but the variegated forms usually grow best with morning sun and afternoon shade or light all-day shade. Average, humus-rich soil generally suits their needs; the more sun they get, the more important it is to have a steady supply of moisture to prevent the leaf edges from browning. If the leaves do become discolored, cutting the plants to the ground and watering thoroughly will encourage healthy new growth. (This trick works nicely for tidying up the clumps after bloom as well.)

**ALTERNATIVE:** For a similar splash of dramatic variegation on slightly smaller-scale foliage, try variegated water figwort (*Scrophularia auriculata* [*S. aquatica*] 'Variegata'). It has light green leaves irregularly edged with cream and often pink-blushed in spring, on 3- to 4-foot-tall flowering stems. Sun to partial shade is fine; dependably moist soil is a must. Zones 6 or 7 to 9.

*Sanchezia speciosa*

*Symphytum × uplandicum* 'Axminster Gold'

# ABUTILON
*Flowering maple, parlor maple*

**Height: Varies**
**Leaf size: 3–5 inches long and wide**
**Full sun to partial shade**
**Zones 9 and 10**

With their handsome foliage and beautiful, bell-shaped blooms, flowering maples are fantastic for outdoor color from spring to fall. Bring them indoors at the end of the season, and you can enjoy them all winter long too.

Variegated flowering maples are best known for their dramatically gold-flecked foliage forms, which get their markings from abutilon mosaic virus. *Abutilon pictum* 'Thompsonii' (also sold under *A. striatum*) is the most common cultivar, with orange flowers and deeply cut leaves heavily freckled with yellow on bushy, upright plants that reach 3 to 6 feet in most areas. 'Thompsonii Yellow' (also sold as 'Yellow Form') has light yellow flowers. *A. megapotamicum* 'Variegatum' has equally speckled but much smaller leaves, with red-and-yellow flowers on arching stems that reach 4 to 6 feet tall; 'Paisley' is similar but with maroon-and-pink or -peach blooms. If crisp white variegation is to your taste, *Abutilon × hybridum* 'Souvenir de Bonn' is sure to please, with its broad green leaves cleanly edged in bright white, plus peachy orange flowers; 4 to 6 feet tall. 'Savitzii' is even more showily marked with white, but it's also much less vigorous and doesn't flower as freely.

**GROWING TIPS:** Flowering maples prefer full sun to light shade with evenly moist but well-drained soil. A bit of afternoon shade helps prevent wilting in hot climates, but too much shade reduces the variegation of spotted types. Regular pinching during the growing season encourages the plants to stay dense and well-shaped.

**ALTERNATIVES:** Annual 'Splash of Cream' shoo-fly plant (*Nicandra physaloides*) has 2- to 4-foot-tall, deep purple stems with wavy-edged green leaves irregularly splashed and speckled in creamy yellow. Full sun; average, well-drained soil. Variegated perennial buckwheat (*Fagopyrum dibotrys* 'Variegatum') produces fast-growing, spreading, 3- to 6-foot-tall plants with nearly triangular green leaves heavily marbled with yellow. Full sun to partial shade; moist but well-drained soil. Zones 4 to 9.

*Actinidia kolomikta* 'Arctic Beauty'

# ACTINIDIA
*Kiwi vine, kiwi*

**Height: 15–25 feet or more**
**Leaf size: 4–6 inches long;**
**    2–3 inches wide**
**Full sun to partial shade**
**Zones 3–7**

Variegated forms of hardy kiwi vine (*Actinidia kolomikta*) aren't the most dependable choice for a fantastic show, but when they're at their best, they're truly spectacular. Often with a bronze cast when they first emerge, slightly older green leaves appear to have been dipped into white paint; varying amounts of pink blushing may also be visible. The greenish white flowers are fragrant but not showy; on female plants, they're followed by small but tasty fruits.

The amount of variegation shown by hardy kiwi plants is variable. Plants labeled 'Arctic Beauty' are typically male and tend to show the best color, although sometimes less brightly marked female plants are also sold under this name. To further confuse the matter, young plants often show no variegation at all, so it's difficult to judge by looking at them in nursery pots. If you do find a potted young plant that shows some white on its leaves, it's worth a try; starting with a cutting from an established plant that you know has good variegation is another option. Or seek out plants labeled 'Pasha'; they seem to be more reliably male and thus well colored.

**GROWING TIPS:** Hardy kiwi vines will adapt to an array of light levels, but sun to light shade brings out the best variegation. (Light shade is ideal in southern gardens.) They appreciate fertile, evenly moist but well-drained soil. Give these vigorous twining vines a large, sturdy support.

**ALTERNATIVES:** For gardeners in warmer climates, kadsura (*Kadsura japonica*) is a better choice for

*Abutilon* 'Souvenir de Bonn'

a variegated, twining vine to about 10 feet tall. Semievergreen to evergreen, the glossy, deep green leaves of 'Variegata' ('Fukurin') have a wide, light yellow edge that fades to cream by winter; the new leaves are often pink-blushed as well. 'Chirimen' ('Chirifu') is irregularly speckled with cream. Partial shade is usually ideal; average soil. Zones 7 to 9.

## AJUGA
*Ajuga, bugleweed*

**Height: 3–4 inches**
**Leaf size: 3–4 inches long;**
    **about 1 inch wide**
**Full sun to full shade**
**Zones 3 or 4–8**

For a carpet of vigorous variegation and pretty flowers, too, ajuga (*Ajuga reptans*) simply can't be beat. Individual plants form dense rosettes of evergreen or semievergreen leaves that send out stolons (aboveground runners); these take root and produce new plants, quickly creating a weed-suppressing ground cover. Spikes of blue blooms to about 6 inches tall appear from early or mid-spring to late spring or early summer. Variegated ajugas are great for brightening up shady spots under trees and shrubs and also in container plantings. Think twice about letting them loose in regular flower gardens, though; they'll spread super-quick in the loose, rich soil, and they're likely to creep into surrounding lawn areas as well. *Note:* The species is considered invasive in some areas of the country.

Ajuga lovers have a number of variegation patterns to choose from. 'Burgundy Glow' is a popular selection with gray-green leaves that are edged in cream to white, with a pink to purplish blush that's particularly noticeable in cool weather. If you like the cream-edged look but prefer less pink, look for 'Variegata' or 'Silver Beauty'. 'Vanilla Chip' (sometimes listed under *A. × tenorii*) has the same color combination, but its leaves are about half the size of other ajugas. 'Arctic Fox' has brighter cream-to-white markings with a crinkled, deep green edge; the amount of variegation may be quite different from plant to plant. 'Multicolor' (also sold as 'Rainbow') offers a much darker effect, with deep bronzy green leaves spotted with cream, yellow, pink, and red.

**GROWING TIPS:** Ajugas will grow anywhere from full sun (in cooler climates) to full shade, but they flower best and have the most distinct variegation when they get plenty of light. Fertile, evenly moist but well-drained soil keeps the leaves looking lush. After the flowers have faded, use shears or a string trimmer to remove the bloom stalks and improve the foliage effect. Remove solid-green rosettes as soon as you spot them.

**ALTERNATIVES:** Fuzzy-leaved *Arabis alpina* subsp. *caucasica* (*A. caucasica*) and smooth-leaved *A. ferdinandi-coburgii* both grow in tidy, evergreen rosettes but spread much more slowly than ajugas. *A. alpina*

*Ajuga reptans* 'Burgundy Glow'

subsp. *caucasica* 'Variegata' has light green leaves with cream edges; 4 to 6 inches tall. *A. ferdinandi-coburgii* 'Variegata' has white edges; 'Old Gold' has a greenish yellow to yellowish white margin; 3 to 4 inches tall. Full sun; average to dry soil. Zones 3 to 7.

## ASTRANTIA
*Masterwort*

**Height: About 1 foot**
**Leaf size: 6 inches long and wide**
**Full sun to partial shade**
**Zones 4–7**

Long overlooked by American gardeners, masterwort (*Astrantia major*) is becoming much more popular, thanks in part to new introductions with richly colored blooms. These perennial beauties flower throughout the summer in white or shades of pink to red over dense clumps of deeply lobed leaves. But for fans of fancy foliage, the flowers are secondary

*Astrantia major* 'Sunningdale Variegated'

to the dramatic display of the selection known as 'Sunningdale Variegated'. It makes an amazing early-season accent, with creamy yellow edges and splashes on its bright green leaves. As the season progresses, the yellow gradually turns white, then light green by the time the pale pinkish white flowers appear atop 24- to 30-inch stems.

**GROWING TIPS:** 'Sunningdale Variegated' tends to look best for the longest period of time in full sun in cool climates; it needs some summer shade in the warmer parts of its hardiness range. It doesn't like to dry out, so give it a dependably moist but well-drained spot, and work plenty of compost into the soil before planting. After the first flush of blooms starts to fade, cut the whole plant to the ground and you'll get fresh, colorful foliage to enjoy through the rest of the growing season. This also helps prevent self-sowing, which can produce an abundance of seedlings that aren't variegated like the parent plant.

**ALTERNATIVE:** Variegated crown imperial (*Fritillaria imperialis* 'Aureomarginata') is another gem for spring foliage interest. Starting in early spring, the large bulbs send up deep purple stalks clad in many narrow green leaves that are edged in yellow. By late spring, each 3-foot-tall flowering stem is topped with another tuft of variegated leaves. The plants die back to the ground by midsummer. Full sun; average, well-drained soil. Zones 5 to 8.

Aucuba japonica 'Picturata'

## AUCUBA
*Aucuba*

**Height: 5–10 feet**
**Leaf size: 5–7 inches long;**
**    3 inches wide**
**Partial to full shade**
**Zones 6–10**

Some gardeners may dismiss aucubas (*Aucuba*) as being too common — but often there's a good reason why common plants *are* common! These dependable evergreen shrubs thrive with a minimum of fuss in sites where others languish or won't fit. The rounded, multistemmed shrubs can be as much as 10 feet tall and wide, although 5 to 6 feet is more likely; cutting a few of the oldest stems to the ground each year lets you keep the plants even smaller, if necessary. Their leathery leaves are normally solid green, but there are also several variegated selections, which supply considerable year-round

interest to borders and shrub plantings. As a bonus, female aucubas produce clusters of long-lasting red berries in winter if you make sure a male plant is nearby.

Variegated aucubas come in two main patterns: either speckled or with a contrasting edge. The cream- to yellow-spotted ones are known as gold dust plants or spotted laurels and are typically sold under the name *A. japonica* 'Variegata'; these can be male or female and vary widely in the amount of variegation they display. 'Gold Dust' is a female selection with fine yellow spotting on narrower, toothed leaves. 'Mr. Goldstrike' is a heavily speckled selection that is supposed to be male; plants labeled 'Crotonifolia' are apt to be female. For even more distinct variegation, consider 'Picturata', a male selection with a bright yellow center and a yellow-speckled

green edge (female or male 'Goldieana' is similar but with variable centers and more speckles); or 'Sulphurea Marginata', a female with a green center and a yellow edge.

**GROWING TIPS:** Aucubas prefer partial to full shade. Evenly moist but well-drained soil is ideal, although they will adapt to quite dry conditions, especially with a generous mulch of compost or chopped leaves. Don't plant aucubas in an exposed, windy site: wind leads to discolored leaves, especially in winter.

**ALTERNATIVES:** *Photinia davidiana* 'Palette' (*Stransvaesia davidiana* 'Palette') has bronze-pink new growth turning green with pinkish white to creamy white splashes. *P.* × *fraseri* Pink Marble ('Cassini') produces reddish pink new shoots; older leaves are white-edged green. *P. glabra* 'Parfait' ('Variegata') has bronze new leaves turning green and gray-green with irregular pink to white edges. All to 10 feet tall or more. Full sun to partial shade; average soil. Zones 7 or 8 to 10.

## CALAMINTHA
*Calamint*

**Height: 12–18 inches**
**Leaf size: To 2 inches long and wide**
**Full sun to partial sun**
**Zones 5–9**

Handsome foliage, attractive flowers, and great fragrance, too — this pretty perennial has it all! Variegated calamint (*Calamintha grandiflora* 'Variegata') produces bushy mounds of deep green leaves that are heavily speckled with creamy white (most distinctly on new leaves), plus tubular, bright pink flowers through the summer. It's a beauty in beds and borders, and it looks terrific in containers too. It's related to mints, but it usually stays in clumps, rather than running rampantly through your garden.

**GROWING TIPS:** Variegated calamint tolerates full sun to partial shade and average, well-drained soil; it appreciates extra moisture in sunny sites, however. Cutting the whole clump to the ground in midsummer prevents self-sowing and encourages a flush of brightly marked new foliage that you can enjoy into fall. Most, if not all, self-sown seedlings are solid green, and they'll quickly crowd out the variegated plants if left in the garden.

**ALTERNATIVE:** Variegated black horehound (*Ballota nigra* 'Variegata'; also sold as 'Archer's Variety') looks

*Calamintha grandiflora* 'Variegata'

like variegated calamint from a distance, but instead of having green leaves speckled with white, the foliage appears basically white with variable green flecking. 'Prancing Jester' is said to be even more heavily variegated. Height is usually 1 to 2 feet. Remove all-green shoots. Full sun to partial shade; average, well-drained soil. Zones 5 to 9.

## CAPSICUM
*Pepper*

**Height: 1–2 feet**
**Leaf size: About 2 inches long;**
   **1 inch wide**
**Full sun to partial shade**
**Zones 9–11**

Colorful and fast-growing, variegated hot peppers (*Capsicum annuum*) are terrific for foliage interest, even if you never plan to harvest their spicy to scorchingly hot fruits. The dense, bushy plants blend well in beds and borders, and they are excellent

as container plants, too; raising them off the ground makes it easier to admire their small purple flowers and bright peppers.

If you buy plants or sow seeds labeled 'Jigsaw', 'Purple Tiger', 'Tricolor', 'Tri-Color Variegata', 'Trifetti', or 'Variegata', you're likely to get plants that have a mix of green, purple, and white marbling in the foliage, as well as small, glossy, deep purple fruits that turn red as they mature. 'Fish' has bright green leaves heavily splashed with white and gray-green; its 2- to 3-inch-long green fruits are striped with cream before maturing to orange and then red. Compact ornamental 'Shu' bears bright green-and-white leaves and short, slender fruits that are all shades of cream, yellow, orange, and red.

**GROWING TIPS:** Peppers thrive in full sun, but they'll get by with a half-day of sun if necessary. Average, well-drained soil is fine. It's easy to start variegated peppers from seed; sow indoors in late winter and keep them warm, and they'll sprout in just a few days. The first leaves may be solid green or purple, but they'll develop variegation as they grow. Remember that peppers hate cold weather, so wait until after your last frost date (once nighttime temperatures are consistently at least 55°F) before you set them outside. In fall, bring potted peppers indoors for the winter, or simply treat them like annuals and start new ones each spring. *Caution:* Protect your skin

*Capsicum annuum* 'Tricolor'

with gloves when handling the fruits, and keep them away from children.

**ALTERNATIVES:** Usually listed simply as 'Variegated' (sometimes as 'Splash of Cream'), variegated tomato (*Lycopersicon esculentum*) has cream streaking and splashing on its medium green leaves and stems. Variegated Jerusalem cherry (*Solanum capsicastrum* 'Variegatum') is related to peppers and tomatoes, but its colorful fruits are definitely not edible. The bushy plants have green leaves heavily splashed with creamy white; about 18 inches tall. Full sun; average, well-drained soil. Zones 8 or 9 to 11.

## CARYOPTERIS
*Caryopteris, bluebeard, blue mist shrub*

**Height:** Usually 2–3 feet
**Leaf size:** 1–2 inches long;
　½–1 inch wide
**Full sun to partial shade**
**Zones 5 or 6–9**

With their clusters of bright blue flowers from late summer into fall, caryopteris (*Caryopteris*) are superb for adding height and color to late-season beds and borders. Unfortunately, they don't offer much interest during the several months before the blooms begin; they're simply large, bushy clumps of relatively undistinguished, green to grayish green leaves. Choosing a variegated cultivar is a great way to get these easy-care plants to earn their keep over a longer period.

There are two kinds of variegated caryopteris to choose from: one that forms small shrubs (*C. × clandonensis*) and one that dies back to the ground each winter (*C. divaricata*). Shrubby *C. × clandonensis* 'Summer Sorbet' grows about 3 feet tall and wide, with narrow, toothed, gray-green leaves that are neatly edged with bright yellow. Herbaceous *C. divaricata* 'Snow Fairy' usually grows 2 to 3 feet tall but may get to 5 feet, with shorter, broader leaves widely but irregularly edged with bright cream to white; 'Pink Illumination' has greenish yellow leaf edges and pink flowers instead of the usual blue.

**GROWING TIPS:** Caryopteris will get by in partial shade but tend to sprawl a bit there; full sun encourages sturdier stems. Average to dry soil is fine; good drainage is a must. Pinching or shearing off the shoot tips a few times in spring to early summer encourages branching and bushier growth; the shrubby form also benefits from a hard pruning just as new growth appears in spring.

**ALTERNATIVES:** Best known as a florist flower, Peruvian lily (*Alstroemeria psittacina*; also listed as *A. pulchella*) looks great in the garden, too. The leaf edges of 'Variegata' are brushed with bright white on upright stems to 18 inches tall. Zones 7 to 9.

*Caryopteris divaricata* 'Snow Fairy'

*A.* 'Glory of the Andes' has cream- to light yellow edged leaves on 2- to 3-foot-tall stems; Zones 6 to 9. Sun to partial shade; evenly moist but well-drained soil.

## CORNUS
*Dogwood*

**Height:** Varies
**Leaf size:** 3–5 inches long,
　2–4 inches wide
**Full sun to partial shade**
**Zones vary**

Dogwoods (*Cornus*) have to be one of the most versatile groups of plants for the home landscape. They come in both shrubby and tree-form species and selections, in a wide array of heights and colors, so you can enjoy them in borders, as informal hedges, in mass plantings, as specimens, and even in containers. Planting dogwoods with variegated foliage adds yet another feature to complement their spring or summer flowers, fall fruits, and winter stems.

Shrubby dogwoods are better known for their colorful young stems than for their flowers. Red-twig dogwood (*C. alba*) grows in clumps of upright stems that are reddish when young. Red osier dogwood (*C. sericea*, also known as *C. stolonifera*) looks similar, but it spreads more vigorously by underground stems to form broad masses. Both are usually hardy in Zones 2 to 7 and grow 8 to 10 feet tall, with white flower clusters and white berries. Here's an overview of the basic variegation patterns that are available.

*Cornus kousa* 'Wolf Eyes'

**Shrubs with green-and-white or -cream leaves.** Several cultivars of *C. alba* have irregular white to cream edges, including 'Elegantissima' (also sold as 'Argenteomarginata' and 'Sibirica Variegata'), Ivory Halo ('Bailhalo'), and Strawberry Daiquiri ('Stdazam'). *C. sericea* 'Silver and Gold' also has white-edged leaves but on bright yellow young stems instead of the usual red.

**Shrubs with green-and-yellow leaves.** *C. alba* 'Gouchaultii' has yellow edges, often with pink tinges; 'Spaethii' is similar but lacks the pink. 'Hedgerow's Gold' has wide yellow edges. 'Cream Cracker' has yellow edges that age to creamy yellow.

Tree-type dogwoods include pagoda dogwood (*C. alternifolia*) and the much larger giant dogwood (*C. controversa*), both of which are prized for the distinct layered look created by their horizontal branching habit. They have clusters of small white flowers in late spring, followed by bluish black fruits. The classic species with showy white or pink bracts in mid-spring and small red fruits in fall is Eastern flowering dogwood (*C. florida*). Japanese dogwood (*C. kousa*) also has showy bracts but blooms about a month later, with large, rounded, reddish fruits in late summer to fall. Cornelian cherry (*C. mas*) — which isn't a cherry at all — blooms as early as late winter with clusters of small, bright yellow flowers that turn bright red by early fall. Here are some of the many cultivars you can choose from.

*Trees with green-and-cream or -white leaves.* *C. alternifolia* 'Argentea' grows 10 to 15 feet tall; Zones 3 to 8. *C. controversa* 'Variegata' may eventually reach 30 feet; Zones 6 or 7 to 9. Variegated forms of *C. florida* are typically less than 10 feet tall but may eventually grow to 20 feet: these include Cherokee Daybreak ('Daybreak'), with white bracts, and 'Welchii' ('Tricolor'), with white bracts and an additional pink blush on the leaf edges; both are usually hardy in Zones 5 to 8. *C. kousa* 'Wolf Eyes' is a stunning selection to about 15 feet, while Samaritan ('Samzam') can reportedly reach to 25 feet; 'Kris-

tin Lipka's Variegated Weeper' is a weeping form to 15 feet or more. Zones 5 to 9. *C. mas* 'Variegata' grows to about 15 feet; Zones 4 to 8.

*Trees with green-and-yellow leaves.* *C. alternifolia* Golden Shadows ('W. Stackman') grows 10 to 15 feet tall; Zones 3 to 8. *C. controversa* 'Janine' can reach 30 feet or more; Zones 6 or 7 to 9. *C. florida* Cherokee Sunset ('Sunset') has pink-tinged new growth and reddish pink bracts, and 'First Lady' has white bracts; 10 to 20 feet in Zones 5 to 8. *C. kousa* 'Gold Star' and 'Sunsplash' eventually reach 10 to 15 feet; Zones 5 to 9.

**GROWING TIPS:** Most dogwoods will grow in either full sun or partial shade, although the shrubby variegates generally like sun and the tree-form variegates seem to prefer morning sun and afternoon shade or light all-day shade. They will adapt to a range of soil conditions, too; fertile and moist but well-drained soil is usually best. Pruning shrubby types heavily in late winter controls their size and encourages the production of more-colorful young stems; either cut out up to a third of the oldest stems at the base of the plant each year or cut down all of the stems to 6 to 12 inches above the ground every other year.

**ALTERNATIVES:** Deciduous 'Creel's Calico' sweet pepperbush or summersweet (*Clethra alnifolia*) forms a dense, bushy clump to about 6 feet tall, with green leaves densely speckled with cream to white. Zones 4 to 9.

'Sunsplash' winterberry (*Ilex verticillata*) is a deciduous holly with irregular spots and splashes of bright yellow (most distinctly on the new growth) on its green leaves; 8 to 10 feet tall. Zones 4 to 8. Full sun to light shade; average to moist soil.

## ELEUTHEROCOCCUS
*Five-fingered aralia, acanthopanax*

**Height: 6–8 feet**
**Leaf size: 3–4 inches long; individual leaflets are less than 2 inches wide**
**Full sun to full shade**
**Zones 4–8**

With its toothed, compound leaves and graceful upright-to-arching stems, five-fingered aralia (*Eleutherococcus sieboldianus;* also known as *Acanthopanax sieboldianus*) is elegant enough to earn a special place and special care in any landscape. It's nowhere near as delicate as it looks, though; this sturdy deciduous shrub will adapt to just about any conditions you put it in — even those tough dry-shade sites.

Variegated forms of five-fingered aralia are even more elegant, thanks to the wide, irregular, contrasting edge on each leaflet. On 'Variegatus', the edge starts out cream and turns white; on 'Aureomarginatus', it starts light yellow and ages to creamy white.

**GROWING TIPS:** Variegated five-fingered aralias can take full sun or full shade, but they generally look their best in partial shade. Average to dry soil is fine. Plants

may spread by suckers. Prune out any all-green stems. *Caution:* Wear gloves when you handle them; there are small but sharp prickles below the leaves.

**ALTERNATIVES:** Japanese aralia (*Aralia elata*) has gigantic compound leaves made up of many dozens of leaflets. The green leaflets are irregularly edged with white on 'Silver Umbrella' and 'Variegata' and yellow fading to cream or white on 'Aureovariegata' and 'Golden Umbrella'; to 15 feet tall or more. Often produce all-green suckers. Full sun to partial shade; average, well-drained soil. Zones 4 to 9. *Note:* The species is considered invasive in some areas.

*Eleutherococcus sieboldianus* 'Variegatus'

*Euonymus japonicus*
'Aureomarginatus'

## EUONYMUS
*Euonymus*

**Height:** Varies
**Leaf size:** 1–3 inches long and wide
**Full sun to full shade**
**Zones vary**

Variegated forms of euonymus (*Euonymus*) are a common sight in home and commercial landscapes in many climates. Although this familiarity inspires contempt from some gardeners, others appreciate the plants' sturdy, adaptable nature and the year-round color splash provided by their leathery evergreen foliage. Besides their white, cream, or yellow markings, the leaves often take on a pinkish to reddish blush in winter.

Generally hardy in Zones 5 to 9, wintercreeper (*E. fortunei*) tends to form 2- to 3-foot-tall, wide-mounded to somewhat sprawling shrubs that may also climb if planted near a tree, wall, or other vertical surface. *Note:* This species is considered invasive in some areas. Selections of Japanese euonymus (*E. japonicus*) tend to be slightly less hardy (usually Zones 6 or 7 to 9), grow taller (6 to 8 feet), and have a more upright, bushier habit, with slightly larger leaves. Both species readily produce variegated shoots in a variety of patterns, so there are a large number of cultivars to choose from (many of them differing only slightly), and more are released each year. Here's an overview of some of the best selections.

**Green with cream-to-white markings.** Selections of *E. fortunei* include the classic 'Emerald Gaiety', with white edges, and 'Silver Queen', which starts out with wide creamy yellow edges that age to white. Some *E. japonicus* cultivars are 'Silver Queen', with irregular, creamy white edges; cream-to-white-edged 'Silver King'; and 'Albomarginatus' and Silver Princess ('Moness'), with narrow white edges. 'Microphyllus Albovariegatus' has tiny, white-edged, deep green leaves on very compact plants.

**Green with yellow markings.** *E. fortunei* Blondy ('Interbolwji') has large yellow to cream centers. 'Emerald 'n' Gold' has broad, bright yellow to creamy yellow edges; Gold Splash ('Roemertwo') is similar but with even wider edges. Sunny Lane ('Roemerone') has bright yellow markings on the new foliage, softening to greenish yellow as the leaves age. *E. japonicus* 'Aureomarginatus' has yellow-to-cream edging; 'Chollipo' has broader, bright yellow edges aging to creamy yellow.

**GROWING TIPS:** Variegated euonymus will grow in anything from full sun to full shade, although they produce the most striking color in sun to light shade. Average, well-drained soil is generally fine, but full-sun plantings appreciate more moisture. Shearing the plants in spring helps to control their size, encourages bushier growth, and promotes more-colorful new shoots. Remove any nonvariegated growth as soon as you see it. Also watch out for euonymus scale, a pest that sucks sap from the stems and leaves, seriously weakening or killing the plants. Spraying repeatedly with an insecticidal soap or horticultural oil may help control scale, but if this is a common, recurring problem in your area, consider planting something other than euonymus.

**ALTERNATIVES:** Cherry laurel (*Prunus laurocerasus*) selections with cream-colored marbling on their evergreen leaves are available under several names, including 'Marbled Dragon', 'Marbled White', and 'Variegata'; to 15 feet or more. Average soil. Zones 7 to 10. For a much smaller plant, consider 'Tubby Andrews' bergenia (*Bergenia*), with glossy, leathery, bright green leaves splashed with cream and yellow; 6 to 8 inches tall. Moist but well-drained soil. Zones 3 to 8. Full sun to partial shade.

## EUPHORBIA
*Euphorbia, spurge*

**Height:** Varies
**Leaf size:** Varies
**Full sun to partial shade**
**Zones vary**

There are thousands of species and selections of euphorbias (*Euphorbia*) to choose from, in a dizzying array of heights, habits, colors, and textures. Among the medium-textured variegates suitable for beds, borders, and containers, two of the best are snow-on-the-mountain (*E. marginata*) and tender 'Yokoi's White' annual poinsettia (*E. cyathophora*; often listed under *E. heterophylla*).

Snow-on-the-mountain is a 1- to 3-foot-tall annual with a single, upright stem that branches toward the top. The oblong, 1- to 3-inch-long and ½- to 1-inch-wide leaves are light green to gray-green on young plants. As the season progresses, the edges of the uppermost leaves are increasingly marked with white, to the point of being nearly or completely all white by the time the tiny greenish white flowers appear in late summer to fall. 'Yokoi's White' annual poinsettia closely resembles the popular Christmas poinsettia, forming well-branched, 1- to 3-foot-tall plants clad in variably shaped leaves that are 3 to 6 inches long and 2 to 4 inches across. Each green leaf is broadly edged with light yellow to creamy white; toward the stem tips, the leaves that are clustered below the tiny flowers develop an orange-red center splash by late summer.

**GROWING TIPS:** Snow-on-the-mountain grows in full sun to partial shade and adapts to just about any soil conditions. It's easy to grow from seed sown directly in the garden in fall or early spring. Be aware that the plants self-sow prolifically, with seedlings often appearing quite a distance from the parents. 'Yokoi's White' annual poinsettia takes full sun to partial shade and average, well-drained soil. It's hardy only in Zones 9 to 11, but you can overwinter it indoors in cooler areas. *Caution:* Wear gloves when working with any euphorbia to protect your skin from the irritating sap, and be especially careful not to get the sap in your eyes.

**ALTERNATIVES:** Snowbush (*Breynia disticha;* also listed as *B. nivosa*) is a slender-stemmed, branching shrub with oval, rich green leaves heavily flecked and stippled with bright white. 'Roseopicta' also has pink and burgundy in the leaves. 6 to 8 feet tall where hardy; 2 to 3 feet in a pot. Full sun to partial shade; evenly moist but well-drained soil. Zones 9 or 10 to 11. *Note:* The species is considered invasive in some areas.

*Euphorbia marginata*

*Filipendula ulmaria* 'Variegata'

## FILIPENDULA
*Filipendula, meadowsweet*

**Height: Varies**
**Leaf size: 8–12 inches long;**
**3–4 inches wide**
**Full sun to partial shade**
**Zones vary**

Filipendulas (*Filipendula*) are often overlooked by perennial gardeners, and that's a pity; they make attractive additions to moist-soil beds and borders. The dense clumps are made up of pinnately compound leaves with toothed and deeply lobed tip leaflets (usually 3 to 4 inches long and wide) and much smaller side leaflets. Plume-like clusters of tiny flowers appear above the foliage in summer. Variegated meadowsweet (*F. ulmaria* 'Variegata') is the most widely available option, with deep green leaflets that have irregular bright yellow to light yellow centers, plus creamy white flowers on stems that are 2 to 3 feet tall. It's hardy in Zones 3 to 9. The selection 'Fuji Haze', often listed under *F. multijuga*, has yellow to cream flecking that is most noticeable in spring, plus pale pink flowers on 12- to 18-inch-tall stems. It performs best in Zones 5 or 6 to 8.

**GROWING TIPS:** Filipendulas can grow in full sun or partial shade; the more sun you give them, the more important it is for the soil to stay evenly moist. Remove the faded flowers to prevent self-sowing. If the foliage looks tattered, cut the entire plant to the ground in midsummer to encourage a flush of brightly variegated new growth. Sometimes, all-green growth will appear; to prevent it from taking over, dig up the clump and cut out the reverted part. (Simply pinching off the solid-green leaves will not solve the problem.)

**ALTERNATIVE:** Best known for the silvery membrane inside its flattened seedpods, biennial variegated money plant (*Lunaria annua* 'Variegata') also produces a great short-term foliage accent. The first-year plants form a dense, 1-foot-tall mound of heart-shaped, medium green leaves. By the next spring, the leaf edges develop cream-colored to white frosting as the central stem shoots up to 3 feet tall by late spring. Full sun to partial shade; average to dry soil. Zones 4 to 9.

## FORSYTHIA
*Forsythia*

**Height: Varies**
**Leaf size: 3–5 inches long;**
   **about 2 inches wide**
**Full sun to full shade**
**Zones vary**

Forsythias (*Forsythia*) are famous for their bright yellow, early-spring blooms, but let's face it: after their short flowering period, they take up a lot of space without adding much to the landscape. These deciduous shrubs produce masses of slender, upright to arching shoots clad in simple or lobed, toothed, deep green leaves. The purplish fall color does provide some interest,

*Forsythia × intermedia* 'Fiesta'

but for a true all-season show, variegated cultivars are a great way to go.

*F. × intermedia*, which is usually hardy in Zones 5 or 6 to 9, offers several variegated selections, including 'Fiesta', which has reddish new shoots with green leaves that have large bright to creamy yellow centers. It's normally 3 to 4 feet tall but can eventually reach 8 feet. 'Golden Times' has bright yellow leaves with an irregular green or yellowish green center; 'Susan Gruninger' has creamy white edges; and 'Ford Freeway' has creamy white flecks and streaks (most noticeable on new growth). All three can reach 6 to 10 feet tall. *F. viridissima* Citrus Swizzle ('McKCitrine') is very compact (to about 2 feet tall), with yellow edges that age to cream; Zones 4 to 8. There are also several variegated cultivars of *F. koreana* (often listed as *F. viridissima* var. *koreana*) that grow 4 to 6 feet tall and are normally hardy in Zones 5 to 8. 'Kumson' has deep green leaves showily marked with a network of cream to bright white veining (which is more yellowish on new growth), and 'Ilgwang' has a green center splash and yellow edges.

**GROWING TIPS:** Variegated forsythias usually grow best with morning sun and afternoon shade or with light all-day shade, but they will adapt to more or less light too. Average, well-drained soil is fine; if they get full sun, they appreciate extra moisture. Prune as needed to shape the plants or control their size immediately after flowering; cut out any reverted shoots as soon as you see them, at any time.

**ALTERNATIVE:** For the same combination of yellow spring flowers and variegated summer foliage on a small tree (in the range of 10 to 15 feet tall), look for 'Double Gold' witch hazel (*Hamamelis × intermedia*), with medium green leaves irregularly bordered with greenish yellow. Full sun to partial shade; average, well-drained soil. Zones 6 to 8.

## GERANIUM
*Hardy geranium, cranesbill*

**Height: Usually 1–2 feet**
**Leaf size: Varies**
**Full sun to partial shade**
**Zones 4–8**

Hardy geraniums (*Geranium*) are classic border favorites for their blue, pink, or white spring or summer flowers on fairly compact, trouble-free plants. Even when not in bloom, the dense clumps of palmately lobed leaves are attractive additions to the front or middle of perennial plantings; they also look great as ground covers and even in containers. Choosing cultivars with variegated leaves may seem like overkill, but it's a fine way to get even more color impact during the months the plants aren't in bloom.

Several geranium species have one or more variegated selections, so you'll be able to find at least one to suit almost any site. *G. thunbergii* 'Jester's Jacket' has light yellow- to cream-speckled leaves with a pinkish blush in spring (they're about 3 inches long and wide), plus small purplish pink flowers on 1- to 2-foot-long, trailing stems that like to weave among other plants. It comes true from seed. *Note:* The species *G. thunbergii* is considered invasive in some areas. Plants sold as *G. yoshinoi* 'Confetti' are very similar, if not identical. Variegated bigroot geranium (*G. macrorrhizum* 'Variegatum') is evergreen to semi-evergreen, with 4- to 6-inch-long and -wide, aromatic, light green leaves edged with cream, plus purplish pink flowers. It spreads by thick rhizomes to form 1-foot-tall carpets. Pink-flowered *G. × oxonianum* 'Spring Fling' forms 1-foot clumps of 3- to 6-inch-long and wide, light green leaves with broad, light yellow to cream edges and sometimes with pink flecking, too (most obviously in cool weather). 'Mourning Widow' (*G. phaeum*) is a distinct clump-former with broad, medium green, purple-marked leaves that are usually 4 to 6 inches long and wide, with deep purple flowers; it's somewhat taller than the other hardy geraniums discussed here (12 to 18 inches in leaf). Its cultivar 'Variegatum' is irregularly splashed with cream; 'Taff's Jester' is marbled with yellow to cream. 'Margaret Wilson' is heavily frosted with light yellow to cream, most brightly in spring.

**GROWING TIPS:** Hardy geraniums will adapt to a range of growing conditions, but most perform best in full sun to partial shade with average to moist but well-drained soil. (*G. phaeum* and *G. macrorrhizum* will tolerate more shade, and the latter can even take dry shade.) Selections with speckled variegation tend to be most brightly colored in spring and early summer; cutting them back to the ground in early to midsummer promotes colorful new regrowth.

**ALTERNATIVES:** Most columbines (*Aquilegia*) with yellow-marbled green leaves are sold under the names 'Woodside' and 'Woodside Variegated', but you may also see them listed as *A. vulgaris* Vervaeneana Group. *A. flabellata* var. *pumila*

*Geranium phaeum* 'Margaret Wilson'

'Silver Edge' has white-frosted leaf edges. Cut them to the ground once the flowers fade for fresh new foliage. About 8 inches in leaf. Full sun to partial shade; average to moist but well-drained soil. Zones 3 or 4 to 8.

---

## HEBE
*Hebe*

**Height: Usually 2–4 feet**
**Leaf size: 2–4 inches long;**
    **1–2 inches wide**
**Full sun to partial shade**
**Zones 9 or 10–11**

Great in the garden and eye-catching in containers, hebes (*Hebe*) form dense, compact shrubs with evergreen leaves that are oblong to lance-shaped. Their individual flowers are tiny, but they're grouped into long, spike-like clusters that create quite a show through the summer. Add in variegated foliage, and you have a plant with guaranteed appeal all through the year.

There are quite a number of variegated hebe selections, but only a few are relatively available. These three have purple summer flowers that age to pale purple or white. *H. × andersonii* 'Variegata' (also listed as *H.* 'Andersonii Variegata') has relatively narrow, deep green to gray-green leaves with creamy white edges; it will eventually grow to 6 feet tall. *H. × franciscana* 'Variegata' (also known as *H.* 'Franciscana Variegata') has oval to elliptical, somewhat fleshy leaves that are broadly edged with yellow to cream on 2- to 3-foot stems. Plants sold as *H. speciosa* 'Tricolor' and 'Purple Tips' have elliptical gray-green leaves that are edged in cream to white, with purple undersides; the shoot tips are also blushed with pink, especially in cool weather. It's usually about 4 feet tall. 'Variegata' is similar but lacks the pink and purple tints.

**GROWING TIPS:** Hebes are bushiest and flower best in full sun, but they'll get by in partial shade as well. Average soil is fine; good drainage is a must. A sheltered site helps to protect the leaves from damage caused by drying winds. Growing hebes in containers makes it easy to bring them indoors before frost; enjoy them

*Hebe × franciscana* 'Variegata'

as houseplants during the winter months. Shear the plants every few years in spring to control their size and maintain a well-branched, rounded form. Cut out all-green shoots as soon as you see them.

**ALTERNATIVES:** Evergreen shrub 'Diamond Heights' California lilac (*Ceanothus griseus* var. *horizontalis*) has solid-yellow and yellow-centered-with-green foliage; 'Silver Surprise' has green leaves edged with creamy white. Hybrid 'Zanzibar' is practically all yellow, with just a thin green center streak on some leaves; El Dorado ('Perado'; sometimes listed under *C. thyrsiflorus*) has glossy yellow foliage with an irregular green center. To about 10 feet tall. Full sun; average, well-drained soil. Zones 8 to 10.

## HELIOPSIS
*False sunflower, oxeye*

**Height: 2–3 feet**
**Leaf size: 3–5 inches long;**
   **2–3 inches wide**
**Full sun**
**Zones 3–9**

While many perennials have somewhat similar variegation, here's one you'll never confuse with anything else. 'Loraine Sunshine' false sunflower (*Heliopsis helianthoides;* also known as 'Helhan') has the same single, golden yellow, summer-into-fall daisies of the species, but its foliage is definitely unique: bright white with a network of deep green veins. It's a knockout in beds and borders, particularly when paired with companions that have deep green or dark purple leaves and/ or blue flowers.

**GROWING TIPS:** Full sun is a must for the brightest variegation; in partial shade, the markings may be light yellow or cream instead of white. Average, well-drained soil is fine, although fertile, evenly moist conditions promote the best growth. Pinching off the shoot tips a few times in spring to early summer encourages bushier growth and ample foliage. Most,

*Heliopsis helianthoides* 'Loraine Sunshine'

if not all, of the numerous seedlings will be similarly variegated; remove the faded flowers if you want to prevent self-sowing.

**ALTERNATIVES:** Looking for other variegated hardy perennials that thrive in similar zones and growing conditions? 'Prairie Frost' purple coneflower (*Echinacea purpurea*) has white-edged leaves on 2- to 4-foot-tall flowering stems. 'Sparkler' has white-to-cream stippling that's showiest in spring; it seems to prefer a little more moisture and/or shade than other coneflowers. Goldenrod (*Solidago*) plants sold as *S. flexicaulis* 'Gold Spangles' and 'Variegata' have green leaves that are heavily splashed with light yellow on 2- to 4-foot-tall stems.

## HEUCHERA
*Coral bells, heuchera*

**Height: To about 1 foot**
**Leaf size: 3–5 inches long and wide**
**Full sun to partial shade**
**Zones 3 or 4–8**

Long known more for their colorful summer flowers than for their dense mounds of shallowly lobed green leaves, coral bells (*Heuchera*) are now available in an amazing range of foliage colors that make blooms practically incidental. Variegated selections (mostly of *H. sanguinea*) are far outnumbered by those in the purple and yellow ranges, but the crisp contrast of bright blossoms against white-marked leaves makes them worth searching for.

With new selections appearing every year, recommending specific cultivars is a challenge. Most of those currently available have green leaves heavily splashed and/or flecked with creamy white, with the brightest markings (and sometimes a pink blush) in cool weather; otherwise, they differ primarily in the shade of their pink-to-red flowers and the amount of vigor they display. 'Snow Storm', 'Cherry Splash', and 'Splish Splash' are three older cultivars that have virtually been replaced by more-vigorous selections, such as pink-flowered 'Snow Angel' and bright red flowered 'Monet' and 'Snowfire' (with nearly white, green-edged and -stippled leaves). These are 8 to 12 inches tall in leaf and 12 to 18 inches tall in flower.

**GROWING TIPS:** Variegated coral bells will adapt to full sun or partial shade with average soil. Good drainage is a must, because they hate having constantly wet roots, but those in full sun appreciate occasional watering; otherwise, the foliage may turn brown on the edges. Removing the spent flowers makes the plants look better and promotes rebloom.

**ALTERNATIVES:** Strawberry begonia (*Saxifraga stolonifera;* also listed as *S. sarmentosa*) looks much like a miniature heuchera, with evergreen rosettes of rounded leaves. On 'Tricolor', the light green foliage is broadly bordered in creamy white, with a pink blush on new growth.

*Heuchera 'Snow Angel'*

'Eco Butterfly' has bright to greenish yellow leaves with an irregular, deep green center. About 6 inches tall. Partial to full shade; humus-rich, evenly moist but well-drained soil. Zones 7 to 10.

# HIBISCUS
*Hibiscus*

**Height:** Varies
**Leaf size:** Varies
**Full sun**
**Zones vary**

Large, trumpet-shaped blossoms in an array of bright colors make hibiscus (*Hibiscus*) a favorite with many gardeners. Some species are hardy enough to grow outdoors year-round in much of the country; others need to come indoors for the winter anywhere there's a chance of frost. Selections with variegated leaves aren't as easy to find as are those with fancy flowers but they're definitely worth seeking out. Once you see the fantastic foliage they produce, you may not care if your hibiscus plants *ever* bloom!

Commonly called rose-of-Sharon, *H. syriacus* selections are typically hardy in Zones 5 to 8, forming 6- to 8-foot-tall, bushy, deciduous shrubs with lobed leaves about 4 inches long and wide. 'Purpureus Variegatus' has grayish green leaves irregularly edged with pale yellow to creamy white, plus reddish purple, double blooms that tend to open only partway. 'Meehanii' is more compact (3 to 5 feet tall), with bright green foliage broadly edged with light yellow to cream, plus pale green splashes on some of the leaves. Its reddish buds open to single, pinkish purple flowers. *Note: H. syriacus* is considered invasive in some areas.

Among the tender types (Zones 9 or 10 to 11) are several selections of *H. rosa-sinensis,* a large, bushy, evergreen shrub or small tree to 10 feet tall or more with glossy, deep green, lance-shaped leaves that are 4 to 6 inches long and 2 to 4 inches wide. Plants sold as 'Snow Queen', 'Silver Queen', and 'Matensis' are streaked and splashed with varying amounts of white and gray-green (occasionally a bit of pink, too), depending on the age of the leaf and how much light the plant receives; the small flowers are bright red. 'Cooperi' looks much the same but is distinctly more compact, making it a better choice for container plantings; 'Rose Flake' has more purple and pink in the leaves. 'Carnival' ('Pink Cooperi') is similar to 'Cooperi' but bears pink flowers. 'General Corteges Variegated' is decidedly different, with rich green leaves splashed with light yellow to creamy white, plus bright red flowers. Variegated selections of mahoe or sea hibiscus (*H. tiliaceus;* also known as *Talipariti tiliaceum*) have heart-shaped leaves to 8 inches long and wide that are splashed and streaked with cream and some pink — reportedly more prominent on 'Albo Variegatus' than on 'Tricolor' — with a distinct bright pink to deep maroon blush over some leaves. The small flowers are yellow fading to orange, then red. *Note:* This species in considered invasive in some areas.

**GROWING TIPS:** Hibiscus generally grow best in full sun and average, well-drained soil, with supplemental watering during dry spells. Those in containers particularly appreciate being fertilized regularly while they're actively growing; hold off on fertilizer and water lightly during the winter if you bring them indoors. Prune off all-green shoots as they appear.

**ALTERNATIVES:** 'Gala' New Zealand Christmas tree (*Metrosideros excelsa*) is another splendid foliage option for warm climates, with small, evergreen, deep green leaves marked by a yellow center splash; 5 to 6 feet tall and about as wide. A unique accent shrub as well as an interesting addition to a foundation planting or large container. It's also handsome as a sheared or informal hedge. Full sun; average, well-drained soil. Zones 9 to 11.

*Hibiscus syriacus 'Meehanii'*

*Hydrangea macrophylla* 'Mariesii Variegata'

## HYDRANGEA
*Hydrangea*

**Height: 4–6 feet
Leaf size: 6–8 inches long;
    4–6 inches wide
Full sun to partial shade
Zones 6–9**

Bigleaf hydrangeas (*Hydrangea macrophylla*) have long been both the joy and the bane of gardeners. These deciduous shrubs are beloved for their large, lacy clusters of summer flowers, but unfortunately, they can easily lose a whole year's worth of bloom if cold temperatures nip the flower buds in winter or if you prune the plants in late summer, fall, or spring instead of immediately after bloom. Choosing cultivars with variegated leaves is a good way to get around this problem: even if they don't flower, you can still enjoy the handsome foliage.

One of the most readily available variegates is 'Mariesii Variegata', with rich green leaves broadly brushed with cream to bright white along the edges. As with most *H. macrophylla* selections, the blooms are bluish when the plant is growing in acid soil and pinkish if the soil is more alkaline. 'Tricolor' (sometimes sold as 'Variegata') has much thinner, cream-to-white margins, along with some gray-green in the green centers. 'Lemon Wave' doesn't flower much in any climate, but its green leaves are so heavily splashed with bright yellow, gray-green, and white that you won't miss the blooms. 'Quadricolor' has a similar color range in its leaves.

**GROWING TIPS:** Bigleaf hydrangeas grow in full sun or partial shade and prefer moist but well-drained soil. In hot-summer areas especially, a site with morning sun and afternoon shade or light all-day shade is ideal. The flower buds are often winter-killed in the northern parts of their hardiness range, but the blooms are basically secondary to the showy foliage anyway; prune back any winter-killed shoots to the emerging new growth in spring.

**ALTERNATIVES:** Looking at it in leaf, you'd probably never guess that climbing hydrangea (*Hydrangea anomala* var. *petiolaris*) is in the same genus as the large-flowered, shrubby forms. It grows as a 15- to 25-foot-tall, clinging climber, with glossy, deep green, deciduous leaves. Plants sold as 'Firefly' or 'Mirranda' have bright yellow leaf edges that age to cream or yellowish green. Light shade; average to moist but well-drained soil. Zones 4 to 7 or 8.

## ILEX
*Holly*

**Height: Varies
Leaf size: Varies
Full sun to partial shade
Zones vary**

Evergreen hollies (*Ilex*) come in a size to fit almost any site, from just a few inches high to well over 50 feet tall. Even leaving out the giants, there are still hundreds of species and selections well suited to smaller landscapes. Narrowing down the field even further by choosing only those with variegated foliage still leaves dozens of top-notch cultivars to provide year-round interest for borders, foundation plantings, hedges, and even containers.

Although not one of the hardiest hollies (usually Zones 7 to 9), English holly (*I.* × *aquifolium*) is one of the best-known species, with deep green, spiny-edged, leathery leaves that are 2 to 4 inches long and 1 to 2 inches wide, plus bright red berries on the female plants. *Note:* This species is considered invasive in some areas. Among the many variegates are 'Argentea Marginata' (also known as 'Albomarginata' and 'Argenteovariegata') and 'Lily Gold', both females with creamy yellow leaf edges. Male 'Gold Coast' has a yellow-green edge; male 'Golden Queen' has a wide yellow edge. 'Silvary' is a compact female selection with a bright creamy white edge. 'Ferox Argentea', a male, has creamy white margins with densely spiny edges and surfaces; 'Ferox Aurea' is similar but with yellow centers instead. 'Honey Maid' blue holly (*I.* × *meserveae*) is a hardier alternative to English holly (Zones 5 to 8) with glossy, deep blue-green leaves about 2 inches long and 1 inch wide, with creamy yellow edges; it's a female. 'Christmas Snow' and 'Stewart's Silver Crown' American holly (*I. opaca*) are equally hardy but have dull, olive green leaves edged with creamy white.

**GROWING TIPS:** Variegated hollies are generally most colorful in full sun but will also grow in partial shade with average to moist but well-drained, acidic soil. Some shelter from drying winds helps to prevent the foliage from browning during the winter. Prune away any damaged growth in spring, and remove all-green growth immediately. If you want berries, you'll have to match compatible male and female selections for pollination to occur.

**ALTERNATIVES:** False holly (*Osmanthus heterophyllus*) looks much like a true holly and thrives in the same conditions. 'Aureomarginatus' bears yellow-green leaves edged with yellow; the leaves of 'Variegatus' are bright green with creamy white edges. 'Goshiki' leaves have heavy cream, light yellow, and gray-green flecking that's most distinct on the younger leaves. Its new growth often has a pinkish tinge. Slow-growing, eventually 8 to 10 feet tall. Zones 6 or 7 to 10.

*Ilex* × *meserveae* 'Honey Maid'

## IPOMOEA
*Morning glory,*
*sweet potato vine*

**Height:** Varies
**Leaf size:** 4–8 inches long;
   3–6 inches wide
**Full sun**
**Zones vary**

Morning glories (*Ipomoea*) are a real treat to grow, especially if you get up early enough to see their large, funnel-shaped flowers before you go to work. But if you're usually able to enjoy your garden only in the evening, all you may see most weekdays are the broad, lobed or heart-shaped green leaves. Growing one of the many selections with variegated foliage is an easy way to make these twining vines do double duty, so you can appreciate their beauty no matter what time of day it is. Most variegated morning glories are commonly listed as selections of *I. nil,* but they may also appear under the name *I.* × *imperialis.* These annuals typically grow 10 to 12 feet tall with irregular light green, gray-green, and cream splashes on the leaves; they differ mainly by the colors and markings on the flowers. 'Blue Silk' and 'Rose Silk' have white-edged blooms, whereas those of 'Mt. Fuji' and 'Tie Dye' are streaked with white and/or purple. Plants or seeds sold as 'Cameo Elegance' and 'Minibar Rose' have smaller leaves and rich reddish-pink flowers edged and centered with white, with a compact growth habit that makes them ideal for planters, in hanging baskets, and as ground covers.

Closely related to the upwardly mobile morning glories, sweet potato vines (*I. batatas*) sprawl along the ground rather than climb, often taking root where they touch the soil. Allow them to creep over the edge of large pots, let them weave among other plants at the front of a border, or plant them in masses for a showy, temporary ground cover to about 6 inches tall and 8 feet or more across. 'Ivory Jewel' ('Spilt Milk') is variable, with heavy yellow-fading-to-cream streaking and splashing on some leaves and little to no variegation on others. 'Pink Frost' has smaller, gray-green leaves irregularly edged with white and pink; the new growth may be a solid bright pink. 'Sweet Caroline Green Yellow' bears deeply lobed green leaves heavily streaked and splashed with light yellow to cream. Hardy in Zones 9 or 10 to 11; annual elsewhere.

**GROWING TIPS:** Both morning glories and sweet potato vines much prefer full sun, but they'll usually tolerate partial shade too. Average to moist, well-drained soil is fine. It's easy to grow variegated morning glories from seed sown indoors in mid-spring or outdoors after all danger of frost has passed. To overwinter sweet potato vines, take cuttings in fall and grow them as houseplants in a warm, bright spot, or dig up the large, tuberous roots and store them in a cool, dry place.

*Ipomoea* 'Mt. Fuji'

**ALTERNATIVES:** Looking for an evergreen twining or creeping vine? Small-leaved 'Tricolor' Asian jasmine (*Trachelospermum asiaticum*) has cream markings and a pink to red blush that's brightest in cool weather. Variegated star jasmine (*T. jasminoides* 'Variegatum') has larger leaves edged and marbled with white, cream, and gray-green and blushed with red to pink in cool weather. Full sun to full shade; average soil. Usually Zones 8 to 11.

*Leucothoe fontanesiana* 'Rainbow'

## LEUCOTHOE
*Leucothoe, fetterbush*

**Height:** 3–5 feet
**Leaf size:** 2–5 inches long;
   1–2 inches wide
**Partial to full shade**
**Zones 5–8**

Gardeners in warm climates have an abundance of excellent evergreen shrubs to choose from, but those in cooler zones have a much more limited selection. Drooping leucothoe (*Leucothoe fontanesiana*) is one of the lesser-known broad-leaved evergreens that are ideal for shady gardens as far north as Zone 5. It produces suckers, and its arching stems will take root where they rest on the soil, eventually forming dense ground-covering thickets of glossy, pointed, deep green foliage accented by sprays of small, creamy white flowers in spring.

The variegated cultivar 'Rainbow' (also listed as 'Girard's Rainbow') offers the bonus of light yellow to cream mottling on the foliage (most colorful on newer growth), plus a pinkish to purplish blush that's most noticeable in cooler weather. 'Trivar' looks similar but is reportedly more vigorous. 'Silver Run' has even brighter creamy white variegation but less pink and is said to be somewhat hardier. 'Dodd's Variegated' coast leucothoe (*L. axillaris*) has some yellow to cream streaking, with a reddish blush on the foliage through the cooler months. It's reportedly more tolerant of hot summers.

**GROWING TIPS:** Drooping leucothoe will tolerate even deep shade, but partial shade tends to bring out better variegation. Humus-rich, moist but well-drained, acidic soil is ideal. (If the soil is moist enough, the plants will tolerate full sun.) Cut a few of the oldest stems to the ground each year to keep the plants looking tidy.

**ALTERNATIVES:** Variegated wayfaring tree (*Viburnum lantana* 'Variegatum') is a deciduous shrub with broad, medium green leaves mottled with bright yellow aging to cream; Zones 4 to 8. *Note: V. lantana* is considered invasive in some areas. Variegated leatherleaf viburnum (*V. rhytidophyllum* 'Variegatum') has evergreen leaves unevenly splashed with light yellow to cream; Zones 5 to 8. Both can reach 8 to 12 feet tall. Sun or partial shade; average, well-drained soil.

## LONICERA
*Honeysuckle*

**Height:** 10–20 feet
**Leaf size:** 1–2 inches long;
   about 1 inch wide
**Full sun to partial shade**
**Zones 4 or 5–9**

It's easy to deck your walls with fantastic foliage — and flowers, too — when you grow honeysuckles (*Lonicera*). Several species produce slender, twining stems with deciduous or semievergreen foliage and long, tubular summer flowers that are often quite fragrant. The young leaves may be deeply lobed, but most have smooth edges.

The cultivar Harlequin (*L. × italica* 'Sherlite'; also listed under *L. periclymenum*) has grayish green leaves irregularly edged with light yellow aging to creamy white, with particularly wide

*Lonicera × italica* Harlequin

margins on the new growth. Its foliage is sometimes blushed with pink as well (mostly in cool weather). The flowers are pale pink and cream and appear sporadically from late spring into fall. Variegated Japanese honeysuckle (*L. japonica* 'Aureoreticulata') has small, oblong leaves that are showily marked with a network of bright yellow veins that fade to cream. *Note: L. japonica* is considered to be seriously invasive in many areas.

**GROWING TIPS:** Full sun encourages more flowers, but if you're growing honeysuckles primarily for their foliage, anything from full sun to partial shade with average, well-drained soil is fine. Train the young vines onto a support or plant them in masses and let them sprawl to form a ground cover. Trim lightly as needed to shape the plants; remove any all-green shoots immediately.

**ALTERNATIVES:** Deciduous 'Aureovariegatum' ('Aureum') common or poet's jasmine (*Jasminum officinale*) has small, deep green leaflets splashed with bright yellow. 'Argenteovariegatum' ('Variegatum') has light yellow to creamy white leaf edges. Zones 7 or 8 to 11. Evergreen variegated bower vine (*Pandorea jasminoides* 'Variegata') has glossy green leaflets edged and splashed with light yellow to creamy white. Zones 9 to 11. Twining vines to 20 feet tall. Full sun to partial shade; average to moist but well-drained soil.

# LYSIMACHIA
*Loosestrife*

**Height: About 2 feet**
**Leaf size: Varies**
**Full sun to full shade**
**Zones 3 or 4 to 8**

If you prefer plants that stay exactly where you put them, then loosestrifes (*Lysimachia*) probably aren't for you. But if you have a large space to fill and want a ground cover with pretty flowers and great-looking leaves, these vigorous perennials could be just the ticket. Many loosestrifes spread by rhizomes (creeping underground stems), and though the variegated forms are slightly less aggressive than the all-green forms, they're usually still thuggish enough to crowd out all but the sturdiest companions. Growing them in pots is another way to enjoy them without fearing they'll take over.

'Geisha' gooseneck loosestrife (*L. clethroides*) grows to about 2 feet tall, with arching, spikelike clusters of small white flowers in mid- to late summer. The 3- to 4-inch-long, 1½-inch-wide, medium green leaves are irregularly edged with light yellow aging to cream. Zones 3 to 8. Yellow loosestrife (*L. punctata*) is about the same height but has bright yellow cupped flowers clustered along the top of each stem in mid- to late summer; the leaves are 2 to 3 inches long and about 1 inch wide. 'Alexander' has a cream edge that ages to white (plus a pink blush in spring); Golden

*Lysimachia clethroides* 'Geisha'

Alexander ('Walgoldalex') has a yellow edge that fades to cream. Zones 4 to 8.

**GROWING TIPS:** Loosestrifes usually grow best in partial shade and moist soil, but they will adapt to just about any site. The farther they are from their ideal conditions (in a dry, sunny site, for instance, or dry shade), the less likely they are to spread. Hot, dry conditions cause the leaf edges to turn brown. Remove all-green shoots as soon as you see them.

**ALTERNATIVE:** *Lysimachia congestiflora* 'Outback Sunset' ('Walkabout Sunset') is a much different-looking loosestrife, with roughly oval, bright yellow to greenish yellow leaves with medium green centers on trailing, pinkish stems; 4 to 8 inches tall. Zones 7 or 8 to 10. Great at the front of a border, along a path, or cascading out of a container. Full sun (in northern gardens) to full shade; average to moist but well-drained soil.

## PELARGONIUM
*Geranium, pelargonium*

**Height: Usually 1–3 feet**
**Leaf size: 2–4 inches long and wide for most**
**Full sun to partial shade**
**Zones 8 or 9–11**

Not to be confused with hardy or true geraniums (*Geranium*), pelargoniums — more commonly called geraniums — are tender perennials prized for their bright blooms as well as their foliage. There is such a diversity of habits, flower forms, and leaf types that specialists divide them into several groups. Three groups that commonly include variegated-leaf selections are zonal geraniums (*Pelargonium* × *hortorum*),

Pelargonium 'Crocodile'

which are upright, bushy plants that usually have a dark ring on each leaf; ivy geraniums (*P. peltatum*), which produce long, trailing stems; and scented geraniums, which boast a number of upright or trailing species and cultivars with delightfully fragrant foliage. Specialty nurseries offer many dozens of variegated geraniums, but you'll find only a few of these at most garden centers. Here's an overview of some of the best to get you started.

*Green with white or cream markings.* Zonal 'Mrs. Parker' is a classic with rounded leaves that have white-brushed borders and large grayish green centers, plus single, bright pink flowers; 'Wilhelm Langguth' has similar leaf colors and double red flowers. 'Freak of Nature' bears nearly all-white leaves with a ruffled green rim and single, bright red blooms. The leaves of 'White Mesh' ivy geranium are veined with white or cream (most distinctly in cool weather), and the blooms are pink. Scented 'Snowy Nutmeg' (often listed under *P. × fragrans*) has small, gray-green leaves splashed with cream and bears white flowers. Variegated lemon geranium (*P. crispum* 'Variegated Prince Rupert') produces small, lemon-scented leaves with densely ruffled, creamy yellow edges and purplish pink flowers. 'Snowflake' has large, light green leaves irregularly streaked with cream, plus purplish pink flowers. 'Lady Plymouth' is a rose-scented type with deeply lobed, light

green leaves edged with cream, plus purplish pink flowers.

*Green with yellow markings.* 'Happy Thought' is a zonal type with a large, bright to light yellow leaf center surrounded by a narrow green border, plus bright crimson red flowers. The ivy geranium 'Crocodile' has yellow-veined, bright green leaves and bright pink flowers. Rose-scented 'Charity' (often listed under *P. × asperum* and *P. graveolens*) bears deeply lobed, bright green leaves with greenish yellow edges, plus purplish pink flowers.

*Tricolors.* Several zonal-type geraniums have green-centered leaves with a reddish or brownish ring and a yellow edge, such as 'Mr. Henry Cox' (often listed as 'Mrs. Cox' and 'Mrs. Henry Cox'), with salmon-pink flowers; 'Mrs. Pollock', with rounded-lobed leaves and orange-red flowers; and 'Skies of Italy', with pointed-lobed leaves and orange-red blooms. 'Dolly Varden' ('Dolly Vardon') is another zonal type with a green center, a wide reddish ring, and a creamy white border, with scarlet flowers.

**GROWING TIPS:** Variegated geraniums prefer lots of light but appreciate some shade during the hottest part of the day, particularly in warm climates. Average, well-drained soil is fine. Remove the faded flowers regularly. Before frost, bring your favorite plants indoors and enjoy them as houseplants for the winter. Wait until after the last frost date in spring to set them out again.

**ALTERNATIVES:** 'Samantha' lantana (*Lantana camara*) forms shrubby clumps of green leaves edged and streaked with light yellow to greenish yellow; 1 to 3 feet tall. Full sun; average, well-drained soil. *Note:* The species is considered invasive in some areas. Semperflorens or wax begonias (*Begonia semperflorens*) in the Charm Series produce glossy green leaves mottled with yellow and cream; 8 to 10 inches tall. Light shade; average to moist, well-drained soil. Zones 9 to 11.

## PERSICARIA
*Knotweed, persicaria*

**Height: 2–4 feet**
**Leaf size: 6–8 inches long; 3–5 inches wide**
**Full sun to partial shade**
**Zones 4–9**

Cultivated knotweeds are hardy perennials that many people view with mixed feelings. Part of the problem is the muddled nomenclature. For instance, you're equally likely to find the most common garden species listed as *Persicaria virginiana*, *Polygonum virginianum*, and *Tovara virginiana*, or even as *Persicaria filiformis* and *Tovara filiforme*. Then there's the whole "weed" issue: although this particular species (which is commonly known as Virginia knotweed or jumpseed) normally isn't classified as invasive, it can qualify as aggressive in some garden settings, mostly through prolific self-sowing.

Despite Virginia knotweed's drawbacks, gardeners grow

*Persicaria* 'Painter's Palette'

and enjoy its variegated forms for their eye-catching foliage. Those with green leaves that are streaked and splashed with light yellow to cream are classified as *P. virginiana* Variegata Group but are often sold as 'Variegata'. The selection 'Painter's Palette' is similar but sports a reddish brown V marking on its leaves. Both may also show a pinkish blush on new growth, and produce stringy reddish flower spikes in late summer.

**GROWING TIPS:** Full sun to partial shade is fine, and moist soil is ideal, although the plants will adapt to drier conditions (particularly if they aren't in full sun). Remove the flower spikes to prevent self-sowing, or be prepared to weed out unwanted seedlings; fortunately, they're easy to identify because they're variegated like the parent plants.

**ALTERNATIVES:** Plants of clump-forming *Fallopia japonica* var. *compacta* sold as 'Milk Boy', 'Spectabile', and 'Variegatum' typically have creamy white leaf splashes; 'Freckles' has brighter white markings; 4 to 6 feet tall. 'Devon Cream' has broad green leaves heavily splashed and sectioned with pink, tan, and cream; to 8 feet. All may be pink-blushed in spring. Full sun to full shade; average to moist, well-drained soil. Zones 5 to 9.

## PHILADELPHUS
*Mock orange*

**Height: 6–10 feet**
**Leaf size: 3–5 inches long;**
**2–3 inches wide**
**Partial shade**
**Zones 4 or 5–8**

If you get the opportunity to sniff mock oranges (*Philadelphus*) in full bloom, you may wonder why everybody doesn't grow them. Come back a week or two later, and you'll know the reason: these rather nondescript deciduous shrubs normally don't have much to offer for the other 50 weeks of the year. Planting a selection that has variegated foliage lets you enjoy the lovely fragrance in late spring to early summer and good-looking foliage from spring to fall.

Variegated common mock orange (*P. coronarius* 'Variegatus'; also sold as 'Bowles' Variety') has medium green leaves so broadly edged with creamy white that the whole shrub looks white from a distance. (This means that the small white blooms are barely visible when they appear, but at least you'll still be able to smell them.) The foliage of hybrid 'Innocence' (sometimes listed under *P. × lemoinei*) is irregularly splashed and streaked with yellow and cream, sometimes turning plain green in the heat of summer. You may want to buy plants of this kind in person, because some sources sell plants under this name that have little or no variegation at all.

**GROWING TIPS:** Variegated mock oranges prefer morning sun and afternoon shade or else light all-day shade; strong sun may cause the leaves to turn brown. Moist but well-drained, humus-rich soil is ideal. Trimming lightly after flowering may promote a flush of bright new growth; pruning a few of the oldest stems each year will control the size. Remove any reverted shoots immediately.

**ALTERNATIVES:** The new growth of variegated Japanese cleyera is brightly bordered and sometimes streaked with yellow to cream, with a pink blush on the youngest leaves and pinkish leaf stems; the older leaves are a glossy deep green. Winter usually brings out a reddish blush on the foliage. While the plant that truly fits this common name is *Cleyera japonica* 'Variegata' (also known as 'Tricolor' and 'Fortunei'), it's mixed up in the trade with the very similar and much more common *Ternstroemia gymnanthera* 'Variegata'. Plants you acquire under either name generally reach 8 to 15 feet tall. Full sun to full shade (partial shade is usually ideal); average to moist, well-drained, slightly acid soil. Zones 7 to 10.

*Philadelphus coronarius* 'Variegatus'

*Phlox paniculata* 'Norah Leigh'

## PHLOX
*Border phlox, summer phlox*

**Height: 2–3 feet**
**Leaf size: 3–5 inches long;**
    **1–2 inches wide**
**Full sun to partial shade**
**Zones 4–8**

Classic border phlox (*Phlox paniculata*) is well known for its showy, fragrant flower clusters atop upright stems that brighten borders from mid- or late summer into early fall. Normally, no one ever remarks on the narrow green foliage unless it's disfigured by dusty gray spots due to a fungal disease called powdery mildew. But when you plant variegated cultivars, the brightly striped foliage will provide an eye-catching accent throughout the growing season, sometimes even making the blooms superfluous. Best of all: even if powdery mildew strikes, you'll hardly notice its spots among the stripes.

Some selections with cream-to-white leaf edges are 'Harlequin', with rich purplish pink flowers; 'Crème de Menthe', 'Frosted Elegance', and 'Norah Leigh', with pale pink flowers that have a deeper pink eye; and 'Silvermine', with pink-centered white flowers. 'Darwin's Joyce' has light yellow to cream edges with light pink flowers; 'Rubymine' is similar but with dark-eyed, medium pink flowers. For bright yellow leaf edges that age to light yellow, consider 'Becky Towe'; it also has bright salmon-pink, darker-eyed flowers. 'Goldmine' has similarly gold-striped margins with stunning pinkish red blossoms that create quite a spectacle against the fancy foliage. Any of these may show a pinkish blush on the new shoots in spring.

**GROWING TIPS:** Phlox bloom most abundantly in full sun, but variegated selections usually look best with morning sun and afternoon shade or light all-day shade. Evenly moist but well-drained, humus-rich soil is ideal. In spring, cut off some of the stems at the base to thin out crowded clumps and help to prevent mildew. Pinching off the shoot tips in late spring produces shorter but bushier plants. Remove the faded flower clusters to prevent self-sowing (seedlings will be all-green) and possibly encourage rebloom. Cut out all-green shoots as soon as you see them.

**ALTERNATIVES:** Variegated white snakeroot (*Eupatorium aromaticum* 'Jocius' Variegate'; also sold as 'Joicus Variegate') starts the season with narrow cream-colored leaves that are flecked with green and sometimes tinged with pink; they age to medium green with greenish cream streaking. The bushy perennial clumps reach 4 to 6 feet tall. Self-sows; seedlings are also variegated. Full sun to partial shade; average to moist, well-drained soil. Zones 4 to 9.

## PHYSOSTEGIA
*Obedient plant*

**Height: 2–4 feet**
**Leaf size: 3–5 inches long;**
    **1–2 inches wide**
**Full sun to partial shade**
**Zones 3–8**

The common name of *Physostegia virginiana* is obedient plant, but gardeners often refer to it as disobedient plant because of its tendency to spread rampantly through beds and borders. Still, the spikelike clusters of purplish pink flowers add welcome interest during mid- to late summer, when many other perennials are taking a break, and cultivars with variegated leaves provide eye-catching color from early spring through autumn. 'Variegata' is a dramatic selection with gray-green foliage that's broadly bordered with cream aging to white. The new leaves of 'Olympus Gold' (sometimes listed as 'Olympic Gold') are light yellow with just a thin green center stripe; later, they turn mostly green. The plants are also more compact (to about 2 feet tall).

**GROWING TIPS:** Obedient plants grow in full sun or partial shade and prefer moist soil, although they will tolerate dry conditions (and spread less vigorously there). Pinching the shoot tips of

*Physostegia virginiana* 'Variegata'

'Variegata' in late spring to early summer encourages bushier growth that's less likely to sprawl. Divide the clumps every year or two to keep them from spreading out of bounds.

**ALTERNATIVES:** Mints (*Mentha*) creep vigorously in moist soil and partial shade; drier and sunnier conditions will slow their spread. Pineapple mint (*M. suaveolens* 'Variegata') has a bright cream to white edge around each aromatic green leaf; 2 to 3 feet tall. Variegated peppermint (*M. × piperita* 'Variegata') is about the same height, with small, deep green leaves irregularly splashed with light yellow to cream. Zones 3 or 4 to 8.

## PIERIS
*Pieris, lily-of-the-valley shrub*

**Height: Varies**
**Leaf size: 3–4 inches long;**
    **about 1 inch wide**
**Full sun to full shade**
**Zones 5–8**

Pieris (*Pieris*) of all kinds are terrific in shady borders and woodland gardens. These upright, bushy shrubs have glossy evergreen foliage for year-round interest; many also produce brightly colored new growth. They also bear nodding or upright sprays of flower buds that develop in fall and look great all through the winter, then open into white or cream flowers in spring.

With all of these wonderful multi-season features, variegation is simply icing on the cake. Japanese pieris (*P. japonica*) offers a number of selections with cream-to-white leaf edges, such as 'Variegata' (4 to 7 feet tall, with pink-tinged new growth); 'White Rim' (which looks very similar from a distance but is said to have slightly more yellow in the markings); and compact 'Little Heath' (2 to 3 feet tall, with reddish bronze new growth). Among the several similarly variegated hybrids are 'Flaming Silver' (4 to 6 feet tall, with bright red new leaves that turn pink, then yellow-green, and finally deep green bordered with cream) and Havila ('Mouwsvila'), which has slightly wider edge markings. 'Evie' is distinctive for its compact growth (2 to 3 feet tall) and upright instead of nodding flower clusters.

**GROWING TIPS:** Pieris will adapt to pretty much anything from sun to shade, but light shade is generally ideal. Their preferred soil conditions are rather more specific: moist but well-drained, humus-rich, acidic soil keeps them looking their best, although they tolerate drier soil after the first few years. A sheltered spot helps to prevent the evergreen foliage from getting damaged by drying winter wind. Trimming off the flower clusters as soon as they fade makes the plants look tidier and may enhance next year's flowering.

**ALTERNATIVE:** 'Shady Lady' Florida anise (*Illicium floridanum*) has narrow, evergreen leaves irregularly edged with cream to white; 6 to 8 feet tall. Light shade; average, well-drained soil. Zones 7 to 9.

## PLECTRANTHUS
*Plectranthus, tropical mint*

**Height: Usually 1–2 feet**
**Leaf size: 1–3 inches long;**
    **about 1 inch wide**
**Full sun to partial shade**
**Zones 10 and 11**

Long appreciated primarily by houseplant and herb collectors, plectranthus have gained a following with gardeners on the hunt for top-notch container plants — due mostly to the many variegated cultivars that are now available. These bushy or trailing, tender perennials are evergreen in frost-free areas; elsewhere they make great houseplants during the wintertime and fine outdoor plants in summer thanks to their vigorous, easy-case nature and colorful foliage. Many of these mint relatives also release a pleasing fragrance when you rub their fuzzy, fleshy leaves. (They produce white or purplish flowers, too, but the small blossoms are not nearly as attractive as the foliage.) Growing plectranthus in raised planters, window boxes, and hanging baskets makes it particularly easy to reach them for petting. The trailing types also make unique temporary ground covers.

The only drawback to plectranthus is their amazingly mixed-up nomenclature. It seems as if every grower uses a different name, often applying the same common or even botanical name to completely different selections. Here's an overview of some of the most commonly available plectranthus,

*Pieris japonica* 'Variegata'

*Plectranthus argentatus* 'Hill House'

with the names they're often sold under. Because of this confusion, you're generally best off buying the plants in person, or at least looking at a catalog or Web site photograph, instead of depending on the name alone to get the features you want.

*Green leaves with white to cream markings.* Variegated Cuban oregano (*P. amboinicus* 'Silver Variegated'; also sold as 'Variegatus') has thick, light green, spicy-scented leaves with white edges and sometimes tinged with pink, on trailing stems. *P. forsteri* 'Marginatus' ('Variegatus') produces large, bright green leaves edged with creamy to bright white on upright plants. Variegated mintleaf or iboza vine (*P. madagascariensis* 'Variegated Mintleaf'; also sold as *P. coleoides* 'Variegatus') has small, white-edged leaves on trailing, reddish stems.

*Green leaves with yellow to cream markings.* 'Ochre Flame' Cuban oregano (*P. amboinicus*) has trailing pink stems with thick, wavy, light green leaves that have a light yellow center. 'Athens Gem' Cuban oregano is similar in habit, with light to deep green leaf margins and a wide, creamy white to light yellow center, sometimes splashed with green. *P. discolor* 'Green and Gold' bears deeply veined, bright to light yellow leaves with a small, green

center blotch on trailing reddish purple stems. Plants sold as *P. forsteri* 'Green on Green' and 'Lemon Twist' have soft, light green leaves edged with yellow on upright plants. *P. argentatus* 'Hill House' produces upright, bushy plants with broad, grayish leaves edged with light yellow.

**GROWING TIPS:** Plectranthus will take full sun in most areas but usually look better with morning sun and afternoon shade or light all-day shade. Average, well-drained soil is fine; the thinner-leaved types tend to need more water than the thick-leaved kinds do. Pinching off the shoot tips encourages more mounded or bushy growth, even on types that normally trail. It's not unusual for variegated plectranthus to produce shoots with markings different from those of the main plant; remove these and discard them, or root them to produce new plants.

**ALTERNATIVE:** Variegated lemon balm (*Melissa officinalis* 'Aurea'; also known as 'Variegata') is another mint relative. It forms bushy clumps that are 18 to 30 inches tall, with bright to deep green foliage flecked with yellow (most distinctly on new growth). The leaves are strongly lemon-scented when rubbed. Full sun to partial shade; moist but well-drained soil. Zones 3 to 8. *Note:* *M. officinalis* is considered invasive in some areas.

## POLYGONATUM
*Solomon's seals*

**Height:** Varies
**Leaf size:** 4–8 inches long;
   2–3 inches wide
**Partial to full shade**
**Zones 4 or 5–8**

The gracefully arching, unbranched stems of Solomon's seals (*Polygonatum*) have a distinctive form that perfectly complements mounded hostas, lacy ferns, and many other lower-growing perennials in shady borders and woodland gardens. They do bloom — with small, creamy white bells that dangle from the upper parts of the stems in late spring to early summer — but you'll hardly notice the blossoms because they're mostly hidden by the foliage. Selections with variegated leaves don't need flowers, though: they provide a combination of green and cream to white

that you'll enjoy throughout the growing season.

The variegates travel under a number of names, but that shouldn't stop you from getting what you want, because the plants themselves look distinctly different. Typically, though, the most commonly available selection is variegated fragrant Solomon's seal (known as *P. falcatum* 'Variegatum', *P. odoratum* var. *pluriflorum* 'Variegatum', *P. odoratum* var. *thunbergii* 'Variegatum', and simply *P. thunbergii* 'Variegatum'), with pinkish, 2- to 3-foot-tall stems and rich green leaves thinly brushed with cream. Variegated common Solomon's seal (*P.* × *hybridum* 'Striatum'; also known as 'Variegatum' and 'Grace Barker') has deep green, sometimes wrinkled foliage that's streaked with creamy white within the leaves as well as on the

*Polygonatum falcatum* 'Variegatum'

edges. Its green stems tend to be more compact (10 to 15 inches tall), and the plants are much less vigorous spreaders. *P. humile* 'Streaker' is even shorter (just 4 to 6 inches), with upright stems and random yellow striping on the green leaves.

**GROWING TIPS:** Solomon's seals grow in partial to full shade and thrive in humus-rich, evenly moist but well-drained soil, although they will adapt to drier soil after the first few years. Where they're happy, they spread steadily to form broad clumps; if needed, divide them in fall or very early spring. Remove all-green shoots immediately.

**ALTERNATIVES:** Fairy bells (*Disporum*) are closely related to Solomon's seals and share their preferred growing conditions. Plants sold as *D. sessile* 'Variegatum' have narrow or broad, white-edged and -streaked leaves; about 18 inches tall and spreads widely. Shorter 'Sunray' has yellow streaking that ages to creamy white. *D. smilacinum* 'Aureovariegatum' is brushed with light yellow to creamy white on the leaf edges and tips; about 8 inches tall. Zones 4 to 8.

# RHODODENDRON
*Rhododendron, azalea*

**Height: Varies**
**Leaf size: Varies**
**Full sun to full shade**
**Zones vary**

Rhododendrons and azaleas (*Rhododendron*) are a remarkably diverse group of shrubs, with flowers in just about any color, deciduous or evergreen foliage, and heights ranging from just a few inches to 10 feet tall or even higher. While the flowers are typically their most eye-catching feature, attractive foliage extends their season of interest all through the growing season, or even all through the year.

When you consider the many hundreds of species, hybrids, and selections, it's surprising how few variegated-leaf cultivars are available. Here are several of the most readily available options (these are all evergreen and usually bloom in late spring or early summer); specialty nurseries offer more.

***Green with white to cream markings.*** 'Silver Sword' azalea bears small, deep green leaves cleanly edged with white and blushed with red in winter, plus bright reddish pink flowers; 'Variegated Hot Shot' azalea ('Girard's Variegated Hot Shot') has small, light green leaves neatly bordered with white, which dramatically set off the rich orange-red blooms; 'Variegated Gem' ('Girard's Variegated Gem') is similar but has pink flowers. These three may be semievergreen in colder areas, with 2-inch-long leaves that are about 1 inch wide, and usually grow 2 to 3 feet tall with a wider spread. Zones 5 or 6 to 9. The bushy, upright plants of *R. ponticum* 'Variegatum' are much larger (usually 8 to 12 feet tall), with glossy, rich green leaves edged

*Rhododendron* 'Variegated Gem'

with cream to white, plus purplish pink blooms. Zones 6 to 9.

***Green with yellow to cream markings.*** 'Goldflimmer' rhododendron typically grows 3 to 5 feet tall, with 4- to 5-inch-long and 1- to 2-inch-wide, deep green leaves that have a narrow, bright to light yellow center splash; the late-spring flowers are bright purplish pink. Zones 5 or 6 to 9.

**GROWING TIPS:** Rhododendrons and azaleas can usually adapt to anything from full sun to full shade, but most of the variegates thrive with morning sun and afternoon shade or light all-day shade. Moist but well-drained, humus-rich, acidic soil is ideal. Removing the spent flowers makes the plants look better. Prune off any all-green shoots as soon as you see them.

**ALTERNATIVES:** Fast-growing, bushy, evergreen pittosporums (*Pittosporum*) offer well over a dozen selections with whorled, green to grayish green, cream-edged leaves, including *P. eugenioides* 'Variegatum', *P. tenuifolium* 'Variegatum', and *P. tobira* 'Variegata' ('Variegatum'). Eight to 12 feet tall if not pruned. Cream de Mint (*P. tobira* 'Shima') and Turners Pitt ('Turner's Variegated Dwarf') are naturally compact (2 to 3 feet tall). Full sun to partial shade; average, well-drained soil. Zones 8 or 9 to 10.

## SALVIA
*Sage, salvia*

**Height: Varies**
**Leaf size: Varies**
**Full sun to partial shade**
**Zones vary**

Common or culinary sage (*Salvia officinalis*) has long been a favorite for its flavorful foliage, while other hardy and tender perennial species have found a home in beds, borders, and container

*Salvia mexicana* 'Kelsi'

plantings for their bright blooms. Now that there are variegated-leaf selections of several species, it's possible to enjoy flavor, fragrance, flowers, and colorful foliage too!

**Green with white to cream markings.** 'Tricolor' common sage (*S. officinalis*) forms 12- to 18-inch tall clumps of 3-inch-long, 1-inch-wide, gray-green leaves that are irregularly margined with creamy white; the new growth is also blushed with pink, and the early-summer flowers are purple-blue. Zones 7 to 9. *S. mexicana* 'Kelsi' grows 5 to 6 feet tall, with 3- to 4-inch-tall and -wide, medium green leaves randomly splashed with creamy white, plus spikes of deep blue flowers in mid-fall. Zones 8 to 10. And then there's 'Fuji Snow' Japanese sage (*S. nipponica*), with 4-inch-long, arrow-shaped green leaves that are heavily frosted with white (most distinctly on cool-weather growth) on 1- to 2-foot-tall stems. The pale yellow flowers appear in late summer to fall. Zones 6 or 7 to 9.

**Green with yellow to cream markings.** Variegated common sage (*S. officinalis* 'Icterina', also sold as 'Aurea Variegata') produces shrubby, 1-foot-tall clumps of 3-inch-long, 1-inch-wide, gray-green leaves that are irregularly edged with bright to creamy yellow; the early-summer flowers are purple-blue. Zones 6 to 9. 'Omaha Gold' blue anise sage (*S. guaranitica*) is much taller (to 6 feet) but less strikingly variegated, with 3- to 5-inch-long and 2- to 4-inch-wide, medium green leaves edged with greenish yellow (most brightly in spring). Spikes of rich blue flowers appear in fall. Zones 8 to 10. Variegated Mexican bush sage (*S. leucantha* 'Eder') grows 3 to 4 feet tall, with 4- to 5-inch-long, 1-inch-wide, grayish green leaves that are narrowly bordered with light yellow to cream; long spikes of rosy purple flower bloom in fall. Zones 9 and 10.

**GROWING TIPS:** Sages generally grow best in full sun, although most can tolerate partial shade, and they normally thrive in average, well-drained soil. The major exceptions are blue anise sage and Japanese sage, which generally prefer light shade; blue anise sage and Mexican bush sage also tend to like more moisture. Pinching off the shoot tips in spring encourages lower, bushier growth. Where the plants are not winter-hardy, treat them as annuals, take cuttings in late summer and grow them on a sunny windowsill, or dig up the plants and store them indoors.

**ALTERNATIVE:** Plants sold as *Kalimeris incisa* 'Variegata', *K. incisa* 'Shogun', *K. yomena* 'Aurea', or *K. yomena* 'Shogun' usually have wide, light yellow to yellowish green leaf edges (often with gray-green shading in the green center as well). The upright, 1- to 2-foot-tall plants grow in spreading patches. The markings often fade in summer; shear plants back by a third in early summer for brighter new growth. Full sun or partial shade; evenly moist but well-drained soil is ideal, but plants can tolerate dry soil. Zones 5 to 8.

## SAMBUCUS
*Elderberry, elder*

**Height: 7–15 feet**
**Leaf size: 10–12 inches long;**
**    8–10 inches wide**
**Full sun to partial shade**
**Zones 4–9**

The ordinary black elderberry (*Sambucus nigra*) isn't especially showy; the variegated selections, however, are an eye-catching attraction in the home landscape. Left unpruned, they form large shrubs or small trees that grow 10 to 15 feet tall, with broad, flat-topped clusters of tiny, creamy white flowers in early summer often followed by drooping bunches of glossy black drupes (berrylike fruits) later in the season. The vigorous plants will also tolerate heavy pruning each spring — to a 1- to 2-foot-tall framework or even down to just above the ground — resulting in larger-leaved but much shorter plants that work well at the back of a mixed border.

All selections of black elderberry have large, compound leaves. On 'Marginata' (also sold as 'Albovariegata', 'Argenteovariegata', and 'Variegata'), each deep green leaflet has an irregular yellow edge that ages to creamy white by midsummer. 'Aureomarginata' looks similar but holds its yellow markings. 'Madonna' has medium green or grayish green leaflets more broadly bordered with bright yellow fading to creamy yellow, to the point that some leaves have little or no green. Leaflets on the

*Sambucus nigra* 'Pulverulenta'

newer shoots of 'Pulverulenta' are so abundantly mottled with white that the whole shrub looks as if it's in bloom throughout the growing season. Its older leaves are light green with less-distinct cream spotting.

**GROWING TIPS:** Elderberries will grow in full sun in northern areas if they have ample moisture; otherwise, they're best with morning sun and afternoon shade or light all-day shade and average soil. Prune away any all-green shoots. If you want to make sure your black elderberry sets fruit, it's best to plant two different cultivars (or a cultivar and a seedling).

**ALTERNATIVES:** Spiketail (*Stachyurus praecox*) is another large deciduous shrub, with 6- to 8-inch-long, pointed, rich green leaves. 'Variegatus' has white leaf edges; 'Aureomarginata' and 'Joy Forever' have bright yellow to creamy yellow edges. The cultivar 'Magpie' (sometimes listed under *S. chinensis*) has light green to gray-green leaves with light yellow to bright cream edges sometimes tinged with pink. Eventually 10 to 15 feet tall. Full sun to partial shade; average, well-drained soil. Zones 7 to 9.

## SEDUM
*Sedum, stonecrop*

**Height: Varies**
**Leaf size: 1–3 inches long and wide**
**Full sun to partial shade**
**Zones vary**

Variegated sedums (*Sedum*) will grow just fine in those hot, dry sites that are too tough for many other variegated plants to handle, but they're adaptable enough to thrive in more-hospitable garden conditions as well. From upright clumpers to carpeting creepers, sedums come in a range of heights, habits, and leaf and flower colors to suit just about any site. The upright sedums grow 12 to 18 inches tall; the creepers typically stay below 4 inches, even in bloom.

*Green with white to cream markings.* The upright selections usually bloom in late summer and have light green to blue-green foliage. *S.* 'Frosty Morn' is neatly edged with white (the flowers are pale pink to white); 'Pink Chablis' looks similar but has more dependably pink blooms. *S. telephium* 'Samuel Oliphant' ('Sam Oliphant') is broadly bordered with cream and rimmed with pink on burgundy stems topped with pink flowers; it tends to be taller than usual (24 to 30 inches). All three are usually hardy in Zones 3 to 9. One lower-growing option is variegated Kamschatka sedum (*S. kamtschaticum* 'Variegatum'), with glossy, spoon-shaped, medium-green, cream-edged leaves; pink buds; and yellow summer flowers that age to orange on trailing stems. Zones 4 to 9. Another is the wide-creeping, evergreen 'Tricolor' two-row sedum (*S. spurium;* also sold as 'Variegatum'), with more-rounded, pale green leaves edged with white and also blushed with pink (most noticeably in cool weather); its summer flowers are also pink. Zones 3 to 8. Variegated carpet sedum (*S. lineare* 'Variegatum') is much less hardy (Zones 6 or 7 to 9), with upright-then-trailing, pinkish stems clad in very narrow, light green leaves neatly margined with cream to white. It may produce yellow flowers.

*Green with yellow to cream markings.* The most common upright-growing sedum in this group has grayish green leaves with wide, bright yellow centers that age to cream by the time the pink-tinged white flowers appear in late summer. You'll find this sedum listed under a number of names, including *S. erythrostictum* 'Mediovariegatum', *S. alboroseum* 'Mediovariegatum', *Hylotelephium roseum* 'Mediovariegatum', and even *S. spectabile* 'Variegatum'. By any name, it's a lovely plant for Zones 3 to 9. The shorter variegated October daphne (*S. sieboldii* 'Mediovariegatum'; also sold as 'Variegatum') has rounded blue-green foliage centered with creamy yellow and rimmed with red, plus pink flowers in fall, on arching stems. It's usually hardy in Zones 4 to 8.

**GROWING TIPS:** Full sun brings out the best in most variegated sedums, although they will tolerate partial shade too (especially the lower-growing types). Average to dry, well-drained soil is fine. On upright sedums, pinching off the shoot tips or shearing them back by half in late spring to early summer promotes bushier growth that's less likely to sprawl. On all variegated sedums, remove solid-green shoots as soon as you see them.

*Sedum kamtschaticum* 'Variegatum'

**ALTERNATIVES:** Variegated heart-leaved ice plant (listed as *Aptenia cordifolia* 'Variegata' and 'Crystal Variegata'; also sold as *A. cordata*) looks very much like a sedum, with succulent, trailing stems and fleshy, bright green leaves edged with creamy white. Typically 3 to 5 inches tall at most. Full sun to partial shade; average to dry, well-drained soil. Zones 9 to 11. *Note:* The species is considered invasive in some frost-free areas.

*Solenostemon* 'Emerald and Snow'

## SOLENOSTEMON
*Coleus*

**Height: 1–3 feet**
**Leaf size: Usually 3–5 inches long;**
   **2–4 inches wide**
**Full sun to partial shade**
**Zones 10 and 11**

When it comes to amazingly variegated foliage, coleus (*Solenostemon scutellarioides,* formerly *Coleus blumei*) are where it's at! They come in a vast array of color combinations, leaf shapes, and heights to suit any scheme you have in mind, either in the garden or in containers. There are already hundreds of named selections and new ones appear on the market every year, so it's not possible to give more than a brief sampling of them here. (Those mentioned below all have green and white or yellow as the primary colors; for those with primarily purple, red, pink, orange, or yellow foliage, see the *Solenostemon* entries in other chapters.) Check out the selection at your local garden center to find the colors you need, or explore the far more diverse offerings of mail-order nurseries that specialize in coleus.

*Green with white to cream.* 'Butter Creme' ('Buttercream') has heavily ruffled, bright green edges and a cream center. Seed-grown 'Kong Green' has extra-large, medium green leaves with wide, cream to white veins radiating from the center. 'Lime Frill' has deeply scalloped, bright green leaves with cream-to-white centers and veining.

*Green with yellow to cream.* 'Emerald and Snow' bears broad, light to medium green leaves heavily flecked with yellow and cream. 'Lemon & Lime' boasts bright green leaves with bright yellow, ruffled edges and faint purple veining. 'Wild Lime' has strongly scalloped, wavy, light green edges surrounding a broad light yellow to cream center.

*Green with yellow or cream and purple.* The foliage of 'Blair's Witch' has scalloped, green-and-yellow edges with a purple-and-red center. 'Flirtin' Skirts' has bright green leaves heavily marked with deep purple striping and usually mottled with yellow and red. 'Japanese Giant' is a taller-than-usual selection (to 3 feet) with large, light green leaves that have a wide burgundy border and a narrow, creamy yellow rim. The distinctly different 'Little Twister' has small, deeply scalloped leaves that are mostly light yellow to cream in the center, with deep green edges, a hint of purple in the very center, and purple undersides.

**GROWING TIPS:** Older coleus cultivars usually prefer some shade, but most of the newer introductions produce their brightest colors in full sun. The more sun they get, however, the more important it is that the soil doesn't dry out. Pinching off the shoot tips every few weeks encourages bushy growth and discourages flowering. You can grow some strains from seed sown indoors in late winter, but the seedlings may be somewhat variable and are usually more apt to try to bloom. To preserve the exact colors and patterns you like, take cuttings in late summer or fall (they're easy to root), then keep them in a sunny spot or under plant lights through the winter. Wait until after the last frost date to set them back outside.

**ALTERNATIVE:** For showy multicolored foliage on a 1- to 2-foot-tall, hardy perennial, chameleon plant (*Houttuynia cordata* 'Chameleon') is an option — if you're prepared to overlook its propensity to creep far and wide. Its heart-shaped, medium green leaves are showily splashed with yellow (particularly along the edges) and brightly blushed with red. Best kept in a pot. Full sun with moist to wet soil; tolerates drier soil in some shade. Zones 5 to 9.

## TALINUM
*Jewels-of-Opar, fame flower*

**Height: 12–18 inches**
**Leaf size: 3–4 inches long;**
   **1–2 inches wide**
**Full sun to partial shade**
**Zones 9–11**

Jewels-of-Opar (*Talinum paniculatum*) is a study in contrasts. Its thick stems and fleshy leaves give the clumps a sense of solidity, while the clouds of tiny, reddish pink summer blooms and beadlike, bronzy orange seedpods are as dainty as could be. 'Variegatum' ('Variegata') brings even more features to the mix, including a reddish pink tint to the stems and a creamy edge

*Talinum paniculatum* 'Variegatum'

around each bright grayish green leaf. Enjoy variegated jewels-of-Opar as a border accent, mix it into container plantings, or let it shine in a pot all by itself. It tolerates heat and humidity better than many other variegates do, so it's a particularly good choice for areas with sultry summers.

**GROWING TIPS:** Full sun is best, but the plants will tolerate partial shade too. Average, well-drained soil is fine. Where they're not hardy, enjoy them as houseplants for the winter. If the stems get lanky, cut off the shoot tips in spring to promote branching. They're very easy to root as cuttings if you want to make more plants.

**ALTERNATIVES:** *Fuchsia triphylla* 'Firecracker' forms upright, shrubby plants with medium green to gray-green leaves irregularly edged in

cream and blushed with pink; 2 to 3 feet tall. Hybrid 'Sun Ray' has smaller leaves on arching stems; about 1 foot tall. Zone 10 for both. *F. magellanica* var. *molinae* 'Sharpitor' has light green, cream-bordered leaves; about 3 feet tall. Zones 7 to 9. Full sun (in cooler areas) to partial shade; moist but well-drained soil.

## TRADESCANTIA
*Tradescantia*

**Height:** About 6 inches
**Leaf size:** 2–3 inches long; about 1½ inch wide
**Full sun or partial shade**
**Zones vary**

Tradescantias have come a long way from their days as common houseplants. They still look good growing indoors, but they're becoming popular in the outdoors too. Their 12- to 18-inch-long, trailing stems make them a natural choice for cascading out of planters, window boxes, and hanging baskets. For something different, enjoy them as temporary ground covers under potted shrubs or right in the garden. They root readily from cuttings and creep around quickly, and can produce roots wherever they touch the soil, so a single plant can give you all the starts you need to fill empty spaces in your beds and borders without spending a bundle.

Most of the commonly available variegates are selections of the white-flowered species *T. fluminensis* (also listed as *T. albiflora*). The names tend to

be a little muddled, but in general, plants sold as 'Albovittata' and 'Quicksilver' are light to medium green heavily striped with white along their length; some may have a purplish underside to the leaves. 'Variegata' has bright green leaves randomly striped with light green, cream, and white (sometimes with a pink blush). Plants sold as *T. fluminensis* 'Quadricolor' (*T. zebrina* 'Quadricolor') typically have green, purple, white, and cream striping on top and purplish undersides. Zones 8 or 9 to 11. *Note: T. fluminensis* is considered invasive in some areas. Plants sold as *T.* 'Maiden's Blush', 'Blushing Bride', and 'Blushing Maid' have upright to trailing stems that are 6 to 10 inches tall, with pink shoot tips (brightest in cool weather) that age to bright green and white, then eventually to mostly or completely green. (Trimming

encourages colorful new growth.) They can fill a space several feet across by the end of the growing season. Zones 6 to 11 (possibly hardier).

**GROWING TIPS:** Morning sun with afternoon shade and average to moist but well-drained soil produce the best-looking foliage, although plants will take full sun in cooler areas if the soil stays evenly moist. Pinching off the stem tips encourages branching. Remove all-green growth immediately.

**ALTERNATIVE:** Variegated basket grass (*Oplismenus africanus* 'Variegatus'; also commonly listed as *Oplismenus hirtellus* and sometimes sold as *Panicum variegatum*) offers narrow, bright green leaves that are striped with white and blushed with pink (and sometimes purple too). Its slender, 18- to 24-inch-long stems trail out of containers or take root as they creep along the ground. Full sun to partial shade; average, well-drained soil. Zones 9 to 10.

*Tradescantia* 'Blushing Bride'

*Tricyrtis formosana* 'Gilt Edge'

## TRICYRTIS
*Toad lily*

**Height: 1–3 feet**
**Leaf size: 3–5 inches long;**
   **1–2 inches wide**
**Partial to full shade**
**Zones vary**

Toad lilies (*Tricyrtis*) are excellent for adding beautiful blooms to shady borders from mid- or late summer into fall, and many of them have attractive foliage for the rest of the growing season. But if you're looking for something a little different from glossy green or green with brown or purplish spots, cultivars with

white- or yellow-variegated foliage are another eye-catching option. Here's an overview of the most commonly available selections, all with white to pale pinkish purple flowers that are spotted with varying amounts of purple.

**Green or yellow with white to cream.** The hairy green leaves of *T. hirta* 'Albomarginata' are neatly rimmed with a narrow white edge, while those of 'Variegata' have a cream-colored edge; both have arching stems. Zones 4 to 9. Plants commonly sold as *T. macropoda* 'Tricolor' have gray-spotted green leaves striped with pink and cream in spring (mostly green for the rest of the year) on upright to slightly arching stems. Zones 5 to 8. (You may also find plants with the same traits sold as *T. macrantha* 'Tricolor' and *T. affinis* 'Tricolor'.) *T. formosana* 'Emperor' is a unique, upright selection with yellow leaves edged with creamy white. Zones 6 to 9.

**Green with yellow to cream.** Two selections commonly attributed to *T. formosana* have glossy green leaves that are bordered with yellow aging to cream on upright stems: 'Gilt Edge', typically hardy in Zones 5 to 9, and the somewhat shorter 'Samurai', which is usually hardy in Zones 6 to 9, although some gardeners report success with it in colder areas. *T. hirta* 'Miyazaki Gold' has hairy, green, yellow-edged leaves on arching stems. Zones 4 to 9. Upright hybrid 'Lightning Strike' has glossy, deep green leaves randomly striped with yellow to

yellow-green (most distinctly in spring). Zones 4 to 9. 'White Flame' is another hybrid with upright stems; its glossy leaves usually emerge with cream centers and age to have cream, light yellow, greenish yellow, and green striping. Zones 5 to 9.

**GROWING TIPS:** In most areas, toad lilies perform best in partial shade with humus-rich, evenly moist but well-drained soil. In cool climates, they will tolerate full sun with lots of moisture; in hot climates, they may prefer full shade. Toad lilies don't like constantly soggy soil, but ample moisture encourages tall stems; the same selections growing with less moisture are commonly much shorter. Too-dry soil causes the leaves to turn brown. Toad lilies spread by rhizomes to varying degrees but rarely enough to be considered aggressive; if needed, divide the plants in early spring to control their size. The new shoots are prone to frost damage, so be prepared to protect them from late-spring frosts.

**ALTERNATIVES:** Variegated Corsican hellebores (*Helleborus argutifolius*) 'Janet Starnes' and 'Pacific Frost' have three-lobed green leaves that are heavily speckled with creamy white, particularly on the new leaves, which may also show a pinkish blush in cool weather. The evergreen, clump-forming plants have upright stems typically about 2 feet tall. May self-sow; weed out any all-green seedlings. Usually hardy in Zones 6 or 7 to 9. Light shade; average, well-drained soil.

## TROPAEOLUM
*Nasturtium*

**Height: Varies**
**Leaf size: 2–3 inches long and wide**
**Full sun**
**Annual**

The bright blossoms of common nasturtiums (*Tropaeolum majus*) are a cheerful addition to sunny gardens from early summer through fall, and selections with variegated leaves add to the fun. These easy-to-grow annuals have light green foliage that's randomly splashed and speckled with cream to white; every leaf is different. Plants in the Alaska Series grow in 8- to 12-inch-tall mounds; 'Alaska Mixed' usually includes cream, yellow, orange, and red flowers. Single colors are also available, such as 'Alaska Gold' and 'Alaska Salmon Orange'. 'Jewel of Africa' produces trailing stems to 8 feet long with flowers in an array of bright and soft colors. Nasturtiums sold as 'African Queen' look the same in leaf but usually bloom only in bright shades of red, orange, and yellow. These two strains are often called climbing nasturtiums, but the stems won't pull themselves up on their own; give the plants taller companions that they can scramble up through, or let them sprawl as a ground cover. Besides looking beautiful, nasturtiums are useful: their peppery-tasting flowers are an excellent addition to salads.

**GROWING TIPS:** Nasturtiums are happiest in full sun and fertile, evenly moist but well-drained soil. (You'll often hear that they like poor soil, but better conditions encourage much better-looking plants, especially if you're more interested in foliage than in flowers.) Sow the seeds indoors in early spring or right in the garden in mid-spring. The plants may self-sow, and the seedlings should be variegated too; remove any all-green seedlings.

**ALTERNATIVE:** Annual 'Moon and Stars' watermelon (*Citrullus lanatus*) has long, ground-hugging stems that produce an 8-inch-tall carpet of deeply lobed, bright green leaves speckled with bright yellow (and tasty yellow-marked green fruits too). Give it full sun, well-drained

*Tropaeolum majus* 'Alaska Mixed'

soil, and room to spread 8 feet or more. Start the seed indoors in mid-spring in most areas; in the South, you can direct-sow a week or two after the last frost date.

---

# WEIGELA
*Weigela*

**Height:** Varies
**Leaf size:** 2–3 inches long;
   1–2 inches wide
**Full sun to partial shade**
**Zones 4 or 5–8**

Even if they never flowered, variegated weigelas (*Weigela*) would still be wonderful plants for mixed borders. Their arching stems produce handsome, spreading mounds, and the deciduous, white- or yellow-edged selections add a delicate touch of color all through the growing season. But they do bloom as well, with narrow, funnel-shaped flowers in various shades of pink in late spring or early summer, and occasionally again later in summer.

*Green with white to cream edges.* The deep green leaves of *W. florida* 'Suzanne' are edged with creamy to bright white on 5- to 7-foot-tall plants; the flowers are typically light pink. *W. praecox* 'Variegata' doesn't exactly fit this color group, because the new leaves have wide, irregular, light yellow margins, but for most of the growing season, the leaf edges are clear white. Its medium pink flowers appear several weeks earlier than on most other weigelas.

*Green with yellow to cream edges.* Among the several selections in this group are 5- to 7-foot-tall *W. florida* 'Variegata' (also listed as 'Florida Variegata') and *W. florida* 'Variegata Nana' ('Nana Variegata'), which is usually more compact; both have medium to light pink flowers that fade to white. These are often mixed up in the nursery trade, and occasionally plants sold under these names have deeper pink flowers. The edges of their green to gray-green leaves are creamy yellow when new and creamy white when older. *W.* 'Sunny Princess' is 4 to 5 feet tall, with an irregular yellow to greenish yellow border; the flowers are medium to bright pink. 'Gold Rush' is similar but with light pink flowers. French Lace ('Brigela') grows 5 to 6 feet tall, with a bright to light yellow leaf edge and rich pinkish red flowers.

**GROWING TIPS:** Full sun is usually best, but for variegated weigelas growing in hot climates, afternoon shade reduces the possibility of leaf browning. Average, well-drained soil is fine. If needed, trim back shrubs lightly after the flowers fade to maintain a neat, mounded shape. On established plants, removing a few of the oldest stems at their base before new growth starts each spring will help to keep the shrubs vigorous. Also be sure to prune away any all-green shoots as soon as you see them.

**ALTERNATIVES:** Deciduous shrub *Deutzia crenata* 'Summer Snow' (also sold as 'Variegata') has medium green leaves splashed with light yellow to cream on new shoots, often turning mostly green later; 2 to 4 feet tall. *D. scabra* 'Variegata' is similar but tends to hold its variegation longer; 5 to 7 feet tall. Full sun to partial shade; average, well-drained soil. Zones 6 to 8. *Note: D. scabra* is considered invasive in some areas.

*Weigela florida* 'Variegata'

## ABELIA
*Abelia*

**Height: Varies**
**Leaf size: 1–2 inches long;**
    **about ½ inch wide**
**Full sun to partial shade**
**Zones 5 or 6–9**

Glossy abelias (*Abelia × grandiflora*) are appreciated mostly for their long blooming period and their fragrant, light pink flowers, which make a pleasing contrast to the glossy, deep green, deciduous to evergreen foliage. Bronzy red new shoots, red to orange fall color, and a reddish winter blush add to the interest. The variegated-leaf forms don't really improve on these features, because the flowers tend to blend into the colored foliage, but they do add a delicate texture to mixed border or foundation plantings for much of the year. Compact selections are also terrific in containers or planted in masses as a ground cover. Abelias readily produce variegated shoots, so there are several selections to choose from, although most look very similar even when you're standing right next to them.

*Green with white to cream markings.* Confetti ('Conti') and Silver Anniversary ('Panache') have bright white- to cream-edged leaves on low, mounding plants that grow 2 to 4 feet tall. 'Mardi Gras' basically looks the same but reportedly has more dependably pink shoot tips.

*Green with yellow to cream markings.* 'Francis Mason' (also sold as 'Frances Mason' and 'Variegata') usually grows 4 to 6 feet tall, with a variable, bright yellow leaf edge that ages to greenish yellow. It often produces shoots with slightly different variegation or with all-yellow leaves. 'Sunrise' is one sport of 'Francis Mason', with a more consistently broad yellow edge on 3- to 5-foot-tall plants.

**GROWING TIPS:** Abelias are sturdy shrubs that will adapt to either full sun or partial shade with average, well-drained soil. Very cold weather may cause some or all of the leaves to drop, but the plants will produce new leaves in spring. Abelias seldom need pruning, but you should remove all-green shoots.

**ALTERNATIVE:** Another fine-textured, multi-season shrub for Zones 8 to 10 (or for containers elsewhere) is *Corokia × virgata* 'Sunsplash'. Its small, glossy, evergreen leaves are silvery white underneath and medium green on top, with splashes of creamy to greenish yellow and sometimes pink. To about 6 feet tall, with a fairly open branching habit, but tolerates heavy pruning if you want to keep it smaller and bushier. Full sun; average, well-drained soil.

*Buddleia davidii* 'Harlequin'

*Abelia × grandiflora* 'Francis Mason'

## BUDDLEIA
*Butterfly bush*

**Height: 6–8 feet**
**Leaf size: 3–5 inches long;**
    **1–2 inches wide**
**Full sun**
**Zones 5–9**

When you're considering a plant that produces so many flowers over such a long season, it may seem like overkill to choose a cultivar that has variegated leaves as well. But these special selections of butterfly bush (*Buddleia davidii*; also listed as *Buddleja davidii*) certainly earn their place in the garden, displaying colorful foliage through spring and early summer, then creating an even more spectacular show when the blooms appear from midsummer into fall. 'Harlequin' is one of the oldest cultivars, with gray-green leaves irregularly edged with light yellow when young and cream to white when mature, plus clusters of reddish purple flowers. Masquerade ('Notbud') looks almost identical but is reportedly less prone to producing all-green shoots. 'White Harlequin' has similar variegation but with white blooms. 'Santana' holds its wide, bright to creamy yellow leaf edges through the growing season, with reddish purple flowers; Strawberry Lemonade ('Monrell') has similar leaf colors with bright pink flowers. *Note:* Butterfly bushes are considered invasive in some regions.

**GROWING TIPS:** Butterfly bushes grow best in full sun and average, well-drained soil. In the coldest parts of their range, they die to the ground by spring; elsewhere, cutting back the stems to about 1 foot in early spring controls their size. Pinching off the shoot tips two or three times in spring to early summer promotes dense, bushy growth. Prune away all-green shoots at their base as soon as you spot them. Regular deadheading encourages rebloom and prevents self-sowing.

**ALTERNATIVES:** 'Aucubaefolia' common lilac (*Syringa vulgaris*) is a deciduous shrub with medium green leaves stippled and splashed with bright to creamy yellow; to 10 feet tall. 'Golden Eclipse' Japanese tree lilac (*S. reticulata*) bears deep green leaves edged in light green when young and bright yellow later in the season; to 20 feet tall. Full sun; average to slightly alkaline, well-drained soil. Zones 3 to 8. Evergreen 'Harlequin' firethorn (*Pyracantha*) has thorny stems clad in small, light green leaves with pink edges that turn creamy white. About 6 feet tall. Full sun; average, well-drained soil. Zones 6 or 7 to 9.

# BUXUS
*Boxwood*

**Height: Varies**
**Leaf size: About 1 inch long;**
    **½ inch wide**
**Full sun to partial shade**
**Zones 6–8**

Elegant evergreen boxwoods (*Buxus*) are ideal for all-season interest in mixed borders and foundation plantings. They've been cultivated for centuries, so it's hardly surprising that there are hundreds of cultivars, including several with variegated foliage — mostly from common boxwood (*B. sempervirens*). These beauties share the dense, bushy habit of the original species, as well as its ability to tolerate regular shearing into topiaries and hedges. Left unsheared, most of these cultivars can reach about 10 feet tall, although it will take them many years to get there.

*Green with white to cream markings.* Several selections with bright cream to white leaf edges are available, most commonly under the names 'Elegantissima' and 'Variegata'. They seem to be mixed up in the trade, which is not surprising given their similar appearance. 'Elegantissima' is usually preferable for its more compact size: it typically grows 4 to 6 feet tall, while 'Variegata' will eventually reach 8 to 10 feet.

*Green with yellow to cream markings.* 'Aureovariegata' (sometimes sold as 'Aurea') has bright yellow new leaves that age to deep green irregularly splashed with lighter yellow. 'Latifolia Maculata' looks similar but reportedly has a denser, bushy habit. 'Aurea Pendula' has deep green leaves that are splashed with yellow (or sometimes solid yellow) on somewhat weeping side shoots. 'Golden Triumph' is a selection of littleleaf boxwood (*B. microphylla*) with greenish yellow leaf edges that age to creamy yellow; it usually grows about 3 feet tall.

**GROWING TIPS:** Although they will grow in full sun with plenty of moisture, a site with morning sun and afternoon shade or light all-day shade and average to moist but well-drained soil is ideal. Maintaining a 2-inch layer of organic mulch around the plants provides good conditions for healthy root growth. For hedges or topiary, shear a few times from spring to early summer. On all established boxwoods, thinning out some of the stems each year allows more air and sunlight to reach into the center of the plant, which helps to keep the plants healthy and vigorous.

**ALTERNATIVES:** 'Midas Touch' Japanese holly (*Ilex crenata*) bears narrow, yellow-edged, deep green leaves. 'Snowflake' has cream-colored new leaves that age to deep green with white edges. 'Variegata' usually has yellow splashes against deep green. All three form bushy, evergreen shrubs eventually reaching 3 to 4 feet tall. Zones 5 or 6 to 8. Full sun to partial shade; average to moist but well-drained soil. *Note:* The species is considered invasive in some areas.

*Buxus sempervirens* 'Elegantissima'

*Chamaecyparis pisifera* 'Snow'

## CHAMAECYPARIS
*False cypress*

**Height: Varies**
**Leaf size: ¼ inch or less (individual**
    **needlelike or scalelike leaves)**
**Full sun to partial shade**
**Zones vary**

False cypresses (*Chamaecyparis*) come in a range of shapes, sizes, and colors to supply interest all year long in a variety of garden spaces. Tall, pyramidal types are ideal as vertical accents and focal points, while rounded or mounding selections add height and structure to the middle of a border. Smaller plants of any

false cypresses are outstanding four-season container plants too. The many needle-leaved or scale-leaved, all-green selections are beautiful in their own right, but those with variegated foliage expand the possibilities for creating eye-catching combinations. Below is a sampling of some smaller cultivars that are typically hardy in Zones 4 to 8; for many more options, check the selection at your local nursery, or seek out specialty conifer nurseries. Note that the sizes below are approximate, reflecting the heights that the plants can reach after 10 years or more. Most of these are relatively slow-growing, so with a little trimming as needed, you can easily keep them in scale with most mixed-border companions.

*Green to gray-blue with white to cream markings.* 'Silver Threads' Lawson false cypress (*C. lawsoniana*) has greenish yellow new growth flecked with cream on narrowly upright plants that eventually reach 8 feet tall or more. 'Snow White' has blue foliage tipped with white on the new shoots; it develops a roughly pyramidal shape to about 6 feet tall. 'Summer Snow' has creamy white new growth over deep green older growth on loosely pyramidal plants to about 6 feet tall. 'Snowflake' Hinoki false cypress (*C. obtusa*) is dull green to bluish green with creamy white flecks and splashes throughout; it starts as a tight ball shape, eventually growing to 6 feet with a more upright, pyramidal habit.

'Cream Ball' ('Creamball') Sawara or Japanese false cypress (*C. pisifera*) tends to maintain its globe-shaped habit as it matures to about 3 feet tall, with gray-green leaves splashed with cream to white. 'Devon Cream' reaches the same height but is a pyramidal plant with white-tipped, gray-blue foliage. 'Silver Lode' forms 2- to 3-foot-tall and much wider cushions that are green with scattered creamy white flecks. Classic 'Snow' starts as a dense round ball of green foliage with white-frosted tips, often developing into a pyramidal plant as it matures to about 6 feet tall.

*Green with yellow to cream.* Many false cypresses that have both green and yellow in their foliage appear solid yellow from a distance, but here are a few that look distinctly variegated. *C. lawsoniana* 'Gold Flake' is blue-green showily splashed with yellow to cream on columnar to pyramidal plants to 8 feet tall or more. *C. obtusa* 'Saffron Spray' has feathery green foliage splashed with bright yellow on broadly upright plants to about 5 feet tall. *C. pisifera* 'Filifera Aureovariegata' is distinctively different, with drooping, threadlike, deep green foliage splashed with yellow on roughly pyramidal plants to about 8 feet tall. 'Gold Dust' is in the same species but grows only 2 feet tall or so, as dense, mounded plants with yellow markings and frosting.

**GROWING TIPS:** False cypresses thrive in humus-rich, evenly

moist but well-drained soil. Although most prefer full sun, the white-variegated selections appreciate light shade during the hottest part of the day, particularly in the warmer parts of their growing range. Protection from strong wind is beneficial too.

**ALTERNATIVES:** Canada hemlock (*Tsuga canadensis*) selections with white- or cream-frosted shoot tips look as if they're dusted with snow even during the "dog days." Try 'Frosty' or 'Gentsch White', both of which grow 4 to 5 feet tall with a globe-shaped habit, or 'Betty Rose', a mounded form that usually reaches 2 to 3 feet tall. Light shade; humus-rich, evenly moist but well-drained soil. Zones 3 or 4 to 7.

## COTONEASTER
*Cotoneaster*

**Height: 2–3 feet**
**Leaf size: ½ inch long and wide**
**Full sun to partial shade**
**Zones 5–7**

When you consider the terrific four-season features of rockspray cotoneaster (*Cotoneaster horizontalis*), it's difficult to imagine how it could be any better. Its spreading framework of densely branched woody stems (to about 6 feet wide) is covered with hundreds of small, pink-tinged white flowers in late spring; then rounded, glossy, deep green leaves emerge for summer. In late summer to early fall, the tiny green berries turn pinkish red, and the leaves turn pink to bright red before they drop to reveal the handsome, berry-clad structure for winter. The fruits last until hungry birds descend to feed on them. 'Variegatus' (*C. atropurpureus* 'Variegatus') has a bonus feature: an elegant white rim around each leaf (sometimes with a pinkish tinge in cool weather). Enjoy this beauty as a ground cover around taller shrubs or trees, or use it in mass plantings on banks or slopes, where its branching habit will show off to advantage.

**GROWING TIPS:** Variegated rockspray cotoneaster grows in full sun or partial shade with average, well-drained soil. Extra moisture is helpful for the first few years;

*Cotoneaster horizontalis* 'Variegatus'

established plantings tolerate drier conditions.

**ALTERNATIVES:** *Coprosma × kirkii* 'Variegata' serves a similar function in Zones 8 to 10. It usually grows 24 to 30 inches tall but may spread to 6 feet or more, with small, glossy, gray-green leaves bordered with creamy white. Hybrid 'Beatson's Gold' has a more upright habit, with rich green leaves centered with greenish yellow aging to bright yellow, sometimes with reddish tints; to 6 feet tall. Full sun to partial shade; average, well-drained soil.

---

## DAPHNE
*Daphne*

**Height: Varies**
**Leaf size: Varies**
**Full sun to partial shade**
**Zones vary**

Daphnes (*Daphne*) have a reputation for thriving for years, then suddenly dying — an alarming trait, to be sure. But these quirky plants are so rewarding when they're happy that many gardeners are willing to put up with their foibles. Several species offer variegated selections (mostly with yellow to cream markings), and the fact that some are deciduous and some are evergreen complicates the decision process a bit. Here's an overview of some of the best.

**Deciduous to semievergreen daphnes.** Burkwood daphne (*D. × burkwoodii*) is a dense, mounded shrub 3 to 4 feet tall, with green leaves that are 1 to 2 inches long and about ½ inch wide, plus clusters of very fragrant light pink to

white flowers in late spring to early summer. In mild-winter areas, it may remain evergreen. 'Carol Mackie' is perhaps the best-known cultivar, with a light yellow leaf edge that ages to bright cream; however, its dense mounds are prone to cracking open under the weight of heavy snow. 'Silveredge' is a lesser-known but excellent selection, with similarly marked foliage on a sturdier, somewhat more upright plant that appears to be more disease-resistant. 'Briggs Moonlight' has the reverse variegation: light yellow to cream centers with a thin, deep green rim. Vigorous 'G.K. Argles' has somewhat broader leaves with a rich yellow edge that ages to light yellow. Zones 5 or 6 to 8.

*D. × transatlantica* has a spreading, mounded habit that's 3 to 5 feet tall, with 1½-inch-long, ½-inch-wide leaves that are usually semievergreen or deciduous. The very fragrant, palest pink to creamy white flowers bloom mostly in spring, with scattered rebloom through the rest of the growing season and sometimes even into winter. 'Beulah' (also sold as 'Beulah Cross') has a creamy white leaf edge, and 'Summer Ice' has a crisp white border. Zones 5 or 6 to 8.

**Evergreen daphnes.** Garland daphne (*D. cneorum*) is a low-growing (to 1 foot tall) but wide-spreading species with tiny, deep green leaves that are less than 1 inch long and ¼ to ½ inch wide. Its late spring flowers are pink

and richly scented. Plants sold under the name 'Variegata' may have creamy yellow edges or creamy white edges; those with the latter markings are more correctly listed as 'Albomarginata'. Zones 5 to 7. Winter daphne (*D. odora*) has a rounded habit to about 4 feet tall; glossy, deep green leaves to about 3 inches long and 1 inch across; and deep pink buds that open to intensely fragrant, paler pink flowers. 'Aureomarginata' (also sold as 'Marginata') has a very thin, yellow leaf edge that ages to creamy white. Zones 7 to 8 or 9.

*Daphne × burkwoodii* 'Briggs Moonlight'

**GROWING TIPS:** Ask a dozen gardeners for the secret to success with daphnes, and you're likely to get a dozen different answers. Generally speaking, the variegates seem to prefer light all-day shade or morning sun with afternoon shade. Excellent drainage is a must; sandy soil is ideal, but you can usually get away with heavier soil if you set the plant with the top of the rootball slightly above the soil surface. Raised beds will also help to provide improved drainage. Traditional wisdom says to keep the soil evenly moist and mulch generously, but many growers report better success in dry conditions with no mulch. One point of agreement is to start with small plants, because they're apt to settle in more quickly after transplanting. Prune away all-green shoots as soon as you see them. *Caution:* All parts of daphnes are poisonous if ingested, and brushing against the leaves may cause skin irritation.

**ALTERNATIVES:** Deciduous, mounded 'Mrs. Gladis Brabazon' tutsan (*Hypericum androsaemum*; also sold as 'Gladys Brabazon') has green leaves streaked with cream to white (pink-tinged in spring); to about 3 feet tall. 'Hidcote Variegated' has cream-edged leaves; 12 to 18 inches tall. Zones 6 to 9. Semievergreen *H.* × *moserianum* 'Tricolor' has bright pink leaf edges aging to cream and then white; 2 feet tall. Zones 7 to 9. Full sun (with plenty of moisture) to full shade (even dry shade).

## EUPHORBIA
*Euphorbia, spurge*

**Height:** Varies
**Leaf size:** Varies
**Full sun to partial shade**
**Zones vary**

Euphorbias (*Euphorbia*) offer an embarrassment of riches when it comes to fabulous foliage, so they make two appearances in this chapter: here for the fine-textured types and elsewhere for the medium-textured selections.

Two of the several variegated, narrow-leaved euphorbias belong to the species commonly called cushion spurge (*E. polychroma;* also known as *E. epithymoides*). Usually hardy in Zones 4 to 9, they grow in tidy, 1-foot-tall, rounded mounds of narrow leaves about 2 inches long and ½ inch wide, with bright yellow, petal-like structures surrounding tiny, greenish yellow blooms at the stem tips from mid-spring to midsummer. 'First Blush' has light green leaves with cream to white edges. The spring and fall growth is also blushed with pink, as are the flower buds. 'Lacy' is about the same height, but its leaf edges are more dependably cream without the pink. Evergreen *E. characias* 'Tasmanian Tiger', for Zones 7 to 10, is more of a rounded shrub with very narrow leaves (3 to 5 inches long and about ½ inch wide) that are blue-green neatly bordered with white. In spring to early summer, the 2- to 3-foot-tall, upright stems are topped with large clusters of greenish yellow blooms.

*Euphorbia characias* 'Tasmanian Tiger'

It's reportedly more vigorous than similar but older selections such as 'Emmer Green' and 'Burrow Silver'. 'Vanilla Swirl' is a more compact cultivar (1 to 2 feet tall) with cream leaf edges.

**GROWING TIPS:** Variegated euphorbias generally perform best with morning sun and some afternoon shade, although they usually grow just fine in full sun too. Average, well-drained soil is ideal. Cushion spurges will tolerate a bit more moisture, but they all dislike heavy, wet soil. On *E. characias* selections, cut out the stems that have flowered right at the base when the blossoms fade. On all variegates, remove solid-green shoots immediately. *Caution:* As with all other euphorbias, avoid getting the sap on your hands or in your eyes.

**ALTERNATIVES:** 'Silberblatte' sundrops (*Oenothera fruticosa*) offers gray-green leaves marked with light yellow to cream; 1 to 2 feet tall.

*O. fruticosa* subsp. *glauca* 'Frühlingsgold' ('Spring Gold') has a cream to white leaf edge (pink-blushed in spring); 1 foot tall. 'Sunspot' (also sold under *O. tetragona*) has green leaves mottled with bright yellow early in the season; about 18 inches tall. Full sun to partial shade; average, well-drained soil. Zones 4 or 5 to 9.

## GAURA
*Gaura, bee blossom, wand flower*

**Height:** 2–3 feet
**Leaf size:** 2–3 inches long; about ½ inch wide
**Full sun**
**Zones 5 or 6–9**

Gaura (*Gaura lindheimeri*) in full flower is a glorious sight, with an abundance of pink to white blossoms over such a long period — most of the growing season, actually — that you seldom even notice the small, narrow foliage.

So why even bother seeking out a variegated cultivar? It's probably not worthwhile for a bed or border setting, but if you're going to take advantage of this pretty perennial in a container, that's a different story. Bringing the plants nearer to eye level, and sitting them where you can get right up close and personal with them, enables you to appreciate the beauty of the foliage as well as the bountiful blooms.

Pale pink-flowered 'Corrie's Gold' is a tall-growing selection (to 3 feet) with yellow-edged leaves that may have some yellow splashes extending into the center. Sunny Butterflies ('Colso') is more compact (to 2 feet tall), with a neat cream to white leaf edge and medium pink blooms. 'Golden Speckles' bears green leaves heavily mottled with yellow and white flowers that age to pink on 3-foot plants. 'Jo Adela' (also sold as 'Jo Adella') has creamy white-splashed leaf centers and white flowers on 2-foot plants. 'Passionate Rainbow' grows to about 2 feet tall, with deep green leaves elegantly rimmed with creamy white and red-tinged mostly in cool weather, accented by short clusters of pink flowers.

**GROWING TIPS:** Gauras need lots of sunlight to do their best, and good drainage — especially in winter — is a must for survival. (If your soil is on the heavy side, improved drainage is another reason to try gauras in containers.) Average fertility is fine. If the flowering slows in mid- to late summer, shear off the flower stems to promote new leafy growth and another flush of flowers for fall.

**ALTERNATIVES:** 'Tequila Sunrise' coreopsis (*Coreopsis*) grows in rounded clumps of very narrow, light green leaves bordered in light yellow to cream and often tinged with pink in cool weather; 12 to 18 inches tall. Zones 5 to 9. *Gymnaster savatieri* 'Variegata' (sometimes sold as *Aster savatieri* 'Variegata') offers narrow, rich green leaves randomly splashed with bright cream in 18- to 24-inch-tall clumps. Zones 5 to 8. Full sun; average, well-drained soil.

*Gaura lindheimeri* Sunny Butterflies

## HEDERA
*Ivy*

**Height:** 2–4 inches as a ground cover; can trail 3 feet or more
**Leaf size:** About 2 inches long and wide
**Full sun to full shade**
**Zones 5 or 6–9 for most**

Long beloved for their elegant evergreen leaves, trailing habit, and fuss-free nature, ivies (*Hedera*) — in particular, some English ivies (*H. helix*) — are starting to get a bad reputation with gardeners for their aggressive and invasive tendencies. We all appreciate sturdy, vigorous plants, especially when they can take tough conditions (like dry shade) that few other plants will thrive in. But there's a fine line between vigorous and aggressive, and neglected ivies can creep right over it, steadily growing out of bounds both horizontally and vertically if they have an upright surface to cling to. And when ivies grow upright, they change from their "juvenile" stage to the "adult" stage; then they're able to flower and produce seeds, which can spread into natural areas and crowd out native vegetation. *Note:* That's why ivies are classified as invasive in some areas.

All that being said, it's possible to safely grow and enjoy ivies in your garden in most regions. If you keep the edges of ground cover plantings clipped regularly, and you snip off shoots that start climbing up walls or trees, they won't get out of hand and you won't have to worry about them

*Hedera helix* 'Mottled Mosaic'

setting seed. Growing variegated ivies makes this simple maintenance even easier, because they tend to be much less vigorous than forms with all-green leaves are. Better yet, stick with variegated selections and grow them only in containers, and you'll be able to enjoy your ivies with no worries at all.

Ivies come in such a diversity of leaf shapes, sizes, and variegation patterns that there are currently several hundred named cultivars, and a few nurseries specialize in collecting, propagating, and selling them to equally dedicated ivy-philes. However, most of us are content to enjoy the more commonly available but still beautiful selections available at our local garden centers. Below is an overview of some time-tested favorites that are usually easy to find. Keep in mind that any of these may also be blushed with pink in cool weather.

*Green with white to cream markings.* 'Glacier' is a classic selection in this color range, with three- to five-lobed, gray-green leaves that have an irregular, creamy white edge and some gray splashes. 'Schaefer Three' has triangular to three-lobed, deep green leaves that are heavily mottled with creamy white. 'Mottled Mosaic' has three-lobed, medium to deep green leaves that are heavily splashed and speckled with white and cream.

*Green with yellow to cream markings.* 'Gold Heart' ('Gold-heart') is a longtime standard in this color range, with pinkish stems that bear three-lobed, deep green leaves with a large, bright yellow to light yellow center splash. 'Gold Child' ('Gold-child') foliage has three to five lobes, with an irregular yellow border that ages to cream, with a green to gray-green center. 'Golden Ingot' ('Golden Inge') has similarly shaped leaves with a medium green center, a bright yellow to creamy yellow border, and a green-flecked rim.

**GROWING TIPS:** Although they'll tolerate just about any amount (or lack) of light — especially if you're growing them as container annuals — variegated ivies typically look their best when they get morning sun and afternoon shade. Average to rich, evenly

moist but well-drained soil is ideal. Remove all-green shoots. If you're not sure your ivies will be winter-hardy, bring them indoors to enjoy as houseplants for the cold season. Those left outside appreciate protection from winter sun and wind. *Caution:* Working with ivy may cause skin irritation, so wear gloves when planting or grooming it.

**ALTERNATIVE:** Evergreen 'Harlequin' wintercreeper (*Euonymus fortunei* var. *radicans;* also listed simply under *E. fortunei*) forms low, broad mounds of deep green leaves edged, streaked, and speckled with white, often blushed with pink in cool weather; to 1 foot tall. Morning sun and afternoon shade or light all-day shade is ideal; average to moist but well-drained soil. Zones 5 to 9. *Note:* The species *E. fortunei* is considered invasive in some areas.

## JUNIPERUS
*Juniper*

**Height:** Varies
**Leaf size:** ¼–½ inch long; about ⅛ inch wide
**Full sun**
**Zones vary**

Some gardeners may sniff at junipers (*Juniperus*) as being too ordinary, but there are good reasons why these evergreens are so widely planted. Besides adding year-round form and color, junipers are sturdy, dependable plants that do their job and seldom need any special care in return. They vary widely in habit, from ground-hugging creepers

to broad, upright mounds to narrowly vertical exclamation points, so there are many ways to enjoy them: as ground covers, in mixed borders and foundation plantings, in masses, as single specimens, even in pots. Growing variegated cultivars lets you enjoy all of these benefits with the added advantage of having something distinctly different from the usual solid-green or powder blue types. It may take a bit of hunting to find them, but they're worth it. Here's a sampling of some variegates on the market.

*Green or blue with white to cream markings.* The Chinese or Hollywood juniper (*J. chinensis*) selection usually sold as 'Variegated Kaizuka' (but also listed as 'Kaizuka Variegated', 'Kaizuka Variegata', and 'Torulosa Variegata') has an upright habit with somewhat twisted branches that can eventually grow 10 feet tall

*Juniperus conferta* 'Sunsplash'

or more. Its rich green foliage is heavily spotted with cream (sometimes light yellow) to white. 'Expansa Variegata' (which is also sold as 'Parsonii Variegata' and *J. davurica* 'Expansa Variegata') has distinctively horizontal branching, forming mounded plants usually 2 to 3 feet tall when mature. Its blue-green foliage is marked with creamy white. Zones 5 to 9. 'Andorra Variegated' creeping juniper (*J. horizontalis;* also sold as 'Andorra Variegata' and 'Andora Variegata') grows with an upright, broad-spreading form to about 2 feet tall. Its feathery, grayish green shoots are flecked with cream and turn purplish in winter. Zones 4 to 9.

*Green or blue with yellow to cream markings.* 'Blue and Gold' juniper (often listed under *J. × media* and *J. pfitzeriana*) forms upright, broad-spreading plants to about 5 feet tall, with slightly arching, blue-green shoots mingled with light yellow shoots. Zones 4 to 9. Shore junipers (*J. conferta*) sold as 'Sunsplash' and 'Brookside Variegated' are low, creeping plants (to about 2 feet tall) with medium green or blue-green foliage and yellow shoot tips scattered throughout. Zones 6 to 9. *J. × media* 'Daub's Frosted' forms low but wide-spreading plants (2 to 4 feet tall), with horizontal to drooping tips that are bright to light yellow when new, aging to blue-green. Zones 5 to 8. 'Sparkling Skyrocket' Rocky Mountain juniper (*J. scopulorum;* also sold as

*J. virginiana* 'Sparkle') has a narrowly upright habit that can eventually reach 20 feet or more, with grayish green foliage intermixed with light yellow to cream shoots. Zones 4 to 8.

**GROWING TIPS:** Variegated junipers thrive in full sun in most areas; in hot-summer regions, a little afternoon shade may prevent the pale shoots from turning brown. Average to dry, well-drained soil is fine. The plants seldom need special care; trim off wayward shoots, if desired.

**ALTERNATIVES:** Several selections of evergreen Scotch heather (*Calluna vulgaris*) have a variegated appearance. 'Spring Cream' is one, with light yellow to cream shoot tips in spring over rich green older growth. 'Easter Bonfire' is another, with red-tinged, creamy white new growth that stays bright into summer. Both grow 12 to 18 inches tall. Full sun; acidic, well-drained soil. Zones 4 to 7. *Note: C. vulgaris* is considered invasive in some areas.

## LAMIUM
*Dead nettle*

**Height: 6–8 inches**
**Leaf size: 1–2 inches long;**
**   about 1 inch wide**
**Partial to full shade**
**Zones 3 or 4–9**

Spotted dead nettles (*Lamium maculatum*) create low, dense carpets of toothed green leaves that look great all through the growing season, with a bonus of pinkish purple or white, clustered flowers in late spring to

early summer. The new shoots are upright at first; later, they trail along the ground and can take root where they rest on the soil. The plants also spread outward by creeping underground stems. *Note:* The species is considered invasive in some areas.

Spotted dead nettle is best known for its many silver-and-green-leaved selections, all of which are invaluable for bringing a touch of brightness to shady sites. There are also a few cultivars with variegated foliage, and their yellow markings add an extra color element you can take advantage of when planning combinations. 'Elizabeth de Haas' has medium green leaves with a silvery white center stripe and bright yellow to greenish yellow splashes, plus bright purplish pink blooms. 'Anne Greenaway' and Golden Anniversary ('Dellam') have the same colors, but the yellow is concentrated around the edges to create a broad border.

**GROWING TIPS:** Variegated dead nettles typically show their brightest colors with morning sun and afternoon shade or light all-day shade, but they will tolerate heavier shade too. Evenly moist but well-drained, humus-rich soil is ideal. Variegated dead nettles perform well as ground covers and also look terrific in shady-area containers. Where you include them in mixed borders, keep an eye on their spread; be prepared to trim their shoots or dig out some of them if they

threaten to crowd out more-delicate companions. If your dead nettle plantings look bedraggled by midsummer, shear them to an inch or two above the ground, and they'll send up fresh new growth that looks good well into the winter season. (If you don't trim them in midsummer, then do it in early spring before new growth begins.) Remove all-green shoots immediately.

**ALTERNATIVE:** 'Yellow Splash' silver-and-gold chrysanthemum (*Ajania pacifica;* also known as *Chrysanthemum pacificum*) produces lobed, medium green leaves covered with silvery hairs that give them an overall gray-green cast, with the added features of a silvery white edge and random yellow markings over the surface; 12 to 18 inches tall. Full sun; average to dry, well-drained soil. Zones 5 or 6 to 9.

*Lamium maculatum* 'Anne Greenaway'

*Lonicera nitida* 'Lemon Beauty'

## LAVANDULA
*Lavender, lavandin*

**Height:** 18–24 inches
**Leaf size:** 1–2 inches long;
¼ inch wide
**Full sun**
**Zones vary**

Lavender lovers rejoice: now you can enjoy its fantastic fragrance, beautiful blooms, handsome shrubby habit, *and* variegated foliage, too! To be honest, variegated lavenders (*Lavandula*) don't have tremendous garden impact; their leaves are so narrow that their markings aren't particularly noticeable from a distance.

But if you keep them close at hand — in a raised planter, for example, or right next to a path or bench — their variegation adds a little extra touch to make these delightful plants just that much more special.

Silver Edge lavandin (*L. × intermedia* 'Walvera'; also sold as 'Walberton's Silver Edge' or under the species *L. angustifolia*) has pale green to gray-green leaves evenly edged in white to cream, plus short, spiky clusters of purple-blue flowers atop slender, 3-foot-tall stems from midsummer into fall. Goldburg lavandin ('Burgoldeen'; also sold as 'Goldberg') is similar but more compact (18 to 24 inches tall in bloom), with light yellow to cream leaf edges. These selections are usually hardy in Zones 6 to 9, although they may survive in colder climates with excellent winter drainage and good snow cover. 'Linda Ligon' French or fringed lavender (*L. dentata*) has narrow, light green leaves with tightly scalloped edges and random splashes of cream, plus light blue flowers atop 2- to 4-foot-tall stems through much of the growing season. French lavender is hardy only in Zones 8 or 9 to 10; elsewhere, bring it into a cool, bright room for the winter to keep it from year to year.

**GROWING TIPS:** Lavenders thrive with full sun and average soil with excellent drainage. Mulching with a ½ to 1 inch of gravel helps to keep the crown dry and minimizes the possibility of rot. Prune back *L. × intermedia* types by about half in mid-spring, as soon as new growth begins, or wait until after the first flush of blooms has faded. Shearing off spent flower stems promotes rebloom. Cut out all-green shoots as soon as you see them.

**ALTERNATIVES:** 'Joyce DeBaggio' rosemary (*Rosmarinus officinalis;* also sold as 'Golden Rain') has needlelike green foliage edged with yellow, while 'Silver Spire' ('Silver Spires') has a creamy white edge; 3 to 5 feet tall. Zones 8 to 10. Variegated wallflower (*Erysimum linifolium* 'Variegatum') bears narrow, gray-green leaves edged with light yellow to cream; 1 to 3 feet tall. Zones 7 or 8 to 9. Full sun; average to dry, neutral to slightly alkaline, well-drained soil.

## LONICERA
*Honeysuckle*

**Height:** Usually 3–4 feet
**Leaf size:** ½ inch long; ¼ inch wide
**Full sun to partial shade**
**Zones 6 or 7–9**

At first glance, you wouldn't guess that boxleaf honeysuckle (*Lonicera nitida*) is a honeysuckle at all. Instead of producing twining vines and colorful, fragrant flowers, it forms a bushy shrub with spreading branches and narrow, glossy, evergreen foliage. You'll hardly notice the tiny, yellowish white spring blossoms. 'Lemon Beauty' has medium green leaves with greenish yellow margins that age to bright to light yellow; 'Silver Beauty' has gray-green leaves with cream to white edges. *L. yunnanensis* 'Pat's Selection' is similar to 'Silver Beauty' but is reportedly more vigorous. Single clumps of any of these are useful for bringing extra color, fine texture, and year-round presence to mixed borders. They show off particularly well next to or in front of companions that have deep green foliage for contrast. They're also attractive in groups as ground covers. Young plants are terrific in containers, too, which really show off the often-arching shoots.

**GROWING TIPS:** Choose a site with full sun to partial shade and average to moist, well-drained soil. A site with shelter from

*Lavandula* Silver Edge

drying winter winds may help to keep the foliage looking good through the colder months. Trim as needed to remove wayward shoots and keep the plants nicely shaped. Prune out all-green shoots as soon as you see them.

**ALTERNATIVES:** Bushy variegated myrtle (*Myrtus communis* 'Variegatus') has small, deep green leaves edged in creamy white; 3 to 5 feet tall. Full sun; average to moist, well-drained soil. Zones 9 to 11. 'Sunspot' sweet bay or bay laurel (*Laurus nobilis*), a large shrub or small tree, offers broader, deep green leaves splashed with yellow. Full sun to partial shade; evenly moist but well-drained soil. Zones 7 or 8 to 10. Both plants are aromatic and evergreen.

*Nerium oleander* 'Variegata'

# NERIUM
*Oleander*

**Height: 8–12 feet**
**Leaf size: 4–7 inches long;**
**about 1 inch wide**
**Full sun**
**Zones 9–11**

Oleanders (*Nerium oleander*) have long been treasured in mild-climate gardens for their summerlong display of single or double blooms, as well as for their handsome evergreen foliage. The vigorous, upright, bushy plants look great alone or in groups; grow nicely in containers as well as in the ground; and laugh at heat, drought, and salt. There are many cultivars chosen for their flower colors, but 'Variegatum' (also sold as 'Variegata') is unique for its light yellow to cream or even white leaf edges, accented by single, bright pink blooms. (Cooler weather seems to bring out more of the yellow in the leaf margins.) 'Variegatum Plenum' differs only in having double flowers; 'Mrs. Runge' looks very similar, but its leaf markings are usually distinctly yellow. *Caution:* All parts of oleander are very toxic if ingested, and the sap can irritate sensitive skin, so choose the planting site carefully or avoid oleander altogether where children or pets are around. *Note:* The species is considered invasive in some areas.

**GROWING TIPS:** Oleanders grow best in full sun with evenly moist but well-drained soil, although established plants will sail through most dry spells without suffering. They may get quite tall in the landscape, but you can keep them smaller with regular pruning (remember to wear gloves); they will also stay smaller — typically in the range of 3 to 6 feet tall — if you grow them in containers.

**ALTERNATIVES:** The light green leaves of 'Glanleam Gold' luma or arrayan (Luma apiculata; also listed under Myrtus apiculata) are just an inch or so long, but they're broadly bordered with pale yellow to creamy white and often pink-tinted when young, creating a very dramatic effect. Eventually reaches 20 feet tall where it's hardy (Zones 7 or 8 to 11). 'Variegated Eureka' lemon (*Citrus limon*) grows 8 to 12 feet tall, with larger green leaves edged in light yellow to cream, sometimes blushed with pink. Zones 9 to 11. Full sun to partial shade; average to evenly moist but well-drained soil.

*Origanum vulgare* 'White Anniversary'

# ORIGANUM
*Oregano, marjoram*

**Height: Varies**
**Leaf size: To 1½ inches long;**
**1 inch wide**
**Full sun**
**Zones vary**

Once relegated to the herb or vegetable garden, oreganos (*Origanum*) are increasingly available in ornamental selections that can hold their own in any flower bed, mixed border, or container planting. They typically grow in spreading clumps with small, spicy-scented leaves and clusters of tiny flowers in summer. Variegated selections have the benefit of extra foliage interest. They typically aren't very flavorful, but they do have a pleasant fragrance when you brush against the leaves, so plant them next to a path or by a bench so they are easy to see and touch. They also make unusual and attractive ground covers.

There are several variegated oreganos; unfortunately, their names tend to be rather muddled. Below are basic descriptions of a few to show you what's available, but in most cases, you're better off buying the plants in person or from a dependable mail-order nursery and relying on their advice on the hardiness of the plants you choose.

*Green with white to cream markings.* Plants sold as 'Country Cream', 'White Anniversary', 'Wellsweep' ('Well-Sweep'), and 'Polyphant' typically have bright green leaves with creamy white edges. These are all usually listed under *O. vulgare,* grow 12 to 18 inches tall, and have pinkish flowers in mid- to late summer. Zones 5 to 9. Variegated sweet marjoram (*O. majorana* 'Variegata') has cream-bordered leaves sometimes tinged with pink, as well as pink flowers on 6- to 10-inch-tall plants in summer. Normally hardy in Zones 8 or 9 to 10.

*Green with yellow markings.* Plants sold as *O. vulgare* 'Jim's Best' and 'Gold Splash' usually have bright green leaves heavily speckled with light green and yellow; new leaves may be entirely light yellow. 'Gold Tip' is distinctive, with green leaves that have bright yellow tips. These are 12 to 18 inches tall, with pinkish flowers in mid- to late summer. Zones 5 to 9.

**GROWING TIPS:** Under any name, variegated oreganos thrive in full sun with average to dry, well-drained soil. Unless you really

want to see the flowers, shear back the plants by about half just as the blooms open to promote lower, bushy growth with good-looking leaves.

**ALTERNATIVES:** 'Pesto Perpetuo' basil (*Ocimum*) is another option for strongly scented (and flavorful) bright green leaves irregularly edged with bright cream to white. It keeps its narrowly upright habit all season; 18 to 24 inches tall. 'Variegated African Blue' has a more open habit, with mildly fragrant, light green leaves narrowly edged with greenish yellow; 2 to 3 feet tall. Full sun; average to moist, well-drained soil. Zones 9 to 11.

## PACHYSANDRA
*Pachysandra*

**Height: 6–8 inches**
**Leaf size: 3–4 inches long;**
   **1 inch wide**
**Partial to full shade**
**Zones 4–8**

Sure, you see it almost everywhere, but there's a good reason for that: Japanese pachysandra (*Pachysandra terminalis*) is one of the few evergreen ground covers that gardeners in a range of climates can depend on for year-round good looks in shady sites. Its short, upright to trailing stems are clad in glossy toothed foliage that's bright green aging to deep green and topped with spiky clusters of tiny white flowers in late spring to early summer. Although the flowers are clearly visible on all-green plants, you'll hardly notice them on the variegated

cultivar 'Silveredge' (also sold as 'Silver Edge' and 'Variegata'), which has an irregular, creamy white border around each leaf. This selection doesn't spread quite as vigorously as the species does, so you can include it in mixed borders without worrying about it crowding out most companions. It's an elegant underplanting for hollies (*Ilex*), boxwoods (*Buxus*), and other solid-green evergreens, as well as for shrubs with colorful winter stems, such as red-twig dogwoods (*Cornus*). It looks great in containers too. *Note: P. terminalis* is considered invasive in some areas.

**GROWING TIPS:** Variegated pachysandra grows best in partial to full shade in average, well-drained soil. Set the plants 4 to 6 inches apart, mulch in between them, and water during dry spells for the first year or two. Once established, they need little care.

**ALTERNATIVE:** Variegated bishop's weed (*Aegopodium podagraria* 'Variegata'), also known as variegated goutweed, has pale green to gray-green toothed leaflets with irregular, pale yellow edges aging to creamy white; about 8 inches tall. It grows just about anywhere, with aggressively spreading rhizomes that are terribly difficult to remove. The self-sown seedlings of variegated bishop's weed are solid green and even more rampant spreaders, to the point of being considered invasive in some areas. Keep in a pot or where nothing else will grow; mow before the flowers open to prevent self-sowing. Zones 4 to 9.

*Pachysandra terminalis*
'Silveredge'

## RHAMNUS
*Buckthorn*

**Height: 10–15 feet**
**Leaf size: 1–2 inches long;**
   **to 1 inch wide**
**Full sun**
**Zones 7 or 8–10**

Italian buckthorn (*Rhamnus alaternus*) creates a dense, bushy shrub that's an interesting possibility for evergreen hedges and screens in mild climates. 'Variegata' (also sold as 'Argenteovariegata') is far more than just another hedging plant, though: between its variegated foliage and its bright berries, it brings a real "wow" factor to the landscape. The small, oval, gray-green leaves are bordered with bright cream to white, and the tiny, pale yellow flowers produce masses of small but brilliant red berries that gradually ripen to black by the end of the summer. Like the all-green version, variegated Italian buckthorn tolerates regular clipping as a formal hedge, but it also looks excellent when allowed to grow with minimal pruning as an informal hedge, screen, or specimen plant — particularly if you site it in front of a larger, deep green evergreen or a dark wall.

**GROWING TIPS:** Although it prefers full sun, variegated Italian buckthorn also performs well with morning sun and afternoon shade, or even light all-day shade. It's fine with average, well-drained soil; once established, it's also quite heat- and drought-tolerant. Prune away solid-green shoots immediately.

**ALTERNATIVES:** Variegated azaras (*Azara*) aren't as densely branched, but they still make an eye-catching choice for use as specimens or

*Rhamnus alaternus* 'Variegata'

hedges. *A. microphylla* 'Variegata' is the most commonly available selection, with small, rounded, glossy, deep green leaves that are edged with cream to white. Can eventually reach 20 feet or more, although regular pruning keeps it smaller. Full sun to partial shade; average, well-drained soil. Zones 8 or 9 to 11.

---

## ROSA
*Rose*

**Height:** Varies
**Leaf size:** Varies
**Full sun**
**Zones vary**

Roses (*Rosa*) certainly aren't one of the common plants that come to mind for foliage interest, particularly for variegated foliage. But for those of you willing to do a little searching, tracking down one of these few available selections repays the effort. The showiest option is variegated

memorial rose (*R. wichurana* [*R. wichuraiana*] 'Variegata'; also sold as 'Curiosity' and 'Goshiki'), with compound leaves composed of several smaller leaflets that are up to 1 inch long and ½ inch across. The spring foliage is bright green heavily speckled with cream and blushed with pink; summer leaves are mostly or completely deep green, but as the weather cools again, variegated shoots again reappear. Scented, single white flowers bloom in late spring to midsummer. The slender, thorny stems are long and trailing, so you can let it sprawl as a ground cover; tie it into a trellis as a climber; or trim it into a 4- to 6-foot-tall, mounded shrub form. Zones 5 to 9. *Note:* The species *R. wichurana* is considered invasive in some areas.

Variegated foliage on hybrid tea roses is a touchy subject for rose aficionados, because yellow-mottled leaves are often a sign of rose mosaic virus. There are, however, a few cultivars that are naturally variegated, with streaks and flecks of light yellow to cream in their medium-textured, deep green leaves (most noticeably on the new growth, which is also blushed with red). 'Verschuren' is the best known, with very fragrant, double pink flowers that bloom from early summer into fall on plants that typically grow 3 feet tall. Its leaflets are 1 to 2 inches long and 1 inch across. To be honest, it's not an exceptional choice for foliage, but it

*Rosa* 'Verschuren'

does make an interesting garden addition if you want something really different. It grows well in a container too. The raised position makes it easier to notice the unusual foliage, and the increased air circulation around the stems discourages black spot. Zones 6 to 10.

**GROWING TIPS:** Like most other roses, the variegates grow best in full sun and fertile, moist but well-drained soil. Variegated memorial rose will also tolerate light shade and needs minimal care; just prune to shape as needed if you're growing it as a shrub. 'Verschuren' takes the same care that other hybrid teas require in your climate: spring pruning to clean up winter damage and promote vigorous new growth, and regular removal of the faded flowers.

*Thuja plicata* 'Zebrina'

**ALTERNATIVES:** Deciduous snowberries (*Symphoricarpos*) grow 3 to 5 feet tall, with a twiggy, rounded habit and small, light green leaves. *S. albus* 'Taff's White' (also sold as 'Variegatus' and *S. orbiculatus* 'Taff's White') has white leaf edges. *S. orbiculatus* 'Taff's Silver Edge' ('Albovariegatus', 'Argenteovariegatus') has creamy white edges. 'Variegatus' ('Foliis Variegatus') has light yellow to cream edges. All can spread by suckering. Full sun to partial shade; average, well-drained soil. Zones 2 to 7.

*Salix integra* 'Hakuro-nishiki'

## SALIX
*Willow*

> **Height:** Varies
> **Leaf size:** 2–3 inches long;
>   ½ inch wide
> **Full sun to partial shade**
> **Zones 3 or 4–9**

Need quick-growing deciduous shrubs to fill a large space quickly? Variegated willows (*Salix*) could be just the thing. Their spring show of colorful foliage is spectacular, and it can last well into summer too — particularly where the weather stays on the cool side. A warning, though: while these easy-to-grow, multi-stemmed shrubs look cute and compact in their nursery pots, you can't count on them to stay that way. Left unpruned, they'll reach 15 feet tall or more and about as wide; it takes heavy pruning in late winter to keep established plants in the range of 6 to 8 feet. (This regular chore gives you the bonus of colorful new shoots.)

The best-known variegated willow by far is *S. integra* 'Hakuro-nishiki' (also sold as 'Albomaculata'), with pink new shoots and light green older leaves that are heavily speckled with creamy white. Its young stems also turn red in winter (another benefit of regular heavy pruning). This willow naturally forms a rather fountainlike shrub with upright-then-arching shoots, but you may also find it sold grafted atop a tall straight stem as a standard. 'Flamingo' reportedly has deeper pink shoot tips. Zones 4 to 9.

*Salix cinerea* 'Tricolor' is similar but its markings are more yellowish, and it's hardier (Zone 3, at least). *Note: Salix cinerea* is considered invasive in some areas.
**GROWING TIPS:** Variegated willows can grow in full sun or partial shade with average to evenly moist soil. Except for occasional pruning, they seldom need any special care.
**ALTERNATIVES:** Shrubby *Spiraea thunbergii* 'Mount Fuji' ('Mt. Fuji') offers narrow, bright green leaves irregularly edged in white. *Note: S. thunbergii* is considered invasive in some areas. *S.* × *vanhouttei* 'Pink Ice' has smaller leaves that are cream-colored when young, turning green finely speckled with cream when older. Both have pink-blushed new leaves and grow 3 to 5 feet tall. Full sun to partial shade; average, well-drained soil. Zones 5 or 6 to 8.

## THUJA
*Arborvitae*

> **Height:** Varies
> **Leaf size:** ¼–½ inch long;
>   to ¼ inch wide (individual,
>   scalelike leaves)
> **Full sun**
> **Zones vary**

Handsome and hardy, arborvitaes (*Thuja*) have become commonplace in northern landscapes as specimens, as hedges, and in foundation plantings. Their upright habit and naturally dense growth look great even without pruning, and the plants are adaptable enough to grow in a range of conditions. The all-green

species and selections are excellent in their own right, but the variegated forms are quite attractive as well, especially if you're looking for something to bring extra winter color to your yard.

The selections mentioned below are from American arborvitae or eastern white cedar (*T. occidentalis*), which is usually recommended for Zones 2 or 3 to 7, and western red cedar or giant arborvitae (*T. plicata*), typically suggested for Zones 5 or 6 to 8. Nurseries that specialize in conifers offer several other selections as well. Keep in mind that you'll see a wide range of heights for these plants presented on labels and in catalogs: sometimes they're for the growth expected after 10 years and sometimes they refer to the size at maturity. Some selections have not been cultivated long enough to actually reach maturity, so the final heights are just guesses.

*Green with white to cream markings.* The new shoot tips of

'Columbia' American arborvitae are frosted with creamy white, set against older, medium green foliage. It has a columnar growth habit, reaching 8 to 10 feet in 10 years and to 30 feet after many years. 'Sherwood Frost' American arborvitae (also sold as 'Sherwood Forest') has bright green foliage with small creamy white tips on columnar to pyramidal plants about 6 feet tall in 10 years and 12 feet or more after many years. 'Wansdyke Silver' American arborvitae is even more compact: 3 to 4 feet in 10 years and eventually to 7 feet or more, with a narrowly pyramidal to columnar form. Its deep green foliage is randomly splashed with creamy white.

*Green with yellow to cream markings.* Narrowly upright 'Emerald Variegated' American arborvitae has bright green foliage splashed with yellow. Its 10-year height is about 6 feet; eventually, it may reach 15 feet or more. The rich green foliage of 'Zebrina' western red cedar is banded with bright to light yellow. The bright color tends to fade in hot weather. In winter, the green parts typically turn bronzy. These fast-growing, broadly pyramidal plants are about 10 feet tall in 10 years and 25 feet or more when mature.

**GROWING TIPS:** Arborvitaes usually grow best in full sun and evenly moist but well-drained soil, although they can stand drier conditions once they've been in the ground for a few years. They may also tolerate a few hours of shade a day, especially in the warmer parts of their hardiness range, but if they get too much, their growth will be open and straggly instead of dense and bushy.

**ALTERNATIVES:** Variegated false arborvitae (*Thujopsis dolabrata* [*T. dolobrata*] 'Variegata') produces patches of creamy to bright white among its glossy, deep green shoots. The broadly pyramidal plants reach about 10 feet in 10 years (eventually to 30 feet). Plants sold as 'Nana Variegata' have a more mounded form to about 4 feet tall. Full sun (or a little afternoon shade in hot-summer areas); evenly moist but well-drained soil. Zones 5 to 8.

---

## THYMUS
*Thyme*

**Height:** Varies
**Leaf size:** ¼–½ inch long; ¼ inch wide
**Full sun**
**Zones 4 or 5–9**

With their compact, mounded to carpeting form and dainty foliage, thymes (*Thymus*) make a terrific choice for edging beds and borders, covering the ground in sunny sites, or accenting container plantings. These sturdy little herbs aren't bothered by heat or drought, so you can even tuck them among rocks or plant them along paved areas that would fry the foliage of more-delicate plants. Their usually evergreen nature provides year-round interest, with the bonus of tiny purplish pink blooms in summer. The foliage also has a spicy or lemony scent when rubbed, so be sure to site it where you can brush by it with your feet or rub it with your fingers to release the fragrance.

Selecting thymes with variegated foliage adds yet another level of garden value to these versatile herbs. And though some of them don't have the rich flavor of the thymes typically used in the kitchen, most are pleasant enough to use in cooking or teas. There are many selections on the market under a variety of names. Those attributed to *T. vulgaris* ought to have a warm, spicy aroma and those sold as *T. × citriodorus* should have a distinct lemony fragrance, but the names are quite mixed up in the trade. If a specific scent is important to you, buy thymes in person so you can sniff for yourself. Otherwise, buying simply by the cultivar name should get you the correct leaf colors. Below is a small sampling of the selections that are available. Keep in mind that any of these may also show a pink blush on their foliage in cool weather.

*Green with white to cream markings.* The most readily available thymes in this color range are sold under the names 'Argenteus' (commonly called silver thyme and sometimes sold as *T. argenteus*) and 'Silver Queen'. They have a shrubby, upright form to about 1 foot tall, with green to gray-green leaves rimmed with creamy white. 'Hi-Ho Silver' and 'Silver Posie' have wider, brighter leaf margins.

*Green with yellow to cream markings.* Plants sold as 'Gold Edge', 'Golden King', and variegated lemon thyme (*T. × citriodorus* 'Aureus') are bushy, upright mounds to about 1 foot tall, with bright green leaves edged in yellow fading to cream. Those sold as 'English Wedgewood' or simply 'Wedgewood' are similar but their leaves have green edges and greenish yellow centers. *T.* 'Doone Valley' is more of a

*Thymus × citriodorus* 'Gold Edge'

carpeter than a mound-former, growing to about 6 inches tall with deep green foliage that's tipped or splashed with yellow (most noticeably on the spring growth). 'Highland Cream' ('Hartington Silver') is a cultivar of creeping thyme (*T. praecox* or *T. serpyllum*) with very tiny, light yellow- to cream-edged green leaves on ground-hugging stems less than 3 inches tall.

**GROWING TIPS:** Thymes thrive in full sun with average to dry soil that's near neutral to slightly alkaline. Good drainage is a must. You'll often see a broad range of hardiness zone ratings for thymes, from Zones 4 to 9 to Zones 7 to 9. Thymes typically are quite cold-tolerant, as long as they're not wet in winter. That's why the same

*Veronica prostrata* 'Goldwell'

cultivar may overwinter in sandy soil under snow cover in Zone 4 but rot in heavier soil during a rainy winter in Zone 6. If your soil isn't sandy, planting in raised beds and/or mulching the plants with gravel should help improve their odds of winter survival. On the bushy thymes, shear the plants nearly to the ground just as growth begins in spring and by about half just before the flowers open to encourage brightly colored regrowth. (Enjoy the fresh summer trimmings in your kitchen or dry them for later use.)

**ALTERNATIVES:** 'Silver Carpet' creeping baby's breath (*Gypsophila repens*) has narrow, white-edged green leaves; about 1 foot tall. *G.* 'Jolien' has yellow-edged leaves; 24 to 30 inches tall. Zones 3 to 7. Variegated rockcresses (*Aubrieta*) offer tiny green leaves in 4-inch-tall carpets. 'Argenteovariegata' ('Albomarginata') has creamy white margins; 'Aureovariegata' has yellow margins; 'Variegata' may have either color on the leaf edges. Zones 4 or 5 to 8. Full sun; well-drained, neutral to slightly alkaline soil.

---

## VERONICA
*Speedwell, veronica*

**Height:** Varies
**Leaf size:** Varies
**Full sun to partial shade**
**Zones vary**

With their usually spiky flower form and beautiful purple-blue color, speedwells (*Veronica*) are always an excellent addition to

perennial plantings. Most have a low, spreading habit that's well suited to edging beds and borders or serving as an out-of-the-ordinary ground cover in small areas. Upright types work equally well near the front or middle of mixed borders. Speedwells typically don't bloom for more than a few weeks, however, so selecting cultivars with variegated leaves ensures that the plants earn their keep throughout the growing season. And when variegated speedwells *do* flower, the combination of purple-blue blossoms and white or yellow leaf markings is certainly elegant. In mild climates, many speedwells are evergreen; elsewhere, their leaves tend to look good into early winter at least.

*Green with white to cream markings.* The lowest-growing selection in this group is 'Miffy Brute' germander speedwell (*V. chamaedrys;* also sold as 'Pam'). Its toothed green leaves are up to 1½ inches long and 1 inch wide, with random splashes of creamy to bright white. Short clusters of bright to light blue flowers bloom mostly in late spring to early summer on 4- to 6-inch stems. It's usually hardy in Zones 3 to 8. Variegated gentian speedwell (*V. gentianoides* 'Variegata') produces rosettes of 3-inch-long, 1-inch-wide, shiny, dark green leaves edged in white; these multiply into spreading carpets. In late spring to early summer, upright, 12- to 18-inch-tall stems

are tipped with spikelike clusters of palest blue blooms. Zones 4 to 8. 'Joseph's Coat' long-leaved speedwell (*V. longifolia*) grows in more-distinct clumps of upright, 3-foot-tall stems topped with long, narrow clusters of light blue flowers from late spring to midsummer. Its new leaves are blushed with pink, later turning green with cream markings. Zones 4 or 5 to 8. 'Noah Williams' spike speedwell (*V. spicata*) has a similar growth habit but is shorter (18 to 24 inches tall in bloom), with long spikes of tiny white flowers from late spring to midsummer over gray-green to deep green leaves edged with cream to white. Zones 3 to 8.

*Green with yellow to cream markings.* 'Corinne Tremaine' (also sold as 'Corrine Tremaine'; sometimes listed under *V. montana*) grows in slow-creeping carpets to about 3 inches tall, with semievergreen, roughly oval toothed leaves that are less than 1 inch long and wide. The light green foliage is edged with pale yellow in spring and cream through the rest of the growing season. Small, purple-blue flowers are scattered over the plant in mid- or late spring to early summer; unlike those of other speedwells, these flowers are not in distinct spikes. Morning sun and afternoon shade or light all-day shade is ideal in most areas. Zones 3 or 4 to 9. *V. prostrata* 'Goldwell' is so bright that it looks solid yellow from a distance, but close up you can see that the narrow green leaves are distinctly edged with light yellow to lemon yellow. It reaches 3 to 5 inches tall, with lovely bright blue flowers in late spring. Zones 6 to 9.

**GROWING TIPS:** One reason you don't see speedwells more often, especially variegated ones, is that it can be a little tricky to find just the right site for them. Morning sun with afternoon shade seems to be ideal for most of them; too-strong sun burns the leaves, and too much shade leads to weak, problem-prone plants. Getting the moisture right is even more important; speedwells hate dry soil, but they can't stand having soggy roots. A spot with that ever-popular "moist but well-drained soil" is ideal. Shearing off the faded flowers tidies the plants for the rest of the growing season. Be sure to remove all-green shoots as soon as you see them, or they'll quickly crowd out the variegated growth.

**ALTERNATIVES:** Moss phlox (*Phlox subulata*) has needlelike, deep green leaves, with cream to white edges on plants sold as 'Nettleton Variation', 'Nettleton's Variation', 'Laura Beth', or 'Laurel Beth'. Sun; average to dry, well-drained soil; hardy in Zones 3 to 8. Variegated creeping phlox (*P. stolonifera* 'Variegata') is a spreader with broader, deep green leaves edged in cream. Partial to full shade; evenly moist but well-drained soil. Hardy in Zones 4 to 8. Both are about 4 inches tall in leaf; evergreen.

# VINCA
*Vinca, periwinkle*

**Height: Varies**
**Leaf size: Varies**
**Full sun to full shade**
**Zones vary**

If vincas (*Vinca*) were more difficult to grow, we'd probably appreciate them a lot more. As it is, they're a common sight in many parts of the country, covering the ground under trees and shrubs, stopping erosion on sloping sites, and trailing out of window boxes and other container plantings.

Held on upright flowering stems and trailing nonflowering stems, the leaves of bigleaf or greater periwinkle (*V. major*) are up to 3 inches long and 1½ inches wide, and those of common or lesser periwinkle (*V. minor*) are 1 to 2 inches long and ½ inch wide. The glossy, evergreen foliage looks great throughout the year, and the blue or white spring blooms are a bonus. But these aren't any pampered garden pets: they'll survive in just about anything you throw at them, from full sun to full shade and just about any soil that isn't either bone dry or underwater. This adaptability explains their ubiquitous presence in yards and gardens — and, unfortunately, their spread into woodlands and other natural areas as well. Vincas' slender, nonflowering stems trail for many feet, and they often take root where they touch the soil, so they can take over large areas quickly. *Note:* Both species are considered invasive in some

areas. At this point, the threat seems to come primarily from plants that have been neglected and allowed to creep from yards into adjacent wooded areas, so if you regularly mow or trim around your patch, or if you grow vincas only in containers, you'll greatly minimize the possibility of them getting out of control. Still, if vincas are a problem in your area, choose a different plant.

Common periwinkle typically grows 6 to 8 inches tall and is hardy in Zones 4 to 9. Bigleaf periwinkle can reach twice that size and is usually hardy in Zones 6 or 7 to 10.

*Green with white to cream markings.* Selections of *V. major* sold as 'Elegantissima', 'Expoflora', and 'Variegata' have light to medium green leaves edged in creamy white. *V. minor* 'Argenteovariegata', 'Ralph Shugert', and 'Sterling Silver' also have creamy white leaf margins.

*Green with yellow to cream markings.* Plants sold under the names *V. major* 'Maculata', 'Aureomaculata', 'Aureovariegata', and 'Surrey Marble' have medium to deep green leaves with an irregular, greenish yellow center splash. 'Wojo's Jem' (also sold as 'Wojo's Gem') has deep green edges and a distinct light yellow to bright cream center. To get yellow-edged green leaves on *V. minor*, look for the names 'Aureovariegata', 'Blue and Gold', 'Golden Bowles', and 'Sunny Skies'. Plants sold simply as 'Variegata' often fit this description

*Vinca major* 'Variegata'

but may have white edges instead. The foliage of 'Illumination' has a deep green rim around a broad, bright yellow center that ages to creamy yellow. 'Golden' has yellow leaf borders and white flowers instead of the usual blue.

**GROWING TIPS:** Vincas will tolerate full sun (with ample moisture) or full shade (even dry shade), they typically prefer sites with light all-day shade, however, and evenly moist but well-drained soil. Mowing established plantings to the ground in late winter or right after bloom every few years will keep them looking fresh and tidy.

**ALTERNATIVES:** The bright to deep green leaves of variegated climbing fig (*Ficus pumila* 'Variegata') are heavily speckled with white; 'Snowflake' has wide white leaf edges. In Zones 8 to 11, the trailing stems can creep to form a ground cover or be trained up a wall, although they're very vigorous and may need frequent trimming. They look great in pots too. Full sun to partial shade; average, well-drained soil.

## ACER
*Maple*

**Height: Varies**
**Leaf size: 2–4 inches long and wide**
**Full sun to full shade**
**Zones 5 or 6–8**

Deciduous Japanese maples (*Acer palmatum*) are well known for their elegant, lacy leaves and fantastic fall color. They are readily available in both upright and weeping forms, and their obvious eye-appeal has earned them

*Acer palmatum* 'Butterfly'

a place of honor in many home landscapes. Selections with variegated leaves add even more interest. Some have such subtle markings that you need to be right next to them to notice (these are especially nice for large containers); others are so striking that they attract attention even from a distance. While there are many variegates to choose from, you're unlikely to find them at your local garden center, so check out specialty nurseries to explore the wide range of offerings. Below is a small sampling of what you can expect to find. *Note:* This species is considered invasive in some areas; Japanese maples can self-sow into woodlands and other natural areas.

*Green with white to cream markings.* Most white-variegated Japanese maples have pink tints at some time during the season. 'Butterfly' and 'Kagiri-nishiki' (also sold as 'Roseomarginatum') have deeply lobed, light to grayish green foliage with irregular cream to white margins and light touches of pink on the edges of the spring growth. Some leaves may have no markings and some may be a solid cream. The upright, vase-shaped plants eventually reach 20 feet ('Butterfly') to 25 feet ('Kagiri-nishiki') and will tolerate more sun than most other variegated Japanese maples do. For a stronger pink effect, consider 'Asahi-zuru', 'Karasu-gawa', and 'Oridono-nishiki' ('Orido-nishiki').

Their leaves may be solid green, solid pink, solid white, or green splashed and streaked with white and/or pink, all on the same branch. These have an upright form and eventually mature at about 15 feet tall. They also need partial to full shade. 'Uki-gumo' has pale green new leaves heavily speckled with pink; later, they turn deep green with white freckles (often still with some pink in the newest foliage). The slow-growing plants can eventually reach 10 feet tall.

*Green with yellow to cream markings.* 'Sagara-nishiki' has new leaves that are light green with pink edges, maturing to deep green with yellow-spotted edges. On some leaves, the yellow mottling extends to cover part or most of the leaf surface. The well-branched plants grow slowly to 10 feet tall. 'Shigitatsu-sawa' is quite distinctive, with new leaves that are cream with light green veining; later, the cream ages to light yellow and the veins darken to deep green. From a distance, the entire plant looks pale yellow. Its fall color is usually orange to a mix of red and green. This small tree can eventually reach 10 to 15 feet tall. Afternoon or all-day shade is a must for both of these selections.

**GROWING TIPS:** In general, variegated Japanese maples enjoy morning sun and afternoon shade or light all-day shade, although some tolerate full sun and most tolerate full shade. Evenly moist

but well-drained soil is ideal. Keep in mind that with many variegated Japanese maples, the amount and color of the variegation varies substantially, depending on the site and on the weather conditions. If a specific effect is a key part of your garden plan, consider another variegated tree; otherwise, just sit back and enjoy the ever-changing show! Also, don't be too quick to prune away all-green shoots; sometimes, vigorous young stems don't show their variegation until their second year.

**ALTERNATIVES:** For equally dramatic foliage on a faster-growing maple, you might consider a variegated box elder (*Acer negundo* 'Variegatum' and 'Argenteovariegatum'), with compound green leaves irregularly edged with creamy white to pure white. Can reach 25 to 30 feet tall; shorter if you cut out some of the oldest stems each year. Sun to partial shade; average to poor soil. Zones 3 or 4 to 8. *Note: A. negundo* is considered invasive in some areas.

## KERRIA
*Japanese kerria*

**Height: Varies**
**Leaf size: 3 inches long;**
**    1–1½ inches wide**
**Full sun to full shade**
**Zones 4 or 5–9**

Japanese kerria (*Kerria japonica*) makes an attractive addition to a large mixed border or foundation planting, not just for its single or double, bright yellow blooms that appear mostly in mid- to late spring, but also for its rich green summer foliage and slender, bright green winter stems. Its shoots start out upright and gradually begin to arch, creating an overall rounded outline. The plants also spread outward by suckers, ultimately forming broad clumps 6 to 8 feet across if left unchecked. A grouping of three to five plants creates an attractive mass that fills a lot of space;

*Kerria japonica* 'Picta'

a row of them makes an interesting compact hedge. *Note:* This species is considered invasive in some areas.

Although the plain green form makes a good background for bright summer flowers, the variegated cultivar 'Picta' (also sold as 'Variegata') makes a more positive color contribution, in the form of gray-green leaves irregularly edged with creamy white. From a distance, the 2- to 4-foot-tall plant has a light grayish appearance. 'Geisha' is usually taller (4 to 6 feet), with green leaves randomly splashed with yellow and cream, as well as double flowers.

**GROWING TIPS:** Variegated Japanese kerrias usually look best in partial shade, although they'll tolerate either full sun (if the soil is moist) or full shade. Average, well-drained soil is fine. Cut out dead stems in spring, prune as needed to shape the plants after flowering, and remove all-green shoots as soon as you see them.

**ALTERNATIVES:** 'Mystique' winter jasmine (*Jasminum nudiflorum*) also has green stems, but in this case they carry three-part, deep green leaves with a bright creamy border around each tiny leaflet. Golden winter jasmine ('Aureum') has a bolder effect, with solid yellow as well as gold-splashed green leaflets. Both grow 6 to 8 feet tall and wide as a shrub; or train on a wall. Full sun to partial shade; average, well-drained soil. Zones 6 to 9.

## PARTHENOCISSUS
*Virginia creeper*

**Height: 20–30 feet**
**Leaf size: 3–4 inches long; about
  1 inch wide (individual leaflet)**
**Full sun to full shade**
**Zones 4–10**

If you're ready to deck your walls (or fences, arbors, or tree stumps) with vibrantly variegated foliage, a selection of Virginia creeper (*Parthenocissus quinquefolia*) might be just the thing. On plants sold as Star Showers ('Monham') and 'Variegata', each leaf is divided into three- to five-toothed, medium green leaflets heavily splashed and speckled with cream to white. In spring they're often blushed with pink, and in fall they turn pink and red before they drop. Clusters of non-showy, greenish white flowers bloom in summer, followed by blue-black berries in fall. This eastern North American native vine clings to vertical surfaces with thin tendrils that end in disklike holdfasts. If there's nothing to climb, the plants also make a nice ground cover for a large space.

**GROWING TIPS:** Variegated Virginia creeper will adapt to just about any light levels and soil conditions, although its showy foliage seems to look best in light shade, and the growth is most vigorous in humus-rich, evenly moist but well-drained soil. Watch for all-green or mostly green shoots, along with all-green seedlings, and remove them right away so they don't take over.

*Parthenocissus quinquefolia* 'Variegata'

**ALTERNATIVE:** 'Ginza Lights' Boston ivy (*Parthenocissus tricuspidata*) climbs like Virginia creeper, but its larger, three-lobed leaves aren't quite as lacy-looking. The deep green foliage is heavily mottled with white, as well as some pink in the new growth, and it turns red to pink in fall. It, too, adapts to a wide range of sites and growing conditions. Zones 4 to 8. *Note:* This species is considered invasive in some areas.

# POLEMONIUM
*Jacob's ladder*

**Height: Varies**
**Leaf size: 8–12 inches long;**
   **2–4 inches wide**
**Partial to full shade**
**Zones vary**

Jacob's ladders (*Polemonium*) are absolutely lovely in bloom, and their ferny foliage clumps make a terrific textural contribution for the rest of the growing season. When variegated cultivars started to appear, gardeners jumped at the chance to buy them, but many were disappointed at their short-lived nature. Fortunately, some of the newer selections seem to be better garden performers over the long run. They are all so beautiful that you might even grow them as annuals just to enjoy their foliage.

All Jacob's ladders have pinnate leaves, which means they have small leaflets arranged in pairs along a center stalk. Common Jacob's ladder (*P. caeruleum*) is a clump-former with upright stems topped with purple-blue blooms in late spring or early summer. 'Brise d'Anjou' (also sold as 'Blanjou') has deep green leaflets edged in yellow aging to creamy white and reaches 18 to 24 inches tall in bloom. 'Snow and Sapphires' has white-bordered leaflets and is about 30 inches in bloom. 'White Ghost' grows to about 2 feet tall, with narrow leaflets that are light green streaked and stippled with varying amounts of cream, and tinged with purple on some of the leaves. It can produce variegated seedlings. All three of these may be hardy in Zones 4 to 8, but they often last only one or two seasons in the garden. Longer-lived 'Stairway to Heaven' is a stunning selection of creeping Jacob's ladder (*P. reptans*) with broad, light to medium green leaflets widely bordered with cream aging to white and often tinged with pink in spring. Its light blue flowers bloom atop 12- to 18-inch-tall stems in mid- to late spring. Zones 3 to 8.

**GROWING TIPS:** Although variegated Jacob's ladders will tolerate full sun in cool climates and full shade in hot climates, they normally look best with partial shade. Humus-rich, evenly moist but well-drained soil is ideal. Snip off the flowering stems once the blooms fade. Remove all-green shoots as soon as you see them.

**ALTERNATIVES:** Ferny-leaved perennial *Sanguisorba menziesii* 'Dali Marble' has blue-green leaflets edged with bright cream to white in 3- to 4-foot-tall clumps. Zones 4 to 8. Strawberry plants sold as *Fragaria × ananassa* 'Variegata', *F. virginiana* 'Variegata', and *F. vesca* 'Variegata' grow in 6-inch-tall rosettes of three-part leaves, with toothed green leaflets edged with bright cream to white. Zones 3 to 9. Full sun to partial shade; average, well-drained soil.

*Polemonium caeruleum* 'Brise d'Anjou'

# PHOTO ACKNOWLEDGMENTS

*Thanks to the following individuals, nurseries, and gardens for their assistance.* — ROB CARDILLO

Annie's Annuals, Richmond, CA

Ray Rogers and Ken Selody, Atlock Flower Farm, Somerset, NJ

The Gardens at Ball, West Chicago, IL

Gerald and Bea Barad, Flemington, NJ

The Pufahl family, Beds and Borders, Laurel, NY

Judy Glattstein, BelleWood Gardens, Frenchtown, NJ

David Culp and Michael Alderfer, Brandywine Cottage, Downington, PA

Brent and Becky Heath, Brent and Becky's Bulbs, Gloucester, VA

Pam Stenger, Brookside Gardens, Wheaton, MD

The Chadwick Arboretum & Learning Gardens, Ohio State University, Columbus, OH

Bill Thomas and Dan Benarcik, Chanticleer, Wayne, PA

Brenda and John Demetriou, Cincinnati, OH

Earthly Pursuits, Windsor Mill, MD

Floral & Hardy, Skippack, PA

George Ball, Grace Romero, and Dina Dunn, Fordhook Farm, Doylestown, PA

Frelinghuysen Arboretum, Morristown, NJ

Tom Winn and Ken Frieling, Glasshouse Works, Stewart, OH

Pete Hedrick, Philadelphia, PA

Heronswood Nursery, Kingston, WA

Thomas Hobbs, Vancouver, BC

Jack Staub and Renny Reynolds, Hortulus Farm Gardens, Wrightstown, PA

Jeff Jabco and Joe Henderson, Swarthmore, PA

JC Raulston Arboretum, Raleigh, NC

Jenkins Arboretum, Devon, PA

Landbohojskolens Have, Copenhagen, Denmark

Landscape Arboretum of Temple University Ambler, Ambler, PA

Adam Levine and Tom Borkowski, Rose Valley, PA

Jerry Fritz, Linden Hill Gardens, Ottsville, PA

Longwood Gardens, Kennett Square, PA

Marina del Rey Garden Center, Marina del Rey, CA

John Story, Meadowbrook Farm, Meadowbrook, PA

Brian Minter, Minter Gardens, Rosedale, BC

Paul Meyer, Morris Arboretum, Philadelphia, PA

Sally Ferguson, Netherlands Flower Bulb Information Center, Danby, VT

Nordic Nursery, Aldergrove, BC

Steve and Julie Perkins, White Stone, VA

Phipps Conservatory and Botanical Gardens, Pittsburgh, PA

Tony Avent, Plant Delights Nursery, Raleigh, NC

Hank Schannen, Rare Find Nursery, Jackson, NJ

Read House and Gardens, New Castle, DE

Roger's Gardens, Corona del Mar, CA

Sarah P. Duke Gardens, Durham, NC

Scott Arboretum, Swarthmore, PA

Stephanie Cohen, Shortwood Gardens, Collegeville, PA

Southlands Nursery, Vancouver, BC

Sperling Nursery, Calabasas, CA

Ilene Sternberg, West Chester, PA

Tim Teahan, Laguna Woods, CA

Tuscan Farm Gardens, Langley, BC

Twombly Nursery, Monroe, CT

Tyler Arboretum, Media, PA

University of Kentucky Arboretum, Lexington, KY

The Variegated Foliage Nursery, Eastford, CT

VanDusen Botanical Garden, Vancouver, BC

Maggie Wych, Western Hills Nursery, Occidental, CA

Winterthur Museum and Country Estate, Winterthur, DE

John Friel, Yoder Brothers, Inc., Lancaster, PA

# INDEX

Page numbers in **bold** indicate main entries; those in *italic* indicate photographs.

Norway spruce. *See Picea abies*
nutrient balance, 29

## O

oakleaf hydrangea. *See Hydrangea quercifolia*
oat grass. *See Arrhenatherum*
obedient plant. *See Physostegia*
*Ocimum* (basil), **124**, *124*
  *basilicum*
    'Dark Opal' ('Opal'), 'Well-Sweep Miniature Purple' ('Minimum Purpurascens Well-Sweep'), 124
    'Osmin', 'Red Rubin', 93, 124
    'Purple Ruffles', 13, *13*, 124, *124*
    'Pesto Perpetuo', 'Variegated African Blue', 272
October daphne. *See Sedum sieboldii*
*Oenothera*
  *fruticosa* (sundrops)
    'Silberblatte', 'Sunspot', 266
    subsp. *glauca*
      'Frühlingsgold' ('Spring Gold'), 266
  *tetragona* 'Sunspot', 266
oleander. *See Nerium*
Olympic mullein. *See Verbascum olympicum*
*Onopordum acanthium*, 150, *150*
*Ophiopogon* (monkey grass, mondo grass), **109**, *109*, 217
  *intermedius* 'Argenteomarginatus', 220
  *jaburan*
    'Argenteovittatus', 'Variegatus', 'Vittatus', 220
  *japonicus*
    'Shiroshima-ryu', 'Silver Mist', 'Torafu', 217
  *planiscapus*
    'Black Knight' ('Black Night'), 93, 109
    Ebony Knight ('Ebknizam'), *94,109, 109*
    'Little Tabby', 217

'Nigrescens' ('Arabicus'), 90, *91*, 93, 109
*Oplismenus* (basket grass)
  *africanus* 'Variegatus', 259
  *hirtellus*. *See Oplismenus africanus*
*Opuntia*, 146
orach. *See Atriplex*
oregano. *See Origanum*
Oriental poppies. *See Papaver orientale*
Oriental spruce. *See Picea orientalis*
*Origanum* (oregano, marjoram), 12, *12*, **77**, *77*, 271, **271–72**
  *dictamnus*, 172
  *majorana* 'Variegata', 272
  'Norton Gold' ('Norton's Gold'), 77
  *onites*
    'Aureum', 'Thumbles' ('Thumbles Variety'), 'Thea's Gold', 77
  *vulgare*
    'Aureum Crispum' ('Curly Gold'), 36, 77
    'Aureum', 36, 49, 77, *77*
    'Country Cream', 'Gold Splash', 'Gold Tip', 'Jim's Best', 'Polyphant', 'Wellsweep', ('Well-Sweep'), 272
    'White Anniversary', *271*, 272
*Orostachys iwarenge*, 181
orpine. *See Sedum telephium* subsp. *ruprechtii*
*Osmanthus heterophyllus* (false holly)
  'Aureomarginatus', 'Goshiki', 'Variegatus', 247
  'Ogon', 80
*Oxalis*, 124, **124–25**
  *alstonii* 'Rubra'. *See O. hedysaroides* 'Rubra
  *depressa*. *See Oxalis triangularis*
  *hedysaroides* 'Rubra', 125
  *regnellii*. *See Oxalis triangularis*
  *spiralis*
    'Aurea', 79
    subsp. *vulcanicola* 'Copper Glow', 79
    var. *vulcanicola*, 125
  *triangularis* (shamrock)
    'Atropurpurea', 93, 105, *105*, 124, *124*

'Charmed Jade', 'Dorothy Chao', 'Fanny', 165
'Charmed Velvet', 'Mijke', 124–25
'Charmed Wine', 93, 124–25
*vulcanicola*
  'Copper Glow', 79
  'Zinfandel', 125

## P

*Pachyphytum*, 181
*Pachysandra*, **272**, *272*
  *terminalis* (Japanese pachysandra)
    'Silveredge' ('Silver Edge', 'Variegata'), 202, 272, *272*
Pacific chrysanthemum. *See Ajania pacifica*
pagoda dogwood. *See Cornus alternifolia*
painted fern. *See Athyrium*
painted lady. *See Echeveria derenbergii*
palmately compound, 11
palmately lobed, 11, *11*
palm grass. *See Setaria palmifolia*
palm sedge. *See Carex muskingumensis*
pampas grass. *See Cortaderia selloana*
panda plant. *See Kalanchoe tomentosa*
*Pandorea jasminoides* 'Variegata', 249
*Panicum* (switchgrass), **159**, *159*
  *amarum* 'Dewey Blue', 159
  *virgatum*
    'Cloud Nine', 'Heavy Metal', 145, 159
    'Dallas Blues', 159, *159*
    'Haense Herms' ('Hänse Herms'), 'Shenandoah', 'Rotstrahlbusch', 109
    'Prairie Sky', 159
paper mulberry. *See Broussonetia papyrifera*
parlor maple. *See Abutilon*
parrot leaf. *See Alternanthera ficoidea*
parrot's beak. *See Lotus*
*Parthenocissus*, **279**, *279*
  *quinquefolia* (Virginia creeper), Star Showers ('Monham'), 279
  'Variegata', 279, *279*

*tricuspidata* (Boston ivy)
  'Fenway Park', 61
  'Ginza Lights', 279
peachleaf bellflower. *See Campanula persicifolia*
peacock ginger. *See Kaempferia*
pear. *See Pyrus*
pearl bluebush. *See Maireana sedifolia*
pearl millet. *See Pennisetum glaucum*
pearlwort. *See Sagina*
pearly everlasting. *See Anaphalis*
*Pelargonium* (geranium), 66, **66–67**, **250**, *250*
  × *asperum* 'Charity', 250
  *crispum* 'Variegated Prince Rupert', 250
  *fragrans* 'Snowy Nutmeg', 250
  *graveolens* 'Charity', 250
  × *hortorum* (zonal geranium), 66
    'Bird Dancer', Black Velvet Series, 'Chocolate Mint', 117
    'Dolly Varden' ('Dolly Vardon'), 'Freak of Nature', 'Happy Thought', 'Mrs. Parker', 'Mrs. Pollock', 'Skies of Italy', 'Wilhelm Langguth', 250
    'Golden Staph', 'Ken's Gold', 'Lotusland', 67
    'Mr. Henry Cox' ('Mrs. Cox', 'Mrs. Henry Cox'), 203, *203*, 250
    'Mrs. Quilter', 'Occold Shield', 'Persian Queen', 66
    'Vancouver Centennial', 25, *25*, 67
  *peltatum* (ivy geranium)
    'Crocodile', 250, *250*
    'White Mesh', 250
*Pennisetum* (fountain grass, millet), **109–10**, *110*
  *advena*. *See Pennisetum setaceum*
  *alopecuroides* 'Little Honey', 222
  *glaucum* (pearl millet)
    'Jester', 'Purple Baron', 110
    'Purple Majesty', 98, *98*, 110
  *macrostachyum* 'Burgundy Giant', 110
  *setaceum*
    'Dwarf Rubrum', 'Purpureum', 'Red Riding Hood', 'Rubrum Dwarf', 109